Urbanization in Large Developing Countries

The International Union for the Scientific Study of Population Problems was set up in 1928, with Dr Raymond Pearl as President. At that time the Union's main purpose was to promote international scientific co-operation to study the various aspects of population problems, through national committees and through its members themselves. In 1947 the International Union for the Scientific Study of Population (IUSSP) was reconstituted into its present form.

It expanded its activities to:
• stimulate research on population
• develop interest in demographic matters among governments, national and international organizations, scientific bodies, and the general public
• foster relations between people involved in population studies
• disseminate scientific knowledge on population

The principal ways through which the IUSSP currently achieves its aims are:
• organization of worldwide or regional conferences
• operations of Scientific Committees under the auspices of the Council
• organization of training courses
• publication of conference proceedings and committee reports.

Demography can be defined by its field of study and its analytical methods. Accordingly, it can be regarded as the scientific study of human populations primarily with respect to their size, their structure, and their development. For reasons which are related to the history of the discipline, the demographic method is essentially inductive: progress in knowledge results from the improvement of observation, the sophistication of measurement methods, and the search for regularities and stable factors leading to the formulation of explanatory models. In conclusion, the three objectives of demographic analysis are to describe, measure, and analyse.

International Studies in Demography is the outcome of an agreement concluded by the IUSSP and the Oxford University Press. The joint series is expected to reflect the broad range of the Union's activities and, in the first instance, will be based on the seminars organized by the Union. The Editorial Board of the series is comprised of:

John Cleland, UK   Henri Leridon, France
John Hobcraft, UK   Richard Smith, UK
Georges Tapinos, France

Urbanization in Large Developing Countries

China, Indonesia, Brazil, and India

Edited by

Gavin W. Jones
and
Pravin Visaria

CLARENDON PRESS · OXFORD
1997

Oxford University Press, Great Clarendon Street, Oxford OX2 6DP

Oxford New York
Athens Auckland Bangkok Bogota Bombay
Buenos Aires Calcutta Cape Town Dar es Salaam Delhi
Florence Hong Kong Istanbul Karachi
Kuala Lumpur Madras Madrid Melbourne
Mexico City Nairobi Paris Singapore
Taipei Tokyo Toronto

and associated companies in
Berlin Ibadan

Oxford is a trade mark of Oxford University Press

Published in the United States
by Oxford University Press Inc., New York

British Library Cataloguing in Publication Data

Data available

Library of Congress Cataloguing in Publication Data

Data available

ISBN 0–19–828974–X

1 3 5 7 9 10 8 6 4 2

Typeset by Alliance Phototypesetters
Printed in Great Britain
on acid-free paper by
Bookcraft (Bath) Ltd.,
Midsomer Norton, Somerset

Preface

This book is based on a seminar held by one of the scientific committees of the International Union for the Scientific Study of Population, the Committee on Economic Consequences of Alternative Demographic Patterns. The seminar was held in Ahmedabad in September 1989, and hosted by the Gujarat Institute of Development Research. As well as those giving papers from each of the large developing countries under discussion (China, India, Indonesia, and Brazil), other members of the IUSSP committee and discussants attended the seminar.

It was agreed during the seminar that the quality of the papers was sufficient to justify the preparation of a book based on them. However, in recognition of the fact that books of conference papers tend to lack a clear theme and focus, the two editors undertook to prepare introductory and concluding chapters, and also to send detailed comments and requests for revision to the chapter authors. This helped both to draw themes together and to improve the quality of papers. With the passage of time it was also necessary to update some of the data in a number of the chapters.

The editors wish to thank the support staff at their respective institutions—the Demography Program, Australian National University and the Gujarat Institute of Development Research—for the assistance they have given over the course of preparing this volume. In particular our thanks go to Daphne Broers-Freeman, the Publications Officer in the Demography Program, Australian National University.

Finally, the editors would like to thank the anonymous reviewers who made useful comments on the earlier draft of this manuscript and thus enabled it to be substantially improved in its final version.

G. W. J.
P. V.

Contents

List of Contributors

GAVIN W. JONES, Professor and Head, Division of Demography and Sociology, Research School of Social Sciences, Australian National University, Canberra, ACT 0200, Australia.

PRAVIN VISARIA, Director, Gujarat Institute of Development Research, Gota 382481, Ahmedabad, India.

JING NENG LI, Professor, Institute of Population and Development Research, Nankai University, 94 Weijin Road, Tianjin 300071, The People's Republic of China.

APRODICIO LAQUIAN, Director, Centre for Human Settlements, School of Community and Regional Planning, The University of British Columbia, 2206 East Mall, Vancouver B.C., Canada V6T 1Z3.

LIN YOU SU, Ex-Ph.D Student, Demography Program, Research School of Social Sciences, Australian National University, Canberra, ACT 0200, Australia.

YOK-SHIU F. LEE, Fellow, Program on Environment, East-West Center, 1777 East–West Road, Honolulu, Hawaii 96848, USA.

MIKE DOUGLASS, Department of Urban and Regional Planning, University of Hawaii at Manoa, Porteus Hall 107, 2424 Maile Way, Honolulu, Hawaii 96822, USA.

IWAN JAYA AZIS, Fakultas Ekonomi, Universitas Indonesia, Jl. Salemba Raya 4, Kampus Depok, West Java, Indonesia; Visiting Professor in Regional Science Program, Cornell University, Ithica, NY, USA.

PETER GARDINER, Insan Harapan Sejahtera, PO Box 44, Mampang, Jakarta 12701, Indonesia.

MUSTARAM KOSWARA, Directorate of City and Regional Planning, Ministry of Public Works, Jl. Raden Patah 1/1, Kebayoran Baru, Jakarta 12110, Indonesia.

DONALD SAWYER, Graduate Program in Demography, CEDEPLAR, Federal University of Minas Gerais, Belo Horizonte, Minas Gerais, Brazil.

GEORGE MARTINE, Director, Institute for Study of Society, Population and Nature, Caixa Postal 9944, Brasilia 70001-970, Brazil.

CLÉLIO CAMPOLINA DINIZ, CEDEPLAR (Center for Development and Regional Planning), University of Minas Gerais, Belo Horizonte, Brazil.

PAOLO ROBERTO HADDAD, Universidad Federal de Minas Gerais, Faculdate de Ciencias Económicas, Rua Curitiba 832, 30 000 Belo Horizonte, Minas Gerais, Brazil.

RAKESH MOHAN, Planning Commission, Government of India, Delhi.

T. S. PAPOLA, Planning Commission, Government of India, Delhi.

List of Figures

List of Maps

List of Tables

1 Urbanization of the Third World Giants

GAVIN W. JONES AND PRAVIN VISARIA

Anybody familiar with the development literature will know that the world is rapidly urbanizing, and that by the year 2005 (less than a decade away) more than half the world's population will live in urban areas (United Nations 1994). This figure, however, hides enormous inter-country variation. Urban growth is the most visible manifestation of the enormous population upsurge of the past four decades. It is one of the major concerns of the planners and governments of most developing countries, because with limited budgets they are finding the task of providing even basic levels of infrastructure and urban services quite daunting. This, along with concern about the political volatility perceived to be focused in cities and, frequently, a class-based concern that migrants to the cities seem to be mainly drawn from the ranks of the rural poor and uneducated, has generated a fundamentally negative attitude to urbanization in most developing countries.[1] In the two largest developing countries, China and India, anti-urban attitudes have historical roots in concepts of the city as parasitic in Maoist and Gandhian thought; such notions are common, too, in the third-largest developing country, Indonesia.

As Montgomery (1988) notes, 'the anti-urbanization perspective achieved its high point in the declarations of the 1974 World Population Plan of Action at Bucharest; since that time, it has gradually been supplanted by more balanced assessments of the contribution made by cities to economic growth'. These more objective assessments of the urbanization process, however, have not character-ized all developing countries, and the more complex set of attitudes which has emerged has been more characteristic of planners and academics than of politi-cians. Certainly, urbanization is more frequently perceived these days as a poten-tially beneficial or, at worst, neutral process, but urban primacy, or the excessive concentration of the population in one city or the few largest cities in a country, is a source of concern. There are varying degrees of recognition of the dynamics of urban growth: that it is due not only to rural–urban migration, but also (in equal or even greater measure) to the high rate of natural increase of the urban popula-tion itself (Jones 1991: 9–10).

---

[1] Examples of attitudes favouring a rural rather than an urban lifestyle are too numerous and stem from too many countries to require documentation. Academic writings blaming urban biases for many of the ills of the development process are represented by Lipton, 1977 and Brown and Jacobson, 1987. An alternative view is given by Lowrey (1989: 2): 'Most of the ills that are blamed on urbanization can be more accurately attributed to population growth, industrialization and prosperity.'

The general interest and concern with issues of urbanization in the developing world tend to focus on the following six aspects:

- rapid rates of growth of urban population
- rising share of urban population in total population
- growth of large metropolises and urban primacy
- problems of providing minimal urban infrastructure
- issues in rural–urban labour transfer and employment
- the linkages between urbanization and regional development issues.

This book analyses urbanization trends and issues in the four largest developing countries—China, India, Indonesia, and Brazil, whose total population of 2.4 billion constitutes over 40 per cent of the world's population (see Fig. 1.1). The justification for writing a book about these countries hinges on two characteristics they share: they are large, and they are developing. In terms of population, they are not equally large, of course; China and India are the giants. But in territorial extent, they differ less, if Indonesia's maritime interstices are included, as we believe they should be for this purpose. (The Indonesian archipelago covers a larger area than India.) Their levels of development are not identical: Brazil is much more industrialized and urbanized than the others. But they all face a range of problems in relation to urban and regional development that are typical of countries generally classified as 'developing'. These problems include, among others, sharply poorer living conditions and levels of human development in rural than in urban areas, but at the same time difficulty in providing even minimal levels of urban infrastructure and services; equity problems of implicit subsidization of living costs in urban areas; and issues relating to the most effective approaches to integrating urban areas into their regional economy.

As will be pointed out below, these four countries are distinguished by many differences in political and administrative systems, level of economic development,

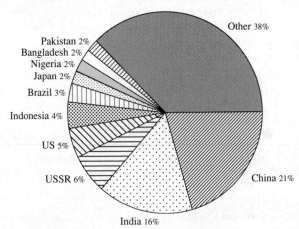

Fig. 1.1. Distribution of the world's population by major countries
Source: United Nations, 1990

and stage of demographic transition. The reason for including them in the one book, aside from their sheer size and importance on the world scene, is the important commonalities in the urban and regional planning issues they face, due to their large territory. Consequent issues of leading and lagging regions, regional urban networks and their integration with the regional rural economy, and decentralization of planning and administration, while they are certainly not absent in countries such as Malaysia or Peru or perhaps even in smaller countries such as Nicaragua or Sierra Leone, attain a particular importance in these territorially extensive countries. The problem often becomes particularly acute in federal systems where entire states or provinces are relatively backward (such as Bihar and Orissa in India, or some of the north-eastern states in Brazil). In unitary systems, including China and Indonesia, it is easier, if desired, to subsidize the poorer states through central government budgetary allocations.

The linkages between regional urbanization patterns and regional development are of particular planning concern. In the chapter by Haddad it is noted that, in efforts to industrialize Brazil's north-east, the industries tended to be concentrated in the three largest cities—Recife, Salvador and Fortaleza. Besides investigating whether there are any mechanisms open to planners to avoid this situation, it is also worth querying whether the situation itself is necessarily bad.

Comparison of Country Situations

Table 1.1 gives some basic comparative information about the four countries covered in this book. To begin with their demographic situation, their population growth rates in the 1980s ranged between 1.4 per cent (China) and 2.1 or 2.2 per cent in India and Brazil. Their expected population growth over the decade 1990 to 2000 ranges between 14 per cent (China) and over 19 per cent (Brazil). In all cases, rates of natural increase are declining, with important implications for urbanization to be discussed in the following section. During the two decades preceding 1992, fertility rates declined by about 43 per cent in Brazil, 47 per cent in Indonesia, 36 per cent in India and a remarkable 66 per cent in China. In India in 1975–7 and in China and Indonesia consistently over a long period, the government has applied strong pressures on people to control their family size (Hull and Yang 1991; Gwatkin 1979). Aside from these pressures, development trends appear to have been making for lower family sizes (McNicoll and Singarimbun 1983; Jones 1990; Merrick and Graham 1979, chapter 10; Visaria and Visaria 1994; Leete and Alam 1993).

Growth of the labour force in the 1980s has been well over 2 per cent per annum in all four countries, as the fertility declines of the 1970s and 1980s had not yet affected numbers entering the workforce. However, in the 1990s, growth of the working age population will slow noticeably: for example, in Indonesia, a growth of 33 per cent during the 1980s is expected to slow to one of 23 per cent over the 1990s, and by the year 2000 the population aged 15–29 will have ceased growing altogether. In China, the growth rate of the labour force in the 1990s will be only half that of the 1980s (Bauer 1990: 617).

Populations in all four countries are very unevenly distributed over the national territory. The most extreme example is Indonesia, where 62 per cent of the population live in Java and Bali, which contain only 7 per cent of the land area. In China, only 6 per cent of the population lives west of a line drawn from Aihue in the north-east to Tengchong in the south-west, on an area containing 57 per cent of the land area (Linge and Forbes 1990: 10–11). There are good historical and environmental reasons for this uneven distribution of population (Fisher 1967); nevertheless, there is a tendency for governments in Indonesia and Brazil, and China as well to some extent, to give normative emphasis to evening the population distribution. The reason for this emphasis is not always clear, though in some cases (e.g. China) it is certainly related to defence considerations.

The 1980s were a period of rapid economic development in China, following the introduction of liberalized economic policies in 1979. In Indonesia, rapid economic growth in the 1970s, fuelled by the oil boom, faltered somewhat in the mid-1980s, but real GDP growth of 5.5 per cent per annum was nevertheless achieved over the decade and strong growth has continued into the 1990s. In India, average annual rates of GDP growth exceeding 5 per cent per annum were achieved for the first time in the 1980s, representing a substantial improvement over the previous two decades. In Brazil, as in much of Latin America, debt crises dominated the picture and growth was the slowest among the four countries.

Development in large countries is heavily influenced by the political-bureaucratic structure. In this regard there are dramatic differences between these countries, which are governed respectively by a communist regime (China), a liberal democracy (India), an authoritarian, military-dominated regime (Indonesia) and in Brazil, a military dictatorship, replaced after 1984 by a democratically elected government. China and Indonesia have unitary, highly centralized forms of government, whereas India and Brazil follow federal systems.

The system of governance appears to have influenced the patterns of urbanization and regional development in a variety of ways. The restrictions on mobility in China have already been mentioned. In India official restrictions are weak despite noises to the contrary; but important *de facto* restrictions are imposed by regional language barriers and 'sons of the soil' policies applied with regard to employment by various states (Weiner 1978, 1983; Papola, Chapter 15 below). Ethnic and language barriers also operate to some extent to restrict mobility in Indonesia, but not in an institutionalized way. Only for a brief time in the late 1950s and early 1960s (Bandung) and the early 1970s (Jakarta) did city governments try unsuccessfully to stem the flow of immigrants through registration approaches (Hugo *et al.* 1987: 355). In Brazil, where the population and language are more homogeneous, only weak attempts have been made to control migration.

The political-bureaucratic structure can also influence the nature and effectiveness of policies to decentralize industry. In China, state enterprises can be ordered into particular areas, selected on grounds such as economic efficiency or strategic importance. This degree of control is not possible in the other countries, but all of them appear to have pursued deliberate policies of industrial decentralization to some extent, using tax and fiscal measures to encourage it. Often there are countervailing forces making for industrial concentration and the net effect is hard to determine. In Brazil, deconcentration of economic activity is evident in the fall in São Paulo's share (Martine and Campolina, Chapter 10 below). In India, there was a tendency towards a decline in inter-state disparities in the share of industrial employment as well as in value added in the manufacturing sector during the 1970s, but the evidence for the 1980s appears unclear (Mohan Chapter 14 below). In Indonesia, there has been an increase in the outer islands' share of industrial production over the 1980s, but within Java, the Jakarta region's industrial primacy has continued to grow (Hill 1992).

India probably has the best basic transport infrastructure of the four countries, because of its excellent railway system. China also has an extensive railway network, but it is inadequate for the task assigned to it because the road network is rather thin. The Indonesian transport network was very dilapidated during the 1960s and though considerable road building and improvement to inter-island shipping has been carried out since then, outside Java the road system is still inadequate and the rail system embryonic.

In terms of actual utilization of transportation services, restrictions on movement have always applied in China, where in any case it is very hard to obtain seats on long-distance public transportation. Though bus and train services are frequent (and subsidized) in India, linguistic differences seem to hinder population mobility; but in Indonesia, increased prosperity and a growing fleet of trucks, buses and minibuses has greatly increased mobility of both people and goods (Dick and Forbes 1992). In Brazil, too, long-distance transportation is well developed and affordable for most of the population, at least in the more settled parts of the country.

Another perspective on differences between these four countries is to consider them either as 'old countries' with a long-established, densely settled population (China, India, and Java–Bali in Indonesia) or as 'new countries' with a much sparser population (Brazil, Indonesia excluding Java–Bali). In the 'old countries' with centuries of adaptation of settlement patterns to resources, the scope for regional re-distribution of population appears relatively limited, whereas in 'new countries' where frontier development based on virgin land or newly discovered mineral deposits is still possible, it is more a question of bringing the people to new areas of economic opportunity, and deconcentrating industry and settlement. In such countries, however, there is still the need for hard-headed evaluation of the costs and benefits of such deconcentration; the fact that it is possible does not mean that it is necessarily desirable.

Indonesia is the only one of the four countries that does not constitute one large land mass. Difficulties of inter-island transport and high shipping costs from ports other than Jakarta and Surabaya inhibit regional development in the outer islands, and until the 1980s, surface transport was poorly developed in the Outer

Islands (Dick and Forbes 1992). In China and India, the surface transport system is adequate for most purposes. However, the inadequacy of the transport system in Brazil has inhibited the mobility of labour and was clearly a major reason for the delayed opening up of large areas of the more isolated inland states such as Para, Rondonia, Acre, and Amazonas.

The bottom section of Table 1.1 presents some basic information about urbanization in China, India, Indonesia and Brazil. In terms of levels of urbanization, Brazil has reached 75 per cent, a level more characteristic of developed countries, whereas the others remain at relatively low levels. The four countries show marked differences in the changes in the proportion of urban population over the three decades between 1960/1 and 1990/1. In Indonesia, this proportion has almost doubled from 15 to 31 per cent whereas in Brazil, the percentage has moved up by over two-thirds from 45 to nearly 76 per cent. India and China show a relatively modest rise in the percentage of urban population: of the order of 30 and 44 per cent, if we accept the estimates based on the 1990 census of China. The latter proviso is crucial because, at one stage, the proportion of urban population in China was rapidly revised upwards each year, from 21 per cent according to the 1982 census to 48 per cent in 1988. The usually cautious World Bank even reported 60 per cent of China's population as urban in 1991 before lowering the estimate to 27 per cent in 1992 (World Bank 1993, 1994, Table 31). This 'gross over-exaggeration of . . . China's actual urbanization level' (Kam 1992: 52) resulted from a new set of criteria for designating towns. Under these criteria, adopted in 1984, thousands of townships (*xiang*), which had previously been classified as rural were granted town (*zhen*) status. Also, many newly designated cities included large expanses of rural areas within their new boundaries, resulting in serious 'overbounding' problems.

According to the measure 'percentage of urban population in cities < 500,000', China and India appear to have a more highly developed network of smaller cities, though the proportions of smaller cities in all four countries are above the average of those developing countries large enough to have at least one city above half a million in population. In all four countries, the number of cities with populations over half a million at least doubled between 1960 and 1990, and it trebled in India and Indonesia. In India, larger cities have been accounting for an increasingly large share of total urban population over a long period of time, as Fig. 1.2 clearly demonstrates. In Indonesia, though, their share increased only slightly over the 1970s, and declined over the 1980s, from 44 per cent to 36 per cent of the urban population.[2] In China, the economic reforms after 1978 led to very rapid growth of small towns and a rise in their share of total urban population (see Laquian, Chapter 3 below).

Urban primacy is usually lower in large countries, because more than one major city grows to serve large hinterlands widely separated from each other. The

---

[2] This apparent decline was somewhat misleading, because much of the urban growth in Java was in localities adjoining large cities, particularly Jakarta, which in functional terms should be considered part of the growth of these large cities.

Table 1.1. Some basic characteristics of the four largest developing countries

	China	India	Indonesia	Brazil
Area (million km^2)	9.6	3.3	1.9	8.5
Population 1990 (millions)	1134	850	178	150
Population growth rate (average annual 1980–90)	1.4	2.1	1.8	2.2
System of government	Unitary	Federal	Unitary	Federal
GDP 1992 (US $billions)	506	214	126	360
GNP per capita 1992 (US$)	470	310	670	2770
ICP estimates 1990 (US$)	1950	1150	2350	4780
GDP growth rate 1980–92 (average annual)	9.1	5.2	5.7	2.2
Percentage of 1990 GDP in:				
Agriculture	27	31	22	10
Industry	42	29	40	39
Services	31	40	38	51
Average annual growth rate of industry, 1980–90	12.5	6.6	5.6	2.1
Percentage of 1990 labour force in:				
Agriculture	71[a]	66[a]	56[a]	23
Industry	19	11	13	23
Services	10	23	31	54
Total long-term debt service as a percentage of exports, 1992	10.3	25.3	32.1	23.1
Total fertility rate 1992	2.0	3.7	2.9	2.8
Percentage change in TFR, 1970–92	–66	–36	–47	–43
Percentage of population urban 1960	20	18	15	45
Percentage of population urban 1990	56[c]	27	31	75
Census estimate 1990/1	26[c]	26	31	76
Projected percentage of population urban 2025[b]	55	45	61	89
Percentage of 1980 urban population in cities < 500,000	55	61	50	48
Percentage of 1992 urban population in urban agglomerations > 1 million	35	34	36	51
Number of cities with population over 500,000:				
1960	38	11	3	6
1990	78	36	9	14
Four- city primacy index[d]	0.43	0.51	1.33	1.06

   [a] Data relate to 1987 in China, 1987–8 in India, 1989 in Indonesia

   [b] Data from United Nations, 1994, Annexe tables

   [c] The controversy over China's level of organization is discussed in Ch. 5

   [d] Population of the largest city divided by population of the next three largest cities. Based on urban agglomeration data derived from UN *Demographic Yearbook 1986*, Table 8, 1991 Population census data for India, 1990 Population census data for Indonesia, and Chinese data from the one-per-hundred simple survey of 1987 (Ebanks and Cheng 1990). Years are 1987 for China, 1991 for India, 1990 for Indonesia, and 1985 for Brazil.

Source: World Bank, *World Development Report* 1992 and 1994, unless otherwise stated.

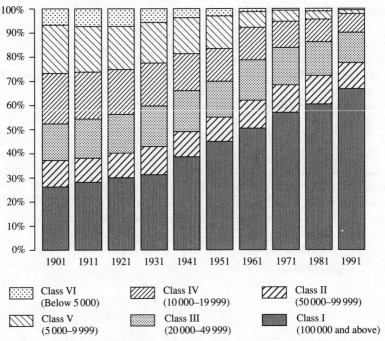

Fig. 1.2.   Proportion of urban population by size class, India 1901–91
Source: Census of India 1991

observed levels of primacy in these four countries are indeed relatively low by
world standards, and they are lowest in the largest countries—China and India.
However, at a lower level (e.g. the provincial level) urban primacy may be much
more marked than at the national level (see, on Indonesia, Jones 1988: 148–50;
and on China, Ebanks and Cheng 1990: 42–7). The Chinese government has been
very successful in avoiding concentration of population in the largest cities, as
evidenced by trends in a range of measures of urban concentration (Ebanks and
Cheng 1990: 42–7). However, where primacy is measured more in terms of urban
function than of size, the picture becomes more complex. In Indonesia, the
centralization of power in Jakarta seems to have increased, if anything, during the
recent period when the rise in Jakarta's demographic primacy halted. Also, cities
can have functional importance across the borders of their province (Vance and
Sutker 1957: 103–4). 'A smaller city in a more developed province may have
greater ecological influence and control across its provincial borders than does the
provincial capital within the provincial border' (Poston, Tian and Jia 1989: 17).
Levels of primacy may be influenced by whether federal or unitary systems of
government are followed, as well as by the relative importance of international
trade in the GDP, the trade policy adopted, industrialization strategies, exchange
rate policies, etc.

Demographic Background to Urbanization

One of the most frequently overlooked facts in the welter of studies dealing with developmental problems of urbanization is that throughout most of the developing world, urban growth results primarily from natural increase (United Nations 1980). Nevertheless, there are some important complexities in the relationship between natural increase, migration and reclassification in fuelling urban population growth.

As village populations grow and engage increasingly in non-farm activities, their classification has to change. The pace of reclassification tends to vary over time and space, and leads to some fluctuations in the trend towards urbanization. China in the 1980s demonstrated an extreme of the likely magnitude of the reclassification effect. The effect was quite substantial in Indonesia over the 1980–90 period. India showed a more moderate effect: the slower pace of urbanization during 1981–91, compared with that of the previous decade, seems to be attributable partly to somewhat limited changes in classification, except in the state of Kerala (where a large majority of the villages have more than 10,000 inhabitants and where there was extensive revision of the number of towns prior to the 1991 census). (Visaria, Chapter 13 below).

As for natural increase and migration, in the short run, the relative contribution of each may be clear. If we adopt a longer time perspective, however, we can argue that the role of migration is larger because much of the natural increase of population in the cities occurs among people who have previously migrated there (most of them in the young reproductive ages). On the other hand, the rural 'pool' from which migrants are being drawn is constantly being enlarged by natural increase (Jones 1988: 139–40; Keyfitz 1980; Keyfitz and Philipov 1981).

In the four countries discussed in this book, the contribution of natural increase and migration to urban growth differs markedly, and in each of the countries there have been substantial changes during the past two decades. The natural increase of the rural population remains fairly high in India, Indonesia, and Brazil, but is much more modest in China. Fertility rates have declined substantially in all four countries. Natural increase of the urban population, though it remains an important factor driving urban growth in each of the countries except China, is no longer the force it once was. This is particularly the case since the usual urban–rural fertility differentials hold true (though offsetting these are lower urban mortality rates and an age structure conducive to natural increase due to the influx of reproductive-age migrants). In Brazil, the rate of natural increase in the metropolitan areas of São Paulo and Rio de Janeiro declined sharply during the 1980s as a result of a rapid fall in fertility (Martine 1993). The same is true of Jakarta in Indonesia.

According to the contributions to this volume, migration has been regulated to a considerable extent in China, although the lifting of restrictions after 1982 led to sizeable rural–urban migration. In Indonesia, rural–urban migration was substantial during the 1980s, though much of the urban population growth rate exceeding 5 per cent per annum resulted from reclassification. In India, natural increase seems to have accounted for about three-quarters of the urban growth during the 1970s and 1980s. A proper analysis of the factors causing urban growth in the different countries merits priority attention by researchers.

What, then, are the prospects for continued rapid urban population growth and (a somewhat different question) rapid urbanization? In regard to both these questions, there are basic differences between Brazil and the other countries. In Brazil, the urban share of the population is now so large that it can no longer be augmented very much from the small rural pool, particularly since the natural increase of this rural population has now slackened. Brazil's heady urban growth rates of the 1960s and 1970s will therefore never be repeated. On the other hand, the rural 'sending populations' in China, India, and Indonesia are enormous and if patterns of economic growth are conducive, massive migration towards the cities can be expected. The lowered national fertility rates will slow down urban growth rates somewhat, as will the increasing tendency to substitute commutation for relocation to urban areas, but rates of urban growth exceeding 4 per cent per annum are nevertheless quite likely, based mainly on urbanward migration.

In a context of declining total population growth rates, such rates would imply particularly rapid urbanization (i.e. rise in the proportion urban). But this should not be unexpected. In relation to the logistic urbanization curves found so frequently in time series, China, India, and Indonesia are located on the pre-inflection point of the curve and might therefore be expected to urbanize rapidly in coming decades.[3] How rapidly will of course depend on macro-economic forces acting on both fertility and migration (Kelley and Williamson 1984: 421).

One implication should be stressed: given the projected slackening in the growth of the younger segment of the workforce already alluded to, and the prominence of young workers in most rural–urban migration, such trends would imply an absolute decline in the youthful component of rural populations, and possibly an absolute decline in the rural population as a whole. Such trends are certainly in prospect in China and Java, though probably not in the near term in India.

Growth of Major Metropolitan Regions

An inevitable feature of very large and populous countries is that as they urbanize, truly vast metropolitan agglomerations will develop. The potential for the growth of such agglomerations has been enhanced by technological developments affecting transport and communications, which makes commuting from longer distances (50 kilometres or so) feasible, and enables business to be

---

[3] It is worth noting that in the Third World as a whole, urban population growth rates and urban inmigration rates were very high over the period when the urban share rose from 35 to 50% (Kelley and Williamson 1984, table 2), the phase of urbanization about to be entered by China, India, and Indonesia.

conducted from home-based telecommunication and computer facilities (Vining 1985).

Such metropolitan agglomerations are in evidence in the four countries under study, and they promise to grow much larger. In China, the three main foci for such developments are the Beijing–Tianjin–Tangshan region, the Shanghai–southern Jiangsu region, and the Pearl River delta, in particular Guangzhou and Hong Kong. A fourth (the Shenyang–Dalien belt in central and southern Liaoning province) is sometimes added (Zhou 1991). In India, the main agglomerations surround Delhi, Bombay and Calcutta, although a number of others are also emerging (Chakraborty 1991, Fig. 14.1). In Indonesia, the main agglomeration is the Jabotabek region surrounding Jakarta, with another one developing in East Java in the Surabaya-Sidoarjo–Mojokerto–Malang region, and incipient developments along the north coast of Central Java and in the Yogyakarta–Surakarta area (Firman 1992). In Brazil, the dominant agglomeration, one of the world's largest, surrounds São Paulo, with another around Rio de Janeiro.

Such mega-urban regions often incorporate two or more large urban cores linked by effective transportation routes. The total metropolitan region includes the major cities, peri-urban zones and an extensive zone of mixed rural–urban land use along such routes (McGee 1991). Characteristics of the 'rural' areas located within the extended metropolitan zone of these large cities include rapid commercialization of agriculture; expansion of transport systems; and an employment shift from farming to other activities, accompanied by migration or commutation to cities. Factories and other non-agricultural activities are also developing within the zone but outside the city proper.

There is a tendency for the population in the periphery of these metropolitan agglomerations to grow faster than that in the urban core. For example, in India, towns within a 100–kilometre radius of Calcutta, Bombay, Delhi, and Hyderabad grew substantially faster than these metropolitan cities between 1971 and 1981 (Chakraborty 1991, Table 14.3). In Indonesia, between the 1980 and 1990 censuses, the population of the Jakarta Special Region grew by only 2.4 per cent per annum, a much slower rate of growth than for the overall urban population of Indonesia. But the population of the *Kabupaten* (districts) of Bogor, Tanggerang and Bekasi, which surround Jakarta and constitute the extended Jakarta planning region, grew by 5.2 per cent per annum; the urban population of these three regencies (although possibly exaggerated by a more generous application in 1990 of definitions of urban which remained unchanged between the two censuses) grew by a remarkable 15.9 per cent per annum. Although the growth of Jakarta proper, then, was relatively slow, the urban population of this core region grew somewhat more rapidly than Indonesia's urban population as a whole (5.9 per cent compared with 5.4 per cent) (Jones 1991: 23–4). Similarly, in Brazil, a tendency has been noted in the larger metropolitan areas for 'an important shift in the momentum of growth from the central municipalities to the peripheral areas' (Merrick and Graham 1979: 328; see also Martine and Campolina, Chapter 10 below; Martine 1993).

Many issues surround the growth of these giant agglomerations. In some cases, not only in these countries but elsewhere (e.g. Bangkok and the Central Plain region of Thailand) they appear to be 'countries within countries', islands of great wealth and high productivity serving as a natural focus for further investments and migration of people from poorer areas. One observer of developments in the Pearl River delta, where growth rates have compared favourably with Taiwan and South Korea in earlier years, sees this as a Cantonese 'newly industrializing economy' (Vogel 1989). Commonly used indicators of labour productivity, often restricted to the manufacturing sector, tend to show the metropolitan regions outperforming other parts of the country and larger cities outperforming smaller cities. For example, in China, per-worker gross value of industrial output (in yuan) ranged from 19,117 in cities of over 1 million inhabitants to 15,085 in cities of between 0.3 and 1 million people and to 12,687 in cities of fewer than 0.3 million (Kim 1989, Table 2; see also Chang and Kim 1989).

Even so, the evidence that higher productivity in large cities results from their largeness is far from watertight. Although evidence of higher productivity in large cities is frequently controlled for differences in capital per worker and size of enterprise, allowance is less frequently made for concentration of talent, education and skilled manpower or better industrial infrastructure. Sometimes the indicators of productivity may be inappropriate, as when the measure of 'production' includes much that from a social accounting point of view should be on the cost rather than the production side of the ledger (e.g. excessive gasoline consumption in traffic jams, extra cleaning and health care costs due to pollution, and higher prices used to ration access to scarce leisure-time activities).

Can these agglomerations remain viable as they grow? Probably so. If not, diseconomies of agglomeration will create automatic adjustment mechanisms affecting the location of enterprises and of the potential workforce (Kelley and Williamson 1984: 421). But 'many of the problems of very large cities in the developing world reflect their rapid growth rather than size per se' (Lowry 1989: 21). When growth eventually leads to scale diseconomies, polynucleation follows, that is, what was a functionally centralized city breaks up into cells, each containing a nearly self-sufficient sub-city, (Lowry 1989: 22) and thereby a very large mega-city becomes viable. Such polynucleation processes can be seen at work in the Jakarta metropolitan region, with formerly small centres developing into major urban nodes in places such as Tangerang, Bekasi, Serpong, and Depok. Similarly, in the Delhi metropolitan area, localities such as Faridabad, Ghaziabad, and Gurgaon are developing into commercial, industrial and residential nodes.

Nevertheless, even if it is true that national economic growth would be maximized by allowing the largest metropolises to grow to a very large size, planners might appropriately opt for slower national growth if faster metropolitan growth meant seriously widened regional income disparities, or lowered quality of life in ways not captured in income measures, or sheer problems of governance and political instability, or suspect environmental sustainability of mega-cities in the longer run (Jones 1991: 24–5). But to opt for slower metropolitan growth implies interventions to slow that growth; the record of such interventions to date does not inspire confidence that planners can always achieve their goals in matters of mega-city growth.

Blurring of the Urban–Rural Distinction

Although the statistical concepts of urban and rural are adopted universally, urban/rural differences actually range along a continuum. The distinctions between urban and rural are tending to become increasingly blurred, as a result of developments in transport and communications and other technological changes which bring within the reach of rural populations, not only goods and services normally thought of as the preserve of urban residents, but also goods and services not available even to urban dwellers only a very short time ago. The percentage of Indian villages with access to electricity grew from less than 5 per cent in the 1940s to 84 per cent in 1992. Developments in communications break down isolation of rural areas, widen the knowledge base and facilitate the rapid dissemination of new ideas. In China, the relaxation of restrictions on village-to-town migration in 1984 led initially to an influx of migrants to small towns, then to more restrictive measures fostering commuting rather than permanent movement. These, however, ensure very close integration of Chinese villages and towns.

Developments in transportation assist the articulation of urban areas with their regions, facilitating the movement of goods and people, breaking down formerly stark differences between rural and urban areas, and enabling rural dwellers to be linked more effectively into the urban labour market, through commuting or temporary or seasonal migration. This helps maintain a relatively cheap labour supply for urban industry, while at the same time increasing income-earning opportunities for rural people. Both because of employment opportunities in nearby urban areas and the growth of non-agricultural employment within rural areas, the rural economy becomes increasingly complex (Jakobson and Prakash 1971; Jones 1983).

Meriting special consideration in the context of the earlier discussion about the growth of metropolitan regions is the tendency for the blurring of urban-rural distinctions to be particularly pronounced in such regions. Indeed, McGee (1991) has coined the term 'desakota' from two Indonesian words, to refer to the development of zones of intense urban–rural interaction, found not only within the extended metropolis but also in the vicinity of major transport corridors between urban areas. Many examples of such zones can be cited in the four countries under discussion: for example, the north coastal corridor of Central Java, or the extended Jabotabek metropolis, in Indonesia; or the zones of intense rural industrialization in China, for example in the Pearl River delta and in Jiangsu and Zhejiang provinces. Features conducive to the growth of such zones appear to include not only the proximity of large metropolitan areas or major transport corridors but also high population density in rural areas. Economic reform in China appears to have made its greatest impact in such peri-urban areas (Pannell and Veeck 1991: 132).

The Major Themes of the Book

In the following sections we propose to highlight a few important findings, grouped according to a set of themes that authors were asked to address.

Structural and spatial economic changes and their implications for urbanization

Urbanization is closely linked with structural shifts in employment and the tendency for certain kinds of employment to be concentrated in urban areas. The now-discredited 'overurbanization thesis' took the postulate of such links to an extreme by arguing that if the rise in urbanization exceeded that in industry's share of employment, it was clear evidence of overurbanization. The argument overlooked the fact that since the Second World War, industry's share of total employment has not tended to go as high as it did in countries industrializing earlier, both because of high capital-labour ratios in modern manufacturing and because the tertiary sector now plays a greater role in advanced economies.

In the four countries covered in this book, agriculture's share of GDP has declined to much lower levels than its share of employment (see Table 1.1), reflecting the lower labour productivity in agriculture. There is also a much wider range in agriculture's share of employment than in its share of GDP. As expected, there was a much higher level of urbanization in Brazil than in the other countries, where agriculture's share of employment was much higher. However, for the other three countries, the correspondence between level of urbanization and share of employment accounted for by non-agriculture was by no means close. This finding could have been affected by inter-country differences in the definition of urban areas, as well as in the recording of agricultural work. However, the link between the shift out of agriculture and urbanization is also not as close as is sometimes imagined (Jones 1983, 1990), because of the possibility of considerable change in the structure of employment within rural areas. The dramatic changes in the employment structure in rural areas of the coastal zone of China, with rural dwellers participating in burgeoning factory employment in the small towns, are sufficient evidence of the possibilities in this regard. The steadily decreasing share of primary industry in the rural employment structure of Java provides another example (Jones 1984).

Agriculture continued to dominate employment in China and India in 1990, whereas its share was falling towards half in Indonesia and was below one-quarter in Brazil. The point at which agricultural employment, with its much lower levels of productivity than other sectors of the economy, ceases to grow has been a significant one in the economic history of many countries. In Brazil, despite all the publicity about agricultural and pastoral development in Amazonia, agricultural employment has been declining since the 1970s. Li (Chapter 2 below) shows that China experienced a slight decline in agricultural employment between 1979 and 1986. In Indonesia and India agricultural employment is still growing, although in Central and East Java, growth has almost ceased (Jones and Manning 1992; Hugo et al 1987, chapters 9, 11). There has been a tendency over time for the share of non-agricultural employment as a proportion of total employment in rural areas to rise in many countries, including the four countries covered in this book. In rural India, the share of the primary sector among male workers declined by nine percentage points and that among female workers by about five percentage points over the 15-year period between 1972–3 and 1987–8 (Visaria, Chapter 13, Table 13.7 below). But the growth of such non-agricultural employment in rural areas has not been even across regions. It has tended to be concentrated in certain well-favoured areas in the vicinity of large cities, or in densely populated regions where labour supply is adequate and transportation networks dense, whereas more isolated rural areas have tended to miss out. The changing spatial distribution of economic activity has naturally led to differences in the pace of urbanization between regions; in the rapidly growing rural areas, more settlements take on the characteristics of urban places and are therefore reclassified as towns. Thus in Indonesia, where there has been a demonstrable tendency for non-agricultural employment to be disproportionately concentrated in areas close to large towns (Jones 1984), the most rapid rise in level of urbanization between 1980 and 1990 also tended to be in such areas (Firman 1992). Similarly, the urbanization process in China is proceeding apace in coastal regions such as Zhejiang and Guangzhou, where rural enterprises are expanding most rapidly. In Brazil, there is clear evidence of deconcentration of industrial employment outside the metropolitan areas (Martine 1993).

As a result of the rapid expansion of non-agricultural employment in rural areas lying within zones of influence of major metropolises and the associated tendency for urbanization to increase more rapidly in these areas than in others, income distribution disparities appear to be widening between such rural areas and more isolated rural areas. The Chinese leadership evidently took a conscious decision to downplay the significance of these growing income disparities as a phase in the process of economic growth. In other countries, the political leadership often finds it difficult to face the issue directly, even if the Chinese view is fully shared.

Effect of regional development policy and national urban development strategies on patterns of urban growth

The authors were asked to address the question of the effectiveness of regional development policy in meeting its stated goals. Is there an articulated national urban development strategy, and if so, how coherent is it and what are its major goals? What approaches can be used to evaluate its success?

In all four countries, regional development policy is given considerable prominence in planning documents and institutional structures. For example, in the Indonesian development planning agency, BAPPENAS, a separate division deals with regional development. The degree of success, however, is difficult to measure. In the nature of the case, development of lagging regions and narrowing of regional income disparities is not easy. The evidence that regional disparities remain wide (Hill 1989) does not necessarily demonstrate the failure of regional planning, because the situation could conceivably have been worse without such planning. In any case, although lessening of regional disparities was a clearly stated goal in India, Indonesia and Brazil, China's case demonstrates that this is not necessarily a goal of regional planning. China made a deliberate policy choice in the late 1970s to turn from a policy favouring the development of the lagging interior regions to one promoting rapid development of the coastal zone, in the interests of faster overall growth, despite the widened income disparities which this would entail (Linge and Forbes 1990, especially chapters 1 and 3).

In Indonesia, regional disparities as measured by 'Williamson' indices[4] and other measures have not widened over the period of rapid economic development. 'The rigid, highly centralized system of government administration has, in a suboptimal fashion, ensured reasonable uniformity in delivering government services' (Hill 1994: 113). Fiscal equalization measures have recycled the windfall revenues from oil and other mining enclaves to ensure that all provinces have shared in the boom to some extent. But there is a downside: regional government is in a fiscal straightjacket, relying heavily on central government subsidies, and is given little incentive to enhance efficiency of tax collection and little capacity to follow policies stressing perceived regional comparative advantage.

Brazil has adopted a wide range of measures, including fiscal incentives, to foster industrialization away from the core region of the South-East (Haddad, Chapter 11 below). They appear to have had only limited success. 'Deconcentration' in Brazil has tended to be more in terms of a geographical expansion of the dominant pole (São Paulo region) rather than an upsurge in investment that creates new poles well away from this region (Martine and Diniz, Chapter 10 below). Entrepreneurs appear to have chosen small cities—within a convenient radius of São Paulo but not necessarily within the state of São Paulo—for purposes of industrial location (Martine 1993: 126).

This brings us to the question of the role of urbanization patterns in regional development and, more generally, as a determinant of economic efficiency and human welfare. What factors influence city-size distribution, and to what extent are they amenable to policy direction? Are the high levels of urban primacy evident in countries such as Thailand or Uruguay the result of geographic 'facts of life' or are they also due to governmental structures and specific policy emphases? As noted earlier, the four large countries covered by this book have relatively low levels of primacy nationally, but sometimes much higher levels regionally. Fierce

[4] Williamson indices are population-weighted coefficients of variation in regional incomes. See Williamson, 1965.

debate continues to rage in the urbanization and regional development literature on optimum urban structures and the extent to which it is appropriate to intervene to alter these. The debate centres on both the desirability and feasibility of altering existing patterns. The 'desirability' debate focuses on the problems associated with the growth of very large cities, and as there are a range of both objective and subjective indicators of such problems, consensus is unlikely to be reached. On the 'feasibility' front, the history of 'growth pole' approaches so popular in the 1970s does not generate confidence (Jones 1991), and intermediate city strategies do not hold out much prospect for major alteration of pre-existing patterns.

A particularly important issue concerns the appropriate urbanization strategy for lagging regions, notably the western zone in China, eastern India, eastern Indonesia, and north-eastern Brazil. For example, in the five easternmost provinces of Indonesia with a total population of 11 million, the level of urbanization is only about 15 per cent, and the largest city has a population of only 300,000, though the second, third and fourth cities are not much smaller. Given the scattered distribution of the population, the continuing very high reliance on primary industry, and the distance to markets, growth centre approaches can hardly be expected to work, and the issue appears to be whether city growth should be left dependent on the spin-offs of a rural development emphasis rather than seen as an entry point to generate regional development.

Effects of implicit policies and institutional factors on urbanization

All four countries face the problem of reconciling inconsistencies between policies designed to influence urbanization and regional development and 'implicit' policies (those designed for other purposes but which do in fact influence urbanization and regional development). 'Implicit policies' can be viewed very broadly as including industrialization strategies, exchange rate policies, transportation, education, health, and defence policies; also influential are institutional factors such as system of government (federal or unitary) and strength of local government (Fuchs, Jones and Pernia 1987, chapter 1). Two examples might be given. The first is from India, where for many years the official policy attempted to prevent the location of industry within a 50-km radius of large cities, (Mohan, Chapter 14 below) but where export promotion was also a declared policy, and the large port cities of Calcutta, Bombay and Madras were prime locations for export-oriented industry. Moreover, advantages such as heavily subsidized city bus fares and water rates had the effect of making it easier for people to live in these cities. Even subsidies for food were concentrated in the urban areas: Bombay, with 14 per cent of the population of Maharashtra State in 1989, accounted for 40 per cent and 31 per cent respectively of the state's share of rice and wheat distribution through fair-price shops (Oberai 1993: 45).

The second example is from Indonesia, where despite a policy stance in favour of the growth of intermediate cities rather than further growth of the big cities, especially Jakarta, the highly centralized planning system, and the need to be near the decision-makers, provides a strong incentive for the location of industry in Jakarta. This is reinforced by the allocation to Jakarta of a much higher proportion of total investments in health and education services, electricity and piped water than is warranted by its share in national population. In 1980, 30 per cent of all households in Jakarta received piped water compared with 23 per cent in Bandung, the capital of West Java, and little more than 10 per cent in other urban centres in West Java (ESCAP 1984).

Urbanization, mobility and labour markets

Neo-classical economics sees migration as an equilibrating mechanism, raising national production and welfare by bringing labour supply into better equilibrium with other resource endowment and with labour demand. However, labour market rigidities and institutional factors may inhibit this favourable outcome. Non-permanent mobility is an important part of the articulation of urban and rural labour markets in China and India (Chapters 4 and 13, by Lin and Visaria, below) as well as in Indonesia (Hugo 1982) and Brazil. Mobility on the scale in which it is encountered in China, Indonesia and Brazil has very important welfare implications for sending and receiving areas, and raises issues including the economic consequences of the age–sex composition of migration flows; private versus social costs and benefits; effect of migration on productivity, income levels, income distribution, availability of entrepreneurial talent, and unemployment; and the role of remittances in development.

Urban poverty poses a particular problem in mega-cities; a study on Rio de Janiero notes that 'the metropolitan poor live in a very competitive environment and cannot turn to small production for self-consumption as a means to supplement their real income.' (Tolosa *et al.* 1991: 102). The urban poor are not concentrated only in the informal sector, nor are they necessarily those who have most recently migrated to the city. (Nor are migrants disproportionately represented in low-income informal sector activities.) Nevertheless, the evidence strongly suggests that the proportion of poor tends to be higher in the informal sector than the formal sector. In large Brazilian cities in 1984, 11 per cent of organized sector workers were poor compared with 66 per cent of unorganized sector workers. In Bombay, 40 per cent of casual workers were below the poverty line compared with 10 and 12 per cent of regular workers in small and large firms, respectively (Oberai 1993: 86). Both unemployment and underemployment stem from the weak labour absorption capacity of the modern sector, forcing the labour force to spill into the informal sector, where wages are generally low and technical progress lags behind that in the modern sector. Even in the modern sector, data for Bombay indicate a pervasive segmentation of productive activity between a small number of highly productive capital-intensive firms (which tend to continue capital-intensification) and a large number of less productive labour-intensive firms. The limited scope for employment in the former pushes labour towards the less productive sector (Oberai 1993: 89).

In India, Indonesia, and Brazil, geographic mobility of labour has been relatively unrestricted, except for the influence of domicile tests applied for public sector employment in some states of India. In Indonesia, migration to new agricultural areas does not appear to have accelerated urbanization in these areas, perhaps because of the generally low incomes of the migrant farmers, which do little to raise consumer demand for urban products. In Brazil, by contrast, urbanization of frontier regions has proceeded apace (see Sawyer, Chapter 12 below). Sawyer attributes this to partial modernization of agriculture, the need of modern agriculture for urban services, the new consumption patterns of Brazil's rural population, the need for urban consumer services, decreased access to land, and, finally, decreased access to ownership and employment in large cities.

China's pattern of mobility remains different (Lin, Chapter 4 below). Restriction on population mobility succeeded in avoiding many of the urban planning problems faced by the other countries. But this was at the cost of totally cutting off the rural people from the process of urbanization and closing the urban system, thus reducing its vitality. Surplus labour built up in the countryside, service industries in the cities were restricted, and welfare in both rural and urban areas probably suffered. The greater mobility of more recent years is by no means unrestricted, and policy focuses on generating new employment opportunities in rural areas and small towns. It is still too early for a definitive assessment of the success of this policy.

Industrial location policy and its implications

In many developing countries, industrial location policy designed to foster deconcentration of industry has not rested easily with trade policies and exchange rate policies designed to foster import substitution industrialization, which tends to concentrate in the metropolitan city or cities. In Indonesia, though ideology supports decentralization, the regulatory environment fosters centralization. In actuality, myriad government interventions in the development process pull in different directions (Hill 1992: 239–44). The general pattern, whereby resource-based activities predominate in the outer islands and footloose industry is concentrated in Java near the main labour force and consumer markets, would probably hold, irrespective of government policy and actions. However, 'there has been no concerted or consistent strategy of spatial industrial development, and growth patterns outside Java have inevitably been very uneven, clustering around a few large mainly coastal centres, and bypassing the interiors and virtually the entire eastern region' (Hill 1992: 244).

Assessment of industrial location policy in India and Brazil supports some of the Indonesian conclusions. Mohan (Chapter 14 below) argues that market forces which induce firms to locate at a particular site are found to be quite strong and only strong policy interventions can lead to a significant change in the cost-benefit calculus that firms typically employ in making their location decisions. Although the Indian government has been concerned to influence industrial location, the instruments of policy appear to have been generally inadequate, particularly as they are frequently in competition with countervailing influences.

In both India and Brazil, government incentives to promote industrialization of peripheral, disadvantaged or backward regions (operating through a wide range of measures, including income-tax incentives, industrial licensing, freight-equalization schemes, concessional finance schemes, industrial estates, distribution and pricing policy for intermediate industrial inputs, and location of public sector plants) do appear to have had some success, though with some perverse effects, for example, on intra-regional income and wealth concentration in Brazil, and in raising levels of unemployment once industrial construction was completed (Haddad, Chapter 11 below). Mohan (Chapter 14 below) argues that, in India, policy has placed too much emphasis on locating industry away from cities, which is not efficient in the Indian context of a balanced hierarchy of cities.

More recently, Indian policy has placed more emphasis on the building of infrastructure as the new incentive for dispersal of industrial location. Infrastructure construction, particularly transportation networks, has also been very important in Indonesia and Brazil, though as Hill (1992) notes, it may be a two-edged sword because as well as providing opportunities through linking the peripheries with the rest of the economy, it can destroy protected local industrial niches.

Housing and infrastructure provision and financing

Housing plays a most important part in determining the welfare of city dwellers. Thus decisions about the way in which housing—especially low-income housing—is provided are of major importance. Should the emphasis be on high-rise flats or slum upgrading? How can such housing and related infrastructure—access roads or paths, sanitation, water and power—be most effectively financed? What is the role of land taxes, betterment taxes, user charges, etc. in financing urban development? In many countries, different housing markets exist side by side, with subsidized housing for government employees and those working in large private firms and an open market operating both in shanty towns and toward the top end of the income scale. There is often mismatch between urban governments' responsibility for public service provision and their revenue authority. Linn (1987) argues that increased flexibility for local governments to raise revenues of their own is probably one of the most important ways in which national authorities can support effective city management.

The case studies on housing policies from China, Indonesia and India, presented in Chapters 5, 9, and 13, provide some interesting contrasts. For a long time, China maintained a low rent policy which led to the premature deterioration of the housing stock. Almost no housing was built in cities such as Shanghai during the chaotic decade from 1966 to 1976. Housing was in desperately short supply, with newlyweds forced to move into cramped parental units. China's aim of encouraging home ownership (begun in 1982) and raising rents from their ridiculously low subsidized levels (begun in 1987) had many teething problems, not the least of which was that parallel reforms were not introduced in the wage system. Employees of state-owned work units enjoyed a disproportionately large share of the new housing stock produced since the early 1980s (Lee, Chapter 5 below).

In Indonesia, where families with limited financial resources are estimated to account for 70 per cent of the population, and where land prices and construction costs are escalating in the cities, provision of housing to the urban poor is a major concern. The Kampung Improvement Programme seeks to upgrade the standard of slum areas by provision of basic access (mainly footpaths), drainage and flood control and low-cost community water supply and sanitation services. The programme is intended to have an indirect effect on housing quality because area upgrading serves to motivate residents to improve their housing and yard areas on their own (Koswara, Chapter 9 below).

In India, while recent estimates of the proportion of urban dwellers living in slums are below earlier estimates, the situation nevertheless remains serious, with about 30 million slum dwellers in 1991, or 13 per cent of the urban population. The percentage of slum dwellers rises to around 30 per cent in Bombay and Calcutta. Limited financial resources hinder efforts to increase the housing stock for the low-income population; thus recent migrants tend to form squatter settlements on public lands, whereas sites and services programs can cater for persons who have already attained a degree of economic stability after some years of urban residence. Strategic provision of credit by public-sector institutions has been shown to support individual and group initiatives in improving living conditions of the slum population (Visaria, Chapter 13 below).

Despite all the lip service paid to housing the urban poor, it seems that no available housing programmes in these four countries actually meet the needs of the poorest 20 per cent of the urban population. Meeting the needs of the lower middle class is hard enough, but housing the lowest 20 per cent of the population remains a seemingly intractable problem.

Although abundant data are available documenting gross deficiencies of housing and of infrastructure (transportation, water, power, waste disposal) in the cities in these four countries, the fact is that in many respects urban dwellers are much better-off than rural dwellers. According to the Indian data based on the Sample Registration System, the expectation of life at birth in urban India exceeded that in rural India by nine years during 1981–5 and by seven years during 1986–90 (Visaria, Chapter 13 below). The infant mortality rate in urban India during 1990–2 was 52 per 1,000, about three-fifths that in rural India (86). Such differences persist despite the continuing effort to provide the rural population with the requisite primary health care. Unfortunately, the wide dispersal of the rural population, with nearly 30 per cent spread over 420,000 villages each inhabited by fewer than 1,000 people, makes it extremely difficult to ensure the desired availability of health facilities.

Conclusions

This chapter has presented an overview of the content of the book, dealing with urbanization in the world's four largest developing countries. Constituting, as they do, more than 40 per cent of the world's population, the urban issues of the four countries discussed would be of enormous importance to the world even if they had no relevance at all beyond national borders.

Special issues in relation to urbanization in large countries have to do with scale, since these countries are large in terms not only of total population but also of land area; and with agglomeration, since large countries tend to generate large metropolises. Economies of scale, though they can also be realised in smaller countries through international trade and through vertical integration of productive activities, remain a particular characteristic of large countries. Their effects on industrial structure, urbanization and the urban pattern, along with their effect on administrative and planning mechanisms dealing with urban areas and regions, require study. It has been argued by one observer (Fincher 1981: 27) that sheer size—particularly the size of the population, but also that of the territory—explains many features of the Chinese scene that are too often attributed exclusively to ideological or cultural variation.

Agglomeration economies and diseconomies also require study, with a view to the formulation of appropriate policies to address the growth of cities of different size classes, particularly the growth of the major metropolitan areas. Offsetting aspects of agglomeration are likely to include (on the positive side) concentration of skills and intellectual and technical resources; economies of scale in the provision of infrastructure and services; and (on the negative side) crowding, traffic jams, pollution, and whatever diseconomies of scale are linked to the provision of infrastructure in large cities. Some of the diseconomies can probably be ameliorated, however, by a polynucleation process within the metropolitan region (Lowry 1989: 22). Though both scale and agglomeration effects are dealt with at various points throughout this book, we cannot claim to have done much more than scratch the surface in discussing the issues involved.

The urban issues faced by the four largest developing countries do have considerable wider relevance. For one thing, there are many other developing countries which are also large in both area and population: Nigeria, Philippines, and Pakistan, to name just three. There is little difference in scale between the issues they face and those discussed in this book. As for much smaller developing countries, their smallness may appear to set their interests apart from those of the four large countries discussed here. They lack very large cities, and their urban hierarchy is composed of relatively few cities. On the whole, however, the differences are of degree rather than of kind. Smaller countries also face issues of urban primacy and urban hierarchies, even if their 'intermediate cities' have populations in the tens of thousands rather than the hundreds of thousands; smaller countries often face sharp regional differences as well.

But the issues are certainly 'writ large' in the case of the giant countries—placed in sharper focus by virtue of their size. Issues of regional government and devolution of decision-making may be equally pressing in medium-sized countries but less so in small countries. Agglomeration economies are hardly a concern in a country whose largest city is only a quarter of a million. Labour markets tend to be less complex in small countries. Thus the relevance of this book to planners will vary according to the size of the country they work in, but we believe all of them will find many matters of interest, and some of them striking parallels, in the case studies presented in this book.

Finally, it might be stressed that the success of all four countries covered in the book in reducing fertility rates is of great significance for their urban futures. A key element of a responsible urbanization policy must be an appropriate policy with regard to population growth. Efforts to control or divert migration from rural areas are difficult even in the best of circumstances, but much more so if the potential supply of rural migrants is being constantly swollen by high rates of natural increase.

Part I

China

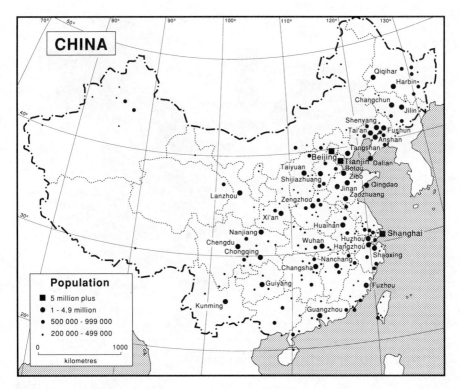

Map 1. Urban centres, China

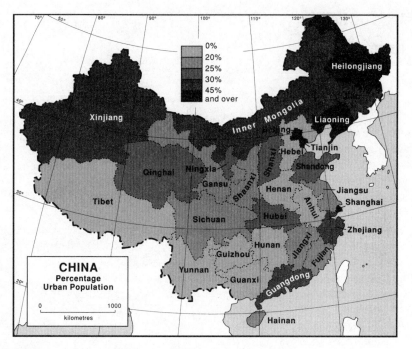

Map 2. Percentage urban by state, China

Introduction

LIN YOU SU

China, the world's largest country, covers an enormous land area with a wide range of geographic conditions, though of the four countries covered in this book, it has by far the largest area subject to cold winters. China has been ruled by a Communist government since 1949, and the attitudes of this government towards urbanization have greatly influenced urbanization trends over this period.

Over the past four decades, China, like the other three largest developing countries, has experienced major structural changes in its economic development and urbanization. The proportion of total urban population increased from 10.6 per cent in 1949 to an official 49.6 per cent in 1988 (China State Statistics Bureau 1989, 1987), though in reality the 1988 proportion was less than 30 per cent. For much of the past four decades, China experienced a unique pattern of urbanization as a result of government policies. The main aims of policy were: to strictly control the growth of large cities and encourage the development of small cities and towns; to control and redistribute the population: on one hand, the government made great efforts to control rural to urban migration, and on the other hand, it organized the resettlement to rural areas of a large number of urban residents; and to expand rural employment through the development of rural industry. Because of China's centrally planned labour allocation system and explicit policy on urbanization and migration, it successfully controlled the rapid growth of metropolitan areas. These efforts, like those to control fertility, have attracted great interest from demographers around the world. Since controlling urban population growth and urban employment has been problematic to many governments of developing countries, it has been widely accepted that China's pattern may offer an alternative approach to development.

During the past four decades, China has achieved tremendous progress in economic development. In 1949, the total value of GNP was only 55 billion yuan. In 1986, it increased to 1,896 billion yuan. The industrial output increased from 14 billion yuan to 985 billion yuan in 1986 (China State Statistics Bureau, 1987: 36). At the same time, the economic structure also changed dramatically. In 1949, the total value of industry accounted for only 29 per cent of GNP; by 1986, this had risen to 69 per cent of GNP (China State Statistics Bureau 1987: 27–39). Such economic development had substantial effects on the pattern and process of urbanization in China. The four chapters in this section briefly review the relationship between economic and regional development and urbanization.

In China, the urban system consists of two parts: cities and towns. For cities, it can be further divided into four levels: extra-largest cities (those with a population of over 1 million); large cities (those with a population of between 500,000 and 1 million); medium–sized cities (those with a population of between 300,000 to 500,000) and small cities (those with a population of under 300,000). According to this classification, by the end of 1988, of China's 431 cities, 81 cities were extra-large, 141 were large, 109 were medium-sized, and 101 cities were small (China State Statistics Bureau 1989: 91). Among China's 50,000 towns, over 9,000 were defined as urban towns in 1987 (Li Jing Neng 1989: 28). Urban towns are defined according to a composite index that includes the location of county-level administrative government, the total population in the residential area, and the population engaged in non-agricultural work.

China's economic development has been unbalanced geographically. The total territory can be divided into three parts: eastern, central and western regions. The eastern coastal region is the most developed region in China. It includes three municipalities and nine provinces. The central region which includes eleven provinces is at a lower level of economic development than the eastern region but is better than the western region. The western region contains six provinces and autonomous regions which are the least developed in China. The level of urban development is greatly influenced by these extensive regional differences in natural conditions and economic development: the absolute number, as well as the proportion, of the urban population declines progressively from eastern to central to western regions. The eastern area, with only 13 per cent of China's land area, contained 46 per cent of the total urban population in 1984; the central area, with 31 per cent of total territory, contained 47 per cent of total urban population; and the western area, with 56 per cent of total territory, contained only 7 per cent of total urban population (Population Research Centre 1985: 811–15). The Chinese government made great efforts to change this unbalanced urban development situation in the past. The major instruments to implement this policy have included the distribution of state construction and investment projects, state finance, allocation of the labour force, and income distribution measures. A detailed discussion of regional development policy and the major policy instruments to implement it, and their influence on the patterns of urban growth in different regions and periods is contained in some of the chapters in this section.

Despite a voluminous literature on China's official urbanization and a tremendous increase in the amount of statistical information available in recent years, the actual figure for urban population continues to be a subject of great debate. This uncertainty is partly caused by changes in the official definition of urban areas in recent years. Partly as a result of such changes, China's official urbanization level more than doubled in the six years between 1982 and 1988, from 20.8 per cent to 49.6 per cent (China State Statistics Bureau 1989: 85–9). The World Bank even cited a figure of 56 per cent for 1990, whereas the official Chinese figure for that year was revised downward to 26 per cent.

2 Structural and Spatial Economic Changes and their Effects on Recent Urbanization in China

JING NENG LI

The economic reforms begun in China in 1979 have had profound effects on the development of the Chinese economy and population, generating many structural and spatial economic changes. Studies of their implications for China's urbanization, as well as deeper analysis of the patterns of urbanization in China's different regions, are therefore needed, despite the serious data problems confronting such an analysis. The data used in this chapter are mainly from China's State Statistic Bureau (CSSB), the Ministry of Public Security, the Institute of Economic Research of the State Planning Commission and relevant surveys made by the Institute of Population and Development Research of Nankai University and other population institutes.

An Overview of China's Economic Changes since 1979

By the end of the 1970s, China's economy had been in serious depression for many years. Production was stagnant, food and daily necessities were in short supply, and the living standard of the great majority of the people had declined. Moreover, more than ten million urban residents were 'waiting for jobs' (unemployed), a hundred million peasants suffered from underemployment, and the labour force lacked initiative, so that their productivity had been stagnant at a very low level or even decreasing for a long time. All these phenomena showed that the planned economy operating under the orders of the central government had reached a dead end.

Some Chinese leaders still dreamed of solving these problems by importing foreign techniques and machinery to raise productivity without modifying the basic social and economic systems. But people soon found out that imported techniques and machinery could not work without modern management, capable manpower and an efficient socio-economic system. Therefore, by the end of the

Apart from some limited updating, this chapter was written before the middle of 1989. The situation in China has since changed. However, the chapter deals with the dynamics of economic and demographic development, and the effects of structural and spatial changes on urbanization, in the period 1979–88. Here the term 'China' refers to mainland China only.

1970s, practical failures pushed the Chinese government step by step towards the adoption of new policies and measures of economic reform.

The period from 1979 to 1984 might be called the first phase of China's current reforms. The economic reforms at first took place in rural areas, beginning with the division of cultivated lands (only the right to use land) by each household, and with the initiation of the responsibility system of production. Then followed the adjustment of the market prices of agricultural products and the overhaul of the price system, along with the improvement of the labour and employment system. In this phase, although China's economic reform was mainly a rural reform, more generally the central government was beginning to transfer some powers and benefits to local governments and enterprises.

The period from the announcement of 'The Decision Concerning Economic System Reforms' by the central committee of the Chinese Communist Party in 1984, to the middle of 1989, might be called the second phase of China's current economic reforms. In this phase, Chinese economic reforms followed more obviously the principles of a market economy, even though this was called the socialist commodity-economy. In addition, the government built up several Special Economic Zones and fourteen Open Cities in order to absorb foreign investments and techniques. Thus Chinese foreign trade developed rapidly, especially in the eastern coastal area. At the same time, enterprises asked for more independent rights to make their decisions and operations, and to a certain extent, private ownership by individuals was allowed to develop, and private companies reappeared progressively.

The economic changes from 1979 to 1988 may be summed up as follows. First of all, under the central government's instructions the planned economy was transformed progressively into a market economy. The market price mechanism played an increasingly important role in developing China's modern economy. As a result, people paid more attention to cost-benefit comparisons in order to raise economic efficiency; in other words, more people were now able to make money and get rich.

In rural areas, besides the institution of the responsibility system in agricultural production, the village–town enterprises of commerce and industry developed rapidly and soon became an important factor in the rural economy and in rural industrialization.[1] By the end of 1983, the number of these village–town enterprises amounted to 1.346 million, absorbing more than 32 million rural surplus workers or about 10 per cent of China's total rural labour force. By the end of 1986, these village-town enterprises numbered more than 1.5 million and occupied about 19 per cent of China's total rural labour force.

Meanwhile, in China's urban areas, especially in its coastal zone, small firms owned by individuals developed very rapidly, though the growth rates of their output in different years were rather unstable (see Table 2.1). There were about five million small urban firms in 1988. At the end of June 1989, the number of small

---

[1] The products of these village-town enterprises in the coastal areas catered almost exclusively for the urban market, and in the inland areas, more than half of them catered to the urban market.

Table 2.1. Comparison of growth rates of industrial gross output values between different ownerships, 1984–7 (%)

Industry	1984	1985	1986	1987
Sum total	14.0	18.0	8.8	14.0
State ownership	8.9	12.9	6.2	11.0
Collective ownership	29.8	30.9	14.6	25.0
including village enterprises	30.3	37.8	28.2	28.2
Urban individual ownership	97.3	125.7	–12.6	48.0
Others	58.6	39.5	33.7	98.0

Sources: China Statistical Yearbooks 1984–8, and *Chinese Statistics Briefing 1988*, used in Watson *et al.*, 1988: 32.

firms owned by individuals throughout both rural and urban areas of China, though smaller than at the end of 1988, was still 12.34 million, employing 19.43 million workers (*Xinhua Ag.*, 22 October 1989). In addition, the number of privately owned enterprises employing more than eight workers in each enterprise was over 1.08 million. Private enterprises, both large and small, had clearly become an important part of the Chinese economy.

The most fundamental economic change following the economic reforms in China has been the creation of a multiple economy, including the following main components: state-owned economy; local or collectively owned economy; individual (private) owned economy; and derived components such as stock companies and joint enterprises (including foreign investment). Local, collective and individual enterprises now have more rights to make independent decisions about their economic activities. Hence the regulation of market prices and competition have played an increasingly important role in developing the modern Chinese economy.

Accompanying the development of the commodity-economy and the increase in productivity, not only have national income and GNP increased sharply, but the economic structures, especially the industrial structure of the labour force, have also begun to change progressively (see Tables 2.2 and 2.3).

From Table 2.2, it can be seen that the GNP index for 1987 is almost 2.3 times that of 1978. If we exclude the effects of inflation (according to my conservative estimation, total inflation in the period 1978–87 was about 35 per cent), then, comparing the figures of 1987 with those of 1978, national income increased in real terms by about 102 per cent, national income per capita by about 79 per cent, GNP by about 106 per cent, and GNP per capita by about 84 per cent.

From Table 2.3 it can be seen that the percentage of GNP in primary industry[2] increased in the first phase of economic reforms (1979–83) and decreased after 1984. By contrast, the percentage of GNP in secondary[3] and tertiary industry[4]

[2] Primary industry includes agriculture, forestry, animal husbandry, fishery, water conservation (*China State Statistics Bureau*, 1988: 125).
[3] Secondary industry includes industry, construction, geological survey and exploration.
[4] Tertiary industry includes transportation, post and telecommunication; commerce, catering trade, supply and marketing of materials and warehouses; public health, sports and social welfare;

Table 2.2.   National income, national income per capita GNP, and GNP per capita, 1978–87

Year	National income (RMB billion)	National income per capita (RMB)	GNP (RMB billion)	GNP per capita (RMB)	GNP indexes (1978 = 100)
1978	301.0	315	348.2	361.73	100.0
1979	335.0	346	387.9	397.67	107.4
1980	368.8	376	433.6	438.28	115.0
1981	394.0	396	462.9	462.57	121.2
1982	426.1	423	503.8	496.15	131.8
1983	473.0	463	562.7	549.00	145.2
1984	565.0	547	676.1	653.39	166.3
1985	703.1	673	833.0	796.89	187.9
1986	788.7	746	945.7	894.52	203.5
1987	932.1	868	1104.9	1022.36	225.1

Sources: China Statistical Yearbook 1988: 26, 41. GNP per capita were calculated. Absolute numbers in this table are at current prices, indexes are at constant prices.

Table 2.3.   Industrial composition of GNP and labour force, 1978–87 (%)

Year	Composition of GNP			Composition of labour force		
	I	II	III	I	II	III
1978	29.1	47.9	23.0	73.8	15.3	10.9
1979	32.4	47.0	20.6	72.5	16.0	11.5
1980	31.3	48.2	20.5	72.1	16.3	11.6
1981	33.3	46.4	20.3	72.0	16.3	11.7
1982	35.0	45.0	20.0	71.6	16.3	12.1
1983	34.9	44.9	20.2	70.7	16.3	13.0
1984	34.0	44.0	22.0	68.4	17.2	14.4
1985	30.5	44.6	24.9	65.9	17.7	16.4
1986	29.1	45.5	25.4	61.1	22.1	16.8
1987	28.8	45.8	25.4	60.1	22.5	17.4

Note I = Primary Industry; II = Secondary Industry; III = Tertiary Industry

Sources: Composition of GNP from *China Statistical Yearbook 1988*: 26. Composition of labour force from *Strategic Transition of Rural Labour Force* (1987), compiled by the Division of Population Research, Institute of Economic Research of State Planning Commission. Figure for 1986 from *China Statistical Yearbook 1987*: 93; and for 1987 from *China Statistical Yearbook 1988*: 125.

generally decreased in the first phase and increased after 1984. The initial rise in the percentage of GNP in primary industry was mainly caused by the following reasons: the prices of agricultural products had been too low, and after 1979 they rose considerably as adjustment measures were taken; the components of

education, culture, art, radio and television broadcasting; scientific research and comprehensive technical services; banking and insurance; governments, parties and other organizations; others.

agricultural output changed in the wake of economic reforms, and, especially in the first phase, the proportion of higher-value industrial crops, fishery, and animal husbandry increased; the total output of primary industry in the first phase of economic reforms increased rapidly, although after the urban economic reforms began in 1984, the gross output value of secondary and tertiary industries increased more rapidly.

Since 1979, the percentage of the labour force in primary industry has decreased substantially, from 73.8 per cent in 1978 to 60.1 per cent in 1987, i.e. by 13.7 percentage points, or almost one-fifth of the 1978 level (see Table 2.3). By contrast, the percentage of the labour force in secondary and tertiary industries in the same period increased by 7.2 and 6.5 percentage points respectively, i.e. by almost a half and three-fifths respectively of the 1978 levels. The second part of this chapter will show a similar trend in the industrial structure of the rural labour force, i.e. the labour force starting to transfer from primary industry to secondary and tertiary industries.

The practice of open policies and the development of the commodity-economy, as well as the setting up of Special Economic Zones and open cities since the beginning of the 1980s, have led to a more unbalanced spatial (regional) distribution of the national economy and labour force, with the coastal areas developing more rapidly. The eastern coastal economic zone is the most developed region in China, followed by the central economic zone (see Fig. 2.1). The western economic zone is the most backward; it lagged far behind the eastern economic zone in 1985 (Table 2.4), and if we include urban areas in the comparison, as in the bottom segment of the table, the differences between zones are even sharper.

Along the Chinese coastal areas, there are three developed regions. The first consists of Guangdong and Fujian provinces, located in south-east China, with the most developed area centred on Guangzhou and the Pearl River delta. Several Special Economic Zones such as Shenzhen, Swatow, Zhuhai, and Amoy have been set up in this region. The second is the region of lower Yangzi River with Shanghai as its centre, located in eastern China. The third is the region surrounding Bohai Bay in north-east China, in which the most developed areas are Beijing and Tianjin metropolitan area, southern Liaoning and the Shangdong peninsula. The commercial economy, especially connected with foreign trade and foreign investment, declines progressively from developed to underdeveloped as we move from south-east to north-west China.

In short, the economic changes in China since 1979 have been dramatic. According to the data of the China State Statistics Bureau (CSSB) and the Economic System Reform Institute, the main achievements of economic reforms in the 1979–88 period (actually comparing the figures of 1988 with those of 1978) are briefly as follows:

1. Total output value increased by 123 per cent.
2. Annual average growth rate of GNP was 9.3 per cent.
3. Annual average growth rate of industry was 11.8 per cent.

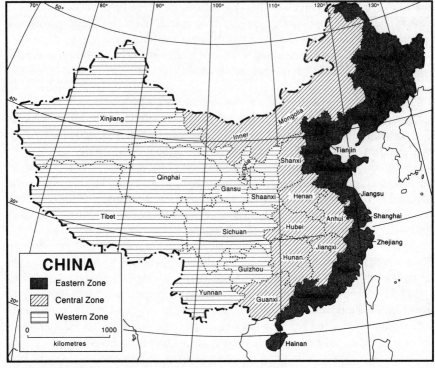

Fig. 2.1.   China's three economic zones
Source: United Nations, 1990

4. Annual average growth rate of agriculture was 6.5 per cent.
5. The proportion of output value of village-town enterprises in total rural output value was 51.4 per cent at the end of the period.
6. Technical investments (i.e. those in new techniques and equipment) aggregated to 200 billion RMB.
7. Urban income per capita increased by 190 per cent; the annual average increase rate was 7.1 per cent (excluding the effects of inflation).
8. Urban self-employed small firms increased from about 10,000 to about 5 million.

According to CSSB data, the GNP of 1988 was 1,395 billion RMB, and its annual growth rate was 11.2 per cent; and the total value of foreign trade (including import and export) in 1988 was US$102.7 billion, with an annual growth rate of 24.4 per cent. It is hard to imagine such great changes and achievements without the current economic reforms. However, it must also be noted that since 1986, many serious problems have emerged in the development process based on recent economic reforms. Those commonly noted include galloping inflation, corruption and speculation, waste of natural resources and pollution, lack of efficiency, lack of free mobility of labour and capital, lack of internal motivation, and lost

Table 2.4. Economic levels of three economic zones of China, 1985, 1987 (%)

Items		Eastern Zone A	Central Zone B	Western Zone C	Total D	A/C
Urban percentage of population		59.2	40.4	32.2		
Percentage of urban population in whole country (1987)		54.5	29.5	15.9	100	3.43
Proportion of rural social gross output value in whole country (1985)	Total	54.1	30.6	15.3	100	3.54
	Per worker (RMB)	2194.5	1583.1	1059.0		2.07
	Agriculture	45.4	35.4	19.2	100	2.36
	Industry	68.3	22.5	9.2	100	7.42
	Commerce and services	52.6	32.7	14.7	100	3.58
Proportion of rural labour force in whole country (1985)	Total	42.2	33.1	24.7	100	1.71
	Agriculture	38.7	34.4	26.9	100	1.44
	Industry	62.8	24.5	12.7	100	4.95
	Commerce and services	52.2	30.2	17.6	100	2.97
Regional gross output Value of agriculture and industry (1987)	(Billion RMB)	1143.1	453.9	251.9		
Proportion of national total		61.8	24.6	13.6	100	4.54

Note: For the distribution of population by province in the different economic zones, see Table 2.10.

Sources: Figures for 1985 calculated from data from *The Strategic Transformation of Rural Labour Force* (1987); figures for 1987 calculated from data from *China Statistical Yearbook 1988*: 40.

control of long-term investments. All these serious problems challenge China's current economic reforms. They also serve as a lesson to Chinese people: economic reforms must be linked with political reforms, because without a democratic and stable political environment, in the long run, economic reforms will never succeed.

Structural Changes in the Rural Economy and Labour Force

Early in the 1980s it was already very clear that after the overall practice of agrarian reforms, especially the introduction of the responsibility system[5] in agricultural production, the problem of employing the rural surplus labour force

[5] The responsibility system, introduced in the late 1970s, first enabled the more energetic and successful work-teams and brigades to retain the surplus income they produced. It quickly developed into the household responsibility system, whereby fields could be contracted to individual households to farm or manage.

would become more and more serious in China. The responsibility system released millions of rural workers from crop cultivation. According to a survey of the Institute of Economic Research of the State Planning Commission, the number of crop-cultivation labourers decreased from 257 million in 1978 to 254 million in 1986, and their proportion in the total rural labour force decreased from 84 per cent in 1978 to 67 per cent over the same period. By contrast, the number of non-crop-cultivation labourers in the rural area increased from 50 million in 1978 to 126 million in 1986, an increase of 154 per cent, and their proportion in the total rural labour force more than doubled from 16 per cent to 33 per cent. These figures doubtless reflect a real shift of large numbers of rural workers from agriculture to non-agriculture, though the location of some of this non-agricultural work may actually be in towns.

Owing to the rapid growth of the rural population and the loss of cultivated lands to construction, the area of cultivated land per capita was only 0.1 hectare in 1987, and the area of cultivated land per rural labourer was 0.25 hectare. The practical needs of labour force for crop cultivation in 1987 were about 145 million, but the number of labourers actually employed in crop cultivation was about 250 million, which means that more than 100 million labourers were underemployed. Meanwhile, the social gross output value (SGOV) of rural areas per rural labourer almost doubled in the 1978–1986 period. These factors no doubt contributed to the shift of the rural surplus labour force from agriculture to the non-agricultural sector.

According to the *China Statistical Yearbook 1988*, the number of village-town enterprises in 1987 amounted to almost 1.58 million, employing more than 47 million workers. It is clear that the processes of transformation, through which the rural labour force is moving from agriculture to non-agriculture, are still going on. At the same time, Table 2.5 shows marked changes in the industrial composition of the rural economy and labour force between 1978 and 1986. The rural SGOV increased by 2.7 times over the period, but the share of primary industry decreased by one-fifth, compensated for mainly by a rise in the share of secondary industry. In terms of employment, the relative losses to agriculture were not as great, but the gains to the secondary and tertiary sectors were very substantial.

The transformation of industrial structures, especially the transformation of rural labourers from agricultural to non-agricultural workers, could be seen as the first step in their transformation from rural labourers to urban workers, thus fostering urbanization.

Just as the economic levels of China's three economic zones were quite different, so too was the industrial composition of their social gross output in rural areas and their rural labour force. The eastern economic zone is the most developed region, with a more vigorous and open commodity-economy, so its industrial composition has undergone the most transformation. By contrast, the western economic zone is the most backward region, so its industrial composition lags behind that of other regions, with a higher proportion of primary industry and lower proportions of secondary and tertiary industry (see Table 2.6).

Table 2.5. Differences between composition of China's rural social gross output value (SGOV) and labour force in 1978 and 1986

Items	1978 (1)	1986 (2)	(2)–(1)	[(2)–(1)/(1)]%
Rural SGOV (in millions RMB)	203,754	755,423	551,669	270.75
included:	(100.0)	(100.0)		
Primary industry	68.6	53.1	–15.5	–22.6
Secondary industry	26.1	39.4	13.3	51.0
Tertiary industry	5.3	7.5	2.2	41.5
Rural labour force (in millions)	306.37	379.89	73.52	24.0
included:	(100.0)	(100.0)		
Primary industry	89.7	80.2	–9.5	–10.6
Secondary industry	6.4	11.7	5.3	82.7
Tertiary industry	3.9	8.1	4.2	109.0
Crop-cultivation-labourer	83.8	66.8	–17.0	–20.3
Non crop-cultivation-labourer	16.2	33.2	17.0	104.9

Source: *The Strategic Transformation of Rural Labour Force*, 1987.

Table 2.6. Differences between industrial composition of rural social gross output value (SGOV) and labour force in China's three economic zones, 1985 (%)

Items	Eastern Zone A	Central Zone B	Western Zone C	A–C
Industrial composition of rural SGOV Sum total (in millions)	342,969	194,085	969,50	246,019
included:	(100.0)	(100.0)	(100.0)	
Agriculture	47.9	66.0	71.6	–23.7
Industry	45.0	26.2	21.5	23.5
Commerce and services	7.1	7.8	6.9	0.2
Industrial composition of rural labour force Sum total (in millions)	156.50	122.60	91.55	64.95
included:	(100.0)	(100.0)	(100.0)	
Agriculture	75.0	85.3	89.1	–14.1
Industry	15.5	7.7	5.4	10.1
Commerce and services	9.5	7.0	5.5	4.0

Source: *The Strategic Transformation of Rural Labour Force*, 1987.

The rapid transformation of the rural labour force from agricultural to non-agricultural sectors in the eastern coastal area could be expected to lead to faster urbanization in eastern China.

The Rapid Development of Urbanization in Recent Years

According to the data of the China State Statistics Bureau (CSSB), the urbanization process was almost stagnant over the 1960s and 1970s; indeed, the proportion of urban population in the total population in 1980 (19.4 per cent) was still lower than that of 1960 (19.7 per cent).

Between 1949 and 1960, urban growth had been rapid, and the urban share of the total population had risen from 10.6 per cent to 19.7 per cent, due to high rates of natural increase, economic development offering opportunities for rural-urban migration, and little official restriction on cityward migration in the 1950s. However, the urban population actually declined during the early 1960s, following the failure of the 'Great Leap Forward', and the urban population grew only slowly during the remainder of the 1960s and 1970s, due mainly to the government's control over migration through the population registration system.

Since 1978, in line with its economic reforms, the Chinese government replaced the previous strict policy on migration and urbanization with more flexible principles. After 1981, the recorded urban population increased remarkably rapidly, with an annual average growth rate in the 1981-7 period of 15.3 per cent, and continuing high growth rates thereafter (see Table 2.7). The most spectacular jump in

Table 2.7.   Growth of urban population, 1975–87

Year	Total population ('0000)	Total urban population ('0000)	Proportion of urban population in total population (%)	Annual growth of urban population ('0000)	Annual urban population growth rate (%)
1975	92,420		17.3		2.8
1976	93,717		17.4		1.9
1977	94,974		17.6		2.1
1978	96,259	17,245	17.9	576	3.5
1979	97,542	18,495	19.0	1,250	7.3
1980	98,705	19,140	19.4	645	3.5
1981	100,072	20,171	20.2	1,031	5.4
1982	101,590	21,131	20.8	960	4.8
1983	102,764	24,150	23.5	3,019	14.3
1984	103,876	33,136	31.9	8,986	37.2
1985	105,044	38,446	36.6	5,310	16.0
1986	106,529	44,103	41.5	5,657	14.7
1987	108,073	50,362	46.6	6,259	14.2

Source: *China Statistical Yearbook 1988*: 75.

the recorded urban population was in 1984, when it grew by 37 per cent or 89.8 million, a number larger than the total urban population before 1956.

From Table 2.7 it can be seen that the total urban population recorded in 1987 (503.6 million) was almost 2.5 times that in 1981 (201.7 million), and the proportion of urban population in 1987 (46.6 per cent) was 2.3 times that in 1981 (20.2 per cent). The annual average growth rate of urban population in the period 1981–7 (15.3 per cent) was more than twelve times the annual average growth rate of total population in the same period (1.2 per cent). As the natural increase rate of the urban population in this period was below 1 per cent, these figures imply that since 1981 the Chinese population has been increasingly concentrated in urban areas. However, it must be pointed out that, for reasons given later, many scholars doubt the validity of the above figures since 1984, arguing that what the State Statistics Bureau recorded as rapid growth of urban population was mostly artificial. I believe that the official figures, while correctly indicating an upsurge in China's urbanization, exaggerate the urban growth that has occurred.

In the 1978–88 period, the number of cities and towns increased sharply. The number of cities doubled between 1978 and 1987, and their population more than doubled (Table 2.8). In the same period the number of towns increased even faster, from about 3,000 in 1978 to 9,192 in 1987, and their population increased from almost 62 million in 1982 to more than 252 million in 1987. This means that, according to CSSB statistics, the total population of towns increased almost three times in only five years, and the proportion of town population to total urban population increased from 29.3 per cent to 48.2 per cent over the same period.

Table 2.8. Number and population of cities and towns, 1953, 1978–90

Year	Total urban population ('000)	Number of cities	City population ('000)	Percentage of total urban population	Number of towns	Town population ('000)	Percentage of total urban population
1953	77,230	166	43,530	56.4	5,402	33,700	43.7
1978	172,450	191	119,290	69.2			
1979	184,950	203	129,400	70.0			
1980	191,400	217	134,470	70.3			
1981	201,710	229	143,320	71.1			
1982	211,310	239	149,400	70.7	2,664	61,910	29.3
1983	241,500	271	178,950	74.1	2,968	62,550	25.9
1984	331,360	295	195,590	59.0	6,211	135,770	41.0
1985	384,460	324	216,110	56.2	7,511	168,350	43.8
1986	441,030	347	233,840	53.0	8,464	207,190	47.0
1987	503,620	381	261,110	51.9	9,121	252,510	48.2
1988	542,490	432	304,050	56.1	8,614	238,440	43.9
1989	573,830	446	318,900	55.6	9,088	254,930	44.4
1990	598,080	461	331,860	55.5	9,115	266,220	44.5

Sources: *China Statistical Yearbook* (1986, 1988, 1990, 1991); figure for number of towns from Ministry of Public Security data.

Thus, even though the growth rate of cities and their population was very high between 1982 and 1987, the growth rate of towns and their population was even higher. These trends changed again after 1987, with a downward adjustment in the number of towns in 1988, leading to a small rise in cities' share of the total urban population.

The trends can be seen more clearly when we observe the distribution of urban population in different sizes of cities and compare them with towns. Comparing the figures of 1986 with those of 1983, in Table 2.9, the rapid growth in town populations caused a falling share of the urban population in all classes of cities, including the rapidly growing mega-cities with populations over one million. In fact, it was the next group of cities—those with populations of between 500,000 and one million—whose share fell relatively little. It was hard to imagine, before the economic reforms began, that almost half the urban population would be living in towns. This might be looked upon as one of the main features of China's urbanization in recent years.

However, as we mentioned before, the conclusion about the recent rapid growth of urban population can only be very superficial and disputable if we use the above CSSB statistics without analysis and evaluation. Although the urban population undoubtedly grew very rapidly following the economic reforms, the recorded urban population growth since 1984 was nevertheless mostly artificial, and mainly due to the loosening of the policy and standards with regard to the designation of cities and towns, in addition to the enlargement of the administrative areas of cities and towns.

According to the stipulations of China's State Council in 1964, a designated town could be established only in residential areas with a permanent resident population of over 3,000 with over 70 per cent non-agricultural population. Moreover, before 1982, only the non-agricultural population which was entitled to buy grain by ration from the government's food stores counted as urban population in the statistics, but in the Third census of 1982, the definition of urban population had changed as follows: all people living in the administrative areas of cities and towns were counted as urban population irrespective of whether they were agricultural or non-agricultural population. Therefore, urban population

Table 2.9. Percentage distribution of urban population in different sizes of city and town, 1983 vs 1986

Year	City							Town*
	Total urban population	Population over 1 million	500,000– 1 million	300,000– 500,000	100,000– 300,000	Below 100,000	Total	
1983	100	35.4	19.5	9.8	7.1	0.3	72.1	27.9
1986	100	25.0	16.2	7.6	4.5	0.2	53.5	46.5

* Owing to different data sources the proportion between city and town is different from those of Table 2.8.

Sources: Calculated from data of the China State Statistics Bureau and MPSC for the relevant years.

numbers would increase simply because the administrative area of a city or town was enlarged, or the number of cities and towns increased. This is exactly what happened after 1984 when the standards for designation as a town were lowered. All the seats of county government became designated towns, and towns with a total population of less than 20,000 could also be set up at the subcounty-seat level if their non-agricultural population exceeded 2,000. In addition, a town with a total population of over 20,000 could be established at the subcounty-seat or county-seat level if its non-agricultural population constituted over 10 per cent of its total population. The restrictions were loosened to an even greater extent in remote areas, industrial and mining districts, and in regions with minority nationalities.[6]

As a result, from 1984 on, not only did the number of cities and designated towns increase sharply, and administrative urban areas enlarge everywhere, but also the urban population numbers counted in CSSB statistics increased artificially because much of the rural agricultural population was thereby counted as urban population. According to the data of the Ministry of Public Security (MPS), the average proportion of agricultural population in each town in 1986 even reached 70.7 per cent. Of all the 324 cities in 1985, 86, or more than a quarter, had an agricultural population constituting over 75 per cent of their total population, despite the stipulation of the State Council that the proportion of agricultural population for a city should not exceed 20 per cent. Many scholars disputed the proportion of urban population shown in the CSSB statistics, arguing that in 1987 this proportion was not 46.6 per cent but under 30 per cent. However, some scholars still considered that the proportion of urban population in 1987 based on CSSB statistics was not overstated, because there were 47 million workers belonging to village-town enterprises and millions of rural labourers working in cities and towns as a floating population without being counted as part of the urban population. If we exclude the agricultural population now counted as urban population according to the ratio shown in MPS data mentioned above, and add those people who worked in village-town enterprises or worked in cities and towns as a floating population over one year, the proportion of urban population in 1987 was a more reasonable 31 per cent. Even this lower figure is well above the figure of around 20 per cent in the early 1980s, and reflects the urbanizing effects of economic development following the economic reforms.[7]

Spatial Distribution of Urban Population and Patterns of Urbanization

After the implementation of economic reforms, as mentioned before, the spatial distribution of economic activity in different regions became more unbalanced,

---

[6] China's Ministry of Civil Affairs is the authority on the designation of cities and towns.

[7] [Editors' postscript] Since the above paragraph was written, China has begun publishing revised statistics on the urban population, which indicate that in 1986 the level of urbanization had reached only 24.5 per cent, and in 1992 27.6 per cent. These figures, along with figures on the agricultural and non-agricultural population, are provided in Table 2.A1 at the end of this chapter.

with the eastern coastal regions developing more rapidly than the western inland region, and the south-east region developing more rapidly than the north-west region. In the Pearl River delta, the most developed commercial economic region, the annual per capita income in 1990 of some cities such as Shenzhen, Faoshan, Dongguan, and Zhongshan, was already over US$800, but in many counties in the north-west region, the income per capita was less than US$100. In line with these economic differences, the spatial distribution of urban population was becoming more unbalanced (see Table 2.10).

Of particular interest in Table 2.10 is the trend in urban population growth in the different economic zones. Between 1982 and 1990 the population of the three municipalities Beijing, Tianjin, and Shanghai increased by only 25 per cent, whereas the urban population in the eastern zone, excluding those three municipalities, increased by 48 per cent, in the central zone by 43 per cent and in the western zone by 41 per cent. Over this period, then, the proportion of the country's total urban population living in Beijing, Tianjin, and Shanghai decreased, whereas in the rest of the eastern zone it increased from 44.9 per cent in 1982 to 47.0 per cent in 1990, and remained more or less constant in the central and western zones. More than half of China's urban population was living in the eastern coastal region, which might be called the highly urbanized area of China. The above situation has been more pronounced since the economic reforms (Yeung and Hu 1992).

From a regional and population-economics perspective, there have been two main patterns of recent Chinese urbanization. The first pattern is based on the rapid development of village–town enterprises resulting in the development of towns, small cities, and even medium-sized cities; at the same time, the rural surplus labour force, after the transformation from agriculture to non-agricultural sectors, has moved and concentrated in towns and cities, primarily as circular migrants, then as temporary residents, and finally as legal immigrants to those towns and cities. In this urbanizing process the chief dynamic is the economic growth and personal abilities of peasants themselves, under the conditions of a vigorous market economy. Some of those moving into towns or small cities set up industrial or commercial firms, mainly to serve the needs of local agricultural production, to process agricultural or other products, and to meet local consumer needs.

The most famous example of this kind of urbanization pattern is the Wenzhou pattern, named after a coastal area of Zhejiang province in south-east China. Early in 1984 this area was already showing a typical pattern of development of small-town and individual private enterprises and the transformation of peasants from agricultural labourers to non-agricultural workers or businesspeople. It was one of the first rural areas in China to get rich. Its industrial gross output value was 4,223 million in 1985, 4,823 million in 1986 and 6,030 million RMB in 1987, an increase of 42.8 per cent over that of 1985. Meanwhile, the urbanization process developed quickly, the number of designated towns rising from twenty-eight in 1983 to eighty-two in 1985 and eighty-seven in 1986. The proportion of

Table 2.10. Urban population and level of urbanization by province, 1982, 1990 (10,000s)

	1982			1990			Difference in percentage urban 1990–1982
	Total popu-lation	Urban popu-lation	Percent-age urban	Total popu-lation	Urban popu-lation	Percent-age urban	
National total	101,541	21,154	20.8	113,368	29,971	26.4	5.6
Eastern zone	43,463	11,321	26.1	48,574	16,364	33.7	7.6
Heilongjiang	3,281	1,309	39.9	3,521	1,661	47.2	7.3
Jilin	2,258	894	39.6	2,466	1,052	42.7	3.1
Liaoning	3,592	1,509	42.0	3,946	2,007	50.9	8.9
Hebei	5,356	740	13.8	6,108	1,165	9.1	5.3
Beijing	919	596	64.9	1,082	791	73.1	8.2
Tianjin	778	532	68.4	879	603	68.7	0.3
Shandong	7,494	1,436	19.2	8,439	2,308	27.3	8.1
Jiangsu	6,089	954	15.7	6,706	1,424	21.2	5.5
Shanghai	1,181	696	58.9	1,334	884	66.2	7.3
Zhejiang	3,924	1,000	25.5	4,145	1,360	32.8	7.3
Fujian	2,604	548	21.0	3,010	642	21.3	0.3
Kwangdong	5,987	1,107	18.5	6,283	2,310	36.8	18.3
Central zone	34,304	5,612	16.4	38,649	8,006	20.7	4.3
Inner Mongolia	1,937	564	29.1	2,146	775	36.1	7.0
Shanxi	2,546	541	21.3	2,876	826	28.7	7.4
Henan	7,520	1,025	13.6	8,551	1,327	15.5	1.9
Hubei	4,801	849	17.7	5,397	1,560	28.9	11.2
Anhui	5,016	721	14.4	5,618	1,005	17.9	3.5
Jiangxi	3,348	643	19.2	3,771	769	20.4	1.2
Hunan	5,452	818	15.0	6,066	1,106	18.2	3.2
Kwangxi	3,684	451	12.2	4,225	638	15.1	2.9
Western zone	23,350	3,797	16.3	25,830	5,355	20.7	4.4
Shaanxi	2,904	548	18.9	3,288	707	21.5	2.6
Gansu	1,975	313	15.9	2,237	493	22.0	6.1
Qinghai	393	80	20.4	446	120	27.4	7.0
Ningxia	393	88	22.4	466	120	25.7	3.3
Xinjiang	1,316	375	28.5	1,516	484	31.9	3.4
Sichuan	10,022	1,416	14.1	10,722	2,171	20.3	6.2
Guizhou	2,875	542	18.9	3,239	613	18.9	0.0
Yunnan	3,283	411	12.5	3,697	544	14.7	2.2
Tibet	189	24	12.7	220	28	12.6	–0.1
Army	424	424		n.a.	n.a.		

Sources: Calculated from the data of the *China Statistical Yearbook* (1983, 1991). Owing to the later revision, the national total figures are somewhat different from those in Table 2.7, which are based on the *China Statistical Yearbook 1988*.

urban population in the total Wenzhou population rose from 21.2 per cent in 1980 to 33.8 per cent in 1986; the annual average growth rate of urban population in the period 1981–6 was 9.3 per cent.

However, generally speaking, this urbanization pattern more frequently happens in inland China, especially in those places located on the main transportation lines, where the commodity-economy developed rather rapidly, even though the effects of mega-cities or medium-sized cities on urbanization were rather weak. The county seat of Jintang in Sichuan province, that of Yongnian in Hebei province, and towns and cities located in the Dongting Lake area in Hunan province, all display this kind of urbanization pattern.

The second kind of urbanization pattern is one in which the rapid development of mega-cities assists the development of the nearby medium-sized and small cities and towns, and in turn supports the development of the nearby rural areas, especially their village-town enterprises. Under the strong influence of the economic centre, some cities become larger both in terms of the scale of the commodity-economy and the size of population, some developed counties become designated cities, some cities are designated open cities or special economic zones, and some of the most developed urban areas start to become metropolitan areas. In this urbanizing process the main force at work is the economic growth of the cities under the conditions of a vigorous market economy, especially the sharp increase in foreign trade and foreign investment. The fastest-growing economic activities in this situation are enterprises newly established to serve the needs of industry, commerce and foreign trade in nearby cities, especially large cities.

The urbanizing dynamics can be divided into four main patterns.

1. *The completed open pattern.*   This is a mixed urbanizing and commercializing pattern whereby rapid growth and concentration of economy and population are closely connected with foreign markets. The rapid increase of commerce, foreign trade and foreign investment results in the rapid development of the market economy, particularly sectors such as the textile and clothing industries, light industry and commercialized agriculture, whose outputs are mainly sold to the foreign market, thus fostering the concentration of economy and population in their urban areas. This dynamic process not only promotes the transformation of the local rural surplus labour force, but also strongly attracts the floating population of nearby regions and even those moving from places thousands of miles away.

In this area, not only is the large city of Guangzhou developing very fast, but many small cities, especially the special economic zones such as Shenzhen and Zuhai, are developing even faster. Let us take the example of Shenzhen. Located on the southern boundary with Hong Kong, the economy of this town was very weak and backward, with almost nothing that could be called industry; its population was no more than 60,000 before 1978. After its designation as a Special Economic Zone, however, investment totalling more than 5 billion RMB, from both domestic and foreign sources, was poured into construction, industry, commerce and foreign trade, under the strong influence of Hong Kong, attracting hundreds of thousands of people to move and work there. By 1986, its population was more than 350,000, a fivefold increase since 1978. Most of Shenzhen's population is made up of temporary residents, as many as 238,000 of them by 1985. In recent years, the annual growth of Shenzhen's population has come mainly from in-migration (see Table 2.11).

A similar situation arose not only in other Special Economic Zones, but also in the whole Pearl River delta. Fushan City is a good instance, with an in-migratory growth rate in the period 1984–6 of over 70 per cent. This indicates that the Pearl River delta area as a whole is now a rapidly urbanizing area, its development based partly on 'overspill' from Hong Kong (Skeldon 1986), in a way that bears some resemblance to the growth of Batam Island in Indonesia, based on the prosperity of neighbouring Singapore.

2. *The semi-open pattern.* In this case, rapid growth and concentration of economy and population are affected directly by a nearby economic centre, the mega-city, and closely connected with local, national and foreign markets. To a certain extent, its urbanizing process is closely connected with rural industrialization and commercialization. Moreover, in this process the local and collective-owned economy plays an important role and becomes the economic bridge between large or medium-sized cities and towns and rural areas.

The most famous example is the southern Jiangsu pattern. Under the strong influence of Shanghai, several medium-sized cities, such as Chengchow, Wuxi and Suchow, developed quickly in recent years, becoming large cities, and resulting in the development of cities and towns based largely on the rapid growth of textiles and light industries. This region has now become one of the most developed commercial and industrial regions in China. In 1986, its social gross output value (SGOV) amounted to 45,817 million, and the SGOV per capita was about 2,443 RMB, higher than the average level of the Eastern economic zone. At the same time, the number of cities and towns and their urban population increased sharply. In 1986, southern Jiangsu's total population amounted to 18.75 million, or 30 per cent of that of Jiangsu province. However, its city population amounted to 5.04 million or 45 per cent of that of the whole province in the same year. It

Table 2.11. In-migratory growth of Shenzhen's population, 1980–5

	1980	1981	1982	1983	1984	1985	Total
Annual growth in total population (A)	13,158	14,280	18,234	48,469	26,434	40,383	160,958
In-migratory growth (B)	11,935	12,481	16,256	35,448	24,498	38,097	135,715
Proportion of in-migratory growth (B/A %)	90.7	87.4	89.1	73.1	92.7	94.3	84.3

Source: *Shenzhen SEZ Economic Statistics Yearbook 1986.*

occupied an area of about 25,000 km², in which there were seven cities and 723 towns (including townships) in 1986. Almost every 100 km² had 2.9 towns and every 10,000 km² had 2.8 cities; the average size of population of its cities was 720,000, almost double that before 1980.

The Shangdong peninsula and southern Liaoning provide examples of a similar pattern excepting that the economic background to the urbanization process in southern Liaoning was mainly the development of heavy industry, strongly affected by the planned economy, but the focus of economic development has now somewhat changed to light industry and foreign trade.

3. *The Shanghai, Beijing and Tianjin pattern.*   In the case of the three municipalities Shanghai, Beijing and Tianjin, a semi-open pattern has been adopted to encourage economic development but strict control of population size. From Table 2.10, it can be seen that except for Tibet, the rates of increase of the urban population of these three metropolises were the lowest in China in 1982–6. As their urban cores (downtowns) were already too densely populated, the density in some districts exceeding 50,000 per km² and in some subdistricts even exceeding 150,000 per km², there was almost no room for further growth of population. However, their economic effects on nearby areas are still very strong, and the urbanizing process in their suburbs and satellites is still outstanding.

Tianjin is a good example: though its total population is growing only slowly, the proportion of in-migratory growth in the annual net growth of total population rose over the 1981–7 period from about 21 per cent to about 30 per cent. Meanwhile, the number of village-town enterprises was increasing quickly, from about 4,000 in 1982 to more than 36,000 by the end of 1988; the number of designated towns rose from 7 in 1982 to 12 in 1987; and the number of non-designated towns increased from 24 to more than 50.[8] The total urban population increased from 4.92 million in 1980 to 5.79 million in 1986. As the population size of its urban core was controlled strictly and was almost stable, so its increasing urban population was distributed mostly in the new urban districts, such as the New Port of Tanggu District and the nearby Special Economic Zone (SEZ)—the oil-production base, Dagang District. The population of Tanggu almost doubled in the period 1978–87, from about 300,000 to 600,000. According to Tianjin's urban planning programme, by the end of the year 2,000, the total population of Tianjin's coastal districts will have increased to about 1.5 million, after the completion of the Beijing–Tianjin–Tanggu Freeway, the first freeway in China. Around the New Port and SEZ there will be a major new urban zone of Tianjin.

4. *Heavy industry-based pattern.*   A final pattern is an urbanizing process closely connected with the construction of heavy industry. In socialist China this pattern could be called the socialist central-planning pattern, because it is part of the economic planning of the central government, and the main motive force of

---

[8] The difference between designated and non-designated towns is that the designated town was designated by the authority as an administrative unit of an urban area, and could constitute its 'town' government officially, have an official budget, urban fixed assets, investments etc., and count its population as urban population with grain rations; non-designated towns have no such benefits.

such an urbanization process is the huge industrial investment carried out by the central government. The dynamics of this urbanizing process might be as follows: first the central government chooses a certain place which has been found to be rich in natural resources as the new industrial base; capital investment and economic construction lead to a continuous inflow of staff members and workers, so the area soon becomes a new town and begins to absorb the nearby rural surplus labour force; after the big companies engaging in some kind of heavy industry put their new factories into production this new town rapidly becomes a city, and may even become a large city within a few years.

Panzihua Mine in southern Sichuan is typical of such a pattern. Its urban population increased quickly when Panzihua developed progressively from a small village into a large mining city. Most of its urban population was composed of migrants from other regions. In the 1965–78 period its in-migratory population amounted to 250,000, and between 1978 and 1985 more than 40,000 more people moved in. The total urban population of Panzihua in 1985 had reached almost 416,000, or almost 49 per cent of its total population in that year.

Conclusion

Economic changes in China during the 1980s, especially the rapid growth of the commodity-economy and the practice of open economic policies, resulted in the transformation of the industrial composition of the rural economy and rural labour force, and led to a process of rapid urbanization. There was great regional diversity in economic development and urbanization. As the spatial distribution of the commercial economy became more unbalanced in later years, that of the urban population was also unbalanced. Generally speaking, the development of urbanization in the eastern and southern coastal regions was more rapid because the development of the commodity-economy was proceeding more rapidly there. At the same time, the different patterns of urbanization could be observed in different regions and even within regions. It is hard to say which is the optimum pattern for contemporary Chinese urbanization. However, along with the practice of the open policy and the rapid development of the commodity-economy and the market mechanism, the influence of the key economic centres and mega-cities on China's urbanization will become more and more important. What has been presented here is only a rough description of China's current economic changes and their implications for urbanization. Further analyses of the quantitative relationships and effects of economic variables on urbanization are still needed.

China's government strictly controls the population size of large cities, in order to prevent the rural population moving rapidly into mega-cities, and furthermore to avoid homelessness and slum-dwelling among the rural–urban in-migrants, common in many developing countries. In this they appear to have achieved great success. However, after the recent economic reforms, China's government emphasized the need to strengthen the economic functions of mega-cities, leading to a sharp increase in the so-called floating population in large cities. Higher rates of in-migration exacerbated many urban population problems such as unemployment, inadequate housing, food and water supply, pollution, and traffic problems. Although China's government planned to move millions of people from coastal areas to inland regions, the reality is that millions of people are still moving from inland to coastal cities, where it is easier to make money. This is also an obvious result of China's economic reforms in the period 1979–88 which had profound effects on the recent urbanization process.

Table 2A1. Urban and rural, agricultural, and non-agricultural population distribution (unit: 10,000)

Year	Total Population	Urban population[a]		Rural population		Agricultural population		Non-agricultural population	
		Amount	Prop.%	Amount	Prop.%	Amount	Prop.%	Amount	Prop.%
1953	58,796	7,826	13.31	50,970	86.69	50,067	85.15	8,729	14.85
1964	70,499	12,950	18.37	57,549	81.63	58,822	83.44	11,677	16.56
1978	96,259	17,245	17.92	79,014	82.08	81,029	84.18	15,230	15.82
1980	98,705	19,140	19.39	79,565	80.61	81,904	82.98	16,801	17.02
1982	101,654	21,480	21.13	80,174	78.87	83,320	81.96	18,334	18.04
1984	104,357	24,017	23.01	80,340	76.99	84,242	80.73	20,110	19.27
1986	107,507	26,366	24.52	81,141	75.48	86,285	80.26	21,222	19.74
1988	111,026	28,661	25.81	82,365	74.19	88,439	79.66	22,587	20.34
1990	114,333	30,191	26.41	84,142	73.59	90,446	79.11	23,887	20.89
1992	117,171	32,372	27.63	84,799	72.37	91,873	78.41	25,298	21.59

[a] Urban population consists of those living in the urban districts of cities and towns.

Source: China State Statistics Bureau (1993), p. 124.

3 The Effects of National Urban Strategy and Regional Development Policy on Patterns of Urban Growth in China

APRODICIO A. LAQUIAN

As a centrally planned economy, the People's Republic of China has an explicit national urban strategy which seeks 'to strictly limit the size of big cities, rationally develop medium-sized cities and encourage the development of small cities and towns' (Li Ximing 1982). This strategy is a key feature of the country's new economic reforms, pursued since 1979. To achieve strategic goals, authority and power have been decentralized to local units, capital and infrastructure investments have been reallocated, pricing policies for goods and services have been altered, and policies on internal migration have been revised.

The implementation of the national urban strategy has significantly changed urban growth patterns in China. First, there has been a higher level of urbanization: the urban proportion of China's population increased from 19.0 per cent in 1979 to about 31 per cent in 1995 (Li Jing Neng 1988b). Second, there has been an increase in the share of urban dwellers in small towns and cities *vis-à-vis* big cities and metropolitan areas. Third, the rate of urbanization in coastal regions has accelerated, widening the development gap between the coast and China's interior regions.

Another feature of China's new economic reforms is a regional development policy that seeks accelerated economic development by concentrating investment resources in two metropolitan regions, fourteen coastal cities and four Special Economic Zones. As a part of China's policy of 'opening up to the outside world', capital investments, economic and social infrastructures, skilled professionals and technicians and other resources have been focused on these cities and zones. Both government-sponsored and temporary migration have contributed to the rapid growth of the metropolitan regions, coastal cities and Special Economic Zones. As a result, the regional concentration of China's urban development has shifted towards the eastern and southern parts of the country.

Historical Context

The distinctly pro-urban bias in China's national urban policy and regional development strategy is of recent vintage. Since its founding in 1949, the People's

Republic of China has pursued largely anti-urban policies. Chairman Mao Zedong and other theoreticians shared the orthodox ideas of Marx and Engels that the city was an evil entity for the exploitation of the proletariat. The large coastal cities of Shanghai, Tianjin, and Guangzhou symbolized the capitalist domination of China. The revolution, after all, was won by the peasants, who encircled the cities until they fell.

Initial urban policies sought to transform 'consumptive' cities into 'productive' ones. Urban infrastructures and capital investments were allocated to cities in the interior not only because coal, petroleum, and other energy resources were there but also to make the cities less vulnerable to foreign military attack. During the Great Leap Forward (1958–60), rural industrialization was pursued. The policy of combining economic and administrative-political functions into 'people's communes', which was begun in the 1950s, was pursued vigorously in an effort to accelerate development in rural areas. Not even the disastrous effects (exacerbated by natural disasters) of the Great Leap Forward and the people's communes campaign dissuaded the government from an anti-urban policy.

The urban proportion of China's population rose only gradually from 10.6 per cent in 1949 to 19.7 per cent in 1960. Thereafter, the urban proportion even declined, as the government pursued the 'rustication campaign' that sent millions of intellectuals, students and other urban dwellers to rural areas. At the start of the Great Proletarian Cultural Revolution in 1966, China's urban population was only 17.9 per cent of the total. By 1971, the proportion had fallen to 17.1 per cent; it did not reach 17.9 per cent again until 1978, when Deng Xiaoping became the new leader of China.

The new leaders of China committed themselves to the Four Modernizations in 1979 (Industry, Agriculture, the Military, and Science and Technology), abolished the people's communes, opened the country up to the outside world, and adopted pro-urban programmes. At the Fourth Plenary Session of the Eleventh Central Committee Meeting of the Communist Party of China in 1979, a resolution on the acceleration of agricultural development was passed. One of the most significant elements of this resolution was the advocacy of the growth of small towns. The encouragement for people to move from villages to small towns, which included the right to change one's household registration from rural to urban, assurances of housing and work, and in some towns, capital loans and training for migrants, was meant not only to achieve agricultural modernization but also to eliminate the disparities between rural and urban workers (Luo 1988).

The adoption of the 'production responsibility system' which allowed farmers to keep and sell products in excess of their production quotas enlivened market towns and increased the linkages between rural and urban areas. Local government was rationalized further with the abolition of people's communes; the administrative-political functions of the communes were absorbed by township governments and village committees and their economic functions by production units and collectives. Traditional townships regained their status with the abolition of communes. Furthermore, settlements of high population densities which used to be the centres of the communes' economic activities were also designated as towns.

The urban proportion of China's population jumped dramatically to 31.9 per cent in 1984 with the passage of a number of regulations. First, the definition of township status, which qualified a place to become urban, was changed. According to the new regulations, all county seats were allowed to become townships. Township boundaries were expanded to encompass adjoining villages. A settlement could become a township if it had a population of at least 20,000 and the non-agricultural population was more than 10 per cent. In October 1984, the government loosened the regulations against rural–urban migration that had been in effect since the 1950s. According to the new regulations, rural dwellers could move from villages to towns provided they did not rely on the government for their grain supply. Millions of rural dwellers responded to this freedom and accelerated China's urbanization.

The government's decision to allow migration to towns also triggered off spontaneous migration to medium-sized and large cities, a phenomenon referred to as the 'floating population'.[1] The economic opportunities in large cities attracted millions of migrants who brought their skills and resources (cash, carpentry tools, bicycles, etc.) with them. The government, realizing the economic potential of these released energies, seems to have relaxed in implementing the strict household registration regulations that officially required any migrant to a city to register with the Public Security Bureau if he or she were staying for more than three days. The number of people living in cities such as Beijing, Shanghai, and Tianjin who were not officially registered in those cities was estimated at about 10 to 20 per cent of the city populations. Even a smaller city such as Hangzhou (1.3 million) had a temporary (floating) population of 300,000, almost 20 per cent of the population (Yang and Goldstein 1989).

The rapid increase in China's urbanization level has been due to the following five factors: (*i*) definitional changes of townships that increased the number of people designated as urban dwellers; (*ii*) definitional changes of municipal boundaries that increased the number of people designated urban by including counties and towns on urban peripheries in municipal jurisdictions; (*iii*) policies and measures such as the coastal cities programme and special economic zones that accelerated the growth of selected urban areas; (*iv*) changes in household registration regulations allowing people to move from villages to towns; and (*v*) relaxation in the implementation of household registration regulations that by 1989 had allowed about 50 million people to move to cities as temporary migrants or parts of the 'floating population'. All these factors should be seen in the light of China's new economic reforms that relaxed central planning and allowed market forces to operate, measures that accelerated urban growth.

---

[1] 'Floating populations' had long existed in China's cities, but only in limited numbers because of the difficulty unauthorized city-dwellers had in obtaining food. The scale of the phenomenon increased vastly after 1984.

Implementing the National Urban Strategy

For the past 45 years, despite the anti-urban policies in China, the concentration of the urban population in very large cities has been a fact of life. In 1952, for example, although large cities of 500,000 and above made up only 12.1 per cent of the total number of cities, they contained 59.1 per cent of the total urban (not city alone) population (see Table 3.1). Small cities of 200,000 and below, which made up 73.3 per cent of the total number of cities contained only 22.5 per cent of the urban population. In 1976, this trend continued, with large cities of 500,000 and above making up 20.4 per cent of all urban units but containing 62.1 per cent of the urban population, while small cities of 200,000 and below, which accounted for 53.3 per cent of urban units, contained only 15.2 per cent of the urban population.

It has been only since the institution of economic reforms in 1979 that the pattern of urbanization in China has started to shift. In 1985, large cities of 500,000 and above made up 16.0 per cent of urban units and contained 58.7 per cent of the total urban population. Small cities of 200,000 and below made up 55.0 per cent of urban units and contained 16.8 per cent of the urban population. If one were to include the population of small towns in the people classified as urban, the proportion of urban residents in large cities would dramatically decrease. Since 1984, when migration to small towns was allowed by the government, millions of people have moved to these. Future trends are expected to be even more marked. It has been estimated that rural surplus labour in China accounts for 30 to 50 per cent of the total rural labour force or about 100 million. If one includes dependents and not just labourers in this estimate, the redundant numbers could be as large as 200 million. The great bulk of these surplus labourers would have to be absorbed in small towns. (Wang 1987a).

Search for Optimal City Size

Urban scholars in China have not been unanimous in supporting the national urban strategy restricting the growth of very large cities and encouraging

Table 3.1. Changes in share of urban population living in different size classes of cities and towns in China, 1952–85 (%)

City size	1952	1965	1982	1985
Over 1 million	40.1	43.0	43.3	39.4
500,000–1 million	19.0	20.5	20.5	19.3
200,000–500,000	17.4	20.7	22.4	24.5
Less than 200,000	22.5	15.8	13.8	16.8

Note: Some columns do not add up to 100 per cent because of rounding.

Source: Zong 1988: 15.

development in small cities and towns. Those who favour further growth of mega-cities use primarily economic arguments, calling such cities the 'super state trea-sury' of the country and the 'locomotive that brings about rapid development' (Zong 1988). They argue that China's large cities are not overdeveloped; in fact, they have been largely neglected and additional investments in them would improve their efficiency and yield better results. They point out that China's transport and communication networks are still inefficient and fragmented except in the very large cities. Economic investments in large cities would take advantage of these efficiencies and increase overall productivity.

As seen in Table 3.2, according to all ten indices measuring outputs and profits, extra-large and large cities consistently out-perform small cities. Zong has con-cluded that 'the larger the cities, the more the industrial output value or the total volume of profits and tax payments to the state' (Zong 1988: 17).

More specific conclusions drawn by Zong are as follows:

Table 3.2.   Economic indices of cities of different scales, 1985

Indices	Extra-large	Large	Large–medium	Medium	Small
Per capita industrial output (Y 10,000/person)	0.62	0.52	0.45	0.46	0.34
Per worker industrial output value (Y 10,000/person)	0.99	0.83	0.74	0.75	0.58
Industrial output value per km^2 (Y 10,000/km^2)	1079	634	138	84	12
Average output value of fixed assets (yuan per 100 Y)	273	208	160	162	147
Average output value of investment (yuan per 100 Y)	577.1	556.3	458.7	516.9	314.1
Per capita profits and tax payments (yuan/person)	1,297	1,016	872	662	548
Per worker profits and tax payments (yuan/person)	2,058	1,624	1,430	1,091	947
Profits and tax payments per km^2 of land (Y 10,000/km^2)	223	124	26.5	12.1	1.95
Average profits and tax payments on fixed assets (yuan per 100 Y)	56	40	30	23	23
Average profits and tax payments on investment (yuan per 100 Y)	120.0	109.3	88.1	74.4	52.0
Per capita investment (yuan/person)	1,085	934	994	891	1,059
Per worker investment (yuan/person)	1,721	1,491	1,628	1,467	1,827

Source: Zong 1988: 16.

1. In terms of economic benefits, those derived from extra-large cities are more than double those from small cities.
2. In terms of profits and tax payments for every 100 yuan of input, the yield from extra-large cities is twice as high as from small cities.
3. In terms of profits and tax payments to the state derived from every square kilometre of land, the value for extra-large cities is seven times higher than that for small cities.
4. In terms of per worker investment, however, it costs 1,827 yuan per worker in small cities and only 1,721 yuan in extra-large cities.

An interesting implication of Zong's analysis is the relative appeal of encouraging the growth of medium and large medium-sized cities (those with populations between 200,000 and 1 million). According to Zong, 'medium-sized cities have an important economic function', and 'they would be developed further with the help of their known facilities'. The rational development of these cities requires their closer linkage with small cities and towns in their peripheries, regional planning schemes that define their relationships with large and extra-large cities, and their linkages with their rural hinterlands. The appeal of developing medium-sized cities lies in their small requirements of per capita and per worker investment, compared with extra-large cities and small cities.

If extra-large cities are beset with pollution, overcrowding and other problems, and small cities do not give fair returns on investments, then, some Chinese scholars have proposed that medium-sized cities would probably meet the 'optimum city size' criterion that planners have been searching for ever since Plato argued that 5,040 was the optimum size for a Greek city.

Fan (1988) proposed several criteria for trying to determine optimum city size for China, among which were: optimum economic returns on investment; optimum social returns; and a high degree of comfort enjoyed by the people in the city. He conceived of the relationship between investments and economic returns on the one hand and urban scale on the other as a U-shaped curve, arguing that 'when urban scale is too small, it will not create any economies of scale; with the expansion of the city, the economies of scale will grow'. However, when the city expands to a certain scale, a series of economic, environmental and social problems such as traffic congestion, shortage of housing, a drop in the quality of services, rising production costs, and environmental pollution, will occur, causing 'diseconomies' (Fan 1988: 27).

Fan analysed data from 324 cities in 1985 and calculated such values as: (a) average net output value per worker at current price; (b) profit tax of original value for every 100 yuan in fixed assets; (c) profit tax from every 100 yuan of investment; and (d) all-personnel labour productivity measured in yuan per person. The results of Fan's calculations (see Table 3.3) consistently showed the direct relationship between city size and the output values analysed. For example, while the average net output value per worker is 7.7 yuan for cities exceeding two million, it was a low 5.6 yuan for cities of fewer than 200,000.

Table 3.3.   The major measures of economic returns of independent accounting industrial enterprises owned by the entire population in China's 324 cities in 1985 (not including counties under the jurisdiction of cities)

Cities	A	B	C	D
Average of the 324 cities	6.180	25.3	26.9	17.211
Average of cities with population exceeding 2 million	7.737	39.1	38.8	22.872
Average of cities with population between 1 and 2 million	6.539	27.4	30.2	18.089
Average of cities with population between 500,000 and 1 million	5.937	22.2	24.7	15.937
Average of cities with population between 200,000 and 500,000	4.958	18.2	19.3	14.603
Average of cities with population less than 200,000	5.677	17.9	19.4	13.042

A. Average net output value per worker at current price (yuan)
B. Profit tax of original value for every 100 yuan in fixed assets (yuan)
C. Profit tax from every 100 yuan of investment (yuan)
D. All-personnel labour productivity (yuan/person).
Source: Fan 1988: 31.

The problem with Fan's analysis, however, is that he did not provide figures on the cost of providing urban services. As he used only 'output' figures, the direct relationship between city size and amounts of output tended to be positive all the time. Perhaps, if Fan had provided figures on the 'costs' of pollution, overcrowded housing, congested traffic, and other negative aspects of larger city size, his analysis would have proved his point. As it is, Fan proved only one side of his hypothesis and Chinese scholars are still searching for an optimum city size that directly applies to the prevailing conditions in China.

Special Economic Zones and Coastal Cities

If there are problems with extra-large cities and small cities for development, China's planning authorities have been trying to avoid these by pursuing a normative strategy of developing medium-sized cities rationally. Concrete measures in pursuing this strategy have been the programme of setting up four Special Economic Zones (SEZs) and fourteen coastal city zones of development. These measures, started in 1980 as part of China's opening up to the outside world, have significantly changed China's urbanization patterns.

The first SEZs were approved in August 1980 by the National People's Congress of China with the passage of the 'Regulations on the Special Economic Zones in Guangdong Province'. Designated SEZs were the cities of Shenzhen, Shantou and Zhuhai, all in Guangdong Province. A small area (2.3 km²) in Xiamen City in

Fujian Province was also designated an SEZ. This was expanded to cover the whole Xiamen Island and other surrounding areas totalling 131 km² in March 1984.

The idea of Special Economic Zones, as embodied in the plans for Shenzhen, followed the policy of transforming the zone as 'the centre of two fans'. The two fans denoted, first, the outward thrust of China's opening up to the outside world and, second, the expansion of international development into the interior of China. Former Premier Zhao Ziyang also called Shenzhen the 'pivot' of China's development (Zhou 1987: 13).

The choice of the four SEZs was based on known locational advantages. Shenzhen is only 27.5 km from the bustling city of Hong Kong, Zhuhai adjoins Macao, and Xiamen is not too far from Taiwan. In the case of Shenzhen, however, the development of the SEZ required massive investment resources. The original built-up area of the old city of Shenzhen was only 3 km², with a total population of 23,000. From 1980 to 1985, a total investment of 6.4 billion yuan (US$1.725 billion) was poured into Shenzhen. A new city of 47.6 km² was built; buildings with a floor space of 9.27 million square metres were constructed; 7,000 new enterprises with fixed assets of 5.8 billion yuan (US$1.563 billion) were set up and a city of 470,000 grew up in barely four years. The plans for Shenzhen expect a city of 800,000 by the year 2000; investment requirements are projected at 21 billion yuan (US$5.660 billion) (Luo 1987: 30).

The SEZ approach of achieving economic and social development by building up cities from scratch has been criticized by a number of Chinese urban scholars. While the net industrial output from the four SEZs has been quite impressive, these critics feel that the same amount of investment, placed in existing urban centres, would probably have yielded better results. In 1984, therefore, fourteen coastal cities were allowed to set up their own economic development zones: Qinhuangdao, Tianjin, Dalian, Yantai, Qingdao, Lianyungang, Nantong, Shanghai, Ningbo, Wenzhou, Fuzhou, Guangzhou, Zhanjiang, and Beihai.

In the development of coastal cities, special economic development zones are chosen, usually in the peripheries of the urban centres. Infrastructure, urban services, production plants and other improvements are provided in these special zones. For example, in Dalian, on the coast of Liaoning province, an economic development zone was set up over an area of 5 km² at Maqiaozi in Jinxian county. Foreign investors, mostly from Japan, were invited to locate within this zone. In Shanghai, Minhang and Hongqiao, districts have been designated by the Shanghai municipal government as centres for inviting foreign investment in advanced technology from abroad.

Implementing these changes has required the delegation of authority to local officials to plan the economic development zones, to approve plans for infrastructure investment, and to negotiate and decide on foreign investments. For example, city officials in Shanghai and Tianjin can approve joint venture projects with capital investments of up to US$30 million. The reduction of bureaucratic formalities (everything used to be decided by the central authorities in Beijing) has greatly accelerated developments in the coastal cities. Even the attitude towards foreigners and their profit motive has changed. Former Shanghai Mayor Jiang Zemih, who has recently been appointed General Secretary of the Communist Party of China, was once quoted as saying, 'We must let foreign investors make money and make more money than we do' (*China Daily*, 1 February 1988).

Another significant measure designed to encourage the growth of coastal cities was the decision of the government to allow municipal authorities to borrow from abroad. In 1987, the Industrial and Commercial Bank of Shanghai started selling bonds worth US$27 million over a two-year period. About US$156 million was also borrowed from the Tokyo financial market by Shanghai authorities. The Shanghai Jiushi Company, a city-controlled company, was set up in 1987 to raise money directly from abroad for investments in the city. The city was authorized capital worth US$130 million and allocated US$100 million in hard currency by the government.

In Tianjin, the State Council of China allowed the Tianjin Commission on Foreign Economic Relations and Trade to borrow about US$1 billion over and above the capital allocations in the city's five-year plan. The loan was to be used for upgrading and reconstructing industries and commercial establishments in the city, to improve infrastructures and to encourage import-substituting industries.

China's implementation of the national urban strategy, especially the SEZ development and the coastal cities programme has released tremendous developmental energies that have transformed the Chinese economy in the past ten years. China's GDP growth rate since 1979 has averaged about 10 per cent. As planned, industrial production and manufacturing have outweighed agriculture at the same time that tourism and trade have expanded China's foreign exchange reserves.

The economic reforms, however, have overheated China's economy and the inflation rate rose as high as 28 per cent in 1989. The construction sector was largely responsible for inflation. When China's national government tried to rein in galloping construction, it was found that the authority delegated to local authorities made the task virtually impossible. The massive financial investments all over the country also had the unsavoury effect of generating corruption among top- and middle-level officials. Thus, while the economic reforms succeeded in accelerating China's economic development, society paid for this in terms of double-digit inflation, official corruption, and a weakening of the power of the Communist Party and the central government. In many ways, the Beijing riots and unrest in June 1989 which significantly set back China's economic growth may be traced to the problems created by the economic reforms mentioned above.

Regional Development Policy

A country as large as China, with a population of 1.1 billion distributed over 9.6 million km^2 inevitably evolves a regional development policy to respond to different geographic, climatic and cultural conditions in various parts of the regions: the highly developed eastern and southern coastal regions; the central developing region with medium-level population densities; and the outlying interior regions which are sparsely settled and relatively underdeveloped (see Fig. 2.1, Chapter 2). Qi and Xia (1986) included in the coastal developed region the cities of Beijing, Tianjin, and Shanghai as well as the provinces of Liaoning, Jilin, Heilongjiang, the eastern part of Inner Mongolia, Jiangsu, Shandong, Zhejiang, Guangxi, Guangdong, and Fujian. In the central developing region, they included Shanxi, Shaanxi, Gansu, Ningxia, Hubei, Hunan, Jiangxi, Sichuan, Guizhou, Yunnan, Henan, and Anhui. In the interior underdeveloped regions, they included Qinghai, western Inner Mongolia, Xinjiang, Tibet, western Yunnan, western Gansu, and western Sichuan.

Historically, urban development in China started in the interior and expanded eastward and southward. However, with the industrial revolution and the linking up of China with international commerce, coastal cities in the east and south developed much more rapidly. In 1933, Professor Hu Huanyong prepared a map of China where he drew a diagonal line from the town of Arhui in Heilongjiang province in the country's extreme north-east to the town of Tengchong in Yunnan province in the south-west (see Fig. 3.1). Professor Hu found that while 64 per cent

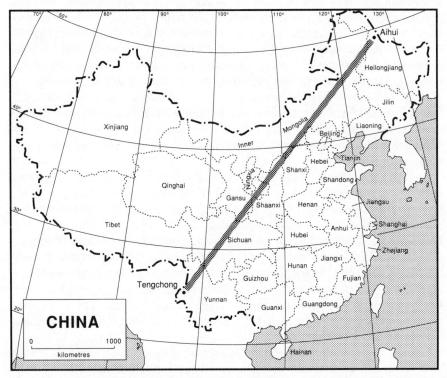

Fig. 3.1. Line roughly separating sparsely populated and densely populated halves of China's land area

of China's land area was north of the line, only 4 per cent of the total population lived there. On the opposite side of the line, 96 per cent of the population lived on 36 per cent of the land (Hu Huan Yong 1984).

Taking economic development, population density, geographic features, and levels of urbanization as important factors, it is possible to distinguish certain regional patterns in China. Essentially, there are three main regional patterns: megalopolitan regions focused on a mega-city as the nucleus; poly-nucleated urban regions; and urban-rural development regions.

Megalopolitan Regions

There are two megalopolitan regions in China focused on the two largest mega-cities in the country: the Shanghai economic zone, officially created in 1983 and the Beijing-Tianjin-Tangshan development region which was the object of a 'territorial planning scheme' prepared in 1984 by the Bureau of Development and Regulation of Territories of the State Planning Commission (Ye 1986).

The economic zone of Shanghai covers 640,000 km^2 which includes the whole municipality of Shanghai and the provinces of Jiangsu, Zhejiang, Anhui, Jiangxi, and Fujian. The zone encompasses 6.6 per cent of China's national territory and 21.8 per cent of the total population (about 220 million people). In 1986, this economic zone was estimated to have manufactured 330 billion yuan (US$8.89 billion) of economic products, fully one-third of China's industrial output value. Aside from Shanghai, the zone includes productive cities such as Suzhou, Wuxi, Changzhou, and Nantong and important ports such as Nanjing, Dagang, and Ningbo. The zone has been planned as an economic region because of the excellent network of transportation and communication that links the various productive nodes. Production and market complementarities, economies of scale, and linkages with international development have been cited as reasons for the planning of this region.

Developments in the Beijing–Tianjin–Tangshan region used to be fragmented as they were mainly focused on the individual urban units. Beijing, originally the political and administrative capital of China, was developed as an industrial city after 1949, despite the fact that its immediate hinterland is poor in raw materials, the city lacks water, and is not ideally located for marketing industrial output. Tianjin, which has locational advantages as the most important port in east China was also developed as an industrial centre but its housing, water supply and other amenities were neglected. The regional development plan evolved in 1984, therefore, linked the development of these two mega-cities (the second and third largest in China). The plan also expanded development potentials to other urban nodes, including the city of Tangshan.

The initial step in the development of the two cities was the transfer of growth to their respective satellite towns and county or prefectural seats. Thus, many industries have been transferred from Beijing and new enterprises have been set up in such satellite towns as Yanshan, Daxing, Tongxian, and Changping. In Tianjin, similar developments have occurred in the towns of Tanggu (the main port), Dagang (site of an oil and petro-chemical complex) and Hangu (marine-chemical production). The setting up of an economic development zone on the outskirts of Tianjin also played a key role in this regional scheme.

The other step in the regional plan was the encouragement of growth in small and medium-sized cities between the two mega-cities. Using the main road and railway line linking Beijing with the port of Tianjin as the main developmental axis, the regional plan encouraged the growth of small settlements such as Langfang, Xixian, and Baxian. Jixian, for example, is almost equidistant from Beijing, Tianjin, and Tangshan in a regional triangle. It was planned as a city for scientific and educational facilities, tourism, light industry, and machine building. Langfang, a prefectural centre between Beijing and Tianjin has been developed as a transportation hub, a food-processing centre, and as a site for light industries and machine building, especially those related to transport.

The rationale for the development of megalopolitan regions in China is based on the kinds of benefits often claimed for the Tokyo–Yokohama megalopolis or the Eastern Seaboard megalopolis in the United States—basically, the aim is to exploit the 'spread effects' of metropolitan development and rationally link production centres, markets, transportation nodes, and service networks into a productive whole. This area-based development planning fills in the interstices between highly developed growth centres and establishes communication and transport linkages among them. Taking advantage of locational potentials, centres of knowledge and expertise, raw materials supply, financial resources, and agricultural bases, megalopolitan planning rationally expands urban agglomerations outwards. The net effect of this regional 'dispersal' strategy is, ironically, to further concentrate urban populations in the well-endowed megalopolis. By increasing the efficiency of the various parts of the regional system through improved transport and communication linkages, the capacity of the megalopolitan area to absorb more and more people is enhanced, thus expanding the megalopolis itself.

Poly-nucleated Urban Regions

On the eastern coastal area of China, a poly-nucleated urban region has grown up situated on the plains of the middle and lower reaches of the Liaohe River. The region includes the cities of Shenyang, Fushun, Beinxi, Liaoyang, Yingkuo, and Dalian, all in Liaoning province. Although agriculture and availability of land were the main magnets that attracted migrants from other parts of China to this region in the eighteenth and nineteenth centuries, it was the rich deposits of coal, iron and other minerals that eventually were responsible for the region's rapid growth. In the early nineteenth century, these rich minerals were exploited by Japan and other capitalist countries. After Liberation, this region became the industrial base of the new China.

Planned as a sub-provincial entity, the poly-nucleated region in Liaoning province contains about 54.1 per cent of the provincial population. Heavy industries are the engines for industrial development and these are mainly concentrated in the large and medium-sized cities. The relatively smaller agricultural population has made agriculture so efficient that the region is basically self-sufficient in grain.

The planning of the region links up the six urban settlements with good communication and transportation axes. An important aspect of the region's development is that two of the cities, Dalian and Yingkuo, are coastal ports that link up with the outside world, mainly Japan. These ports serve not only the region but two of the three industrial provinces in eastern China as well.

Rural–Urban Regions

Hierarchically below the poly-nucleated urban region is the rural–urban region composed of a number of secondary urban centres regionally linked together to achieve higher efficiency through planning. An excellent example of this type of region is the Suzhou–Wuxi–Changzhou region in southern Jiangsu Province. The cities of Suzhou, Wuxi, and Changzhou were well-known settlements in ancient China. As their populations increased after 1949, they were faced with the problem of where to expand.

To conserve the ancient city, Suzhou authorities decided to expand development toward the eastern and western sections of the settlement. Wuxi, hemmed in by Taihu Lake, has decided to create two self-contained districts in the north, towards the Yangtze River, to make room for a city of 1 million. The medium-sized city of Changzhou is fast expanding southward and northward into a city of 500,000.

Although this region in southern Jiangsu has now become one of the most urbanized sections of China, it originally owed its prosperity to intensive agriculture. Wuxi has traditionally been known as one of the rice baskets of China, owing its productivity to the abundant water from Taihu Lake and the marshes fed by the Yangtze River. Suzhou, with its world-famous silk, thrived on grain and fish production and other rural industries. At present, although the rural development of the region is still one of its main sources of income, industry, and manufacturing have taken over as the region's main resource. Although the region is only 17.1 per cent of the territory of Jiangsu, it currently accounts for 39.2 per cent of the province's total industrial and agricultural output value.

By aggregating a largely rural population around traditional urban centres and then linking up the small-scale agglomerations into a planned region, Chinese planners have strengthened the productive relationships between urban and rural areas. An aggressive policy of rural industrialization based on private efforts or collective enterprises is providing the energy for China's new-found grassroots development. This approach to regional planning has encouraged the growth of small and medium-sized cities. It has also served to strengthen rural productivity by opening up the linkages between rural enterprises and urban markets and services.

Small Towns Development

The most important recent trend in the urban growth of China is the accelerated development of small towns. From 1978 to 1985, China's urban population increased by 200 million. Much of this growth has been due to the increase of the population of small towns, which accounted for 62.4 per cent of the growth. Of course, much of the 'growth' of the small town population was due to definitional changes that 'designated' many formerly rural areas as towns.[2] However, since 1984, when migration from villages to towns was officially allowed by the Government, the real growth of small towns has been very significant (see Table 3.4).

The main impetus for the growth of towns has been rapid increases in rural incomes due to the production responsibility system. In 1979, Chinese farmers were allowed to keep and/or sell products in excess of their production quotas. Selling the products in the open market enhanced productivity, the savings deposits of peasants expanded tremendously, and most of them started engaging

Table 3.4. Growth of small towns in China

Year	No. of towns	Total population	Percentage of non-agricultural population
1953	5,402	23,530,000	—
1965	2,902	37,931,000	81.3
1979	2,851	41,828,000	—
1980	2,784	56,931,000	77.6
1982	2,664	61,909,000	—
1983	2,786	62,340,000	72.0
1984	6,211	134,474,000	38.9
1985	7,511	163,322,000	35.4

Note: These figures do not tally with those given in Table 2.8. However, because of the varying definitions used in Chinese statistics, this is not an unusual occurrence.

Source: Luo 1988: 28.

[2] A major change was introduced in 1984 in the criteria for being designated a town. Since 1964, a town had been defined as an area inhabited by at least 3,000 permanent residents, of whom 70% or more were non-agricultural residents, or an area inhabited by 2,500–3,000 permanent residents, with 85% or more being non-agricultural population. Since 1984, a new definition has been adopted, by which a town may be established as long as it is also the location of the county government; or it is a township with a population of over 20,000, where the township government is located and the non-agricultural population is over 10% of the township population; or it is an area where it is necessary to establish a town (e.g. in a frontier area, a minority region, a mining centre or a tourist centre) though the above criteria are not met.

in so-called 'sideline occupations' and rural enterprises. By 1985, the number of open markets where farmers could freely sell their goods jumped to 60,000.

A national free-market system was planned to be in full operation in China by 1990, to replace the state markets. One market was planned for every 30,000 to 50,000 residents in big and medium-sized cities and one market for every 10,000 to 20,000 people in small cities. Investment in the markets was expected from local governments, collective enterprises and private entrepreneurs.

Between 1983 and 1984, about 437,200 new rural enterprises were established all over China; almost all of them were collectives and two-thirds were in towns. In June 1985, it was reported that 11 million enterprises existed in China. They employed 16 million workers (11.6 million in rural areas and 4.4 million in cities). In addition, the government estimated that there were 20 million private business entrepreneurs and self-employed workers all over the country.

In a study of thirty-six towns located in eight coastal provinces carried out between 1985 and 1987 (Liu 1989), it was found that the population of the towns practically exploded between 1984 and the time of the survey. The great bulk of the population increase was due to in-migration. For example, the average increase in the population of four towns in Shandong province was 61.3 per cent within three years. In the four towns in Zhejiang province, a total of 30,709 rural labourers moved in between 1984 and 1986. In four towns located in the suburbs of Shanghai, about 630,000 rural labourers had shifted from farming to non-agricultural work, which classified them as urban under the new household registration regulations. In fact, in the prosperous province of Zhejiang, it was found that out of 19.1 million rural labourers in 1986, about 6.5 million or 34 per cent shifted from agricultural to non-agricultural categories.

The most serious problem that China faces in the future is how to find jobs, housing, education, health and other services for the 200 million or more rural people who will have to move from agricultural to non-agricultural callings by the year 2000 (Wang 1987b). In most small cities and towns, the migrants hope that they will be able to find employment in the formal sector (government, collectives, state enterprises). However, most of the jobs found in small towns and cities are in the informal sector—food stalls and restaurants, beauty parlours and barber shops, dressmaking salons, or petty trading. While these informal-sector jobs tend to be labour-intensive and can absorb significant numbers, there are questions about their economic efficiency and productive potential.

In their efforts to find ways of achieving socio-economic development in China's rural areas, the authorities have evolved two so-called 'models' of development: the Southern Jiangsu model, based on experiences in the region around Suzhou, Wuxi and Changzhou and the Wenzhou model, patterned after developments in Wenzhou, Southern Zhejiang province. The Southern Jiangsu model is founded on the merits of the 'collective enterprise', while the Wenzhou model relies on the 'household factory' for its development energy.

Because in the Southern Jiangsu model, especially in the cities of Suzhou and Wuxi, most of the enterprises are owned by the state or collectives, the scale of production is larger than in the Wenzhou model, capital intensity is greater, and more workers are employed in each enterprise. About 90.8 per cent of the total industrial and agricultural output value in 1985 was derived from collective enterprises. In that year, the cities of Suzhou, Wuxi, and Changzhou alone had 52.4 billion yuan in industrial and agricultural output value. In the city of Suzhou, rural enterprises increased their output by 34.5 per cent in 1984. This rapid rate of economic growth was mainly responsible for the fact that about 40 per cent of the total rural labour force in Suzhou, Wuxi, and Changzhou changed jobs and worked in rural enterprises instead of continuing to work on the farm (Tao *et al.* 1988).

Wenzhou, in southern Zhejiang, has a population of 6.2 million living in about eleven counties and districts. In 1985, the city of Wenzhou had 107,000 household factories and 25,000 joint-household enterprises employing about 400,000 persons. The total output value of the enterprises was 1.1 billion yuan in 1985, which represented 61.5 per cent of the rural output value. Among the total transport enterprise efforts, private enterprises accounted for 70 per cent, and in the catering industry private households accounted for more than 70 per cent of output.

Rural enterprise in Wenzhou relies very heavily on commodity markets of which there were 417 in the city. Some of these commodity markets were very large—out of the 417 mentioned above, ten had an annual turnover of about 100 million yuan. The activities of the commodity markets have also been strongly supported by private financial institutions (e.g. savings and loans associations, pooled capital funds, agricultural banks). In Pingyang county, for example, 97 per cent of the household factories and 83.9 per cent of the trading families have established ties with these financial institutions.

The importance of the Wenzhou model is that by establishing linkages between urban and rural areas, the various rural enterprises have absorbed thousands of rural labourers. In recent years, it was estimated that household factories and other enterprises have absorbed more than 600,000 workers, about 75 per cent of the total rural labour surplus in the region. The proportion of workers engaged in agricultural activities in Wenzhou dropped drastically from 89 per cent in 1978 to 28.5 per cent in 1985. The Wenzhou model, therefore, showed the ability of the private sector to absorb redundant population from the countryside.

Conclusion

Since 1979, China has pursued a national urban strategy and a regional development policy that together have started to change urban growth patterns significantly. The national urban strategy has attempted to limit the growth of large and extra-large cities. In ten years, this goal has not shown signs of succeeding because of the rediscovered economic benefits of urban agglomeration and the threatening spectre of uncontrolled urban growth due to spontaneous (temporary) migration that has led to what has been called the 'floating population' problem. The planned development of 'megalopolitan regions' centred on Shanghai and Beijing has served to concentrate urban populations further by enhancing developmental efficiencies and economies of scale in these regions.

The second goal of the national urban strategy—the rational development of medium-sized cities—has met with more success. Urban growth around medium-sized cities is being achieved by planned development of satellite cities and towns around them and the regional planning efforts linking a number of medium-sized cities together. Some medium-sized cities have also been strengthened by planned efforts to link them up more rationally with small towns and their rural hinterlands.

The third goal of the national urban strategy—the development of small cities and towns—has only started to be successful. Regulations allowing people to move from villages to towns provided they take care of their food-grain needs have been passed and they have accelerated rural–urban migration. Economic development in small towns has been enhanced, through greater employment in collective or family-centred enterprises. Much of the migrant labour has been absorbed by informal-sector industries and services in small towns. In less than five years, since migration was encouraged, millions of people have changed their status from agricultural to non-agricultural workers. This change has rapidly raised the urbanization level in China to almost 46.6 per cent at the end of 1987.

More rapid urbanization and greater urban concentration in the traditionally richer areas of China have resulted from regional development policy. The setting up of Special Economic Zones and building cities from scratch have entailed very heavy costs but the four SEZs have been very successful. Development in the fourteen coastal cities has been slower because of large capital needs. The heavy construction demands of regional development have overheated the Chinese economy and caused serious inflation. The rapid economic growth in the chosen areas also helped to spawn corruption, which has, in turn, created anti-government feeling. The upheavals in Beijing and other parts of China that so adversely affected Chinese development in the early 1990s may be partly traced to some of the economic and physical planning approaches that have been responsible for China's rapid growth in the preceding decade.

Like other developing countries, China has been attempting to balance the goal of achieving rapid economic development on the one hand, and more egalitarian and shared welfare goals on the other. Since 1979, the Chinese government has decided to strive for rapid economic development first. Because of the close association between urbanization and development, regional development policies were pursued that promoted urbanization and extended urban growth to wider settlement networks. The execution of such policies has strained the Chinese economic situation and political stability has been hampered. It may take some time before China is able to maintain the economic-political balance it seeks and prevent the spatial and class polarization that may arise from the economic and urban development policies it so energetically pursues.

4 Migration and Urbanization in China

LIN YOU SU

Migration is one of the most important areas of contemporary research on development issues in developing countries. The process of migration is closely related to the structural transformation of a country from an agrarian society to an industrial society. Recent studies show that in many developing countries city-ward migration is a significant factor contributing to the growth of the urban population (Yap 1975: 6–10; Fuller 1981: 55–66; Goldstein and Goldstein 1985: 3–21), and China is no exception. However, because of the paucity of material on migration in China, very little is known about this. This chapter will begin to fill the gap by focusing on migration to urban China. It is mainly based on two sets of data: Registration data and Migration Survey data from 1986.

The Migration Survey was conducted by the Population Research Institute of the Chinese Academy of Social Sciences between 1 September and 30 November 1986. The total sample size was about 25,000 households in seventy-four cities and towns. In each city and town, the survey followed stratified random sampling principles, the size of the sample in each city varying according to the number of households in that city. The principle was that small cities and towns would have large sample sizes in order to make sure that small areas also had enough sample cases. One of the advantages of this survey is that it collected information on each member of the selected households, no matter whether his or her official residence was in the city. For example, if there was a rural woman who had been working privately in a household for years, which is now common in China, the survey would collect information about her even though her official residence was in the rural areas. In this sense, the survey data are more reliable than registration data which ignore the officially unrecognized migrants in urban areas such as the one mentioned above. One limitation of this survey, however, is that it did not collect information on those who did not live in households but in hotels, dormitories or construction camps. Thus, the survey failed to catch all of the temporary migrants or so-called 'floating population'. Some estimates suggest that temporary migrants who lived in households only accounted for 30 per cent of the total temporary migrants.

Based on data collected in the Migration Survey, it is possible to derive rough estimates of the share of urban growth in China contributed by the following three sources: the natural growth of the urban population; the expansion and reclassification of urban areas; and migration. Over the entire period 1949–86 the share of each factor was estimated to be: 35 per cent due to the rate of natural increase among urban residents; 31 per cent due to expansion of urban areas and their reclassification; and 34 per cent due to migration. However, the proportions varied over time. From 1949 to 1960, the share of natural growth was approximately 39 per cent, and boundary expansion and migration accounted for 61 per cent of the total. From 1961 to 1970, the main source of urban population growth was the natural rate of growth of the urban population (68 per cent), suggesting that the government policy of strict control on migration was successful during the 1960s. From 1971 to 1975, city expansion, reclassification and migration accounted for 43 per cent of total urban growth, and this share progressively increased to 77 per cent during the period 1976–80 and to 87 per cent from 1981 to 1986.

General Review of Migration in China

This section will examine general migration patterns and trends in China between 1949 and 1986, with special emphasis on urban areas. In order to provide the context, it will first review the geography of population distribution in China.

The geographic context

The population of China is unevenly distributed due to extensive regional differences in natural conditions and economic development. Population density in the twenty-nine provinces and autonomous regions ranges from 1.6 persons per square kilometre in Tibet and five persons per square kilometre in Qinghai to 590 persons per square kilometre in Jiangsu. The territory of China can be conveniently divided into two by a straight line from Aihui in Heilongjiang province in the north-east, to Tengchong in Yunnan province in the south-west (Map 1). The region east of this line accounts for 36 per cent of the total area but contained 94 per cent of China's population at the 1982 census. It has a warm and moist marine climate, with fertile land that has been cultivated for thousands of years. Compared with the western region, eastern China is more economically developed. The value of industrial and agricultural production from this region accounts for almost 90 per cent of the total value of industrial and agricultural production in China. The region west of the Aihui–Tengchong line constitutes 64 per cent of the total territory but contained only 6 per cent of the population in 1982. The climate in this part is dry and cold, and the area of cultivated land is limited.

The geographical distribution of the urban population in China follows a similar pattern: the absolute number, as well as the proportion of the urban population progressively declines from the east and south-east to the west and south-west, as noted earlier in the introduction to this part of the book and as evident in Map 1. Such an unbalanced spatial distribution of population has induced the Chinese government to implement policies to redistribute population from east to west, from coastal regions to the inner hinterland, and from cities to the remote border regions.

Types of migration

There are many different ways of classifying migration. For example, according to the nature of the places of origin and destination, migration can be categorized as rural–rural, rural–urban, urban–urban and urban–rural. Alternatively, migration can be classified into four categories of duration in the place of destination: permanent migration, temporary migration, circular migration and daily commuting. In this section, migration is divided into two types according to the level of government involvement. The first type will be called sponsored migration. The second is not government-organized, and will be called private migration.

Sponsored migration

Few governments have made as much effort as the Chinese to redistribute population. It has tried to redistribute population from urban to rural areas, from the east coast to the inner hinterland, and from densely populated areas to remote border regions through officially sponsored migration programmes. Migration schemes have been of three types: the 'settle-down campaign in rural areas'; the 'border region settlement'; and the 'inland industrial shift'.

Of the three, the 'settle-down campaign' was the largest. This movement started in 1957, by the end of which year about 2 million city youth had been moved to rural areas (Lau 1977: 552). The cultural revolution raised this kind of movement to new levels. From 1968 to the early 1970s, about 17 million city middle-school graduates were sent to rural areas, many of them to remote mountain areas or border regions. The original purpose of this 'settle-down campaign' was not merely to reduce the urban population, but to train 'revolutionary successors' in the rural areas. The government also hoped that by sending educated young people to the backward regions, the cultural and economic level of those areas would be raised. The 'settle-down campaign' failed to achieve these goals but succeeded in reducing the urban population, although only temporarily. The campaign lasted until the late 1970s, when it was quietly shelved.

Another government-organized movement, known as the 'border region settlement' was also initiated in the late 1950s. Since then, millions of young city-dwellers have been dispatched to China's border regions of Heilongjiang, Inner Mongolia, Yunnan, Xingjian, and even Tibet. In addition to young urbanites, many peasants from densely populated areas were also sent to the border regions. For instance, during the 1960s, about 500,000 peasants were moved from Hunan Province to Xinjian in north-west China. One objective was to bring virgin territory into extensive agricultural production. Up to 1985, about 2,000 state-owned farms had been established in border regions, with 4.9 million workers and staff. Many of these farms were equipped with advanced technology and their productivity was much higher than that of traditional agriculture. Some centres of agricultural production have developed into towns and small cities that play an important role in local social, economic, and cultural life. A typical example is Shihezi city in Xingjian region. In 1950, this city was built in the Gobi Desert. After forty years, it has become a medium-sized city with a population of 549,000 in 1985, most of them migrants from Shanghai or their children.

The third government-organized migration is called the 'inland industrial shift'. Since the mid-1950s, many big cities along the eastern coast of China have dispatched technicians and skilled workers to inland regions, mainly to Sichuan, Shaanxi and Gansu provinces. It has been estimated that between 1949 and 1979, approximately 10 million such people were shifted from the east to the west of China. Approximately 1.3 million skilled personnel were sent from Shanghai alone (Lu 1986: 51–4). This kind of transfer was intended to reduce rapid urban growth in the sending areas, and to promote economic development in the receiving areas by the inflow of skilled human resources.

Private migration

In China, there were two traditional routes for private migration: the migration stream from Shandong, Hebei, and Henan provinces to the north-east of China, formerly Manchuria; and from Guangdong and Fujian to South-East Asia. After 1949, the second stream was suspended but the first continued. This is reflected in the rapid population growth of Heilongjiang province in the north-east. The population in Heilongjiang increased from 10 million in 1949 to 30 million in 1985, approximately 7 million of the increase resulting from net migration (Tian *et al* 1986: 82–4). However, from the mid-1950s to the late 1970s, migration, especially rural to urban migration, was generally restricted by government regulations.

The situation changed completely after 1977. As China's economy has become more market-oriented, private migration has increased because the new policy encourages peasants to leave the land and seek employment opportunities elsewhere. The 1982 census revealed that approximately 6.4 million people had moved from their permanent place of residence for periods of more than one year. Some 4.8 million people reported that their residential registration had not been settled. This is not the complete picture. Chang (1986: 3–7) estimated that, by the end of 1985, about 20 million peasants were working away from their official places of residence. Studies in cities have also shown that more and more migrants were living in urban areas. For example, a survey in Beijing on 20 April 1985 recorded 662,000 non-permanent residents who spent that night in Beijing. This was about 12 per cent of all permanent residents in the city. Among these, 38 per cent lived in the households of Beijing inhabitants, 36 per cent in hotels, 21 per cent in construction camps and 5 per cent in markets and stations (Du 1986: 12–14).

There is increasing evidence that, since 1977, people have increasingly migrated on their own initiative, moving for more income, better living standards, higher

education or family-related reasons. At the same time, there has been less government-organized migration. This constitutes perhaps the most dramatic change in
China's migration pattern since 1949.

Patterns and trends of migration: 1949–86

The period 1949–86 can be divided into four phases:

Phase 1 (1949–60) Migration levels were high throughout China. According to
official registration data, by 1954 over 22 million people had changed their place
of residence. In 1955, the number increased to 25 million. In 1960, those who had
changed their place of residence reached a peak of 33 million (Ma Xia and Wang
Weizhi 1988: 1–7). During this period, the urban migration pattern was characterized by a large number of in-migrants and a small number of out-migrants.
This was especially true in the late 1950s. As a response to the 'pull' factor of
industrialization in urban areas, about 20 million rural dwellers moved into the
cities during the late 1950s: in the case of Beijing, about 3 million people moved in
during the 1950s, while the total number of out-migrants was about 1.8 million
(Lin 1986: 25–38).

Phase 2 (1961–5) was marked by sudden and substantial changes in the volume
and patterns of migration. The pace of migration was much slower than in the
1950s. For example, the numbers who officially changed their place of residence
dropped from 33 million in 1960 to 19 million in 1961, and to 13 million in 1963,
(Ma Xia and Wang Weizhi 1988: 1–7). The migration pattern in urban areas also
changed markedly in this period. Again taking Beijing as an example, the number
of in-migrants was only 1.3 million compared with 1.9 million out-migrants (Lin
1986: 25–8). The main reason for this low level of population movement was the
economic situation. The early 1960s was a period of economic depression in
China. Whereas by the end of 1959 there had been approximately 263,000 industrial enterprises, by 1965 only 158,000 remained (China State Statistics Bureau,
1983: 213).

Phase 3 (1966–76) was a period of political turmoil in China with low levels of
migration. Between 1966 and 1976, the average annual number of people who
officially changed their place of residence was 5–6 million, the lowest since 1949.
On the one hand, thousands of urban youth were sent to rural areas, while on the
other many rural migrants flowed into the cities in order to meet the demands of
the urban labour market. One estimate has suggested that, during the period
1966–76, over 14 million peasants transferred from rural to urban jobs and 17 million urban youth were dispatched to rural areas (Ren 1988: 19–23).

Phase 4 (1977–86) Migration in China increased again after 1977, due to economic reform. According to official figures, the number of people who changed

their place of residence ranged from 14 million to 25 million annually (Ma Xia and Wang Weizhi 1988: 1–7). This figure is not as accurate as the corresponding figure in the 1960s because, due to the relaxation of controls, many more migrants did not register their movement. After 1977, many seasonal workers, handicraft workers, construction workers and household servants from rural areas moved to urban areas, some travelling long distances. An important change is that these were no longer government-organized migrants, but private migrants.

The Pattern of Migration to Urban Areas

The pattern and volume of migration to urban areas in China has long remained a mystery due to lack of data. This section will use Household Registration data and the 1986 Migration Survey to examine the pattern, trends and volume of migration in urban China between 1949 and 1986.

China's Household Registration data provide general information on the volume of urban migration in different periods, although the accuracy and completeness of the data varies over time. Three terms are used here to measure migration volume:

1. In-migration rate, defined by: $mi = (Mi / P) * K$, Where mi is the in-migration rate, Mi is the total number of in-migrants to a particular urban area in a specific time period, P is the total population in the same urban location during the corresponding period, K is a constant.

2. Out-migration rate, defined by: $mo = Mo / P * K$, Where mo is the out-migration rate, Mo is the total number of out-migrants to a particular urban area in a specific time period, P is the total population of the same urban area during the corresponding period, K is a constant.

3. Net migration rate: $n = mi - mo$, where n is the net migration rate.

According to Household Registration data (Ren 1988: 19–23), from 1951 to 1986, the average annual in-migration rate in all urban areas was 6.8 per cent, the average out-migration rate was 5.6 per cent and the net migration rate was 1.2 per cent. However, the volume of migration varied considerably over time. From 1951 to 1953, the annual urban in-migration rate averaged 10.4 per cent, the out-migration rate 7.1 per cent, and the net in-migration 3.3 per cent. From 1954 to 1960, both in-and out-migration increased, and all cities in China experienced a large volume of population mobility. During this period, both in-migration and out-migration rates were high, with in-migration rates approximately 3 per cent higher, on average. The following period, 1961 to 1965, was a low tide of population mobility in urban China. The failure of economic strategy to achieve over-ambitious goals in industry and the disaster of the commune system in agriculture forced the government to dismiss 18 million workers and staff from state-owned enterprises and send over 20 million urban residents to rural areas. Consequently, out-migration from urban areas exceeded in-migration.

From 1961 to 1965 average annual in-migration was only 3.6 per cent, while the out-migration rate was 5.4 per cent, resulting in a net out-migration rate of –1.8 per cent annually. Between 1966 and 1970, Household Registration data were not usable due to the political turmoil of the 'Cultural Revolution'. It is estimated that out-migration from urban areas must have been quite high because of the 'settle-down campaign', in which 17 million city youth were sent to rural areas. Between 1971 and 1977, urban in-migration exceeded out-migration but overall population movement remained at a low level. During this period, the average annual in-migration rate for urban areas was 3 per cent, compared with an out-migration rate of 2.2 per cent. From 1978 to 1986, more migrants moved to urban areas. Average annual in-migration reached 3.5 per cent, while out-migration was 2.1 per cent.

Based on these statistics, net urban in-migration over the period 1951–86 would be 60 million persons, with five years (1966–70) of data missing. Assuming that the average annual number of in-migrants in these five years was 2 million (the average annual number of the 30 years, 1951–69 and 1971–86), the total number of migrants to urban China would be 70 million during the period 1951–86.

The Migration Survey conducted in 1986 also provides some information on the volume of urban migration. According to the survey data, the proportions of lifetime migrants among urban residents in different-sized cities were as follows: 33 per cent in extra-large cities (those with a population of one million and over); 46 per cent in large cities (those with a population between 500,000 and 1 million); 34 per cent in medium-sized cities (those with a population between 200,000 to 500,000); 39 per cent in small cities (those with a population under 200,000); and 45 per cent in towns. Since China's official urban population is exaggerated by over-boundedness, this study will use the non-agricultural population to estimate the total number of lifetime migrants in urban China. According to recent data, (Ministry of Public Security 1987: 9–22), the non-agricultural population in each level of urban areas was 49 million in extra-large cities; 23 million in large cities; 17 million in medium-sized cities; 22 million in small cities and 60 million in urban towns. Based similarly on the non-agricultural population, the number of lifetime migrants in each category of urban areas was 16 million in extra-large cities; 10 million in large cities; 6 million in medium-sized cities; 8 million in small cities and 27 million in towns. The total number of lifetime migrants in all urban areas would be 67 million in 1986: a conservative figure, since it is based on the non-agricultural population, which is less than the official urban population.

Certain historic features of migratory flows in urban China stand out. First, the extra-large cities experienced a larger volume of in-migration in the 1950s than did other urban areas. As shown in Table 4.1, in-migrants arriving during the 1950s accounted for 30 per cent of all migrants living in extra-large cities in 1986. By comparison, only 11 per cent of the in-migrants in the towns arrived during the 1950s. The large number of in-migrants to the extra-large cities in the 1950s reflects government industrialization efforts in metropolitan areas at that time. Under the slogan of 'turning the consumer cities into productive cities', a large

Table 4.1.   In-migrants by year of move and city size (%)

City size	1949–60	1961–70	1971–78	1979–86	All years
Extra-large cities	29.6	13.2	20.8	36.4	100.0
Large cities	14.4	27.2	28.1	30.3	100.0
Medium-sized cities	19.5	19.8	22.1	38.6	100.0
Small cities	16.5	18.0	20.1	45.4	100.0
Towns	10.2	16.1	20.2	53.5	100.0

Source: Population Research Institute, Chinese Academy of Social Sciences, Beijing, China, 1986.

number of factories were set up in big cities, creating many job opportunities for rural–urban migrants. Second, towns have enjoyed significant in-migration since 1979: the majority of in-migrants (53 per cent) moved in after 1979 (Table 4.1). In small cities, the proportion of in-migrants arriving after 1979 (45 per cent) was also quite high. Compared with this, large cities show a smaller concentration of recent in-migrants.

The increased number of in-migrants in small cities and towns during recent times reflects the successful implementation of the government's urban strategy of 'actively developing small cities and towns'. In recent years, the importance of the small cities and towns in China's urbanization process has been repeatedly stressed. According to the forecasts of the agricultural ministry, approximately 200 million peasants in rural China will have moved from farming during the 1990s. Some of these people will have to be relocated in small cities and towns.

The migration pattern in China is mainly influenced by two factors: government policy on migration which has been discussed in the previous section; and industrial development, which will be discussed in this section.

During the past four decades, there have been four phases of industrial development which led to four waves of migration in China (Ma 1986: 13–25). The first occurred in the 1950s. During this period, the Chinese government adopted a development strategy emphasizing heavy industry, and characterized by the building of large factories in big cities. This 'pull' factor of industrial development caused the first wave of urban population growth through a large aggregate volume of rural to urban migration. It is estimated that over 30 million rural peasants moved into urban areas during the first wave of migration (Ma 1986: 5–8).

The second phase of industrial development took place in the 1960s and was characterized by the shift of industry from the eastern coastal region to the western and inner hinterland. The main reason for this shift was defence and military considerations due to China's deteriorating relations with both the USA and USSR during the 1960s. This inland industrial shift provided the basis for the second wave of migration in China. From 1962 to 1969, hundreds of factories were shifted to the western regions, together with thousands of skilled workers from coastal regions.

The third phase of industrial development was the diffusion of industry from cities to rural areas. It was initiated in the late 1950s but the real development occurred in the 1970s. In recent years, the development of rural industry was even more considerable, and the number of employees working in rural industry jumped from 20 million in 1981 to 43.9 million in 1986 (China State Statistics Bureau 1987: 37). Most of these rural enterprises were located in towns and small urban centres. This industrial diffusion generated the third wave of migration, which was characterized by a migration stream from rural to small urban areas and towns.

The fourth phase of industrial development occurred during the 1980s. In this phase, China's east coastal region became the focus. The establishment of four special economic zones and the opening up of fourteen coastal cities created a new momentum in migration in this region. By 1988, over 10,000 foreign investment enterprises and joint ventures had been set up in these areas, absorbing much surplus labour not only from the local region but also from other provinces.

The Economic Situation of Migrants in Urban Areas

Do migrants become concentrated in certain industries or occupations after they move into urban areas? Are they economically better-off than the non-migrants in the communities of destination? Studies on migration in developing countries have provided different answers to such questions on the performance of migrants in urban areas. Some have found that migrants to the cities were more likely than non-migrants to be employed in less-skilled occupations, tended to be relatively more numerous in service and tertiary sectors and usually received less pay than non-migrants (Zachariah 1968: 148–211; Standing 1978: 5–16). Other studies have found contradictory results. Premi and Tom (1985: 69) found that in Indian cities, a significantly higher proportion of migrants than non-migrants of both sexes were engaged in professional, technical, administrative, executive and managerial jobs. Similarly in certain South-East Asian countries the economic position of many migrants compared favourably with that of urban natives. Migrants tended to have a higher proportion in white-collar jobs and to earn more than non-migrants (Fuller 1981: 55–66).

In this section, the employment status, occupation and income of migrants and non-migrants in the different-sized cities of China will be examined, based on the Migration Survey data of 1986. The migrants referred to in this study are two categories of permanent migrants: those who have official registration in urban areas; and those who have no official registration in urban areas but have been there one year or longer.

Since age structure has a great influence on labour force participation and income of individuals, this section will first review the differences in age structure of migrants and non-migrants. In general, the current age structure of the urban non-migrant population is much younger than that of the urban migrant population (Table 4.2). In extra-large cities, only 5 per cent of migrants are in the age group 0–14, compared with 24 per cent among non-migrants. In towns, the differentials are even larger: about 10 per cent of migrants as against 31 per cent of non-migrants are in the age group 0–14. Contrary to the situation in many developing countries, even the young working-age population (15–29) is over-represented among non-migrants compared with migrants. However, a much higher proportion of migrants fall in the older working-age groups, 30–44 and 45–59 in all selected urban areas. This age differential between migrants and non-migrants affects the employment, occupation and income of migrants, to be discussed below.

An analysis of sex ratios of migrants and non-migrants provides a clear picture of differentials between the two population sub-groups in different-sized cities of China (Table 4.3). Among the migrants, males are predominant in all urban areas,

Table 4.2.   Migrant status by age group and city size in urban areas (%)

Age group	Extra-large cities		Medium-sized cities		Towns	
	Migrants	Non-migrants	Migrants	Non-migrants	Migrants	Non-migrants
0–14	5	24	6	28	10	31
15–29	23	34	28	34	32	33
30–44	32	18	31	18	30	15
45–59	28	13	25	10	22	10
60+	12	11	10	10	6	11
Total	100	100	100	100	100	100

Source: Population Research Institute, Chinese Academy of Social Sciences, Beijing, China, 1986.

Table 4.3.   Sex ratio by migration status and city size

	Migrants (male/female)	Non-migrants (male/female)
Extra-large cities (A)	116	97
Large cities (B)	136	108
Medium-sized cities (C)	117	99
Small cities (D)	109	101
Towns (E)	121	102

A. Population of 1 million or over.
B. Population 500,000–1 million.
C. Population 200,000–500,000.
D. Population 50,000–200,000.
E. Population 2,000–50,000.

Source: Population Research Institute, Chinese Academy of Social Sciences, Beijing, China, 1986.

the sex ratio ranging from 109 to 136. Among non-migrants, females form a higher percentage in extra-large and medium-sized cities, whereas in other kinds of cities, the sex ratio is almost equal. The sex differential between migrants and non-migrants may also affect differentials in employment status, occupation and income.

Employment of migrants in urban areas is not only important in its own right, but it has been viewed as an essential step for their subsequent adjustment in urban areas (Stromberg *et al.* 1974: 309–23; Clark 1986: 47). In China people between the ages of 15 and 60 are considered to be economically active. Table 4.4 provides a general picture of the employment situation of migrants and non-migrants in different categories of cities in China.

The data in Table 4.4 show that both male and female migrants had a higher work-participation rate than non-migrants in all categories of cities. Age structure may be the main reason. Non-migrants included a higher proportion of those under age 15, and as a result, a higher proportion of students. Migrants included a lower proportion unemployed than non-migrants, and this is especially true in

Table 4.4. Employment status of migrants and non-migrants aged 6 years and over (%)

	Male		Female	
	Migrants	Non-migrants	Migrants	Non-migrants
Extra-large cities				
Employed	81	75	66	63
Unemployed	2	3	2	3
Retired	11	15	16	17
Student	6	7	4	7
Unpaid housework	0	0	12	10
Total	100	100	100	100
Medium-sized cities				
Employed	83	75	68	63
Unemployed	1	6	3	7
Retired	11	10	11	9
Student	4	8	4	8
Unpaid housework	1	1	14	13
Total	100	100	100	100
Towns				
Employed	82	74	56	54
Unemployed	3	7	6	9
Retired	9	7	6	3
Student	5	12	7	10
Unpaid housework	1	0	25	24
Total	100	100	100	100

Source: Population Research Institute, Chinese Academy of Social Sciences, Beijing, China, 1986.

medium-sized cities and towns. Age structure may again be a contributing factor, as unemployment rates tend to be higher among young people, who constitute a larger percentage of non-migrants than of migrants. The other possible explanation is that since migration to cities occurs primarily for economic and work-related reasons, migrants are more willing to accept any working opportunities available to them. By contrast, non-migrants have grown up in urban areas, and may prefer to have more choices and try to select better and easier jobs.

In urban China, there are three forms of employment: employment in state enterprises, employment in collective enterprises, and self-employment. In the past, people working in state-owned enterprises enjoyed the best conditions and had higher incomes and a secure welfare and medical system. Those who worked in collectively-owned enterprises tended to have lower incomes, harder working conditions and a poor welfare system. The self-employed had the lowest prestige, irregular incomes and lacked access to medical care and the general welfare system. In recent years, some employees of collectively-owned enterprises have begun to earn more than in state-owned enterprises, and some of the self-employed have become quite rich. However, state-owned employment still enjoys higher prestige and the shift from collective and self-employment to state-owned employment can still be considered a form of upward social mobility.

In all three levels of urban areas, both male and female migrants included a much higher proportion working in state-owned employment than did non-migrants (Table 4.5). A smaller proportion of females than of males worked in state-owned employment.

The occupational classification of the Migration Survey in 1986 is based on that used in the 1982 census. For the purpose of the present analysis, seven broad categories have been used: industrial- and production-related occupations, such as manufacturing, construction, and transport; agriculture-related occupations,

Table 4.5. Employed migrants and non-migrants (aged 15–60) by status of ownership of the enterprise, sex of employee and level of urban areas (%)

	Migrants			Non-migrants		
	State	Collective	Self	State	Collective	Self
Extra-large cities						
Male	85	14	1	65	33	2
Female	62	37	1	54	44	2
Medium-sized cities						
Male	87	12	1	51	44	5
Female	65	32	3	46	51	3
Towns						
Male	74	24	2	37	59	4
Female	51	44	5	35	61	4

Source: Population Research Institute, Chinese Academy of Social Sciences, Beijing, China, 1986.

including farming, fishing, animal husbandry, and forestry; administration and management occupations, including government employees, and senior and supervisory staff in enterprises; professional occupations, including teaching, medicine, science, technical work, engineering, and design; clerical occupations; sales and services occupations; and other.

Table 4.6 suggests that a higher proportion of migrants had white-collar occupations, such as administrative, management and professional work. In extra-large cities, over 38 per cent of migrants were in white-collar occupations compared with only 21 per cent of non-migrants. In small towns, the differentials became even more substantial: 34 per cent of migrants were in white-collar groups as against only 14 per cent of non-migrants.

The 1986 Migration Survey collected information on the income of each member of selected households in the survey. Individual income included wages, salary and bonuses, income from private business benefits and the value of agricultural products. A lower proportion of migrants fell in the bottom income group (under 50 yuan) and migrants were over-represented in the top income group for each level of urban areas (see Table 4.7). In extra-large cities 17 per cent of migrants as against 24 per cent of non-migrants were in the bottom income group (under 50 yuan). In medium-sized cities, the over-representation of non-migrants in the lower income group was even more marked.

Gross comparison of employment status, occupation and income, then, shows that migrants had higher social and economic status than non-migrants. However, this kind of comparison does not take account of other factors affecting occupation and income, such as age and education. A valid comparison of the performance of migrants and non-migrants in urban areas must therefore control for these factors. In order to do this, Multiple Classification Analysis (MCA) was

Table 4.6.   Migrants and non-migrants (aged 15–60) by occupational category and level of urban areas (%)

Occupation	Extra-large cities		Medium-sized cities		Towns	
	Migrants	Non-migrants	Migrants	Non-migrants	Migrants	Non-migrants
Production	50	58	48	50	46	45
Agriculture	4	13	7	22	8	28
Administration/ management	20	10	18	9	21	8
Professional	12	6	13	5	6	3
Clerk	6	5	7	4	7	4
Sales/services	5	6	5	7	7	9
Others	3	2	2	3	5	3
Total	100	100	100	100	100	100

Source: Population Research Institute, Chinese Academy of Social Sciences, Beijing, China, 1986.

Table 4.7.   Income of migrants and non-migrants (aged 15–60) in different categories of urban areas, 1986 (%)

	Monthly income (yuan)				Total
	Under 50	51–100	101–150	151+	
Extra-large cities					
Migrants	17	51	26	6	100
Non-migrants	24	54	18	4	100
Medium-sized cities					
Migrants	24	54	19	3	100
Non-migrants	42	48	8	2	100
Towns					
Migrants	35	47	15	3	100
Non-migrants	51	39	7	3	100

Source: Population Research Institute, Chinese Academy of Social Sciences, Beijing, China, 1986.

used to test the variables affecting occupation and income of migrants and non-migrants. One of the advantages of MCA is that it does not assume linearity. This provision is attractive since some of the independent variables may have no clear linear relationship with the dependent variables, as is the case with the relationship between age and educational attainment. Another important assumption of MCA is that independent variables may have additive effects on dependent variables. This assumption allows us to isolate the net or adjusted effects of an independent variable, controlling for the additive effects of other independent variables. The control variables are entered as factors (categorical variables) and the table gives the mean value of each variable by migration status (Tables 4.8 and 4.9). Beta indicates the relative importance of the variables. It is the multiplier of the independent variables when the variables are expressed in the standardized form. The significance level of F indicates the significance of the difference between migrants and non-migrants after removing the effect of control variables. The relationship would not be significant if F exceeds the .05 level. R square refers to the relative importance of each factor.

Table 4.8 dichotomizes the occupations of migrants and non-migrants into white and non-white collar occupations. The white-collar occupations include administrative, managerial, professional and clerical work. The numbers of those engaged in white-collar work are converted into proportions. The first column shows the unadjusted mean of the proportion of white-collar occupations; the second column has been adjusted for the age differential between migrants and non-migrants; the third column shows the proportion of white-collar workers when the effect of education is removed; and the last column indicates the proportion of white-collar occupations of migrants and non-migrants after adjustments have been made for all controlled variables and interaction between them.

Table 4.8. Multiple classification analysis of proportion of migrants and non-migrants (aged 15–60) in white-collar occupation

	Unadjusted mean	Mean adjusted for		
		Age	Education	Altogether
Extra-large cities				
Migrants	0.38	0.33	0.31	0.30
Non-migrants	0.21	0.18	0.20	0.22
Beta	0.19	0.18	0.13	0.11
Significance *F*	0.000	0.000	0.000	0.000
R square		0.035	0.267	0.308
Medium-sized cities				
Migrants	0.38	0.35	0.32	0.30
Non-migrants	0.18	0.18	0.20	0.20
Beta	0.22	0.21	0.14	0.10
Significance *F*	0.000	0.000	0.000	0.000
R square		0.055	0.250	0.315
Towns				
Migrants	0.34	0.32	0.31	0.31
Non-migrants	0.14	0.16	0.21	0.21
Beta	0.21	0.19	0.16	0.11
Significance *F*	0.000	0.000	0.000	0.000
R square		0.050	0.213	0.274

Source: Population Research Institute, Chinese Academy of Social Sciences, Beijing, China, 1986.

Before the adjustment, migrants had a much higher proportion in white-collar occupations than non-migrants, and when the effect of age and education were removed, they still had a higher proportion in white-collar occupations, although the differential had narrowed considerably. This was the case in all levels of cities.

Data on the monthly average personal income of migrants and non-migrants, measured in yuan (Table 4.9), show that, before adjustment, migrants earned 10 to 17 yuan more than non-migrants in the different levels of cities. When the factors of age and education were held constant, the differences in personal income persisted, but the differential narrowed to approximately 5 yuan in extra-large cities and towns, but remained quite marked in the medium-sized cities. The multivariate analysis therefore shows that the factors of age and education have considerable effects on personal income, especially age, which has a higher *R* square than education. However, after removal of the factors of age and education, the income differential between migrants and non-migrants still persists. One explanation for this may be the sex differential between migrants and non-migrants. Since males predominated among migrants, it would be expected that they would have better occupations and higher incomes than those of non-migrants.

Table 4.9. Multiple classification analysis of monthly income of migrants and non-migrants (yuan)

	Unadjusted mean	Mean adjusted For		
		Age	Education	Altogether
Extra-large cities				
Migrants	94	93	93	91
Non-migrants	84	85	85	86
Beta	0.10	0.14	0.12	0.06
Significance *F*	0.000	0.000	0.000	0.000
R square		0.068	0.041	0.141
Medium-sized cities				
Migrants	82	82	81	79
Non-migrants	65	66	66	67
Beta	0.22	0.20	0.19	0.14
Significance *F*	0.000	0.000	0.000	0.000
R square		0.089	0.074	0.156
Towns				
Migrants	82	80	81	78
Non-migrants	68	70	69	72
Beta	0.14	0.10	0.13	0.07
Significance *F*	0.000	0.000	0.000	0.000
R square		0.071	0.025	0.100

Source: Population Research Institute, Chinese Academy of Social Sciences, Beijing, China, 1986.

Summary and Conclusion

Over a period of four decades, the Chinese government carried out a policy of controlling population movement and growth, especially rural–urban migration and urban population growth. Furthermore, it made great efforts to redistribute its population from urban to rural, from east to west, and from densely populated regions to remote regions. One positive result of this development strategy was that China successfully avoided overurbanization. China has few of the squalid, densely populated slums that are common in many developing countries. Under central planning, the urban population has been guaranteed their daily basic needs by the state. The majority of urban residents have secure jobs, and income distribution is relatively equal compared with many other developing countries.

Another important achievement has been the establishment of a more balanced urban hierarchy, with a number of large cities at the top and many small cities and towns at the bottom (see also the discussion of this in the first chapter of this book). Under the government policy of strictly controlling the growth of big cities, properly developing medium-sized cities and effectively developing small cities and towns, China avoided a heavy concentration of population in its metropolitan areas. The growth of big cities has been effectively controlled.

In spite of these positive results, government intervention in migration and urban development also caused many problems. First, for a long period the registration system divided China's population between non-agricultural or urban population and agricultural or rural population. Combined with a rigid labour-allocation system, this system prevented the rural people from moving into urban areas, totally cutting them off from the process of urbanization and closing the urban system, thus reducing its vitality. A large amount of surplus labour built up in rural China and serious underemployment occurred in agriculture. Furthermore, the policy of limiting labour mobility, which deprived individuals of opportunities to choose their jobs, led to extremely low efficiency in the urban economy because many people were forced into jobs that they disliked.

The second weakness of China's urban development strategy was a neglect of the function of services in the urban economy, which arose from the government's heavy industrial-oriented strategy in the 1950s and 1960s. A typical slogan at that time was 'turning the consumer cities into productive ones'. Overemphasis on this goal and the expansion of capital-intensive heavy industry ignored the reality of China's vast human resources. The chronic shortage of services and the absence of an informal sector in the urban economy limited the ability of urban areas to absorb rural labour. As a result, the process of urbanization stagnated and China's potential advantage of human resources and cheap labour was not fully utilized.

The third weakness of China's migration policy was the very high cost of the government-sponsored migration and population redistribution. Although it is hard to know exactly how much the government has spent on its resettlement programme, the cost must have been very high. For example, during the 'settle-down' campaign in rural areas in the late 1960s and early 1970s, the average spending for each urban youth was 200 yuan as a settle-down fee from the government. Thus, for nearly 20 million urban youths, expenditure amounted to at least 40 billion yuan, not including other costs such as transportation. Furthermore, since almost all of those urban youths later returned to their home cities, the government spending yielded no long-term benefit.

The trend in recent years indicates that China has been moving toward a more typical urbanization pattern since economic reform. The decades-long policies of anti-urbanization and anti-cityward migration have been abandoned. The Chinese government has finally realized that the transfer of labour from rural to urban areas is an integral part of the process of economic development. However, it is still trying to minimize the scale of direct migration to big cities by generating new employment opportunities in rural areas and small towns. It is still too early to conclude whether China's new urban development strategy will allow the country successfully to complete its transformation from an agricultural and traditional society to an industrial and modern society.

5 Urban Housing Reforms in China, 1979–89

YOK-SHIU F. LEE

Introduction

In early 1989, the *China Daily* printed an apprehensive account of the ongoing reform experiments in urban housing. Under the headline 'Reform in housing at crossroads', the author noted that 'progress over the whole country last year [1988] failed to meet government expectations. Many large cities, including some provincial capitals, have been less than enthusiastic about implementing reform' (31 January 1989). This worrying observation, increasingly found in the official Chinese press, is revealing because it was made just one year after the State Council announced in early 1988 its decision to enforce housing reforms in all urban areas in China within three years (Tong Zengyen 1988: 11). It signifies the existence of major difficulties in extending reform programmes beyond a few cities and hints at some fundamental flaws in the overall approach and policy design of the current reform programmes.

One of the major purposes of this chapter is to demonstrate that evidence uncovered through a detailed examination of a major urban housing reform programme in the city of Yantai lends overwhelming support to the above disquieting view. Thus, of immediate research concern is not just the legitimate question of whether or not the reforms will be implemented according to the proposed plans (Barlow and Renaud 1989: 84), but more importantly at this moment, whether or not the current reform policies and programmes are appropriately formulated to address the fundamental problems in urban housing.

This study holds that although earlier remedial measures introduced from 1979 to 1986 have resulted in an increase in the supply of new housing, current reform programmes are largely ineffective in ameliorating two basic problems in urban housing—shortage and inequality. Shortage remains a problem despite increased investment in housing from 1980 to 1985. Some of the reform programmes, through deliberate design or inadvertence, actually reinforced housing inequality among urban dwellers. Before focusing attention on the reform policies and programmes, it is useful to review briefly the problems of shortage and inequality in China's urban housing sector.

Urban Housing Shortage

The extent of the problem of urban housing shortage is documented in Table 5.1. In 1977, 6.26 million urban households had insufficient floor space. Ten years

Table 5.1. Urban housing shortage in China

Year	Number of urban households with insufficient floor space[a] (million)	As percentage of total number of urban households
1977	6.26	n.a.
1978	6.89	35.8
1980	7.90	n.a.
1982	7.49	31.3
1985	7.54	28.8
1987[b]	6.23	31.6

Note: n.a. = not available

[a] Households with insufficient floor space include three main categories: (1) households with no residential units, (2) inconvenient households, and (3) congested households. Households with no residential units refer primarily to people who do not own their residences but live in hotels or guest houses attached to their units. Inconvenient households often refer to those of newly-weds who cannot find their own residences and still have to live with their parents or share living quarters with other families. Congested households refer to those households whose per-capita residential floor space is below the national average (Lee 1988: 389).

[b] The recent official urban population estimates are much larger than before and thus they may suggest that the proportion of urban population with insufficient floor space should have fallen a lot. The new urban population estimates, however, have been systematically inflated by the inclusion of *de facto* rural residents. To maintain data consistency over time, Chinese authorities in charge of urban development have continued to refer to de facto urban residents in their writing. For details, see Lee 1989: 771–86.

Sources: 1977, 1978, 1980, 1982: Lee (1988: 389).
1985: Wu Wanqi (1988: 13).
1987: The number is from Liang Xiaoqing (1989: 18). The percentage figure is from *Renmin ribao* (*People's Daily*), 3 August 1987.

later, in 1987, the number of urban households with insufficient floor space declined only slightly to 6.23 million, or equivalent to 31.6 per cent of all urban households.

The data in Table 5.1 reveal that the urban housing shortage has persisted through the 1977–87 period despite the government's attempts to resolve this problem since the early 1980s. What, then, are the principal causes of China's urban housing shortage and its persistence through the 1977–87 period? First, most Chinese planners would agree that inadequate state investment in the urban housing sector from the late 1950s to the late 1970s is responsible. Urban housing in China was regarded as 'non-productive' investment and accordingly received low priority relative to 'productive' investment such as building factories and large industrial projects (Lee 1988: 388–90).

Second, the government's decision to keep rents low in the urban areas has also contributed to the problem. Artificially low rents have led to the premature deterioration of existing housing stock: because rental income is too low to keep normal maintenance on schedule, necessary repairs are deferred. In addition, under the low-rent policy, each new housing unit represented nearly a full, direct grant of limited public funds, which severely limited the number of units that could be built each year.

Third, the shortage problem can be linked to rising urban housing standards since the early 1970s. Better standards, however, translate into higher construction costs. In the context of a tight or a slow-growth housing investment budget, this constrained the increase in new housing units.

Since the early 1970s standards of design and building materials have gradually been improved. Whereas in the 1960s several households would share common kitchen and lavatory facilities, by the mid- and late 1970s each new individual residential unit would frequently be equipped with such amenities. Another important standard for urban housing that was repeatedly upgraded from the early 1970s to the early 1980s was the floor area per residential unit: the national standard was raised between 1972 and 1982 from 34 m^2 to between a minimum of 42 and a maximum of 90 m^2. While this increase in housing standards has undoubtedly led to higher living standards, it has been criticized by a number of leading Chinese planners as being excessive, when measured against the scale of the existing housing shortage problem and the limited resources available (Lee 1988: 394–5).

Urban Housing Inequalities

There are basically three distributional aspects of inequality in the urban housing sector: housing, housing investment, and housing subsidies.

As a result of increased state investment in urban housing in the early 1980s, per capita residential floor space in urban areas jumped from 3.60 m^2 in 1978 to 7.61 m^2 in 1987 (Table 5.2). Although the figures showed improvement, substantial inequalities existed in housing conditions among urban dwellers. In 1987, 37.8 per cent of all urban households residing in both cities and towns had living quarters with greater than 8 m^2 per capita. At the same time, however, 20.9 per cent of the urban households had only 4 to 6 m^2 per capita and another 18.3 per cent had insufficient floor space (Table 5.3).

The unequal distribution of housing is, to a great extent, the consequence of unequal allocation of government investment in housing. In 1982, for instance, per capita housing investment (197 yuan) in state-owned enterprises was almost six times more than that (34 yuan) in collectively owned enterprises (Lee 1988: 399). The housing construction boom since the early 1980s has actually accentuated existing housing inequalities. Primarily because of the enormous gap in housing investment funds between state-owned and collectively owned sectors,

Table 5.2. Per capita residential floor space in urban areas[a] (in m^2)

Year	National average
1978	3.60
1985	6.66
1986	7.19
1987	7.61

[a] Per-capita residential floor space does not include kitchen, lavatory or corridor.

Sources: 1978: *Renmin ribao* (*People's Daily*), (5 August 1980: 5).
1985: Barlow (1988: 82).
1986, 1987: *1987 Quanguo* (1988: 77).

Table 5.3. Housing conditions of urban households in cities and towns, 1987

Housing conditions	As percentage of total no. of urban households
Households with insufficient floor space	18.3[a]
4–6 m^2 per capita	20.9
6–8 m^2 per capita	23.0
> 8 m^2 per capita	37.8
Total	100

[a] Urban residents living in towns on the average enjoy a much larger per-capita floor space than urban residents who live in cities. The inclusion of urban (town) population in the analysis of urban housing conditions, such as in this 1987 survey report, has therefore led to a lower estimate of urban households with insufficient floor space than if only urban (city) households are considered.

Source: 1987: *1987 Quanguo* (1988: 44).

only workers in certain sectors (electronics, heavy industry) benefited from increased housing investment and enjoyed larger per capita floor space (11 and 9.8 m^2 respectively). On the other hand, 37.5 per cent of commercial and textile workers still faced serious housing shortages (Lee 1988: 404–5).

The third type of housing inequality stems from the way that rent subsidies are distributed. Rent subsidies in China's cities are not distributed according to each household's financial needs. Rather, they are given out by the state through the work units on a per-m^2 basis, regardless of the size of a household's living area. For instance, a family of four (A) living in a 20-m^2 apartment in Beijing would receive an annual housing subsidy in cash of 91.2 yuan, whereas a family of the same household size (B) living in a 40-m^2 apartment would receive 182.4 yuan annually (Wu Cunzhong and Wu Cunxiao 1980: 53). Not only did family (B) live in a more spacious apartment, but precisely for this reason it also enjoyed a larger government subsidy. In other words, there is a built-in incentive for an urban household to secure housing with the maximum amount of floor space. The outcome is persistent inequality in the distribution of housing and rent subsidies.

Remedial Measures, 1979–86

Increasing the proportion of capital construction funds allocated to the urban housing sector was the Chinese government's first most conspicuous attempt to resolve the urban housing shortage problem. The share of the capital construction budget assigned to urban housing almost doubled from 7.8 per cent in 1978 to 14.8 per cent in 1979. For two consecutive years, later, in 1981 and 1982, it was further increased to one-quarter of the annual capital construction budget (Table 5.4).

Of the total housing investment in each year, about 60 to 70 per cent came from the enterprises (Gu Yunchang 1988: 37). Many enterprises had been able to expand housing investment only by using funds that were intended for the upgrading and maintenance of production facilities. Since the mid-1980s, the urban housing sector was under increasing pressure to relinquish its share of the capital construction funds in favour of the industrial sector. Subsequently, the proportion of capital construction funds allocated to urban housing dropped markedly

Table 5.4. Percentage of capital construction funds allocated to urban housing

Year	%
1976	6.1
1977	6.9
1978	7.8
1979	14.8
1980	20.0
1981	25.1
1982	25.4
1983	21.1
1984	18.1
1985	20.0
1986	16.1
1987	13.5

Sources: 1976–80: *Zhongguo tongji nian-jian 1981* (1981: 309).
1976–87: *Zhongguo tongji nian-jian 1988* (1988: 567).

from 20.0 per cent in 1985 to 16.1 per cent in 1986 and to 13.5 per cent in 1987 (Table 5.4). Thus, increased government expenditure in new housing is obviously not a sustainable, long-term strategy.

Coinciding with the increased housing investment in the early 1980s came the recommendation by some Chinese planners to commercialize urban housing. Reformist planners urged that, to solve the housing shortage problem, rents should be increased and the sale of housing to individuals should be officially sanctioned (Zhao Jincheng 1985: 11–14; Zhang Libo 1985: 18–22).

The Chinese government promptly embraced the idea of selling housing to individuals, though carefully and on a limited basis. With regard to rent increases, however, it has acted much more cautiously and slowly. Whereas residential units were first sold to individuals under a pilot scheme introduced in 1982, experiments to raise the rents were conducted five years later, starting in 1987 in several selected cities with careful calculation. The government's cautious attitude toward rent increases was understandable. A rent increase or a restructuring of the rent subsidies would have required a total rearrangement of the economic system, and the beneficiaries of the old system would have been adversely affected. To preserve the overall economic well-being of the urban dwellers and to avoid social unrest, the Chinese government therefore acted prudently in designing and implementing the rent increase programme.

The sale of urban housing to individuals, first tried in four cities in 1982 and then extended to include more than 160 cities by 1986, basically involved a subsidized sale method. Residential units allocated for individual purchase were sold at prices below their investment cost. The individual paid one-third of the total construction cost of a residential unit, with the government and the buyer's employer providing an equal share of the outstanding balance (Liu Mingxin 1984: 23).

The most obvious advantage of the scheme was that at least one-third of the initial investment could be recovered and reinvested to build more new housing. The state would also save money because it would no longer be responsible for the maintenance and repair cost of private housing. Critics of the scheme, however, pointed out that the subsidized sale programme placed a heavy burden on both the state and the work units and that it could not realistically be maintained over a long period of time (Zhou Zheng 1985: 76).

By 1986, the remarks of the critics had been proved correct. The sale price of housing under the subsidized sale scheme averaged less than 20 yuan per m^2, when the actual housing construction costs were 300 yuan or more per m^2. The method was therefore considered unsustainable, incapable of solving the urban housing problem, and was discontinued (Barlow 1988: 16).

As already stated, Chinese planners moved slowly and cautiously on the other component of the housing commercialization proposal—rent increase. Even by late 1987, rents remained very low in major cities and in most parts of the urban areas (*Jingji guanli yanjiu* [*Economics and Management Research*] 1988, No. 2: 48). As a result, in 1987 alone, the state still needed to spend 20 billion yuan in housing subsidies (Lu Wei 1988: 29). The low-rent problem was heightened by the realization that urban residents' spending on housing—as a proportion of their total expenditure—actually declined in recent years (Guan Jian 1988: 49), although between 1978 and 1984, the average real wage increased by 30.1 per cent and the real disposable income of the average urban household jumped by 61 per cent (Barlow and Renaud 1988: 83).

Whereas rural residents' annual investment in housing increased steadily from 3.67 yuan in 1978 to 51.23 yuan in 1986, urban residents' average yearly rental payment increased slightly in the past 30 years from 5.16 yuan in 1957 to 7.2 yuan in 1986 (Barlow 1988: 13). (Expenditure by rural residents on housing may be rightfully called investment because rural housing, unlike urban housing, is primarily privately owned). The income share spent on housing for urban households actually dropped from 2.3 per cent in 1957 to 0.9 per cent in 1986. In contrast, during the same period, the proportion of housing costs to total expenditure of the peasants increased from 2.1 to 14.4 per cent (Table 5.5).

Partly because they were confronted with these startling figures on housing expenditure gaps between the rural and the urban households, and partly because the state was still under enormous pressure to finance huge housing subsidies every year, policy-makers in 1986–7 decided it was time urban workers spent a greater portion of their increasing income on housing.

Reform Policies and Programmes, 1987–9

At first, urban housing reform policies and programmes after 1987 were simply reaffirming two basic components of the housing commercialization scheme—the sale of housing to individual workers and rent increase. However, unlike the half-hearted remedial measures of 1979–86, when the sale of housing was heavily subsidized, individual buyers after 1987 were asked to pay for the full cost—or as

Table 5.5.   Housing costs in proportion to total expenditure (%)

Year	Proportion of housing costs to total living expenditure (total living expenditure = 100)	
	Urban households	Rural households
1957	2.32	2.10
1964	2.61	2.80[a]
1981	1.39	n.a.
1983	1.52	n.a.
1984	1.39	11.70
1985	0.96	12.40
1986	0.90	14.40

[a] Figure is for 1965.

Note: n.a. = not available.

Source: Adapted from Barlow (1988: 13).

much of it as possible—of new housing. Moreover, whereas rents were basically untouched until 1986–7, by mid-1987 experiments to raise rents were drawn up and implemented on a trial basis in a number of cities. Furthermore, central planners after 1987 identified the sale of both new and old housing—a major step toward the privatization of housing—as the ultimate goal of urban housing reform (Renaud 1989; Wang Zuxin 1988: 20; Yantai City Economic Research Center 1988: 36).

Underlying the emphasis on the sale of new housing at full cost and old housing at discounted prices, is a major macro-economic aim of reducing urban residents' liquidity, which in turn can help lower demand for durable consumer goods and dampen inflationary tendencies (*China Daily* 20 March 1989; Barlow 1988: 4; Li Weijie 1989: 16). Rent increase has become a means to help achieve the larger goal of the sale of housing: that is, rents are raised not only to help reduce the state's subsidy burden but, more importantly, to make buying a housing unit a comparable and attractive financial alternative to renting (Gu Wen 1989: 16).

The Yantai Programme

The following sections will (1) describe the basic features of the housing reform programme in the city of Yantai, which is a coastal city in Shandong province, (2) examine the way the programme was implemented, and (3) evaluate its accomplishments and limitations. The decision to focus discussion on the Yantai housing reform programme (hereafter called 'Yantai programme') is not because it is the only major programme or represents the most promising solution, but is based on two major considerations. First, the Yantai programme is one of the few major attempts to overhaul an entire city's housing system and has attracted the maximum attention of central government leaders. Placed under the watchful eyes of the central government as well as interested researchers and policy analysts in China, the programme's success or failure will therefore have a disproportionate effect on the future course of national urban housing reform policy. Second, because the programme generated and commanded national attention, a substantial volume of information was collected and subsequently made available in the West, thereby permitting us to examine more closely the opportunities available to and the constraints faced by policy-makers.

The Yantai programme consists of two major components: the sale of housing and rent increase. Housing is to be sold to individuals at full cost, or as close to it as possible, and a lending (mortgage) system to individuals established. Except for a small number of wealthy persons, however, purchase of a home is far beyond the financial capacity of the average urban resident; and the development of viable housing finance systems is still in a preliminary stage. However, the second component of the Yantai programme—rent increase—has been formulated in detail and its implementation has attracted much attention inside and outside of China. The following phrase sums it up: 'Increase the rent, issue vouchers; empty circulation as a starting-point' (*tizu faquan; kongzhuan qibu*). How was this rent-increase strategy designed in the first place?

Determining the rate of rent increase

In Yantai two general guidelines were observed in deciding the new rent: the first specified that rents should be raised to make purchasing a home a financially comparable or attractive alternative to renting (China's Urban Housing Problem Study Society 1987: 27); the second stipulated that the planners should steer a middle course in designating the rate and amount of rent increase. Although the full cost should not be imposed instantly, nor should the rent increase be incrementally introduced over many years (Yu Zhengxing 1988: 86).

Therefore, instead of immediately charging the full cost of housing, which is equal to the commercial rent, maintenance rent is used as the baseline to calculate the actual rent charged to urban households. Currently, commercial rent includes the following eight factors: depreciation, maintenance fee, interest on investment, management fee, real estate tax, land management fee, insurance, and profits. Collecting the commercial rent from urban households is the ultimate objective of the urban housing reform programme (Barlow 1988: 15). Maintenance rent, on the other hand, includes only the first five items listed under commercial rent. Although collecting the maintenance rent does not make the housing industry financially self-sustaining, Chinese planners believe it would generate enough rental income to cover housing maintenance and repair costs. In Yantai, the monthly commercial rent in 1988 was 2.40 yuan per m^2 and the maintenance rent was 1.53 yuan per m^2 (Table 5.6).

The standard rent is the basis on which the actual rent for each individual housing unit is calculated. For reasons unknown, the standard rent was equivalent to 83.7 per cent of the maintenance rent and, in 1988, was 1.28 yuan per m^2 each month in Yantai. The rent actually charged for each individual dwelling is further adjusted to account for the differences in location, quality, and floor plan, among other factors, of the housing stock. In 1988, the average actual rent each month in Yantai was 1.17 yuan per m^2, or about 6.3 times that of the pre-reform level of 0.187 yuan per m^2 (Table 5.6).

Determining the ratio of rental subsidy

There is no question that an instantaneous rent increase by 6.3 times in China's low-wage urban economy would have to be cushioned by rental subsidies to make it financially feasible and politically acceptable to the majority of the urban households. Accordingly, in Yantai, rental subsidies were distributed on the principle that the amount of subsidies might be slightly greater than the rent increase (China's Urban Housing Problem Study Society 1987: 27).

The formula used in calculating the subsidy coefficient is (new rent – old rent)/old wage = subsidy coefficient. Hence, the size of rental subsidies is based primarily

Table 5.6.   Housing rent in Yantai, 1988

Rent	Average (yuan/m^2/month)
Commercial rent[a]	2.40
Maintenance rent[b]	1.53
Standard rent[c]	1.28
Actual rent charged after reform[d]	1.17
Pre-reform rent	0.187

[a] Commercial rent includes: (1) depreciation, (2) maintenance fee, (3) interest on investment, (4) management fee, (5) real estate tax, (6) land development fee, (7) insurance, (8) profits.

[b] Maintenance rent includes: (1) depreciation, (2) maintenance fee, (3) interest on investment, (4) management fee, (5) real estate tax.

[c] The standard rent is determined based on maintenance rent. For reasons yet to be determined, it was equivalent to 83.7 per cent of the maintenance rent.

[d] The rent actually charged after reform is based on the standard rent but the exact amount for each housing unit is adjusted to account for the variations in the location, quality, and floor plan of the housing stock. The fact that the actual rent is lower than the standard rent indicates that, *inter alia*, the quality of a large number of the housing units in Yantai is substandard.

Sources: For commercial rent, maintenance rent, and standard rent: Barlow (1988: 23).
For actual rent charged after reform and pre-reform rent: Yu Zhengxing (1988: 86–7).

on the extent of rent increase. In Yantai, the subsidy coefficient was calculated at 23.5 per cent (Yu Zhengxing 1988: 87; Yantai City Economic Research Center 1988: 37). That is, each worker on average would receive a rental subsidy equivalent to 23.5 per cent of his/her monthly basic wage to help pay for the higher rent.

To save money, however, housing vouchers were never printed and distributed to the workers. Instead, housing vouchers were distributed and collected through a city-wide accounting system set up by the city's housing reform office and managed by the city's finance department, with no physical transaction involved.

'Empty circulation' (*kong zhuan*) versus 'real circulation' (*shi zhuan*)

'Empty circulation as a starting-point' refers to the fact that during the initial stage of the reform programme, there was no real transfer of funds between enterprises. Through the city-wide housing accounting system, vouchers—which could not be converted into cash—were first given by individual enterprises to their workers, who would then use the vouchers to augment their own cash to pay for the higher rent. Because not all enterprises have their own housing, vouchers issued by non-property-owning enterprises would therefore end up in the hands of property-owning enterprises. If the housing vouchers could be converted into money, then a rent increase would actually transfer money away from non-property-owning work units to enterprises that do own housing.

One of the purposes of stipulating 'empty circulation as a starting-point' is, therefore, to avoid suddenly increasing the financial burden of those non-property-owning enterprises, which usually have limited financial capacity to begin with (Nie Yan 1987: 22–3; Yu Zhengxing 1988: 87). However, the method of 'empty circulation' using coupons is applicable only to housing completed before 1 November 1986. The Yantai programme stipulated that housing built after this date must use cash to subsidize the higher rent (i.e. 'real circulation') (Liu Shuhui and Wang Jian 1987: 43).

In the initial stage of the Yantai programme, all housing vouchers collected by property-owning enterprises were thus turned over to the city's finance department, which in turn redistributed the vouchers to every individual voucher-issuing enterprise based on the amount of vouchers issued by each work unit. This procedure ensured that each enterprise could recoup the same number of vouchers—or as many of them as possible—as it had issued (Yantai City Economic Center 1988: 37). Chinese planners were also concerned that if cash, instead of vouchers, was given to workers as rental subsidies, that could be akin to a wage increase and could lead to greater inflationary pressure.

In addition to the preceding considerations, a fundamental reason for issuing vouchers and not cash is simply that use of cash would result in an unbearable financial burden for every enterprise in Yantai as well as the local and central government budgets (Zheng Fuheng and Zuo Ling 1988: 144). For instance, if the method of 'real circulation' was adopted in Yantai, allowing the use of cash and permitting property-owning enterprises to keep all of their rental receipts, then an estimated annual sum of 30 million yuan would have to come from operating funds of the city's enterprises and the financial budgets of local and central governments (Yantai City Economic Research Center 1988: 37). Such a financial burden, however, is completely unacceptable to policy-makers in Yantai.

Assessing the Yantai Programme

As mentioned earlier, the Yantai programme is only one of several major housing reform programmes in China. Two other programmes may be briefly noted here because of their slightly different approaches. In the city of Shenyang in Liaoning province, housing reforms were implemented by stages and in groups. Large enterprises which have public housing rented to their employees and have better economic conditions were slated to carry out reforms ahead of other enterprises. In the city of Changzhou in Jiangsu province, housing allowance is awarded to workers in cash, not housing vouchers. As with Yantai, both Shenyang and Changzhou allot the housing allowance in accordance with a certain percentage of the workers' wages. The differences are that Shenyang's implementation of the reform programme was initially limited to larger and financially healthier enterprises and Changzhou raised workers' compensation prior to increasing rent (Barlow 1988: 21).

Both Shenyang and Changzhou, therefore, differ from Yantai in that they apparently pay more attention to the enterprises' financial capacities in determining the scope and pace of their housing reforms. The question of whether or not Shenyang's and Changzhou's approaches signify more promising alternatives to Yantai's programme could be adequately addressed only through a detailed, comparative analysis of these three programmes.

This section will analyse the accomplishments and complications of the Yantai programme and will address two specific questions. First, can the Yantai programme be considered as a model for other cities and its strategies transferred to and proliferated in other urban areas? Second, are the basic strategies of the Yantai programme appropriately formulated to tackle the basic housing problems of shortage and inequality?

The problem of transferability

Whether or not the reform strategies of the Yantai programme could feasibly be transferred to other urban centers largely depends on whether the programme is politically and economically acceptable to all the parties concerned. Policy-makers in every city are aware that the major players involved in housing reform include almost every facet of society: households, enterprises, city authorities, and central government officials. They also know that objections to the reform effort will become stronger and sometimes even insurmountable if any of the major parties involved perceives reform as a real or potential threat to its own welfare. If officials in many major cities are indeed unenthusiastic about housing reform, as reported in the *China Daily*, then there must be some strong reservations—by one or more of the major players—about the housing reform programmes that discouraged their proliferation. What are these reservations?

Empty circulation still costs money

Contrary to intuition and to the belief of some Chinese researchers, the strategy of empty circulation still requires continuing subsidies from both the enterprises and the central government. Although empty circulation stipulated the use of vouchers and no real transfer of funds between enterprises, additional housing subsidies were required in Yantai for three reasons. First, precisely because only vouchers were used, regular housing construction and maintenance expenses had to be continuously financed by individual enterprises and the central government (China's Urban Housing Problem Study Society 1987: 5).

Second, more subsidies were needed in Yantai to give financial backing to the extra vouchers that many households had received under the reform programme. One purpose of the Yantai programme was to make households occupying larger and better-than-average housing pay more rent out of their own pockets. Conversely, families living in smaller and worse-than-average apartments would expect to see their higher rent more than adequately compensated by rental subsidies.

In the aftermath of implementing the Yantai programme, 52.4 per cent of the households discovered that they had left-over vouchers after paying the post-reform rent (China's Urban Housing Problem Study Society 1987: 29). At the initial stage of the reform programme, however, the vouchers could not be converted into cash, and these households were required to deposit their extra vouchers in a special housing account that they could use in the future either to rent more housing or to buy their own apartments (Barlow 1988: 26). Money from the enterprises, local authorities, or the state, was therefore needed as a reserve in the banks to back up these vouchers.

Third, additional subsidies were requested from the central government to help finance a provision that would reduce, exempt, and further subsidize certain households for the increased portion of their rent (Yu Zhengxing 1988: 90; Gu Yunchang 1988: 39). In Yantai, 47.6 per cent of the city's households found that after reform they had to pay additional rent out of their own income because they occupied larger-than-average housing, and subsequently their higher rents could not be fully compensated by vouchers.

Interestingly, a World Bank study revealed that two-thirds of the households whose post-reform rents were greater than the vouchers that they had received were government officials (Barlow 1988: 27). Partly for this reason—although policy-makers in Yantai had tried to downplay its significance—and partly because the other one-third of such households were low-income families, the Yantai programme added a provision to reduce, exempt, or further subsidize certain households for the increased portion of their rent. In 1987, the city of Yantai requested and received from the central government 2 million yuan to finance these additional reductions, exemptions, and subsidies (China's Urban Housing Problem Study Society 1987: 28).

Obviously, such a provision is directly contradictory to the objective of achieving greater equality in housing distribution. Nevertheless, its inclusion was deemed necessary to make the Yantai programme politically acceptable to the affected government officials and economically feasible for the low-income households. Thus, this stipulation aptly illustrates one aspect of the set of political and economic constraints within which reform policy-makers had to operate.

Rapid increases in prices for new housing

Another reservation about the housing reform programme is that the prices for new, commercialized housing have increased dramatically, beginning in the mid-1980s. Many cities are facing enormous difficulties in implementing the reform programme of the sale of new housing (Ma Piao 1988: 97). The ever-increasing prices of new housing have made the option of buying a home beyond the reach of almost all of China's wage-earning urban households.

Proponents of the sale of new housing had invariably based their calculation of affordability to buyers on the assumption that the construction cost of new housing was between 200 and 250 yuan per m^2 (*Jingji cankao* [*Economic Reference*], 14

January 1988; Zhang Jinzhong *et al.*, 1988: 26). For instance, in Yantai, a supporter of the sale programme used 200 yuan per m² as the basis to conclude that a two-income (150 yuan a month) family, supplemented with housing subsidies (40 yuan) from their work units, would be able to afford the monthly mortgage payment (83 yuan), provided they could also come up with a 4,000 yuan down-payment for an 11,000 yuan apartment (Nie Yan 1987: 23).

The problem is that not many urban households, particularly those that need housing the most, could afford such a huge sum of money as down-payment. A more serious difficulty that limits the expansion of the sale programme is that in many cities, new housing in 1987 was on the average costing about 1,000 yuan per m² (Table 5.7). The exceedingly low housing prices in Yantai seem more like an exception than the rule. With a typical college graduate earning 100 yuan a month (*China Daily* 29 March 1989), and most urban workers earning less than that, it means that buying commercialized housing—which by now costs 55,000 yuan to 100,000 yuan a unit—is beyond most people's reach.

What are the reasons for the upwardly spiralling prices of new, commercialized housing throughout China's major cities? Two major factors have been identified by Chinese researchers:

1. steadily rising housing construction costs. Housing construction costs have risen continuously as a result of mounting prices of construction materials, and higher standards for housing design and construction methods.
2. a multiplication of taxes and fees imposed on the builders (*Renmin ribao* [*People's Daily*] 24 December 1987; Ma Piao 1988: 98).

The second is the more important factor. These taxes and fees usually include land-use fees, and compensation for requisitioned farmland and relocating former residents (*China Daily* 25 December 1987). Many cities by the mid-1980s

Table 5.7. Prices of commercialized urban housing (in yuan per m²)

	1986	1987	1988
Yantai	n.a.	200	n.a.
Guangzhou	600–1,250	700–1,300	n.a.
Shanghai	800	1,000–1,800	1,250
Nanjing	n.a.	1,200	n.a.
Beijing	n.a.	n.a.	1,500–2,000

Note: n.a. = not available

Sources: Yantai: *Renmin ribao (People's Daily)*, 4, August 1987.
Guangzhou: 1986: Liu Shuhui and Xie Yiwen (1987: 27).
1987: Ho Yiwen (1988: 10).
Shanghai: *Jingji yu guanli yanjiu* (*Research on Economics and Management*), 1988, No 2, p. 47.
Nanjing: *Renmin ribao* (*People's Daily*), 24, December 1987.
Beijing: *Chengxiang jianshe* (*Urban Rural Construction*) 1989, No. 2, p. 18; *China Daily*, 20, February 1989.

also started to ask builders to help pay for municipal services as well as urban infrastructure and utilities, subsequently raising these taxes and fees by 93 per cent between 1984 and 1986 (Ho Yiwen 1988: 10). In Beijing, these taxes and fees can now add up to about two-thirds of the price of a new apartment (*China Daily* 25 April 1989).

Whether or not to impose these new taxes and fees in the production cost of residential buildings is the subject of a continuing debate between different quarters within the Chinese government. Although the central authorities and certainly the housing reform planners oppose the inclusion of such taxes and fees because it may impede the commercialization programme of urban housing reform, many city officials strongly believe that new housing construction projects should provide the bulk of investment money for urban infrastructure and related facilities (Gao Liugen 1988: 20; China's Urban Housing Problem Study Society 1987: 16).

Housing inequality reinforced

The current housing reform programmes are disappointing when measured against another criterion: equality in housing distribution. One of the intentions of rent increases is to reduce inequality in housing distribution by charging rent primarily based on the size of the apartment. In Yantai, as mentioned, more than 47.6 per cent of the households involved in the reform programme had to pay more rent out of their own income, which indicated that they were occupying larger and better-than-average housing. These households were given the option to trade for smaller apartments to lower their rents. However, only 3 per cent of them decided to take up such an option (Zhang Xiouzhi and Zhang Zhixin 1988: 42).

A major reason for such an apparent indifference towards the higher rent has already been revealed: many of these households could ask for and be granted reduction, exemption, and further subsidization for the increased portion of their rent (Gu Yunchang 1988: 39). Not surprisingly, some Chinese writers are now expressing concern over the problem of misuse of such a provision, particularly by those who are in power (Qi Mingshun 1989: 23; Zhu Yin 1989: 18).

As mentioned earlier, even before the current reform programmes, the method of distributing rental subsidies had been criticized by Chinese researchers as one of the sources of housing inequality. Under the Yantai programme, the old method was replaced by a new approach: every worker involved in the reform was given a housing subsidy equal to 23.5 per cent of his/her basic monthly income. This distribution method, however, led to a new form of inequality because everyone received the same rate of subsidy regardless of income level. Thus, in the words of two Chinese writers, 'the higher the salary, the [greater] the subsidy coupon, the better the bargain' (Zhang Xiouzhi and Zhang Zhixin 1988: 44).[1]

[1] For instance, if two households (A and B) occupied housing of the same floor area (40 m^2) then under the stipulation of the Yantai programme the monthly rent for both households would be increased by the same amount (42.8 yuan). However, if the monthly income of household (A) was 200

Concerning the sale of commercialized housing, only a small percentage of China's urban households can afford the incredibly high prices involved. The small quantity of housing that was actually sold to individuals was mainly bought 'by people who have overseas support, by individual business people and by professional writers, artists and performers' (Xiao Liang 1988: 19; *China Daily* 25 April 1989). It is virtually impossible for wage-earners to purchase commercialized housing. Moreover, about 80 per cent of commercialized apartment units were bought by government institutions and state-owned enterprises, which then allocated them to their workers free of charge. (*China Daily* 25 April 1989). In a way, therefore, despite the reform rhetoric to achieve greater equality in housing distribution, the reality is that workers employed in state-owned enterprises continue to enjoy a privileged access to housing denied to workers in the non-state sector.

Conclusion

What are the major lessons that we can draw upon from the preceding analysis of China's urban housing reform programmes, particularly of that conducted in the city of Yantai? Are there any policy directions that show greater potential for success than the current approaches in tackling the problems of housing shortage and housing inequality? Finally, what is the prospect of urban housing reform in China, in view of the ousting from political power of Zhao Ziyang—a principal supporter of current housing reform policies—and his pro-reform advisers after the 4 June 1989 bloodshed in Beijing?

First, one of the more urgent tasks that housing reform planners should undertake is to slow down the upwardly spiralling prices of commercialized housing. The continuously rising prices, if left unchecked, will ultimately defeat the entire strategy of commercialization of housing, the core of urban housing reform, and will eventually make it impossible for any Chinese urban resident to purchase a home. Moreover, because the levels of rent increases are supposedly tied to housing prices to make renting and buying comparable, steadily soaring prices are certainly not going to make the 'increase rent; issue vouchers' programme financially viable for either the enterprises or the government.

The initial step that policy-makers can take to lower housing prices significantly is to limit the components of housing prices, primarily by excluding certain fees and taxes that city governments rely on to finance infrastructure investment. Many of these fees and taxes can properly and feasibly be replaced by other revenues such as the proposed urban land-use fee that is applied to all users—industrial, commercial, and residential.

yuan and for household (B) 160 yuan, household (A) would receive a comparatively larger subsidy (47 yuan) than that of (B) (37.6 yuan). Consequently, the higher-income household (A) would have 4.2 yuan of subsidy left over after paying for the higher rent, and lower-income household (B) would have to make an additional payment of 5.2 yuan from its own income to supplement the subsidy (Gu Yunchang, 1988: 38). In certain circumstances, then, the rent increase reform programme may actually exacerbate the income gap between urban households.

Housing construction costs can also be reduced, though to a rather limited extent, to help put a brake on prices. Policy-planners can adopt less advanced building codes and somewhat lower standards such as a more moderate apartment size and more common facilities.

Second, despite the reform-planners' claim that promoting the sale of housing is the ultimate goal of housing reform, the reality is that an overwhelming majority of Chinese urban dwellers will for a long while continue to be tenants. For those who have already been assigned good and comfortable housing, there is simply no financial motivation to purchase their own housing. However, most wage-earners who are dissatisfied with their housing conditions are unable to purchase affordable housing, even at the currently lowest housing price levels.

The basic strategy of employing rent increase primarily as a means to foster buying therefore needs to be re-examined. Policy-makers should remember that rent increase by itself constitutes a legitimate, important and useful goal of urban housing reform. Rent, however, should be increased gradually first to help relieve the state's subsidy burden and then to make buying a comparable option. Accordingly, the method of determining the rate of rent increase should also be revised. An undeniable fact is that any rent increase in China's low-wage urban economy will have to be subsidized by the enterprises and the state government. Any long-term, sustainable rent increase programme should therefore be based on a realistic assessment of the financial capabilities, not only of the workers, but more importantly, of the enterprises and the state government. The Yantai approach of increasing rent and issuing vouchers simultaneously, without regard to the financial capacities of the city's enterprises and the state government, will prove to be a futile attempt to bypass the wage system to reform the housing sector if carried out in isolation.

Third, despite significant increases in housing investment throughout the early and mid-1980s, urban housing shortage remains a tenacious problem. A major explanation for its persistence is that China's urban housing production and distribution structure is inherently unequal. Urban housing is largely produced by and distributed within each individual work unit, or group of enterprises under the same ministries. State-owned enterprises are usually in a financially superior position to privately owned enterprises to invest in more and better housing. Employees of the financially stronger, and often state-owned, work units therefore enjoy a disproportionately larger share of the new housing stock produced since the early 1980s.

As a result, behind the improved figures for per capita floor space, which increased from 3.60 m^2 in 1978 to 7.61 m^2 in 1987 (see Table 5.2), there actually lie greater inequalities in housing. In Beijing, for instance, while 27 per cent of the city's households in 1988 were able to live in apartments with per capita floor space of greater than 8 m^2, 30.7 per cent of the city's families were still classified as 'households with housing difficulties', crowding in apartments with per capita floor space of less than 2 m^2 (Wu Zhaoxing and Wen Wanping 1989: 19).

Unless the existing housing production and distribution structure can be significantly modified or replaced, for example by gradually expanding the role of the real estate industry, the housing inequality and the housing shortage problems that stem partly from the biased distribution system will probably remain intractable for some years to come.

Finally, it is all too apparent that the overall tone of the current strategies to commercialize housing in China's urban areas is to privatize the urban housing sector over the long run. One of the immediate effects of the removal of Zhao Ziyang from political power is that criticisms directed against the idea of privatization have escalated. This means that attempts to commercialize urban housing may be slowed or suspended altogether.

The analysis in this study suggests, however, that regardless of whether or not the pro-reform policy-makers remain in power, the long-standing problems of shortage and inequality, reinforced and compounded by difficulties emerging from the current reform programmes, will probably necessitate some fundamental revisions of the overall approach to reforming housing as well as other segments in the urban economy.

Most of the major housing reform proposals are based on the premise that the root of the housing problem lies within the housing sector, particularly its 'irrational' low-rent policy. However, as the 'increase rent; issue vouchers' strategy aptly illustrates, the low-rent policy itself has been dictated by the state's low-wage policy. It also tells us that, by instituting a housing voucher system, housing reform policy-makers were trying to sidestep the equally enormous problem of wage-system reform.

This therefore raises an important policy question: should urban housing reform be put forward as one of the first steps in implementing reform programmes affecting the entire complex urban economy? Will it be more productive to begin with the rationalization of the wage system and the urban land-use system before introducing reform measures in the urban housing sector? Or should urban housing reform and wage reform be conducted simultaneously? Similar issues arise with respect to whether infrastructure investment costs should be borne by new housing projects or through broader reform of the system of municipal finance. These are some of the intriguing policy questions that need more attention at this juncture of the ongoing housing reform experiments.

Postscript, July 1995

Five years have elapsed between the time this chapter was finalized in September 1990 and this postscript was prepared in July 1995. The fundamental problems afflicting China's urban housing sector discussed in the above have, however, remained more or less intact. The major conclusions reached in the chapter have stood the test of time and some have been validated by development in China's urban housing sector in the past five years. For instance, a Beijing newspaper,

Jingji Ribao (Economics Daily), reported in late 1994 that the number of 'households with insufficient floor space' in China's urban areas would jump from 5.5 million in 1992 to over 8.0 million by the year 2000. There is no evidence to suggest that any of the multitude of housing reform programmes implemented in various Chinese cities since the early 1980s has successfully resolved the central issues of housing shortage and housing inequalities. The fact that China's urban housing reform efforts seem to have produced very little positive results over all these years only reinforces the argument that the root of the urban housing problem lies beyond the housing sector *per se*. Whether or not the housing sector is a strategic entry point to reform China's complex urban economy is a question that needs to be carefully re-examined.

Part II

Indonesia

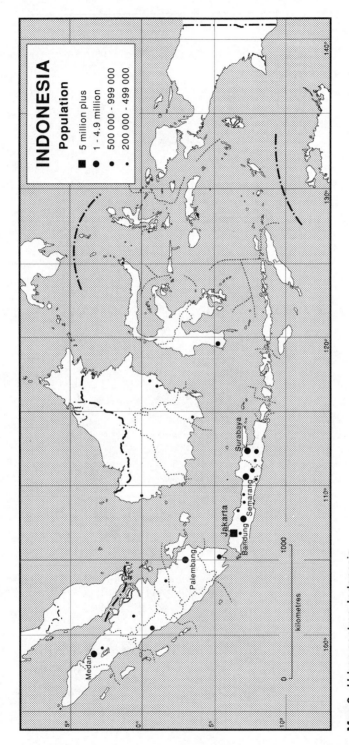

Map 3. Urban centres, Indonesia

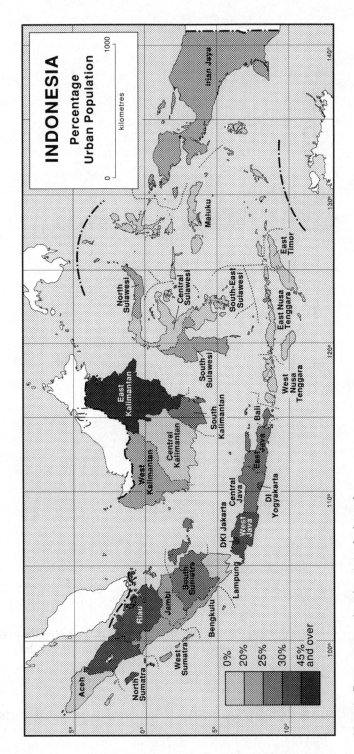

Map 4. Percentage urban by state, Indonesia

Introduction

GAVIN W. JONES

In terms of population, Indonesia is the world's fourth-largest country, with a 1990 population of 179 million. Although its land area is less than that of a number of countries with smaller populations, it is a far-flung archipelago, stretching across a distance greater than that from London to Moscow. The island of Borneo, most of which lies within Indonesia, is the third-largest island in the world, after Greenland and New Guinea, almost half of which also lies within Indonesia.

Indonesia is located entirely within the tropics. Although its people comprise more than 300 distinct ethno-linguistic groups and live in an archipelago of more than 13,000 islands, more than 92 per cent of the population live on the four islands of Java, Sumatra, Kalimantan, and Sulawesi; the Javanese, Sundanese, Madurese, Minangkabau, Batak, and Buginese appear to be the only ethno-linguistic groups whose numbers exceed three million.

The island of Java, though it contains only 7 per cent of Indonesia's land area, accommodated 60 per cent of its population in 1990. This percentage has been slowly declining over time, as the rate of natural increase is lower in Java than elsewhere and Java has been experiencing a net migration outflow, partly as a result of the government's transmigration programme which moves people from Java, Bali, and Lombok to the more sparsely settled outer islands. Nevertheless, Java's population continues to grow, and reached 107 million in 1990. Java is one of the most densely settled areas on earth, with a population density of 794 per km^2 (1990). Only 36 per cent of Java's population live in urban areas (1990), although many of its rural areas, particularly those close to the large cities, have many urban characteristics, including a relatively small proportion of the workforce in agriculture.

Most of Indonesia's islands are dominated, virtually from end to end, by rugged mountain backbones, containing volcanic cones some of which rise above 3,500 metres. Transportation difficulties due to the archipelagic nature of the country and the rugged or swampy terrain in many areas perpetuated the isolation of much of the population. With increasing prosperity and political calm through the 1970s and 1980s, however, roadbuilding proceeded apace and communications improved immensely, thus opening formerly isolated areas to outside influences.

Real per capita GNP grew at over 4.0 per cent per annum over the 27 years to 1992, reaching US$670, which placed Indonesia just below the group of middle-income countries. Education has expanded rapidly; health services have improved and mortality has fallen, though it remains well above the level in neighbouring Malaysia and Thailand. The infant mortality rate (66 per 1,000 live births in 1992) was lower than in India but twice as high as in China.

Since 1970, Indonesia has pursued a vigorous family planning policy, which, allied with economic and social development, has led to a slowing of the rate of population growth. Indonesia's population growth rate was down to slightly below 2 per cent in the 1980s, and six provinces—Jakarta, Central Java, Yogyakarta, East Java, Bali, and North Sulawesi—had fertility at or approaching replacement level in 1990.

The proportion of Indonesia's population living in urban areas rose from 17 per cent in 1971 to 22 per cent in 1980 and 31 per cent in 1990. The urban structure in Indonesia has been influenced by inter-island and intra-island transportation difficulties and the importance of the provinces (of which there are 27) as administrative units. The level of primacy at the national level does not approach that of Thailand or even the Philippines, but primacy is much more evident at the province level. Each province tends to have one large city, and in the case of some of the largest provinces (West Java, Central Java, East Java, North Sumatra, South Sumatra), this city exceeds one million in population. Even so, Jakarta, located in a national capital district surrounded by West Java, had reached 8 million in 1990 and was tending towards increased dominance, particularly when the additional population within the extended metropolitan area was taken into consideration. During the 1980s, in Java at least, more rapid urbanization tended to occur in corridors linking major cities, including the north coast from Jakarta to Semarang, from Semarang to Yogyakarta, and from Surabaya to Malang.

6 Structural Change and Urbanization in Indonesia: From the 'Old' to the 'New' International Division of Labour

MIKE DOUGLASS

Introduction

Indonesia's economy shares many structural characteristics with other large countries of Asia. It has remained a substantially agrarian society throughout its post-independence era, with more than half the population working in or having employment dependent upon agriculture. Until very recently, the shift of employment away from agriculture has been moderate and has tended toward tertiary activities rather than the manufacturing sector, with the latter sector having among the lowest shares of employment in Asia.

The island composition of the nation has given its urban system a number of unique characteristics, such as an emphasis on the growth of inter-island port cities occasioned by the vast sea distances between the thousands of islands making up the Indonesian archipelago. But as with other very large developing countries in Asia, Indonesia's vast area, long history of settlement and agrarian base have worked to keep both the level and concentration of urban population relatively low. The official share of only 22 per cent of the population living in urban places in 1980 was shared among nine cities having populations greater than 500,000, thirteen between 200,000 and 500,000, and a total of forty-two cities with more than 100,000 inhabitants (NUDS 1985: 66).

Differences in soil fertility and historical development processes favouring Java have, however, resulted in a pronounced regional concentration of population, with slightly more than three-fifths of the nation's citizens and approximately 70 per cent of the nation's 31 million urban inhabitants living on this island. Furthermore, just three metropolitan regions—Jakarta, Bandung, and Surabaya—account for 42 per cent of Java's urban population. As with such large countries as India and China, although a number of regional centres share in the distribution of the urban population, the urbanization process in post-independence years has proceeded slowly in rural regions away from metropolitan centres and coastal areas.

Given Indonesia's similarities with other large agrarian nations of Asia, a striking feature of the 1980s is that many of the parameters guiding the urbanization process are showing signs of change which appear to be directing the 'space-economy' of the nation toward a substantially different path of development than that followed over the previous two decades. Events at the world level have undermined Indonesia's past model of development, and new policy initiatives to stimulate export-oriented manufacturing have begun to induce structural changes in the economy that are both accelerating rates of urbanization and the polarization of development in Jabotabek, the greater Jakarta metropolitan region. With the urban population expected to increase at more than 5 per cent per year compared with a rural population growth rate of only 1.2 per cent per year, some projections suggest that as much as 60 per cent of the population increase in the nation in the coming decade will be absorbed by cities (NUDS 1985). Jabotabek, which accounted for almost one-third of Java's urban population in 1980 and is the fastest-growing metropolis of the nation, is likely to absorb at least half of these projected increases to make it one of the ten largest metropolitan regions in the world.

The purpose of this chapter is to explain recent patterns of urbanization by introducing an international dimension to their conventional treatment as a 'national' process contextualized solely by a state and society acting in isolation of external forces. This closed-nation treatment has been particularly prevalent among the very large developing countries of Asia which, because of their large area and potentially vast domestic market, have been seen as receiving less impact from global actors. It has also been perpetuated by narrow measurements using shares of imports and exports in the GDP as the indicators of the relative strength of external linkages. Missing from the analysis have been a wide array of equally powerful international relations formed through direct investment in production and services, licensing agreements, concessionary contracts for the extraction of natural resources, and finance by transnational enterprises, their home governments, and international donor agencies. All of these linkages have, in fact, been expanding much more rapidly than international trade, and when seen together they comprise an increasingly formidable set of parameters on Indonesia's future economic and spatial development.

In addition to the inclusion of specific extra-national linkages in the discussion of structural change and urbanization within a particular national setting, the dynamics of the international economy must also be taken into account. The major theme of this chapter is that transformations in the world economy in the 1980s have made the experience of the 1970s of doubtful utility in understanding the pressures and opportunities for development in the coming decades. The fall of OPEC from centre stage, the rise of Japan as the world's major centre of capital accumulation, including the rapid transnationalization of Japanese corporations, and the emergence of the Pacific Rim as a new world economic region are among the major new dimensions imposed upon national development. In contrasting the decade of the 1970s with that of the 1980s, a second purpose of this chapter is to argue against a 'single-development-path-for-all-nations' view of development. By placing the discussion within the context of the relationship between the internal and external dynamics of development, neither of which is predetermined or unidirectional in time or space, the discussion leaves open the possibility for alternative paths and outcomes.

The discussion is divided into three sections below. The first presents a brief overview of the implicit national economic development strategy adopted in the 1970s and traces its impacts on patterns and processes of urbanization. The next discusses recent changes in national policies and external relations which are already having significant impacts on the national space-economy. The third section concludes by raising key economic and spatial development policy issues for the coming years.

The 1970s: Indonesia's 'Golden Decade' of Development

With President Soeharto's establishment of a New Order Government in 1965 and the subsequent launching of the first five-year development plan, Repelita I, in 1969, the national stage was set for a decade of sustained economic growth. The state's guidance of economic restructuring during this period rested on three cornerstones. Two of them—import-substitution industrialization and the green revolution—were designed to internalize and shield the economy from the vagaries of the external world market. The third—resource exploitation for international markets—worked in the opposite direction. Cutting across each component was an equally powerful dimension of the post-independence era: direct foreign investment into all sectors of the economy. The interaction of national development policies with the logic of foreign investment set a new framework for the restructuring of the national economy; it did not, however, create the conditions for the elusive 'take-off' toward sustained economic growth. By the 1980s each component had run its course as a leading force of economic expansion.

Import-substitution

Of the three major components of Indonesia's implicit national development strategy that emerged from policies and events under Repelita I (1969–74), the one receiving most attention from the state was one widely adopted throughout the Third World, namely, the import-substitution policy of protecting infant domestic industry from international competition. By erecting tariff barriers and banning the import of certain categories of manufactured goods, such as fully assembled automobiles, Indonesia was to be launched along a path of accelerated industrialization which had been blocked by 300 years of colonial rule and two decades of 'socialist' mismanagement.

The industrialization drive offered the promise of rapidly catching up with the West as well as with Indonesia's Second World War colonial master, Japan. The prospects presented by the Lewis (1955) model in currency at the time were as tantalizing as they were elegantly simple. Only a few years before, one of the best-known observers of the history of economic development in Indonesia, Clifford

Geertz (1963: 143), had suggested the possibilities by declaring that the only significant difference between Japan and Java of the nineteenth and early twentieth century was not that the vast majority of the people of Java suffered under colonialism—the peasantry of Japan perhaps suffered even more—but that, unlike the Japanese, the Javanese 'suffered for nothing' because their surpluses were appropriated by Holland instead of being reinvested in urban industry in Indonesia. The Javanese had thus been left in an 'involutionary' syndrome of increasing stress on rural resources and ever more intricate cultural patterns of poverty-sharing. Adopting the import-substitution policy, the state could lead the way out of this syndrome by creating the conditions for a structural change in employment away from agriculture.

The actual outcomes of import-substitution left much to be desired. High levels of protection contained biases toward capital-intensive, low labour-absorbing industries which often operated substantially below capacity and were heavily dependent upon direct and indirect government subsidies. They also magnified already well-known problems of corruption and nepotism through government contracts, monopoly rights, and special dispensations allowed only to firms—domestic and foreign alike—which could gain privileged access to protection and subsidies under the import-substitution legislation. The net result was a moderately expanding industrial sector composed of large firms in basic industries, many of which were state-owned, with highly concentrated ownership patterns. Such attributes made import-substitution poorly geared for generating a manufacturing-led transformation of the Indonesian economy.

Table 6.1 summarizes the employment outcomes of the industrial strategy during the 1971–80 period. It shows that although the number of workers in the

Table 6.1.   Structural change in employment, 1971–80

Sector	Employment				Share of change (%)	Average annual growth(%)	Rp. 1000/ worker[a]
	Number (million)		Share (%)				
	1971	1980	1971	1980	1971–80	1971–80	1980
Agriculture	26.5	28.6	67.4	56.6	18.7	0.9	573
Mining	0.1	0.4	0.2	0.7	2.7	18.3	39,268
MFG	2.7	4.7	6.9	9.3	17.9	6.3	1,568
Construction	0.7	1.6	1.8	3.2	8.0	10.3	2,452
Trade	4.3	6.7	10.9	13.3	21.4	5.1	1,520
Transport	1.0	1.4	2.5	2.8	3.6	4.7	2,031
Services[b]	4.1	7.1	10.4	14.1	26.8	6.3	955
Total[c]	39.3	50.5	100.0	100.0	100.0	2.4	1,303

[a] GDP in constant 1983 prices + labour force by sector.
[b] Includes public service.
[c] Excludes 'other' sectors;
Source: World Bank (1986), Annex, Table 2.2.

manufacturing sector doubled, its small base meant that its share of national employment increased from 6.9 to only 9.3 per cent. Manufacturing absorbed fewer members of the labour force than even the exceptionally slow-growing agricultural sector. The fact that the majority of manufacturing job increases were neither in small, medium, nor large-scale industry but were in self-employment in individual enterprises and family cottage industries further demonstrated the low absorptive capacity of the protected industrial sector. Agriculture itself continued to have a level of productivity of only about one-third that of the manufacturing sector. The bulk of the increase in the labour force was absorbed in what are generally considered to be the non-basic sectors of construction, transport, trade and services.

The green revolution as rural development

The slow growth of employment in the agricultural sector during the 1970s is substantially attributed to government policies which, in effect, redefined rural development as a technical matter of increasing the production of rice. High population growth rates and the absence of any sustained process of rural development during the first two decades of independence had left an agricultural sector marked by declining labour productivity and a country heavily dependent upon grain imports. In the late 1960s Indonesia moved to join the rest of Asia in the quest for national grain self-sufficiency. Java, with rich rice soils, relatively high levels of irrigation and a long tradition of rice cultivation, became the major focus of the green revolution and witnessed yield increases which for the first time in contemporary history produced enough rice to satisfy domestic demand in the early 1980s.[1]

This success notwithstanding, the impact on the labour force was, like the import-substitution policy, less than ideal. Along with the new technology came new social relations of production resulting in a widespread decline in the labour-absorptive capacity of agriculture on Java. In a situation of already very high rural densities with most good land on Java already under rice production, alternative sources of agricultural employment were found by pushing production into the ecologically fragile upland areas of the major watershed regions surrounding the major metropolitan regions of the island (Douglass 1987). And while some workers worked more efficiently and made higher wages than before, many who had access to farm work and sharing in harvests via technologies and social relations of the past were now foreclosed from these opportunities (Collier, *et al.* 1982; Wiradi and Manning 1984).

---

[1] Between 1968 and 1981 the area of land under rice cultivation increased by 15% and the productivity of wet rice land increased by 45% (MOA, 1983). During the same period, the area of land on Java devoted to maize, cassava, and sweet potatoes declined (Paauw, 1984). Rice production accounts for over 50% of the national calorie consumption and has typically accounted for 10% of the GDP, making it the single largest contributor to the national income after oil.

Natural resource extraction and export crops

The third component of Indonesia's national development strategy directly linked the national to the international economy and was centred on the use of international markets and foreign investment to extract Indonesia's considerable endowments of natural resources, particularly oil and timber, and, to a much lesser extent, promote the export of cash crops from the outer islands. With oil prices still low, and with Thailand and the Philippines just beginning to sell off their then plentiful forest reserves to Japan and other world markets in the 1960s, these two major resources in Indonesia had remained surprisingly untapped until the early 1970s when the fortuitous skyrocketing of oil prices and expanded mining of forests quickly became the principal sources of government finance and national economic growth. Both also reduced pressure on food-crop production to finance urban-industrial expansion and assisted in pursuing the green revolution.

The extraction of natural resources, which was largely accomplished through the awarding of concessions and contracts to transnational corporations, also became the major point of negotiation and leverage over the government and the national economy as the price of oil waxed and waned in the coming years. With little direct involvement by either the state or domestic capital in the actual exploration for and extraction of oil and timber, the primary roles assigned to the government were in the areas of contract management and bargaining. Although these roles were unevenly executed, the billions of dollars brought annually to the economy proved to be so substantial that even with near-bankruptcy of the national oil ministry, Pertamina, and the uncontrolled depletion of a significant portion of Indonesia's forest reserves, enough money trickled through the hands along the way to generate a number of important national development programmes (Oong 1986; Dickie and Layman 1988). Oil and timber concessions proved to be the single most important source of what can be called Indonesia's golden decade of economic growth, with oil revenues alone providing as much as three-quarters of the revenues used for national development programmes. The contradiction set up by industrial policies dependent upon rural surplus transfers and an agricultural policy requiring the reinvestment of surpluses in grain production was thus neatly sidestepped. Both industry and agriculture could be financed from the export of natural resources. To its credit, rather than allowing oil revenues to provide the excuse for abandoning other sectors of development, as such oil-rich countries as Nigeria and Venezuela appear to have done, the Indonesian government was able to secure impressive gains in basic industries, rice production, health, education, and transportation.

Employment shortfalls accompanying the import-substitution industrial policy and the impacts of the green revolution were also partially compensated by transfers from oil revenues used to generate urban and rural public works programmes. Through such programmes, these revenues brought about one of Indonesia's three 'revolutions' of the 1970s, namely the lacing of Java's countryside with highways allowing for mini-vans to bring most of the inhabitants of the island within commuting and temporary migrating distance of the island's large metropolitan regions. Rice self-sufficiency and almost universal primary education were the other two successes which, in light of Indonesia's more than three centuries of colonial rule and early post-independence decades of poor economic performance, could be seen as miraculous achievements.

Foreign investment

As the discussion above suggests, Indonesia's development in the 1970s was tightly linked to the world economy through trade and direct foreign investment. It was non-Indonesian enterprises which explored for and extracted Indonesia's oil reserves, felled its forests, and initiated a significant proportion of the nation's medium-and large-scale manufacturing operations. For a decade these linkages with the world economy presented the nation and the government with unprecedented opportunities for economic growth and improvements in national welfare.

Foreign investment also revealed the many paradoxical relationships between policy intentions and outcomes. The import-substitution policy, for example, was designed to protect domestic enterprises from foreign competition. In practice, however, it accelerated the penetration of foreign enterprises by both requiring direct investment to gain access to the Indonesian market and, at the same time, protecting investing firms from competition with other transnational enterprises producing outside the country. This phenomenon is exemplified by studies showing that virtually all of the investment from Japan in manufacturing during the 1970s, which dominated foreign investment in this sector, was for the sole purpose of gaining access to Indonesia's domestic market; that is, investment substituting for trade rather than building upon any presumed comparative advantage of the Indonesian economy itself (Panglaykim 1983; Kinoshita 1986; Kano 1981). Although this led to the establishment of important basic industries, linkages with domestic firms remained weak, and in at least some sectors the subsidies provided to foreign investors helped to undermine traditional rural cottage industries (Kano 1981).

Table 6.2 shows the sectoral distribution of actual cumulative investment made in Indonesia between the years 1967 and 1981. Before assessing the data, it should be noted that most of the foreign involvement in oil and timber extraction, which is generally in the form of concessions rather than equity investment, is not included in the official BKPM (Investment Coordinating Board) accounts.[2] Furthermore, actual or realized investment, which does not include loans, is typically half or less of the amount of approved investment. In 1981, for example, approved investment totalled more than US$10 billion, but implemented investment equalled only US$4 billion. With these caveats in mind, we can see from Table 6.2 that foreign investment was heavily concentrated in two types of

[2] Between 1971 and 1980 foreign oil companies spent an estimated US$9.5 billion in Indonesia, of which approximately US$6 billion could have qualified as foreign investment under definitions used by BKPM.

Table 6.2.   Sectoral distribution of implemented foreign investment, 1967–81

Sector and sub-sector	Amount (US$ million)	Share (%)
Agriculture and Fishing	197.5	4.9
Agriculture	94.6	2.3
Fishing	102.9	2.5
Forestry	377.7	9.3
Mining	543.5	13.4
Manufacturing	2850.7	70.5
Food	193.5	4.8
Textiles/leather	999.1	24.7
Wood and wood products	28.1	0.7
Paper and paper products	49.3	1.2
Chemicals and rubber	458.9	11.4
Non-metallic minerals	326.8	8.1
Basic metal	256.7	6.4
Metal products	512.0	12.7
Other	26.3	0.7
Construction	52.3	1.3
Trade	13.3	0.3
Hotels	97.5	2.4
Transportation	15.2	0.4
Communications	35.8	0.9
Services	120.8	3.0
Trade services	102.4	2.5
Personal services	18.4	0.5
Other	114.6	2.8
Total	4041.2	100.0

Source: Bank of Indonesia, 1982.

activity: basic industries related to natural resources (mining and forestry) and resource processing (chemicals, minerals and metals), and, secondly, textiles. Together they accounted for three-quarters of the total foreign investment during the 1967–81 period. Forestry and mining together absorbed almost one-quarter of the total. In addition to the high concentration of foreign investment in a few sectors, another striking feature of the data is the very low level of investment in agriculture, which received a lower share than even hotel construction. Given that from one-half to almost two-thirds of the nation's labour force was engaged in agricultural activities during the 1970s, the small share of less than 3 per cent of foreign investment in this sector had obvious implications for increasing out-migration from the densely-settled rural regions of Java.

Sources of foreign capital displayed a marked Pacific Rim character. Forty per cent of all the non-oil investment came from a single country, Japan, with Hong

Kong, the United States, Taiwan, and Singapore comprising a substantial proportion of the remaining amount.[3] In linking the industrial interests of the respective investor with the resources and markets of Indonesia, the relationships between country of origin and sectors of investment proved to be exceptionally strong. Investments in textiles, for example, were highly associated with Japan (Tsurumi 1980). Japanese companies also used investment in automobile assembly operations to capture more than 90 per cent of the domestic automobile market in Indonesia by 1980. Whereas US-based transnational enterprises concentrated their investment in oil and timber extraction from the outer islands, firms headquartered in Japan focussed on import-substitution industries located on Java. In making these investments, Japanese firms also began to dominate the market for imported capital goods. In 1980 almost half of the value of Indonesia's total imports of manufactured goods, including machinery and transport equipment, originated from Japan (Suhartoyo 1983).

Structural change and urbanization, 1971–80

The conjuncture of national development policies with international markets and foreign investment served as the principal context for the restructuring of the 'space-economy' of the Indonesian archipelago in the 1970s. First, the combination of import-substitution policies and foreign investment in Indonesia's fledgling manufacturing sector began to accelerate the polarization of development in the Jakarta metropolitan region (Douglass 1984). Between 1974 and 1979 Jakarta and its surrounding province of West Java increased their shares of the total value added in medium-and large-scale manufacturing in Indonesia from 38 to 42 per cent (BPS 1986).

Equally important to the polarization process was the concentration in Jakarta of a rapidly expanding civil and military service—again largely financed by oil revenues—accompanied by massive public investments in highways and other infrastructure in the capital city. The civil service has also been the major avenue for pribumi (indigenous) participation in the ownership and management of industrial enterprises. With its high concentration of government functions, Jakarta was the locus of the expansion of employment in public administration and defence, which grew at an annual rate of 13 per cent for the decade of the 1970s. Foreign investors also started to build hotels and establish financial institutions in Jakarta. Within a decade most of the dilapidated Dutch buildings of this old colonial city were being replaced by multi-storey office buildings aimed at catering to local headquarters of transnational finance, trade and manufacturing firms. The inflow of foreign businesses and employees working for oil companies,

[3] Together with West Germany and Holland, these countries accounted for two-thirds of the cumulative investment between 1967 and 1981. The inclusion of the oil and energy sector would have made companies headquartered in the United States, which invested approximately US$4 billion in Indonesia in the 1970s, the single largest source of investment during the 1970s. Indonesia has also been a highly-favoured country by Japanese investors, receiving more than half of all investment in Asia and 15% of all investment worldwide from Japan between 1967 and 1981 (Panglaykim, 1983).

donor agencies, foreign enterprises and consultancy firms was greatly responsible for the development of a luxury housing market and creation of new markets for higher order services.

All of these factors led to an acceleration of the growth of Jakarta and its immediate hinterland. Although the government attempted to temper this growth by adopting direct controls on migration through the issuing of Jakarta resident permits in the early 1970s, these efforts were soon abandoned, and for the decade of the 1970s Jakarta experienced an annual 4.5 per cent population growth rate. If continued, it would double the city's population of 6 million every fifteen years.

In addition to the accelerated growth of Jakarta, the second major spatial trend was the expansion of key port cities linking Java's northern coast with resource enclaves and ports in the outer islands. As cities on Sumatra, Kalimantan, and other islands began to expand around oil and timber ports and cash-crop plantations, northern port cities of Java expanded their roles in the inter-island trade of consumer goods from Java in exchange for raw materials from the outer islands. Since state revenues from outer island exports and concessions were delivered first to Jakarta for subsequent national distribution through the government bureaucracy, and given Jakarta's position as the nation's principal port, these linkages also aggrandized its pivotal position in the economy.

As stated, much of both natural resource exploitation and modern manufacturing activities expanded through foreign investment. Figures 6.1 and 6.2 display the principal spatial impacts of this investment. Figure 6.1 shows how it augmented the two dimensions of urbanization noted above, namely, a high concentration around Jakarta and in natural-resource-rich areas of the outer islands—and, conversely, a neglect of densely-settled but resource-poor rural regions of Java, Bali, and Eastern Indonesia. Other studies have also noted the high regional concentration of foreign investment. Hill (1988: 42) found that 60 per cent of approved investment (excluding timber and oil) between 1967 and 1985 was located in only two regions: the extended metropolitan region of Jabotabek where most of the consumer-oriented industries have located, and North Sumatra where the huge Japan-sponsored Asahan project combining dam construction with aluminum processing is located.[4] These findings are consistent with those of Kelly (1985), who concluded that even when controlling for industrial sector and size of firm, foreign firms operating in Indonesia were significantly more spatially concentrated than domestic firms receiving BKPM approval.

A partial view of the spatial dimension of economic restructuring promoted through foreign investment is presented in Fig. 6.2, which shows the provincial distribution of sectoral investments by Japanese transnational corporations. The

[4] The Asahan hydro-electric power and aluminum refinery was the second largest Japanese investment in Asia in the latter half of the 1970s (Kitazawa, 1977). Largely financed through loans, it suffered from disputes over ownership which resulted in the government's suspension of aluminum shipments to Japan in 1989. Kitazawa states that the twelve Japanese firms identified by the Japanese government as owning 75% of the company actually invested no capital at all in the project. In 1987, Indonesia's Ministry of Finance attempted to restructure the loan and investment formula to raise its ownership from 25% to 41%, which Japan refused to acknowledge.

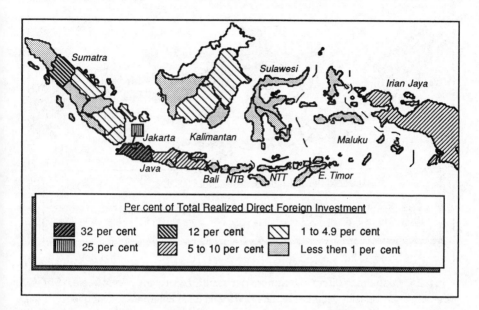

Fig. 6.1A. Distribution of direct foreign investment by province, Indonesia, 1967–82
Source: Bank of Indonesia, 1982

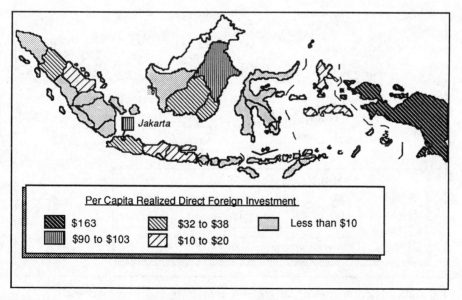

Fig. 6.1B. Average annual realized foreign investment per capita, Indonesia
Source: Bank of Indonesia, 1982

122   *Mike Douglass*

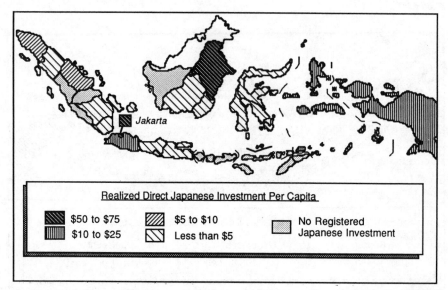

Fig. 6.2A. Japanese direct investment per capita, by province, Indonesia, 1967–79

Source: Ampo, special issue on 'Japanese Transnational Enterprises in Indonesia', 1980, 12: 4

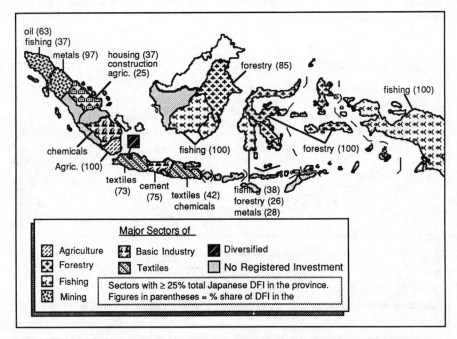

Fig. 6.2B. Major sectors of Japanese investment by province, Indonesia

Source: Ampo, special issue on 'Japanese Transnational Enterprises in Indonesia', 1980, 12: 4

figure indicates that in contrast to the diversification of the industrial structure promoted through foreign investment in Jakarta, the trend in other regions has been to increase their specialization in a limited number of activities.[5] Thus while the metropolitan core of the nation has been able to expand new sectors of growth and stabilize its economy by developing a number of alternative economic sectors, the outer islands and their cities have become highly dependent on the export of a limited number of commodities. As the experience of the early 1980s would confirm, the fostering of a highly specialized spatial distribution of labour presents inherent risks of 'boom–bust' growth and decline as the ripples of price fluctuations for specific commodities at the world scale increase in amplitude when reaching the sub-national level.

Patterns of industrialization and foreign investment combined with the green revolution to provide the third dimension of urbanization in the 1970s: the rapid out-migration of labour from rural areas of Central and East Java and Yogyakarta. The principal urban destinations of these migrants were, first, Jakarta, and secondarily Surabaya and other cities along Java's northern coast. The only major factors diffusing population movements away from these areas were the government's ambitious transmigration programme resettling rural households in the outer islands, migration to the resource enclaves in the outer islands, and international migration to the oil-rich countries of the Middle East. Even when combined into a single number, however, migration to the outer islands was substantially less than inter-provincial migration on Java directed toward a select number of coastal cities and metropolitan regions.

The failure of advances in rice production to significantly expand employment in agriculture and non-farm employment in rural areas of Java was manifested in the growth of cities whose economic base was in inter-island transport, government services and import-substitution manufacturing growth. With very low backward and forward linkages, rice production was unable to generate employment related to either increased upstream demand for inputs or downstream agro-processing industries. Rural towns remained low-level service centres growing at rates equal to natural population increases and having only those basic functions that can be sustained by the generally very low incomes of the households in their immediate hinterlands (de Jong *et al.* 1983). Cities—big and small—located away from Jakarta and the expanding inter-island crescent of urbanization thus grew at very low rates.

The economic results of this pattern have been twofold. One has been heightened access to more remunerative seasonal and temporary employment opportunities in core urban regions, such as Jakarta, Bandung, and Surabaya (Hugo 1985; Jones 1984). The other, moving in the opposite direction, is the penetration of rural markets by manufactured goods made in large cities. Many goods for daily use

[5] Hill also supports these findings by noting that investment in each province away from Jabotabek tended to be dominated by a single sector: timber in Kalimantan, mining in Sulawesi and Irian Jaya, textiles in West Java, cement in Central Java, breweries and cigarettes in East Java, and fertilizer in North Sumatra.

that might have been fabricated locally before, which range from clothing to food products, are now made in the metropolis. A study by Kano (1981: 360), for example, showed that Japanese investment in textile production, which concentrated in Jakarta and Bandung, led to an absolute decline of manufacturing employment, or deindustrialization, of Yogyakarta and much of Central Java in the 1970s. Educational advances have also created a new generation which expresses less desire to enter into agricultural work and is more capable of moving to distant metropolitan regions.

In sum, patterns of regional economic growth and urbanization during the 1970s displayed two opposing trends: the incipient polarization of development around Jakarta, and an outward expansion along an inter-island crescent of port cities linking resource-rich regions with Jakarta and other key trading cities along the north coast of Java. The channelling of revenues from oil and timber exports directly to the national government in Jakarta accentuated the development of the inter-island chain of cities. But with little private or government investment in non-primary sectors in the outer islands, much of the urban expansion there was characteristically of a 'hot-house' variety that would be sustained only as long as the very capital-intensive resource-extraction and oil exploration activities continued to create demand for construction and urban services.

As Fig. 6.3 shows, almost all of the cities of the archipelago which grew at rates greater than that of the national population were inter-island ports. Although some of these cities, such as Palembang, were the sites of fossil-fuel-related industries, most of the economies of the rapidly-growing cities on the outer islands were

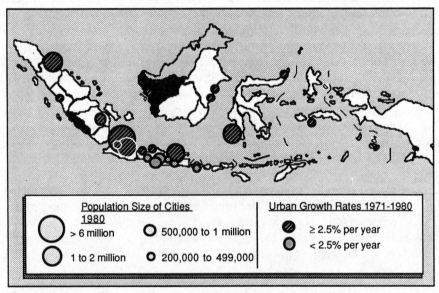

Fig. 6.3. Major cities by size and growth, Indonesia, 1971–80
Source: Douglass, 1994

based on export of natural resources and cash crops either abroad or, in the case of key estate crops such as copra, to Java for further processing. Trade between settlements of the outer islands remained extremely limited, with linkages to Java usually being stronger than those with more proximate cities.

From the 'Old' to the 'New' International Division of Labour

By the early 1980s the foundations for Indonesia's decade of success were nearing points at which further reliance on them was resulting in severely diminished returns. Import-substitution industries had accomplished the easier tasks of creating basic industries and developing a national textile industry. Many were running well below capacity and, particularly in the case of the large number of state-owned enterprises which dominate natural resource-based processing industries, were poorly managed, yet without incentives to improve their performance. Further expansion of employment in a sector having such an institutional base was likely to proceed even more slowly than in the past. The industrial sector was itself highly dependent upon the export of oil and other natural resources and cash crops to create domestic markets for its products. The surge in manufacturing growth rates immediately following world-wide oil price increases and, conversely, the sharp drop in the manufacturing growth rate accompanying the fall in oil prices in the early 1980s, were clear indicators of the crucial role played by oil revenues in generating government-spending-led increases in domestic demand underlying the expansion of the medium-and large-scale manufacturing sectors. Much of the spending in the state-owned industrial sector was also directly tied to oil-related processing and basic industries such as LING, fertilizer, and chemical production.[6]

In sum, with the expected persistence of substantially lower prices for petroleum into the foreseeable future, the driving force of Indonesia's industrialization process under the formula of the 1970s could not be relied upon to carry the economy forward. Added to the fall of oil prices was a pervasive drop in prices for Indonesia's other natural resource and cash-crop exports, including copra, palm oil, and rubber. In some cases commodity prices fell by as much as 60 per cent in the early 1980s. The ban placed on further log exports, while to be applauded from both an environmental and longer-term economic perspective, also cut deeply into outer island exports.[7]

---

[6] Most manufacturing growth after 1975 was in intermediate and capital goods industries, with the production of consumer goods growing very slowly and actually declining after 1981. Light industry as a share of the GDP also fell. Many of the nominally private firms are 'so inextricably linked to the state apparatus that they hardly qualify for the label "private". These links refer not only to dependence on bureaucratic largess and patronage, but also to the so-called cukong, arrangements involving close ties between Chinese business interests and senior armed forces officials' (Hill 1988: 19). Other studies have also noted the propensity for foreign investors to link either with Chinese Indonesians or the military elites (Tsurumi 1980: 304).

[7] Kinoshita (1986: 35) states that the heavy protection of the Japanese market against processed and manufactured goods resulted in Japan importing 56% of Indonesia's log exports but only 1.7% of Indonesia's plywood in 1982.

All of these changes had important implications for the nation's urbanization process. First, since the international marketing of resources had provided the economic basis for the expanding inter-island trade and, therefore, urbanization in the outer islands, the declining revenues were also likely to dampen both investment and employment growth in the cities on these islands. In five key outer-island provinces, receipts for exports fell by at least 20 per cent, while the impact was negligible or very low on Java. The fall in commodity prices was exacerbated by a precipitous drop in direct foreign investment in the economies of the outer islands. Japanese companies, which until the early 1980s had persisted in trying to break into oil exploration and other resource-based activities, began to withdraw from Indonesia, and six Japanese companies in the cash-crop sector were liquidated (Kinoshita 1986: 46).

Table 6.3 shows the overall impact of changes in the economy during the 1978–85 period. The erstwhile leading sector of the economy, mining (primarily oil) dropped from 28 to 18 per cent of the GDP. Manufacturing, which increased its share from about 9 to 13 per cent, was unable by itself to make up the losses in oil exports. Forestry, under a new ban on log exports outside of concession areas, also witnessed a negative growth rate. Although of limited importance to the GDP, forestry had nevertheless been an important source of government revenues. The overall growth rate of the economy fell from a high of 5.3 per cent during what the rest of the world perceived as the 'second oil shock' of price increases in the late 1970s to 2.5 per cent during the 1981–5 period. As the data on the per

Table 6.3.   GDP sectoral distribution and growth rate, 1978–85

Sector and sub-sector	GDP (Rp. trillion) (in constant 1983 prices)					Percentage Share GDP		Total increase		Average annual growth rate	
	1978	1980	1982	1984	1985	1978	1985	1978–81	1981–5	1978–81	1981–5
Agriculture	14.4	16.4	17.4	18.7	19.2	24.7	24.3	20.9	26.7	4.6	2.8
Food crops	8.4	9.7	10.7	11.9	11.9	14.4	15.1	16.7	17.2	6.1	2.9
Non-food crops	1.4	1.8	2.0	2.3	2.5	2.5	3.2	4.2	7.2	8.6	6.1
Estate crops	0.4	0.5	0.6	0.4	0.5	0.8	0.6	0.6	–0.1	4.3	–0.3
Livestock	1.2	1.6	1.7	1.8	2.0	2.1	2.6	2.8	5.6	6.8	5.9
Forestry	1.9	1.7	1.1	0.9	0.9	3.2	1.1	–4.5	–5.5	–9.4	–9.4
Fisheries	1.0	1.1	1.2	1.3	1.3	1.7	1.7	1.2	2.3	3.8	3.6
Mining	16.4	16.1	13.9	14.8	14.0	28.1	17.7	–0.2	–31.8	0.0	–3.8
Manufacturing	5.1	7.3	8.0	9.5	10.0	8.8	12.7	20.6	29.2	11.4	6.3
Non-oil/LNG	4.2	5.4	6.0	6.6	7.0	7.3	8.9	13.1	13.5	9.1	3.9
Construction	5.0	5.8	6.2	5.7	5.7	8.6	7.2	8.2	–5.4	5.1	–1.7
Trade	8.2	10.1	11.8	12.3	11.8	14.1	14.9	20.2	11.0	7.4	1.8
Transport	2.5	2.9	3.5	4.3	4.6	4.3	5.8	6.0	17.3	7.2	8.6
Services	5.9	6.8	8.1	9.1	9.7	10.1	12.3	11.8	30.6	6.2	6.9
Other*	0.7	1.3	2.5	3.8	4.1	1.3	5.1	12.4	22.4	34.5	14.1
Total	58.2	66.7	71.4	78.2	79.0	100.0	100.0	100.0	100.0	5.3	2.5

* banking, ownership of dwellings, electricity, gas, water.

Source: World Bank, 1986, Annex, p. 138.

cent share of total increase indicate, the decline of oil and timber during the 1981–5 period were compensated by a slow-growing agricultural sector, manufacturing (almost half of which was in LNG), and the service sector broadly defined to include trade, transportation and services. They also confirm that the fall in oil revenues brought a sharp drop in public and private construction activities.

Because of the high capital-intensity of such sectors as mining and manufacturing, employment expansion does not necessarily parallel that of the changing sectoral distribution of the GDP. Thus intercensal survey data show that despite the substantial increase in manufacturing GDP during the 1978–85 period, the proportion of labour absorbed in this sector was half of that of the 1970s, and its share of total employment remained almost constant. Agriculture, trade, and services, the three sectors with the lowest levels of productivity, together absorbed 84 per cent of the increases in the labour force during the first half of the 1980s. Although caution must be used in interpreting these figures, they do support the premise that with regard to the critical issue of employment expansion, the early 1980s stands in marked contrast to the halcyon decade of the 1970s and that the slowdown in the rest of the economy once again saw labour rely on low-productivity agricultural employment as its safety net.

Coupled with the slow employment expansion of the manufacturing sector was its continuing high concentration on Java. In 1985, Java held a 76-per-cent share of all manufacturing employment. When broken down by rural and urban categories, and with the support of studies showing that most rural employment in the manufacturing sector is in very low-productivity individual and cottage enterprises, an equally striking statistic is that only 14 per cent of all urban-based manufacturing employment in Indonesia was found to be outside of Java, and most of this (8 per cent) was on Sumatra around Medan and Palembang. At the same time, 72 per cent of all rural and urban construction work was located on Java. In a situation of declining or stagnating prices for primary-sector commodities from the outer islands, this continuing concentration of non-agricultural and non-primary sector employment opportunities on Java has obvious implications for national urbanization patterns in the coming years.

On Java, the 1970s trend of shedding labour from agriculture seemed by the mid-1980s to be poised for a new, more pronounced cycle. First, agricultural production, including rice production, had reached a plateau beyond which further gains were increasingly difficult to achieve. For the agricultural sector as a whole, the growth rate fell from 4.6 per cent per year during the 1978–81 period to 2.8 per cent during the 1981–5 period. By the early 1980s high-yielding varieties of rice had already been adopted on 94 per cent of the wet rice area, and yield increases levelled off after 1984. The withdrawal of subsidies on inputs and the expansion of agriculture into ecologically fragile upland regions further decreased the likelihood of repeating the types of gains made in the 1970s. Adverse weather combined with these factors to see annual increases in rice production continue to drop, with recent government data showing that annual production gains were below 2.5 per cent in each of the years from 1985 to 1988.

Of greatest potential impact on labour was another trend which only began in the early 1980s, namely the rapid spread of mechanization—threshers, padi-tractors, weeders—across the island, which is not only leading to the disappearance of water buffalo, but also to lower use of labour per hectare.[8] In addition, falling government revenues have meant a decline in the capacity to sustain previous levels of rural public works programmes which were a major source of non-agricultural employment in agricultural regions in the past. When coupled with a higher growth rate of the labour force in the 1980s and 1990s over the 1970s and new preferences of the now literate youth of Java for non-agricultural work (Collier *et al*. 1988), the prospects for urbanward movement from rural regions of Java seem much greater now than at any time in the past, including the decade of rapid urbanization in the 1970s.

All of these changes suggest a simultaneous process of a nation-wide 'contraction', and acceleration of the urbanization process. Or, in other terms, the trends of the early 1980s all pointed towards a significant slowing-down of migration to cities and settlements in the outer islands and an increased focus on Jakarta and other major northern coastal cities on Java. Concurrence with this view was found in the 1985 intercensal population survey showing that Java experienced an estimated population increase of almost 9 million people during the 1980–5 period, or an annual rate higher than that of the 1971–80 period—despite lower birth rates (BPS 1987). Economic data from the late 1980s suggests a continuation of this trend: in 1976 the per capita GDP of the outer islands as a whole was higher than that for Java; by 1987 Java was 25 per cent higher than the outer islands, with the Jakarta metropolitan region leading this reversal (World Bank 1988).

Other changes in government policy which were not explicitly macro-economic in design or purpose will also play a role in the spatial redistribution of population towards Java. The major shift in this regard is the *de facto* curtailment of Indonesia's massive transmigration programme, which between 1979 and 1984 resettled approximately 2 million peasants from Java into subsistence agriculture schemes in the outer islands. An average of more than 1,000 people per day were estimated to have moved to newly cleared land and government-built houses in the outer islands during this period. From the receiving region perspective, the movement was so great that in some districts up to two-thirds of the population increases during the 1970s came from transmigration (Douglass 1985). Unable to successfully sustain this pace and under external pressure from environmentalists, economists, and human rights activists, the Ministry of Transmigration was compelled in 1986 to discontinue sponsored resettlement in favour of upgrading existing sites and encouraging spontaneous migration to the outer islands. In the short run this move is expected to result in a sharp drop in migration from Java to the transmigration areas in the outer islands.

[8] Collier *et al*. (1988) found in their 1987 recensus of thirteen Javanese villages that water buffalo had declined by as much as 50% during the previous five years. They also found that landlessness and the concentration of land ownership had increased, with large landowners having a higher propensity to use tractors and, therefore, reduce the number of workers per area of land under production.

Although the hundreds of thousands of people who were sent to the outer islands each year did not reduce the absolute size of the population of Java, in many sending areas of Java, the programme was seen as a viable alternative to the prospects of landlessness and near-landlessness under increasing demographic pressure and further concentration of land ownership. Yet densities in lowland rural areas of Java, which were already in excess of 1,000 people per square kilometre, continued to increase, and median farm size shrank to about one-quarter of a hectare by the early 1980s. Rural underemployment remained high, with 40 per cent of the rural population of Central and East Java working fewer than thirty-five hours per week (Douglass, 1987: 10).

Table 6.4 compares population census data for Indonesia's population distribution in 1971, and 1980 and 1990. Although Java's share of the national population has continued its slow decline, most of this change is now due to differences in natural population growth rates. Of particular importance in this regard are the data which show that although Central and East Java and Yogyakarta have continued to experience falling shares of the national population, Jakarta and its surrounding province of West Java have increased their shares. Together, these two provinces moved from 22 to 24 per cent of the national population and, more strikingly, from 34 to almost 41 per cent of Java's population during the 1971–90 period.

As previously noted, inter-provincial migration within Java is many times that of migration to the outer islands. For the 1980–5 period, 71 per cent of all migrants leaving their home province in Java stayed on Java. Slightly more than two-fifths of this inter-provincial migration on Java was directed toward Jakarta, a city which comprises only 7 per cent of the island's population. Jakarta and West

Table 6.4. Population growth and distribution by province, 1971–90

Island and province	Population (million)			Average annual growth rate (%)		Percentage share					
						Total			Island		
	1971	1980	1990	1971–80	1980–90	1971	1980	1990	1971	1980	1990
Java	76.1	91.3	107.5	2.0	1.6	63.8	62.1	59.9	100.0	100.0	100.0
Jakarta	4.6	6.5	8.2	4.0	2.3	3.8	4.4	4.6	6.0	7.1	7.7
West Java	21.6	27.5	35.4	2.7	2.5	18.1	18.7	19.7	28.4	30.1	32.9
Central Java	21.9	25.4	28.5	1.7	1.2	18.4	17.3	15.9	28.8	27.8	26.5
Yogyakarta	2.5	2.8	2.9	1.1	0.4	2.1	1.9	1.6	3.3	3.0	2.7
East Java	25.5	29.2	32.5	1.5	1.1	21.4	19.9	18.1	33.5	32.0	30.2
Sumatra	20.8	28.0	36.5	3.4	2.7	17.5	19.1	20.4	—	—	—
Kalimantan	5.2	6.7	9.1	3.0	3.0	4.3	4.6	5.1	—	—	—
Sulawesi	8.5	10.4	12.5	2.2	1.8	7.2	7.1	7.0	—	—	—
Bali/NT	6.6	7.9	10.2	2.0	2.6	5.6	5.4	5.7	—	—	—
Maluku/I.J.	2.0	2.6	3.5	2.8	3.0	1.7	1.8	2.0	—	—	—
Indonesia	119.2	147.5	179.2	2.3	1.9	100.0	100.0	100.0	—	—	—

Sources: BPS, Statistik Indonesia 1986, Table 3.1.2. Results of the 1990 Population Census, Series S2, BPS, Population of Indonesia, Table 5.9, p. 24.

Java combined, which includes both Jabotabek and Bandung, received 78 per cent of the inter-provincial migration. In net terms, Jakarta gained 205,000 migrants from other provinces of Java, and West Java gained 183,000 migrants. Central Java and East Java combined to have a net loss of 400,000 migrants. By these accounts, Java is clearly witnessing a rapid polarization of development in Jakarta and along its rapidly expanding 'Jabopunjur' corridor towards Bandung.

At the same time, however, even the extraordinarily high rates of migration to the metropolis are not sufficient to the task of reducing rural population densities. To the extent that non-agricultural employment is gravitating to coastal cities and is not being generated in rural areas, increasing rural densities are disturbing. Village-level studies on Java carried out in the early 1980s found that agricultural employment comprised 70 per cent of the income received by the main income earners and 57 per cent of the combined income of second and third household income earners (Wiradi and Manning 1984). This share was almost exclusively made up of income derived from wet and dryland rice farming. Non-farming activities were dominated by either cottage (handicraft) industries, pedi-cab (becak) driving, and trade in agricultural (including food) products. This same study found that manufacturing activities were accounting for a declining share of household income, with transportation, trade and government employment having become the major income-earning alternatives to work in agriculture. More than 50 per cent of non-agricultural activities were found in the 'self-employed' category, and a substantial proportion also involved seasonal and circular migration to metropolitan regions (especially becak driving and construction work). In many cases former rural producers had become pure vendors of metropolitan factory-made products.

Incorporation into the 'new' international division of labour

By the late 1980s Indonesia had reached a crossroads at which the government could either try to continue to lever gains from the international economy by attempting to revitalize its past model of development or try to join the select league of city-states and medium-sized countries in Asia by radically diverging toward a new course of export-oriented manufacturing. With the tremendous growth of transnational corporations in the 1970s and equally prodigious advances in international transportation and communications technologies, the comparative advantages of Third World countries were rapidly shifting away from natural-resource endowments, many of which were either severely depleted or experiencing low market prices, towards their supplies of low-cost yet now literate labour. In other words, Indonesia could join the 'new' international division of labour in which industrial labour rather than oil, timber, or cash crops would be the principal attraction for transnational capital and the driving force of structural change in the economy.

In addition to a literate and compliant labour force, which Indonesia now had in abundance, the pursuit of the new development path required a substantial reformation of relations between the state and transnational capital. State enterprises formerly girded by protectionist policies giving them monopoly positions would be left to struggle in a more competitive market. The intricate pathways of permits and approvals established by the bureaucracy as a means of linking with global capital to create small domestic tributaries of unproductive wealth would have to yield to the transnational imperative to accelerate the global circulation of capital as a basic condition for attracting foreign investment. Competing with other Asian economies for foreign investment in manufacturing would also be likely to result in lower, perhaps even negative, state income from foreign firms (ESCAP/UNCTC 1988).

The promulgation of Repelita V, the fifth national development plan covering the 1989–93 period, seemed to confirm that the government was willing to begin taking the necessary steps to accommodate the policy changes needed to join the new international division of labour. In calling for greater reliance on the private sector to spur economic development, the government also announced deregulation policies, including financial reforms allowing for greatly expanded foreign participation in banking and insurance. Shares in invested firms were raised from less than 50-per-cent to 85-per-cent foreign equity in joint ventures. Restrictions on more than 200 areas of investment were subsequently lifted, with restrictions waived for ventures exporting 100 per cent of their production (Crone 1989: 7). For the special island of Batam, located just 20 km from Singapore, investors who export 100 per cent of all production were allowed 100 per cent equity for the first five years of operation and 95 per cent thereafter. All these moves represented fundamental changes in the posture of the Indonesian government toward transnational capital.

The pressures on the middle class and ruling elites to push for these changes are not difficult to identify. Austerity measures following declining oil prices had quickly led to cutbacks in the civil service and in the subsidies and perks, such as free automobiles, provided to the upper echelons of the bureaucracy. A squeeze on the new urban middle class was rapidly becoming apparent by the middle of the 1980s, and was being registered by increasingly open dissatisfaction with the continuing concentration of wealth in the hands of the very top national leaders and their business partners. Politically, pressures for an economic, if not political, change had reached a level not experienced over the previous two decades.

At the same time that these pressures were mounting in Indonesia, a new factor was rapidly emerging at the international level which, by the end of the decade, would initiate fundamental changes in the economic integration of Pacific Rim countries. This factor was the tremendous rates of capital accumulation in Japan which, following the revaluation of the yen at the end of 1985, resulted in a pronounced offshore movement of labour-intensive manufacturing activities orchestrated by Japanese corporations (Douglass 1989a). The motive for this new wave of investment was radically different from that of the past, and would be of potentially crucial importance to Indonesia's future role in the Pacific Rim economy. Unlike Japanese foreign investment in the past, which was motivated by imperatives to capture expanding markets to keep pace with expanding production of manufactured goods in Japan (Panglaykim 1983; Yoshihara 1978; Kinoshita 1986), the new motive was to gain access to cheap labour in developing countries to remain competitive in the production of commodities for international markets (Douglass 1986; 1988).

The resulting expansion of Japanese direct foreign investment in Asia and the world has been stellar. In 1968 Japanese firms accounted for only 1 per cent of the total investment by transnational corporations in the world; by 1980 the share had reached 7 per cent (Stopford and Dunning 1983). Recovery from the second oil shock unleashed a substantially amplified round of foreign investment in the early 1980s, with the amount doubling by 1985 when Japanese corporations accounted for 147 of the Fortune top 500 non-US firms, seven Japanese corporations had moved into the ranks of the top twenty corporations in the world, and Japanese banks accounted for five of the six largest international banks. None of these trends was able to compare with the leap in Japanese foreign investment after revaluation of the yen. In just two years, 1986 and 1987, the level tripled to reach an official level of US$33 billion.

The new labour-orientation of Japanese investment began to be increasingly directed toward Asia. Particularly after 1985, Japanese firms began to accelerate what they call 'integrated globalization' of production through the integration of higher-technology segments of production in Japan with labour-intensive segments relocated to East and South-East Asia. By the end of 1986 half of the companies in Japan with 1,000 or more employees had adopted plans to set up production units outside the country (*Shukan Toyo Keizai.* 1988). Although the principal targets for these investments were initially Japan's former colonies of Korea and Taiwan, their rising labour costs and perceived political instability led to an unexpected thrust into the ASEAN region of South-East Asia. In 1987 Japanese investments into South-East Asia increased by 87 per cent over the previous year, and Asia's share of annual world-wide investment by Japanese enterprises nearly doubled from 10 per cent in 1986 to 19 per cent in 1987.

With regard to Indonesia, by the mid-1980s Japan was already the largest foreign investor in the manufacturing sector. In 1987 Japanese investments approved by the Indonesian government totalled US$400 million, or 1.6 times the 1986 level of US$250 million.[9] In terms of number of Japanese companies, the 231 in Indonesia in 1987 ranked it thirteenth in the world. In the same year 60,000 non-Japanese workers were reported to be directly employed by these companies.[10] Such figures suggest that Indonesia, as a 'favoured' nation for Japanese investment,

[9] Indonesia's share of annual Japanese foreign investment increased from 1.1% in 1986 to 2.5% in 1987 to become the third highest Asian recipient after China (6.9%) and Hong Kong (4.1%) for that year (Shukan Toyo Keizai, 1988). Disagreement over the Asahan Dam led to a sharp drop in Japanese investment in 1988, but 1989 figures showed a renewed surge in investment, particularly after events in China led to a sharp drop in that country.

[10] Kinoshita (1986: 39) estimates that if all sources of Japanese loans, export credits, special loans, and indirect financing from subsidiaries in Hong Kong, Singapore, and other countries are tallied, Japanese investment in Indonesia up to 1984 was already second only to that in the US.

could position itself to participate in the strategy of industrial integration on the Pacific Rim. Yet with international borrowing instead of oil revenues having quickly become the major source of the government's development budget, and with more than 40 per cent of Indonesia's outstanding debt being financed in yen, and the appreciation of the yen substantially raising the level of debt liabilities to Japanese lenders, Japanese investors have gained enormous political as well as economic advantage in setting the terms for foreign investment. With 45 per cent of Indonesia's exports going to Japan, 35 per cent of all approved foreign investment and one-third of the total development funds to Indonesia for the government's 1988-9 budget coming from Japan, the linkages and points of pressure are multi-faceted and increasing.

Furthermore, even with new opportunities and policies encouraging foreign investment in export-oriented manufacturing, Indonesia has a long way to go in competing with Thailand, Malaysia, and Singapore for a significant share of transnational capital. The other economies have several advantages not yet credited to Indonesia: higher levels of demand in their domestic markets for electronics and other transnational products; governments that are perceived to be less corrupt and more predictably hospitable to foreign investment; financial markets that are well-developed; superior physical development of cities, sea, air and road transportation, infrastructure, and communications; and more highly educated, factory-experienced workers (Yoshihara 1978: 48; Kinoshita 1986: 49). For these reasons, and although foreign investments in recent years have experienced a boom in Indonesia, those directed toward export-oriented manufacturing were higher elsewhere in the ASEAN countries, notably Thailand.

These problems notwithstanding, Indonesia has compensating attractions. Real wages are among the lowest in Asia—less than one-third of those of Singapore—and have remained almost constant over the past decade. Even though the reliability of infrastructure and energy supplies such as electricity are a constant cause of concern, both are heavily subsidized and utility costs are also low. Deregulation and streamlining of investment and port procedures have greatly improved the investment climate. And of all the ASEAN countries Indonesia is the most attractive target for investment in at least one respect—size. With a population of 179 million (1990), it is potentially the largest market in South-East Asia for the manufactured goods being produced both in Japan and in the East-Asian newly industrializing countries (NICs). To the extent that reforms allow investors both to capture portions of the huge domestic market and, as a bonus, to produce for export, investors now seem willing to give Indonesia a level of consideration not granted a few years ago. In this regard, and in view of the prevailing characteristics of its economy, labour force, and unpredictable bureaucracy, Indonesia's major competitor for foreign investment is most likely to be China, not South-East Asia. Thus the current political repression and instability in China may well bring more attention to Indonesia.

The new dimension of Japanese investment is already having significant impacts on the Indonesian economy. In the past Indonesia has been seen as the most reluctant of the East and South-East Asian market economies to pursue the export-oriented manufacturing strategy of economic growth. Its government resisted external efforts to create a large number of export-processing zones, and its import-substitution policies were heavily biased against export-oriented manufacturing. Throughout the 1970s, manufactured exports as a percentage of total exports from Indonesia never exceeded 2 per cent. From 1986 onwards, however, the value of selected manufactured exports, such as automobile components, began to double. In 1988 approved foreign investment in Indonesia tripled in value over the previous year to reach US$4.4 billion, and non-oil exports rose by an estimated 35 per cent. A small but significant share of the increases in these exports has been in manufactured goods.

Although the export-oriented manufacturing investments are new, the internal political and economic ramifications may not be as novel as some observers expect. Most of the new export-oriented manufacturing linkages between Japan are, in fact, shoring up and expanding the monopoly positions of well-known military-bureaucrat-Chinese conglomerates formed under Sukarno or in the early years of the New Order Government. A principal example is Astra International. Established in 1957 and rapidly expanding in the 1970s on the basis of its position as the sole agent for the import of commodities from such companies as Toyota, Fuji Xerox, Westinghouse, and Kodak, in 1987 it initiated a US$75-million engine plant to combine with its Toyota franchise to begin to export almost fully Indonesian-produced 'Kijang' vans to South-East Asia and China.[11] Some Toyota automobiles produced by Astra are already being sold in Papua New Guinea and Fiji, and a small number of Indonesia-produced Honda motorcycles have been sent to China. It has also begun the construction of an automobile windshield and industrial glass factory for glass exports under licence with a US firm.

The major roles played by Astra and other Indonesian corporations in all of these ventures are not 'industrial' in the sense of internalizing the full production process or research and development capabilities in Indonesia.[12] As in the past, their principal functions are, first, to smooth access to government bureau overseeing investment and, second, to secure loans for equity investment from domestic and foreign markets. As such, the new form of international industrial

---

[11]   Astra, which is now the exclusive agent for Toyota, Daihatsu, Peugeot, Renault, BMW, and Fiat already controls most of the domestic automobile industry. It is also the major partner with Honda motorcycles, Komatsu Heavy Equipment, and Digital Equipment, and owns real estate, logging and plywood, palm oil, coconut, cassava and fruit plantations, and other subsidiaries in Indonesia. It has also joined with the US-based Scott Paper Company to build an integrated timber, pulp and wood-chip plant in Irian Jaya and with Korea's Samsung Corporation to produce monosodium glutamate. The company is owned by an Indonesian-Chinese associate of Mrs Soeharto and was a major target during the anti-Japanese Malari Riots accompanying Prime Minister Tanaka's visit to Indonesia in 1974 (Robison, 1986: 165).

[12]   Among these are the business empires of such Indonesian-Chinese as Liem Sioe Liong (Sudono Salim), sole agent for, *inter alia*, auto assembly and reportedly one of the richest men in the world; Tan Siong Kie (Hanafi), the largest industrialist outside of the automobile industry; and Tan Tjoe Hing (Hendra Rahardja), sole agent for Yamaha and owner of major shopping complexes in Jakarta (Robison, 1986).

partnerships cannot be expected to radically alter the political economy of business in Indonesia.

The monopoly positions and high concentration in Jakarta of Indonesian partners in new export-oriented manufacturing ventures can be expected to accentuate the polarization in the capital and only secondarily promote the growth of a few port cities on Java's north coast. As with the urbanization processes in Japan, Korea, and Taiwan, all of which experienced phenomenal rates of primate-city-directed rural–urban migration in the 1960s and 1970s, an exclusive economic focus on export-oriented industry would appear to have little hope of reaching into densely settled rural regions, particularly in a situation of abundant labour that is quite willing to migrate in search of work. The portent of this process has moved the question of how to cope with the twin problems of accelerating growth of Jakarta and the likelihood of continuing slow growth of agriculture and rural regions to centre stage in devising new urban and regional development strategies for a new period of structural change.

The 1990s and beyond

Events in the 1990s are accentuating trends that emerged in the mid-1980s. The 1990 census revealed that cities absorbed 70 per cent of the national population growth during the 1980s, with migration from rural areas accounting for about two-thirds of urban growth. By 1990 Java was officially 36 per cent urban. The urban population of Jabotabek, at 13 million in 1990, grew at 5.8 per cent per year during the 1980s, increasing its share of the national urban population to 24 per cent. Two other metropolitan regions on Java—Surabaya, with 3.5 million, and Bandung, with 3.3 million—came in a distant second and third in size. With an estimated population of 15.5 million in 1994 and a population-doubling time of about 12 years, Jabotabek is projected in the national plan, Repelita VI (1993/4–98/9), to reach 33 million in population by the end of the current long-range planning period (PJP II) in 2018, placing it among the world's largest urban agglomerations.

Three trends in particular have amplified the reconcentration of development around the capital city. The first, and largely unanticipated, trend has been the transnationalization of capital pouring out of the newly industrialized economies of Korea, Taiwan, Hong Kong, and Singapore. Since 1986 they have joined with Japanese direct foreign investment (DFI) to increase exponentially the levels of DFI in urban manufacturing in the ASEAN countries of South-East Asia, including Indonesia (Douglass 1991). From 1989–90 alone DFI increased by almost 90 per cent, with 72 per cent going into industrial projects, particularly labour-intensive textiles, shoe-making, and car assembly, most of which is located in West Java and Jakarta (*FEER* 1991). By 1993, the Asian NIEs had together surpassed every country except Japan in amounts of foreign investment approved by the Indonesian government, accounting for more than US$2 billion in investment compared with Japan's US$700 million and US$400 million from the US (*AWSJW*, 1994). With more than 80 per cent of all foreign investment projects approved in 1990 located in Jabotabek, Bandung and Surabaya, the government's estimate that this investment would generate 200,000 new jobs suggested a very high degree of spatial concentration of new employment.

The second trend, which is closely allied with increases in direct foreign investment in urban-based manufacturing, is the expansion of an international spatial network of connectivity composed of transportation and communications linkages focused on key cities and development corridors on the Pacific Rim that are linked to Indonesia through Jakarta (Rimmer 1994; Douglass 1996). Telecommunications, sea and air transport infrastructure, and the growth of centrally located business and finance services required to maintain a key position in the new international urban hierarchy, have almost wholly focused on Jakarta.

Although still in embryonic stages, the development of a highly integrated hierarchy of cities on the Asian arc of the Pacific Rim is well underway. While Tokyo currently holds the position as a major world city on this arc, Hong Kong and Singapore are already explicitly attempting to fashion a world-city role for themselves. Other capital cities such as Bangkok, Kuala Lumpur, and Jakarta form an important second tier of cities linking national economies to the higher circuits of distribution and accumulation. Reaching outwards from each of these cities are coastal corridors that are being extended with expressways for vehicular transportation, high-speed trains, electrification, telephone lines, inter-urban air traffic, and shipping lines. Just as the development of these corridors widens the gaps between them and the rest of their respective nations, huge projects, such as a proposed land bridge linking coastal ports in Vietnam to north-east Thailand, are planned to integrate these corridors across international borders. Growth triangles, the most well known of which combines Singapore with Johor Baru in southern-peninsular Malaysia and Batam Island of Riau Province in Indonesia, and other transborder regions are being touted by governments as key loci for creating new international spaces along these corridors.

The expansion of international and domestic corridors produces feedback loops of capital and labour flows that further expand Jabotabek ahead of corridors and other urban regions connected to it. By 1989, for example, more than half of the value of Indonesia's imports was channelled through Jakarta (Soegijoko 1992). The need to invest in this region to keep pace with ever higher demands for more expensive and grander forms of mega-infrastructure is manifested in the completion of the new international airport, the manifold increase in major regional toll roads, the appearance for the first time of condominiums and apartment rentals for foreign businessmen and women, a commercial building boom that has substantially raised the skyline of the city from its earlier *kampung* and low-rise family-run commercial establishment profile, and the construction of new towns housing as many as half a million people. The concentration of economic activities and population around Jakarta is thus not just the result of quantum increases in direct foreign investment in export-oriented manufacturing, although this is substantial; it is more broadly implicated in the creation of an international spatial network required by transnational systems of resourcing, production and distribution that, after decades of dependency on primary-product exports from outer islands, have begun to dominate the economic geography of Indonesia.

The extension of corridors from Jabotabek and other major cities has been part of a third crystallizing pattern, namely, the economic and spatial transformation of rural Java. At least two-thirds of the urban population of Java resides in and around the two major extended metropolitan regions, Jabotabek–Bandung and Surabaya–Malang, and major corridors extending outwards from them to cities on the north and to Yogyakarta and Solo in Central Java. In the recent report of an ongoing twenty-five-year study of villages across Java, Collier *et al.* (1993) found three major new trends emerging over the previous decade in rural areas within close proximity to these corridors:

- Within a 60-km range of large cities, the vastly improved transportation and communications infrastructure and services are allowing ever greater numbers of villagers to move between village and city on a daily, monthly and yearly basis for factory and service jobs. Most landless rural families in these areas now have at least one person who is working outside the village and in a factory or service job. A very large proportion of migrants to cities— probably more than half—consists of young women going to textile and other labour-intensive light industry. Factory managers are sending agents to villages in search of labourers, and factories often send buses to pick women up every day.

- Mechanization of rice production has continued to spread throughout lowland Java. At the same time, rice production on Java may have reached a limit, and the further absorption of labour into agricultural cultivation activities in rural Java is thought to be unlikely. An accelerated decline in the agricultural work force on Java is expected in the future.

- The proportion of landless households in villages is increasing as land markets are active in rural Java. Communal pastures in villages are declining as commercial agriculture expands and land prices rise. Consolidation of small into large holdings is occurring and sales to outsiders are prominent. The growth in employment in cities outside the village tends to compensate for growing landlessness, resulting in wages for jobs carried out by rural migrants staying almost constant despite high rates of urban–industrial and national economic growth.

Taken together, the implications of increased international economic and spatial linkages focused on Jabotabek and extended inter-city corridors, plus the increased ease of rural–urban population movement and declining absorptive capacity of traditional agricultural crop production, are profound. On the positive side, in well-located lowland villages most indicators show a decrease in the share of population in poverty (although absolute numbers of poor have not declined), national economic growth rates have remained high, and Indonesia's rise as a next-generation newly-industrializing country has many believers. Most children even in rural areas are now able to finish junior secondary school (SMP). Rural electrification is also well underway, and a very large share of rural households have television sets, daily newspapers, and hourly or more frequent bus services (Collier *et al.* 1993). For upland and more remote villages, however, all of these gains remain severely dampened and permanent out-migration is becoming a dominant trend.

The many short-term benefits of the amplified polarization of development around Jabotabek and other metropolitan regions must be weighed against the prospects for their long-term sustainability. Great stress is being placed on Jabotabek's natural and built environment to accommodate its stellar economic growth. As many as ten major new towns have either been built by private developers or are in final proposal stages (Dharmapatni and Firman 1996). At the same time, the depletion of ground water by residential and commercial users has resulted in sea-water intrusion reaching up to 12 km inland in Jakarta. Coastal development is also leading to serious loss of mangrove forests, and industrial pollution reaching the Java Sea is reported to be causing a decline in what has been a US$1-billion-a-year shrimp industry.

Traffic volumes are increasing at rates in excess of 15 per cent per year in Jakarta, which already has among the highest levels of air pollution in the world (World Bank 1993a). In areas of heavy traffic, lead, sulphur-dioxide and nitrogen-oxide pollution—each of which has very damaging health effects—is high and likely to worsen as industry and automobile ownership grow. The World Bank (1993a) predicts that without drastic measures, BOD (biological oxygen demand) from water pollutants will increase tenfold by 2020; emissions of suspended particulates into the air will increase fifteenfold; and emissions to all media of bio-accumulative metals (mercury and lead) are projected to increase almost twentyfold. Since increasing incomes are associated with increases in per-capita solid waste, urban solid waste is expected to increase more than twice as fast as population. An estimated 30 per cent of solid waste ends up in rivers and canals. In Indonesia unsafe water is a major source of such common causes of infant mortality as diarrhoea, typhoid, and cholera. Almost all cities lack basic sewerage systems, and existing piped water systems often deliver contaminated water due to leakages and low pressure levels (World Bank 1993a).

Although in the short term enterprises and households are able to push the costs of their negative environmental impacts on to the city at large, their cumulative effects are expected to have a serious impact on the economic performance of the region. For 1990 the estimated monetary costs of environmental degradation in terms of the health effects of pollution was US$500 million (World Bank 1993a). And even though significant investments have been made in public infrastructure, extraordinarily high urban growth rates have kept overall service levels in, for example, water and sewerage among the lowest in Asia. Rectifying the backlog in environmental infrastructure would call for an estimated investment of

US$1 billion per year during the 1990s, a sum which is twice the current levels and does not cover operation and maintenance costs (World Bank 1993b).

The growth of manufacturing in peri-urban areas is also intensifying rural–urban land and resource conflicts. In Bandung the indiscriminate growth of textile industries at the edge of the city has, for example, led to gross depletion of ground water. Water supplies that adjacent *kampung* have been relying on for decades and longer have completely dried up. The conversion, pollution, and diversion of water from prime agricultural land where some of the best rice in Indonesia is produced will have a negative effect on Indonesia's gains in grain self-sufficiency as well. While the government has a policy to protect irrigated agri-cultural lands, in practice they are disappearing rapidly. Dharmapatni and Firman (1996) report that in the 1980s the rate of loss of agricultural land was in excess of 8 per cent per year in Jabotabek.

These and other concerns, such as that over prospects for political stability when the Suharto era draws to a close, point towards a consideration of whether Indonesia can continue to rely on direct foreign investment as its principal source of industrialization and economic growth. There are already indications from cities such as Bangkok that regions which allow themselves to be environmentally degraded and to fall seriously behind in basic infrastructure and services will find themselves abandoned by investors as alternative sites present themselves in other regions and countries. The Government of Indonesia is keenly aware of such a possibility, particularly as the opening of China and Vietnam to foreign invest-ment presents direct competition for the very low-wage light manufacturing that it has been attracting. In 1993 DFI and manufactured exports began to show signs of faltering. Partly due to recession in Japan and competition from China, the decline has also been attributed to a perennial problem, corruption, that adds sub-stantial costs for investors and slows down the implementation of investment (Van der Eng 1993). Labour unrest on Java due to poor working conditions, including those in foreign-run textile and footwear industries, is also becoming more active (Manning 1993).

In sum, the new manufacturing export motor of the economy is fraught with a number of actual and potential weaknesses that suggest an over-reliance on it will result in economic swings that will in turn create policy crises covering a wide array of issues ranging from environment and infrastructure management to administrative overhauls and labour struggles. Acknowledging these possibilities raises yet another question, namely, what policies should be adopted for the rest of Indonesia, including rural Java where approximately 75 million people cur-rently reside.

For those on Java who live within commuting range of large cities, a major issue is whether to continue to encourage manufacturing to locate in the immediate periphery of these cities, thereby creating the necessity of daily long-distance commuting or, conversely, massive increases in low-cost housing at the urban fringe. To take advantage of existing rural housing stock by encouraging the growth of manufacturing enterprises in rural areas, a model of sub-contracting

from major enterprises in cities to small-scale rural enterprises is under consideration. Currently, however, the government is giving greater attention to the emerging business conglomerates that promise quantum leaps into high-technology
manufacturing, including the independent production of aeroplanes in Indonesia.

Within the agricultural sector on Java there is great opportunity to achieve
higher incomes. Higher education levels, greater access to urban markets and a
diminished need to remain in subsistence farming, suggest that policies to encourage a more diversified, high value-added regime of food production could have
high pay-offs. If these opportunities are to be realized beyond the immediate
commuting range of cities, a host of off-farm infrastructure and services, including vastly improved micro networks of all-season inter-village and village-to-
town roads linked to major arterial systems will be needed. In addition, such
improvements would encourage commercialization of cash-crop production and
processing as well as animal husbandry for domestic consumption and export
(Paauw 1984; Collier *et al.* 1993). Increasing rural incomes would also stimulate
the growth of rural towns through increased demand for services of a higher
quality. Java is now at a point at which television could be used to teach business
and other skills to expand marketing opportunities for small producers in city and
countryside alike. Finally, if the current *de facto* strategy of migration to the city
is to be counterbalanced by a more rural-based process of farm and non-farm
economic growth, the focus on large infrastructure projects as the strategy for
rural development adopted in the past will need to give way to a more decentralized promotion of small-scale, locally initiated economic programmes that are
supported by rather than initiated and operated from Jakarta.

Devising strategies for developing the outer islands, particularly the densely settled and very poor areas of eastern Indonesia, faces more entrenched problems.
Prices for the major outer-island exports remain depressed, and oil and logging
have finite horizons. Although coal exports from Kalimantan have done well, as
have timber and oil, employment generation is limited in comparison to the levels
of capital investment. The government has recognized the need to devise special
policies for eastern Indonesia, but as of the mid-point of Repelita VI they remain
sketchy. Much can nonetheless be done to lay the foundations for a coherent
growth strategy for this area, which would include the provision of basic economic infrastructure—roads, power, water—and services such as education,
health, and local government training.

The government has responded to these issues by, in part, using Repelita VI to
call for a thorough decentralization of public planning and administration down
to the sub-provincial *kabupaten* level across the nation. In addition, overlaying
this decentralization of governance in the plan is a national spatial development
strategy that identifies a functional hierarchy of cities spanning the archipelago.
Work is underway in the central government to reach agreements among various
ministries on the integration and co-ordination of national planning with this
spatial template, namely, to allocate packages of infrastructure and services
appropriate to the functional role of each designated city. Given the long history

of a highly centralized government with decision-making divided among powerful ministries, few expect substantial results overnight from the new approaches embodied in the national plan. There is, however, a high degree of agreement among the ministries in Jakarta that decentralization and development opportunities must be spread more evenly across the nation. What remains to be seen is whether this agreement can be translated into practice in a manner that actually links the scale of decentralized public administration with growth potentials and strategies at the local level. So far, the emphasis on government functions appears to be far ahead of devising strategies to counterbalance the growing spatial unevenness of national economic development.

The people of Indonesia have experienced important gains in economic welfare over the past two decades, first largely from the translation of windfall gains from OPEC-driven oil-price increases and, beginning from the mid-1980s, from the influx of direct foreign investment in manufacturing from East Asia. The government has proved itself astute in seizing the shifting economic opportunities of the day. At the same time, however, it has remained plagued by underlying problems of cronyism, and suppression of labour and other social movements. These chronic issues are intertwining with serious urban environmental problems and urban management, infrastructure and service shortfalls. Standing in the foreground are also the persistence of social inequalities and poverty, Islamic fundamentalism as a major source of political opposition, and the absence of any clear successor to President Suharto.

With the social and demographic shift towards a more highly-educated urban population and labour force, the stakes involved in ignoring these issues are being raised by the heightening spatial imbalances focusing on Jabotabek. From these perspectives, faith in Indonesia's participation in a new international division of labour can be justified only to the extent that it can be expected to be sustained in the longer term. While much of the government's attention on the economy is being directed towards adjusting to new competition from other Asian countries for foreign investment in export-oriented manufacturing, the equally telling indicators are those that show how the social, environmental, and spatial consequences of these investments are being addressed inside the country.

7 The Increasing Role of the Urban Non-formal Sector in Indonesia: Employment Analysis within a Multisectoral Framework

IWAN J. AZIS

Introduction

The analysis of employment and labour movements often stresses the growth of the urban formal sector *vis-à-vis* the expanding commercial agricuiture (farm) sector. Yet, various problems in developing countries more often than not involve issues such as rapid urbanization versus limited expansion of industrial employment, suggesting the potential growth of the less visible non-formal sector in the overall development process. It is in this context that the multisectoral framework approach could be very useful for analysing employment patterns and estimating labour movements.

The multisectoral framework applied in this chapter will specifically disaggregate the Indonesian economy into six types, including the category of the non-formal sector (both urban and rural). The information is taken from the data tapes of Susenas (national economic and social survey) 1982 and 1987.[1] The time-trend analysis should be read with care due to lack of data comparability between Susenas 1982 and 1987. It is for this reason that the cross-sectional analysis for 1982 will be discussed in detail before an attempt is made to obtain some indications from time-series observations.

Following the aforementioned analysis, the phenomenon of industrial location in relation to employment patterns and trends of urban migration is discussed. The observation is based on data tapes of industrial surveys covering the period 1978-81 (designed to support the preceding analysis of Susenas 1982). It is suspected that patterns of industrial location will reinforce flows of migrants to urban areas.

Employment Analysis of Susenas 1982

The classification in the multisectoral framework is based on three types of dualism: rural–urban, formal–non-formal and farm–non-farm. In an environment

[1] The Susenas surveys covered rural and urban areas throughout Indonesia, except for parts of Irian Jaya and Timor Timur which were not covered in 1982. The sample size for the 1987 Susenas was approximately 55,000 households.

where equity and poverty eradication are of concern to policy-makers, disaggregation by location, activity and form of organization is necessary. The extent to which differences between sectors tend to persist can be analysed within the framework.

Based on Susenas 1982, the bulk of Indonesia's employment was in the non-formal sector (83.2 per cent), in which the majority (71.9 per cent) worked in rural areas.[2] Of these rural non-formal workers, more than one-quarter were involved in the non-farm sector. Viewed from a regional perspective, Java dominates the number of workers in this activity. With respect to the urban non-formal sector, as expected, Java is also dominant; it accounts for more than 70 per cent of the nation's employment in this category. In fact, four Java provinces (East, West, and Central Java and DKI-Jaya[3]) are the only regions in Indonesia having more than one million urban non-formal workers each (see Table 7.1).

In the formal sector there was also more employment in rural than in urban areas, with most employment in non-farm activities. Again, only the aforementioned Java provinces, except of course DKI-Jaya, had more than one million employed in rural areas. At the same time, each of these had more than two million workers in non-formal, non-farm activity. In terms of earnings per worker, in most of the provinces the urban formal-sector worker earns less than the urban non-formal worker. The exceptions are: Jambi, South Sumatra, Bengkulu, DKI-Jaya, Yogyakarta, and East Kalimantan. Due to the dominance of DKI-Jaya, on average the whole island of Java has higher earnings per employee in the urban formal than in the urban non-formal sector, the opposite of the situation prevailing in other regions (see Table 7.2).

It is important to note, particularly for DKI-Jaya and Yogyakarta, that the lower earnings of urban non-formal workers in the six provinces were recorded in the face of Java's much greater and still-growing employment in this sector. The standard argument of 'the bright lights of the city' and the view that non-formal temporary employment and formal job search are complementary are often used

[2] The characteristics of the non-formal sector in Susenas 1982 are determined as follows:

Type of work	Work-status			
	Self-employed	Employers	Employees	Family workers
Professional, technical workers				Non-formal
Management and administrators				Non-formal
Farmers and agricultural workers	Non-formal		Non-formal	Non-formal
Others	Non-formal			Non-formal

For other studies on the non-formal (informal) sector in Indonesia, see Sethuraman 1974; Moir 1978; Van Gelder and Bijlmer, 1989.

[3] DKI-Jaya refers to the Jakarta municipality.

Table 7.1. Indonesia: Urban and rural employment, by type of activity and province, 1982 (in thousands)

Provinces	Urban Formal	Urban Non-formal	Urban Total	Farm Formal	Farm Non-formal	Farm Total	Non-farm Formal	Non-farm Non-formal	Non-farm Total	Total employment Formal	Total employment Non-formal	Total employment Total	Total labour force Rural	Total labour force Urban	Total labour force Total
Aceh	18	48	66	1	746	748	100	134	234	119	929	1,048	1,008	70	1,078
North Sumatra	219	382	601	5	1,967	1,972	216	305	521	440	2,654	3,094	2,542	644	3,186
West Sumatra	39	78	117	7	833	840	81	224	305	126	1,135	1,262	1,159	126	1,285
Riau	66	100	166	8	367	375	48	81	129	122	548	671	532	185	717
Jambi	23	29	53	4	308	312	37	121	158	64	458	523	480	55	535
South Sumatra	108	245	356	4	1,102	1,106	78	231	309	190	1,578	1,767	1,439	373	1,812
Bengkulu	3	20	23	1	271	272	18	37	55	22	328	350	329	24	354
Lampung	44	118	163	1	1,186	1,187	66	230	296	111	1,534	1,646	1,497	174	1,671
Dki-Jaya	995	1,028	2,023			—		—	—	995	1,028	2,023	—	2,184	2,184
West Jaya	648	1,107	1,755	28	4,429	4,457	1,401	2,369	3,770	2,076	7,905	9,981	8,563	1,880	10,443
Central Java	738	1,042	1,780	21	5,569	5,590	1,280	2,537	3,817	2,039	9,148	11,186	9,627	1,851	11,478
Yogyakarta	85	162	246	1	729	730	132	348	480	217	1,238	1,456	1,228	255	1,483
East Java	793	1,273	2,066	39	6,729	6,768	1,321	2,477	3,798	2,153	10,479	12,632	10,803	2,184	12,988
Bali	39	98	137	3	634	637	145	243	388	187	975	1,162	1,030	140	1,170
West Nusa Tenggara	26	96	122	1	685	686	72	295	368	99	1,077	1,176	1,066	125	1,191
East Nusa Tenggara	17	43	60	2	1,009	1,011	22	104	126	41	1,156	1,196	1,141	63	1,204
East Timor	3	7	11	0	5	5	3	5	7	6	17	23	13	11	24
West Kalimantan	46	75	121	0	863	863	36	74	110	82	1,012	1,095	984	126	1,109
Central Kalimantan	7	27	33	0	243	243	39	87	127	47	357	404	384	35	418
South Kalimantan	37	96	133	1	464	465	47	152	199	85	712	797	680	140	819
East Kalimantan	67	82	148	0	214	214	46	54	101	113	350	463	320	156	477
North Sulawesi	36	72	108	2	409	411	62	184	246	100	665	764	674	114	788
Central Sulawesi	9	28	37	2	368	370	29	67	95	39	463	502	468	39	506
South Sulawesi	77	218	295	10	935	945	112	369	480	199	1,522	1,721	1,475	317	1,792
South East Sulawesi	6	18	23	1	252	252	11	66	77	17	336	353	334	24	359
Maluku	12	32	44	0	310	311	26	74	100	39	416	455	420	47	467
Iran Jaya	4	10	14	0	31	31	7	17	24	10	59	69	58	15	72
Indonesia (total)	4,165	6,534	10,701	143	30,658	30,801	5,435	10,885	16,320	9,738	48,079	57,819	48,254	11,357	59,610

Source: Processed from SUSENAS- 1982 data tapes, Central Bureau of Statistics.

Table 7.2. Indonesia: average earnings per worker by industry group, computation of sectoral averages and by five regions, 1982 (Rp. 1000 per month)

Regions	Industry groups[a]	Urban		Rural	
		Non-formal[b]	Formal[b]	Non-formal[b]	Formal[b]
Sumatra	Others	60.7	58.8	41.1	41.9
	Agriculture	14.4	0.7	5.5	5.1
	Mining	119.8	145.2	48.7	92.3
	Industry	39.7	60.6	16.9	49.0
	Public utilities	64.5	0.0	78.4	0.0
	Construction	0.0	0.0	0.0	0.0
	Trade/hotel	44.0	56.7	34.3	44.7
	Transport	55.5	58.7	43.5	47.1
	Banking	113.6	77.6	0.0	0.0
	Social Services	64.9	45.5	56.6	37.4
Java	Others	55.8	63.3	36.1	36.5
	Agriculture	12.9	0.0	6.6	6.5
	Mining	0.0	128.3	21.3	28.0
	Industry	31.2	43.6	12.7	24.7
	Public Utilities	70.9	0.0	29.1	0.0
	Construction	0.0	0.0	0.0	0.0
	Trade/hotel	36.1	59.5	23.3	29.3
	Transport	51.3	54.7	38.8	36.8
	Banking	115.9	86.1	0.0	0.0
	Social Services	65.2	37.9	44.0	23.9
Kalimantan	Others	74.0	74.0	84.0	136.4
	Agriculture	6.9	6.9	0.0	0.0
	Mining	128.1	128.1	161.5	16.0
	Industry	50.4	50.4	69.3	42.6
	Public utilities	61.6	0.0	157.0	0.0
	Construction	0.0	0.0	0.0	0.0
	Trade/hotel	48.6	48.6	85.4	2.3
	Transport	60.7	60.7	59.4	65.8
	Banking	114.6	114.6	0.0	0.0
	Social Services	77.7	77.7	53.3	7.7
Sulawesi	Others	99.6	58.1	42.1	42.3
	Agriculture	11.3	0.0	6.6	6.6
	Mining	56.4	65.0	45.6	49.1
	Industry	55.1	51.3	15.1	35.3
	Public utilities	0.0	0.0	0.0	0.0
	Construction	0.0	0.0	0.0	0.0
	Trade/hotel	47.3	50.5	30.7	34.3
	Transport	57.0	51.7	46.8	38.9
	Banking	169.42	0.0	0.0	0.0
	Social Services	69.0	39.9	56.1	28.8

Table 7.2. (*cont.*)

Regions	Industry groups[a]	Urban		Rural	
		Non-formal[b]	Formal[b]	Non-formal[b]	Formal[b]
Others	Others	53.5	43.3	39.4	51.8
	Agriculture	7.1	4.3	3.7	1.6
	Mining	25.9	25.0	0.0	30.7
	Industry	24.6	45.2	12.2	23.2
	Public utilities	67.7	0.0	0.0	0.0
	Construction	0.0	0.0	0.0	0.0
	Trade/hotel	31.7	67.4	23.5	33.1
	Transport	58.7	52.4	48.7	45.0
	Banking	94.6	0.0	0.0	0.0
	Social Services	68.8	28.9	60.0	28.3
Indonesia	Others	60.8	62.7	38.6	38.5
	Agriculture	12.4	1.4	6.1	5.9
	Mining	0.0	135.2	25.8	42.9
	Industry	34.1	45.9	13.6	28.9
	Public utilities	0.0	0.0	22.1	0.0
	Construction	0.0	0.0	0.0	0.0
	Trade/hotel	38.1	59.9	25.3	31.8
	Transport	52.9	55.4	40.7	39.3
	Banking	117.8	84.4	0.0	0.0
	Social Services	66.2	39.0	48.9	26.1

Notes:
  [a] The sectoral definition is based on the following coding system: 11–19 agriculture, 21–9 mining, 31–9 industry, 41–9 public utility (gas, electricity and water), 51–9 construction, 61–9 trade/hotel, 71–9 transport, 81–9 banking, 91–9 social services and 01–09 others. With this classification the data fail to find formal workers registered under public-utility and construction sectors.
  [b] Y/E is the average per-worker earnings.

Source: Processed from Susenas 1982 data tapes, Central Bureau of Statistics.

to explain the phenomenon. Another often-cited explanation, especially in relation to rural–urban migration, is the interplay of various non-economic factors in the migrants' decision whether to migrate or not. These arguments seem to weaken the importance of earnings per employee as the key factor in the growing urban non-formal sector in Indonesia. A more detailed analysis, taking into account other possible explanatory variables, needs to be conducted to establish the truth.

Susenas 1982 also reveals that the high earnings of urban non-formal workers occurred mostly in the public-utilities and social-services sectors (Table 7.2). It is therefore to be expected that rural–urban migrants who failed to enter the urban formal sector would make these non-formal sectors their next choice. Contrary to the case of agricultural activity, in the rural industrial sector the average earnings in the formal category are generally higher than in the non-formal category.

Ranked according to the ratio between percentage share of total earnings and share of employment, the urban formal sector was at the top, followed by urban non-formal, rural non-farm formal and non-formal (see Table 7.3). Contrary to the general belief, in the formal and non-formal earning category Java is not in the top rank. This most developed region is surpassed by Sumatra, Kalimantan, and others in terms of its formal-sector earnings, whereas in non-formal activity it is surpassed by Sulawesi. Nevertheless, in all regions the attractiveness of employment in the urban areas, whether formal or non-formal, seems to be supported by higher earnings than in rural areas. Should earnings be the prime indicator or interregional-cum-intersectoral labour movements, the expected flows would be from the farm sector in the rural areas to urban areas, formal or non-formal, or to the rural non-farm formal and non-formal sector. To confirm this observation, however, intertemporal data ought to be used. It should be clear that the approach of matching the trend of earnings with the employment path is essential in the analysis of labour movements especially when data on actual labour movements are non-existent.

Earnings in real terms are often more representative of the true purchasing power, and hence the actual attractiveness of a region or a sector. Table 7.4 displays per-employee real earnings by province and formal–non-formal as well as by urban–rural classification. It is important to observe that regions in Java generally have a narrower gap of earnings between urban and rural, as well as between formal and non-formal, sectors. The highest ratios of urban–rural earnings are found in West Kalimantan, East Nusa Tenggara and North Sulawesi. Interestingly enough, Aceh, a province with major mining and refinery activities, also falls in this category. In fact, Aceh has the highest ratio of earnings in formal to non-formal sectors. This special province, rich in resources, especially natural gas, is ranked at the top in its formal-sector earnings but it is at the very bottom with respect to non-formal earnings. The standard 'enclave development' hypothesis may well be the explanation, since similar cases are also found in East Kalimantan and Riau, Indonesia's two other major oil provinces.

Given the fact that employment is largely in the rural and non-formal sectors, the above patterns indicate that the narrow gap in Java is probably due to the island's relatively high rural and low urban earnings in comparison with other provinces. This is evident from the data in Table 7.4. At any rate, Java's small gap may contribute to the attractiveness of the island, particularly of those provinces with very high non-formal real earnings, ie. DKI-Jaya and West Java.

Factors Affecting Interprovincial Urban Migration

If we confine our analysis of urban migration to interprovincial migration, it is revealed that during 1980–5 more than half the interprovincial migrants to urban areas had indeed chosen DKI-Jaya, followed by West Java (26.2 per cent)[4]. Thus,

---

[4] The interprovincial migration data are obtained from the 1985 intercensal survey, referring to the population (five years of age and over) who, during the survey, resided in urban areas of the observed

Table 7.3. Indonesia: percentage share of total earnings divided by percentage share of total employment by rural–urban, types of activity and by five main regions, 1982

| Region | Urban | | | Rural | | | | | | Total earnings | | |
| | | | | Farm | | | Non-farm | | | | | |
	Formal	Non-formal	Total	Formal	Non-formal	Total	Formal	Non-formal	Total	Formal	Non-formal	Total
Sumatra	2.99	2.53	2.69	0.27	0.29	0.29	2.42	1.98	2.22	2.61	0.79	1.00
Java	2.26	2.09	2.16	0.30	0.31	0.31	1.34	1.20	1.25	1.73	0.82	1.00
Kalimantan	3.26	2.70	2.90	0.22	0.25	0.25	2.15	1.85	1.94	2.67	0.78	1.00
Sulawesi	2.41	2.58	2.53	0.32	0.32	0.32	1.78	1.68	1.70	1.95	0.89	1.00
Others	3.25	3.01	3.07	0.11	0.23	0.23	2.61	2.09	2.23	2.73	0.82	1.00
Indonesia (total)	2.46	2.26	2.34	0.29	0.29	0.29	1.57	1.40	1.47	1.93	0.81	1.00

Source: Processed from SUSENAS-1982 data tapes, Central Bureau of Statistics.

Table 7.4. Indonesia: real earnings per employed worker by urban–rural, types of activity and by provinces, 1982 (Rp. 1000 per month)

Provinces	Urban	Rural	Urban/ Rural	Formal	Non- formal	Formal/ non-formal
	(1)	(2)	(1)/(2)	(4)	(5)	(4)/(5)
Aceh	94.4	17.0	5.5	124.4	12.4	10.0
North Sumatra	79.5	20.7	3.8	73.2	25.3	2.9
West Sumatra	81.2	25.0	3.2	74.7	25.3	3.0
Riau	93.8	32.3	2.9	101.7	35.4	2.9
Jambi	77.3	28.8	2.7	65.8	29.2	2.3
South Sumatra	76.0	20.1	3.8	75.1	25.9	2.9
Bengkulu	63.3	14.3	4.4	50.4	15.4	3.3
Lampung	55.9	12.9	4.3	49.5	14.8	3.3
Dki-Jaya	96.4	—	—	99.3	93.7	1.1
West Java	67.4	37.5	1.8	63.6	37.3	1.7
Central Java	53.5	32.8	1.6	62.0	30.3	2.0
Yogyakarta	55.0	24.8	2.2	57.2	25.1	2.3
East Java	61.7	27.2	2.3	57.6	27.7	2.1
Bali	55.8	21.7	2.6	55.3	20.0	2.8
West Nusa Tenggara	46.5	17.0	2.7	61.3	16.2	3.8
East Nusa Tenggara	68.0	10.5	6.4	58.7	12.6	4.7
East Timor	96.5	n.a.	n.a.	n.a.	n.a.	n.a.
West Kalimantan	80.4	12.5	6.4	82.3	14.9	5.5
Central Kalimantan	81.1	33.6	2.4	86.0	31.2	2.8
South Kalimantan	87.6	30.6	2.9	74.3	36.1	2.1
East Kalimantan	118.9	33.8	3.5	116.8	43.1	2.7
North Sulawesi	93.2	33.0	2.8	77.4	36.1	2.1
Central Sulawesi	70.2	24.8	2.8	62.3	25.2	2.5
South Sulawesi	68.9	23.0	3.0	53.8	27.9	1.9
South East Sulawesi	92.1	16.2	5.7	55.8	19.7	2.8
Maluku	103.1	26.5	3.9	90.8	28.7	3.2
Irian Jaya	119.0	57.6	2.1	100.7	64.5	1.6

Source: Processed from SUSENAS- 1982 data tapes, Central Bureau of Statistics.

despite the importance of other economic and non-economic factors, real earnings still seem to have some weight in explaining interprovincial migration patterns. Another economic factor, as the standard Todaro model has suggested, is the probability of obtaining a job in the region of destination.

Finding a perfect measure of the probability of obtaining a job is extremely difficult. A simple proxy would be the ratio of the numbers in formal employment to the total numbers in the labour force[5]. As expected, Java is ranked first in terms

province and five years before had lived in the province of origin. It should be noted that interprovincial rural–urban migrants are only a fraction of all migrants to urban areas, many of whom migrate within a given province.

[5] Alternative measures for employment opportunity are open unemployment and disguised unemployment. However, given the fact that in the Indonesian case open unemployment does not reflect

of this measure. By province, DKI-Jaya offers the greatest probability. West Java is also ranked in the top five. Two provinces with high probability, East Timor and East Kalimantan, deserve an explanation. In the case of East Timor, the small number in the labour force, and the infancy of its economic development due to the province's newness, result in the relatively small size of non-formal employment, and hence a greater probability ratio. A small labour force characterizes East Kalimantan, a province with the nation's third-lowest population density. In fact, for the same reason, the whole island of Kalimantan has the second-greatest job probability within the five-region classification, with a slightly greater ratio than that of Sumatra (0.1157 compared with 0.1124 (see Table 7.5)).

It is therefore suspected that two economic factors, earnings and job probability, could be essential in the analysis of labour migration. The extent of their roles is yet to be examined. Within the multisectoral framework, the examination could be enriched by the provision of trends in the urban and rural earnings variables as well as in the formal and non-formal earnings classification.

The unexpected minus signs of the coefficient in the regression analysis shown in Table 7.6 suggest that the earnings level in the urban sector is not the prime consideration in the migrants' choice of destination. On the other hand, employment opportunity as measured by formal job-probability seems to affect significantly the migrants' choice of destination. One striking example is the high job-probability in DKI-Jaya and West Java cited earlier, which coincides with the largest flows of migrants coming into these regions. Whichever model is used, the signs of coefficients are normally significant and positive.

Table 7.5.   Employment opportunity by five regions, 1982

Region	Employment opportunity index*
Sumatra	0.1124
Java	0.1939
Kalimantan	0.1157
Sulawesi	0.1030
Others	0.0926

* Employment opportunity index = ratio of numbers in formal employment to total numbers in the labour force.

Source: Processed from SUSENAS-1982 and 1987 data tapes, Central Bureau of Statistics.

the true condition or the crux of the problem (only 3% in 1982, see Table 7.1), while disguised unemployment is almost impossible to measure, the above indicator becomes an acceptable choice. The concern as to whether the indicator really reflects the development of a region is not more serious than the problem at the other extreme suffered by the two alternative measures, namely whether they really represent underdevelopment.

Table 7.6. Regression results of interprovincial migration model for Indonesia, 1980–85

Equation number	Independent variables					R^2	DW
	Eyurban	Eyrural	Eyformal	Eynformal	EDPP		
1	−1311.3				1296100	0.6799	1.7704
	(−1.6663)				(7.1263)		
2 (27)				2507.6	844712	0.7111	1.2548
				(2.3820)	(3.7581)		
(26)				540.9	1250810	0.7491	1.2979
				(0.3798)	(4.1825)		
3					1207650	0.6428	1.6344
					(6.7081)		
4 (27)				5189.5		0.5411	0.6192
				(5.4299)			
(26)				5540.6		0.5583	0.6106
				(5.5078)			
5 (27)			−731.7	3301.7	763972	0.7246	1.3882
			(−1.0614)	(2.5610)	(3.2271)		
(26)			−1520.5	1209.99	1285620	0.7978	1.4614
			(−2.3007)	(0.9034)	(4.676)		
6 (27)	−2134.3			3502.2	844728	0.7985	1.5887
	(−3.1578)			(3.6796)	(4.4050)		
(26)	−1893.7			2767.6	973245	0.7995	1.5271
	(−2.3511)			(1.7191)	(3.2685)		

Notes: Figures in parentheses are t-ratios; (26) and (27) refer to the number of regions covered.

The importance of job probability surpasses the role of real earnings. Notice in equation 5 of Table 7.6 that, as in the case of urban earnings, the negative and significant signs of formal real earnings do not indicate the importance of the variable in the migrants' choice. On the contrary, in equation 5 real earnings in the non-formal sector is positive and significant although with a lower degree of confidence compared with the job-probability variable. It could be deduced therefore that, in general, migrants' choice has been more determined by (formal) employment opportunities in the region of destination. The assertion is of course confined to the case of interprovincial urban migration being analysed in this study. But the real earnings of this sector, as well as in urban jobs, do not seem to be very important for their decision. Should migrants fail to enter the formal sector, the non-formal sector appears as the alternative choice. At this point migrants may begin to include earnings in their considerations. Again, this is merely a tentative conclusion and should be confirmed by the analysis of intertemporal data. Further generalization also requires a greater coverage of migrant flows to include within-province migration to urban areas.

The multisectoral framework will be much more useful when the analysis is carried out for different time periods. Susenas data are actually available for different years, but the problem of data comparability is rather serious.

The first obstacle is the unit of observation. The basic unit of Susenas 1987, the latest available so far, is the household, while Susenas 1982 is based on individuals. Consequently, in Susenas 1987 there are no data available on income of each member of the household. The 1982 Susenas covers 60,000 households or 357,062 members[6]. On the other hand, only 208,128 members of 49,317 households are available for the analysis of Susenas 1987. Another source of incompatibility is the survey period. While Susenas 1987 refers to the month of January 1987, Susenas 1982 is based on the September–December period. In addition to these distinctions, perhaps the most serious one for our analysis is the definition of formal–non-formal. Due to data limitation, a special approach to define formal–non-formal sectors in Susenas 1987 data is required. Discriminant analysis has been applied to this task[7].

Having described these problems it is clear that outcomes of the time-series analysis can only provide an indicative trend. Notice in Table 7.7 that the ratio

Table 7.7. Index of ratios between percentage shares of total earnings and employment by rural–urban area and types of activity, 1982 and 1987

	Urban			Rural total	Total (Urban + rural)
	Non-formal	Formal	Total		
A. Percentage share of total earnings divided by percentage share of total employment					
(a) 1982	2.26	2.46	2.34	0.70	1.00
(b) 1987	1.15	0.95	1.03	0.99	1.00
B. The same as (A) designating urban nonformal = 1					
(a) 1982	1.00	1.09	1.04	0.31	0.44
(b) 1987	1.00	0.83	0.90	0.86	0.87
C. Average annual growth rates of (B), 1982–7	0.00	–5.37	–2.86	22.92	14.47

Note: Total urban + rural set equal to 1
Source: Processed from SUSENAS-1982 and 1987 data tapes, Central Bureau of Statistics.

[6] Originally, there were records for 357,073 members in the data tape, but due to data damage (as indicated by the SAS programme), eleven fewer records could be analysed.
[7] A multivariate analysis of variance (MANOVA) is first used to select some variables capable of distinguishing formal from non-formal sectors. The two selected variables (with F-test = 212.35) appear to be household cost of production (OPER) and household incomes (PPER). By making use of discriminant analysis, the following non-liniar probability functions are then generated:
$$f_i(X) = (2)^{-p/2}.|V_i|^{-1/2}.\exp(-0.5d_i^2(^2X))$$

between percentage shares of earnings and employment for the urban–non-formal category is set to equal one. This is done to facilitate observation of the changes of each category's position relative to the urban non-formal category. Furthermore, since our emphasis in using the multisectoral framework is particularly on the urban non-formal sector and the distinction between urban and rural, only these categories are shown in Table 7.7.[8]

As indicated in Table 7.7, there has been a tendency for a decline in the position of the urban formal *vis-à-vis* the urban non-formal sector with respect to rates of earnings. While in the early 1980s the urban sector (both formal and non-formal) proved to be an attractive alternative to rural employment, the trend throughout the late 1980s changed somewhat. The development process characterized by a series of reforms, promulgated during the mid-1980s, appears capable of raising earnings per employee in the rural sector relative to those in the urban[9]. This suggests that improvements in rural standards of living combined with slow employment growth in urban areas will probably affect mobility between rural and urban labour markets in such a way that less urban migration is expected. However, at least two conditional factors deserve attention. Although the relative position of rural earnings has markedly improved, the average rate remains lower than that in the urban areas (row A of Table 7.7).[10] Secondly, the assertion regarding the expected trend of urban migration above is based merely on earnings-per-employee data. Other non-monetary factors are ignored. Thus, should the actual number of urban migrants have indeed increased, these ignored factors must have been quite significant in the migrants' decision.

In urban areas, the non-formal sector earnings begin to surpass those of the formal, indicating an increased relative attractiveness of the urban non-formal sector. Such a trend may help to explain the continuing flows of migrants to urban areas. Table 7.7 shows that by 1987 the urban non-formal sector had the highest earnings per employee, even higher than those of the urban formal sector. In fact, earnings per employee in the urban formal sector were also less than rural earnings. This, of course, is very suspicious. Many studies utilizing Susenas data (e.g. Booth 1992) show that the income and expenditure data of the upper income

where t = 0 (for non-formal) and = 1 (for formal),
    X = Vector of household production cost and incomes,
    p = number of group(=2),
    V_t = the tth group's matrix of variance-covariance, and
    d_t^2 = general square distance.
The following criteria are then applied:
   non-formal, if the value of the function –0> that of function –1
   formal, if the value of the function –0< that of function –1

[8] It should be clear to readers that this will not have anything to do with the strength and limitation of the multisectoral framework for employment- and labour-movement analysis.

[9] This observation is consistent with the author's finding on the nation's relative income distribution, indicating a slight improvement during 1980–7.

[10] The stronger improvement of rural workers during the 1980s is supported by the consumption expenditure data of Susenas, in which during 1984–87 the real growth rate of per-capita consumption among the rural poor (lowest 40%) was higher than the rate among the urban poor, i.e. 54% versus 3.1% annually.

group are underestimated. Not only is the sample coverage unrepresentative but more relevant to our case is the fact that income and expenditure answers given by respondents in this category are probably lower than the actual levels.

As indicated earlier, an analysis of time-series data could be expected to provide only rough indications. Many factors have hampered the comparability of data. Before these problems are solved, any attempt to generate a more convincing analysis will not be possible. In the next section we examine patterns of industrial location and the expected consequence on the increasing pull-factor of urban areas.

Patterns of Industrial Location and their Impacts upon Urban Migration

At least until the early 1980s a clear policy on industrial location was practically non-existent.[11] The well-known spatial configuration of the industrial sector is that more than 80 per cent of large and medium industrial establishments are in Java. In terms of value-added production, Java's dominance varies from 98.4 per cent for textile industries to 24.3 per cent for wood-related manufactures. In the small-industry category the variation is from 53.8 per cent (wood-related) to 93.5 per cent (textile). Since the government banned exports of logs in the early 1980s, processed-wood manufactures have grown fast, favouring a Javanese location. In the case of rattan, for example, the concentration has been intensified by a deliberate government decision in the late 1980s to select Java's three largest cities, plus Medan in North Sumatra, as the central locations of the rattan industry.

Quite contrary to expectations, the attractiveness of Java is even greater under the recently adopted external-oriented strategy. Many advantages flow from locating on this most densely-populated island, compensating for the higher cost of transporting raw materials from outer islands. In addition, better port facilities and more developed infrastructures (software and hardware) appear to play crucial roles despite the fact that transportation costs for exports may be more expensive than if they originate in the outer islands.

The relative shipping costs have been recently affected by two events. The November 1988 deregulation, known as Paknov, was basically aimed at easing the flows of commodities to support the national programme of expanding exports of non-oil and gas. Among others, the new policy removes restriction on the use of foreign-owned shipping within the Indonesian territory and allows the national shipping company to determine the route to be serviced. The second event was the increase of fuel prices, which eventually raised costs of practically every mode of transportation. While flows of goods have indeed been increased, both interregionally and overseas, the process of concentration appears to have been reinforced. This is evident, for example, from the trend of exports by region (port of origin) shown in Figs. 7.1 and 7.2

[11] This is despite the fact that the concept of *Wilayah Pusat Pertumbuhan Industri* (regional centre of industrial growth) stemming from article 20, Law No. 5, 1984, is designed to optimize industrial location based on available resources and environmental considerations.

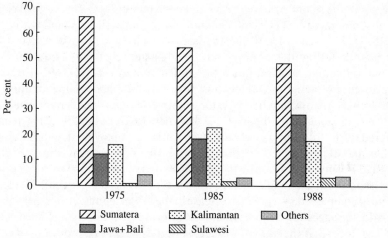

Fig. 7.1. Share of total exports by region, Indonesia, 1975–88

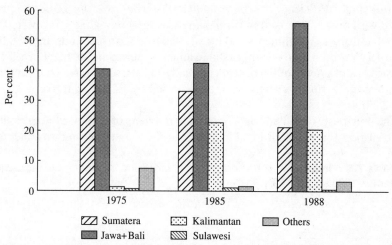

Fig. 7.2. Share of manufacturing exports by region, Indonesia, 1975–88

The recent surge of non-oil and gas exports has been mostly (70 per cent) originated in manufactured products. During the period of deregulation (1985–8) by regional composition Java and Bali are practically dominating the increase (Fig. 7.2). As a result, a similar regional composition of total non-oil and gas is observed (Fig. 7.1).

The increasing concentration in Java–Bali is also evident from the trend of regional 'revealed comparative advantage' (RCA). Many commodities originally directly exported from the outer islands are now exported from Java. Quite a substantial number of them required further processing and many of the processing industries are located in Java. A few examples can be cited. Increasing level of RCA in Java–Bali being accompanied by declining RCA in the outer islands is noticeable in the following cases: cows and oxen hides (SITC 211110), collection and collection pieces (SITC 8960590) and imitation jewellery plated with other metal (SITC 8972900). Meanwhile, the case in which decreasing RCA level in the outer islands followed by completely new existence of export activities in Java–Bali is found in reservoir tanks and similar containers (SITC 692110).

The absence of an industrial location policy has also had an impact upon the urban–rural configuration. By 1981, for example, about 47 per cent of establishments were in the urban category, a marked increase from the preceding years.[12] Measured by the total number of employed workers, employment in the large and medium manufacturing enterprises increased by 6.9 per cent annually from 1978–81. The annual rate of growth in urban manufacturing appears to have been greater than in rural manufacturing, 7.5 per cent versus 6.2 per cent. The trend was also accompanied by a greater increase in the urban manufactures' per-labour value-added, suggesting a more significant improvement in urban efficiency (see Table 7.8). Indeed, if the ratio of input to output is taken as a proxy for an efficiency measure, improved efficiency in the urban areas was more prevalent than in the rural areas. Efficiency in urban manufacturing improved by 5.6 per cent compared with only 3.2 per cent in rural manufactures. During the same period new manufacturing establishments had mostly chosen urban locations. In 1978 there were 4,196 rural manufacturing establishments, increasing to 4,239 in 1981, an average rate of growth of 0.3 per cent annually. For the same period the number of urban manufacturing establishments increased by 1.2 per cent, from 3,574 to 3,702 units.

The previously cited pattern of growth in numbers of employed workers leads us to suspect that the additional labour in urban manufacturing was due to the

Table 7.8.   Indonesia: some indicators of large and medium manufacturing sector, 1978 and 1981 (by year)

	1978		1981	
	Rural	Urban	Rural	Urban
Number of establishments (units)	4,196	3,574	4,239	3,702
Labour (persons)	435,047	388,535	521,376	483,333
Wage/labour (Rp. 00,000)	3.17	5.20	5.88	8.69
Value-added/Labour (Rp. 000)	1,334.74	1,707.86	2,678.33	3,858.72
Labour per establishment (persons) = L/E	103.68	108.71	123.00	130.56
Input per unit of output	0.65	0.75	0.59	0.63

Source: Processed from data tapes on industrial surveys, 1978 and 1981.

[12] The term urban refers to *kotamadya* (municipalities) and *kota administratip* (administrative towns) outside *kotadadya*. Changing definitions of urban–rural during the period of observation may affect the analysis, but the observed trends are likely to persist. Furthermore, the coverage of industrial surveys has only recently improved, affecting data from 1986 onward. Actually, retrospective figures have been generated but their accuracy is still in question. Therefore, industrial data for 1978 and 1981 used in this study are those of non-retrospective series.

greater number of new manufacturing establishments, but this turns out not to be the case. Measured by the number of workers per establishment, hereafter L/E, the growth rate in urban manufacturing reached 6.3 per cent annually while in the rural areas it was only 5.9 per cent. Between 1978 and 1981 no fewer than eight provinces experienced a decline in their rural manufactures' L/E while only four provinces had a decline in their urban manufactures' L/E (Table 7.8). It is also important to note that the L/E in urban manufacturing has always been higher than in rural establishments. At any rate, the greater attractiveness of urban manufactures in comparison to the rural industrial sector is clearly observed. Such a trend could reinforce inflows of migrants, permanent as well as temporary, to urban areas.

Based on the rural–urban classification of large and medium industrial establishments, faster growth of employment in urban areas was supported by higher wage rates. In urban areas the rate was between 1.5 and 1.6 times higher than in rural areas. Thus there was an indication that the restoration of equilibrium in the labour market had been prevented, among other things, by the inflexibility of wage rates in urban manufacturing.

The explanation for wage rigidity in the modern manufacturing sector usually centres around at least three possibilities. First is the workers' resistance to wage cuts *vis-à-vis* a greater preference for firings and layoffs, especially in the absence of their ability to detect whether a firm is accurately representing the demand for its products. The second possibility pertains to impediments to lowering wages. Finally, there is also a possibility that, fearing an efficiency reduction in its workforce, a firm's management would resist wage cuts.[13] In order to better evaluate the extent of these possibilities for Indonesia, further examination is needed, preferably at the firm level, with a rural-urban distinction. Such an approach is crucial in order to avoid erroneous conclusions arising from using aggregate data concerning the role of wages in labour-market adjustment.

The discussion above is aimed at demonstrating the link between patterns of industrial location and the analysis of inter-sectoral labour movements (or, in our case rural-urban manufacturing by province), particularly in the absence of actual data on labour movements. It has been shown that the growth patterns in the large and medium manufacturing sector during the late 1970s and early 1980s tend to support further inflows of migrants to urban areas.

Concluding Remarks

Although many discussions on development patterns in less-developed countries put the emphasis on the growth of the urban formal sector and formal farm activities, the increasing contribution of the non-formal sector suggests that neglecting that sector is likely to distort the overall analysis. During the oil-boom period of

---

[13] A discussion on these possibilities can be found in Levy and Newman 1989, among others.

the 1970s, the urban formal sector in Indonesia grew substantially. Employment absorption was high but at the same time the urban population grew rapidly due to migration, especially in Java. The size of the urban non-formal sector has consequently shot up, leading to expanding urban non-formal employment, with its corresponding socio-economic repercussions. Such a trend has forced the government to design a series of policies to cope with the problem. Without a good understanding of labour movements between sectors and forms of organization, particularly those pertinent to the non-formal sectors (rural farms, rural non-farms, and urban), policies will probably fail to work effectively. It is along this line of argument that the study is carried out.

Although the emphasis is on the increasing role of the urban non-formal sector, more generally the study represents an attempt to elucidate the factors affecting urban migration, particularly that of the interprovincial category. By using a multisectoral framework, Susenas 1982 data are shown to be capable of supporting useful analysis regarding changes in the relative position of each sector in terms of real earnings and employment. It is revealed from the regression analysis that (formal) employment opportunities appear to play much stronger roles than real earnings in the analysis of interprovincial urban migration. Only when migrants fail to enter the urban formal sector will real earnings in the non-formal sector matter.

The geographical patterns of industrial location also have the potential to reinforce further urbanward migration. Higher average wage rates together with improved efficiency in large- and medium-sized urban manufacturing enterprises increase the attractiveness of urban areas. This is obviously true if we refer to the industrial survey data of 1978–81. In the absence of a clear and concrete industrial location policy, new establishments have mostly chosen urban locations, particularly in Java. It is therefore often suggested that rural industrialization would help reduce the urbanward migration trend.

Data incompatibility is perhaps the most serious obstacle to making the time-series analysis. Although some refinements have been made, only rough conclusions may be drawn. Despite some suspicions about data showing a drastic increase in rural wages per employee, the expansion in numbers of employees in the urban non-formal sector appears to be substantial. The trend also features a fast-increasing ratio of relative wages per employee. In the midst of intensified economic reforms, in which the elasticity of substitution favouring the use of non-labour inputs tends to be greater (through the removal of rigidities in import activities), such a finding raises some doubts. It may be that those of the non-fixed-income group, including the urban non-formal sector, are in a more favoured condition during and after the reforms. But given the data incompatibility, any conclusions on this issue would be decidedly premature.

A quantitative approach using a simultaneous econometric model has been developed by the author. The model basically attempts to relate the central–regional transfer of government funds known as Inpres with the trend of urban migration. The results so far indicate that the strong relation between the two appears to be transmitted through regional incremental capital stock and infra-structures induced by the transfer. It is therefore not too surprising that the more urban-biased transfer generating further infrastructure development in urban areas would eventually induce greater urban migration. The model is capable of showing such a conclusion.

In the light of the premise that urban migration is a phenomenon not independent of the overall economic policy, a model of this kind would be necessary to enrich and enhance a more comprehensive analysis of urban migration, hence of the urban non-formal sector.

8 The Indonesian National Urban Development Strategy and its Relation to Policy and Planning

PETER GARDINER

Introduction

Concepts and approaches to strategic planning are now fairly well entrenched in the literature, although only a few fully national planning exercises have actually been carried out specifically for urban development. Egypt and Pakistan are perhaps the best examples of major studies predating the work in Indonesia discussed in this chapter. Nevertheless, more integrated planning has increasingly been seen by administrators as a means of dealing with such problems as increasing urban–rural disparity, escalating development costs connected with congestion and environmental degradation in primate cities, and distortions in regional development caused by imbalances in the functional and economic linkages between cities, and between these cities and their rural hinterlands.

This chapter deals with the National Urban Development Strategy (NUDS) prepared for Indonesia and issued in 1985. It attempts to focus on the relation of this strategy to the policy-making and planning process as it is actually carried out in Indonesia. An initial discussion of how NUDS dealt with various urban development issues confronting Indonesia emphasizes issues related to levels and spatial patterns of urban growth. This is followed by an examination of the relation of these outputs to the policy and planning process, in effect to try to understand some of the administrative and structural constraints affecting the acceptability of the proposed strategy, Finally, there is a limited discussion of the spatial implications of selected national level policies, partly to indicate their spatial importance, but also to point out some of the difficulties of integrating concepts of efficiency (reflected in overall economic growth) and equity (reflected in spatial balance in implementation) within the context of Indonesian development planning.

Urbanization—The Perceived Need for a National Strategy

Rapid urban growth and, perhaps more important, the emergence of large, relatively complex, metropolitan areas, has been a relatively recent phenomenon in

Indonesia. During the colonial period, the difficulties of regional integration and interregional communication, coupled with direct policies aimed at decentralizing political control and at stifling the development of an urban industrial base, served both to limit the growth of urban areas generally and to prevent the emergence of any one centre into a position of national primacy (Milone 1966; Hugo 1978).

By the end of the first third of the twentieth century less than 7 per cent of the population lived in designated urban areas (either areas with formal municipal status or towns without such status but treated as urban in the 1930 census). The largest city, Jakarta, contained barely 500,000 people and there were some six other centres of 100,000 inhabitants or more, including the pre-colonial court centres of Jogjakarta, Surakarta, and Palembang, the major Javan port cities of Surabaya and Semarang, and the major administrative and regional service centre of Bandung. Two other major port cities, Medan in Sumatra and Ujung Pandang in Sulawesi, were also rapidly approaching the 100,000 mark. The remainder of the urban population was scattered among a large number of smaller trade and administrative centres, seldom exceeding a population of 30,000, many of which, particularly on Java, served mainly as collection and shipping points for the primary agricultural commodities that formed the heart of the colonial economy (Milone 1966).

Following independence, however, the situation changed. The political turmoil both during the independence struggle and in the years following, along with attempts to consolidate a national and regional bureaucracy, led to more rapid urban growth and, in particular, spurred the growth of a few of the larger urban centres. Over the roughly 30-year period between the censuses of 1930 and 1961 Jakarta grew from roughly 500,000 to nearly 3 million people and Surabaya and Bandung had either passed or were approaching the 1 million mark by 1961 (Table 8.1).

Urban growth slowed somewhat during the 1960s and then apparently picked up dramatically during the 1970s (Table 8.1). This upsurge, however, was largely explained by a major change in the urban definition between the 1971 and 1980 censuses (BPS 1979) which resulted in the reclassification of a considerable number of areas from rural to urban status. Taking this into account led a number of analysts to revise the 1971–80 estimate of the urban growth rate downward to around 3.8–4.0 per cent (World Bank 1983; NUDS 1985a), much closer to that observed during the 1960s. On the other hand, the recorded urban growth rate and the continuing rise in the absolute size, if not the overall primacy, of the capital city, Jakarta, did achieve a purpose in raising the consciousness of administrators and planners of the scope of urbanization and urban growth in Indonesia and the need for a more comprehensive and integrated approach to solving basic urban-development problems.

The urban definition, however, has not changed since 1980 and, thus, the results of the 1985 intercensal population survey (BPS 1987) are of particular interest, as they indicate a substantial upswing in the urban growth rate, and particularly,

Table 8.1.   Selected indicators of urban growth in Indonesia, 1930–85

Indicator	1930	1961	1971	1980	1985
Urban population (000)	4,034	14,358	20,465	32,846	43,030
Urban-rural population ratio	0.081	0.174	0.207	0.288	0.356
Urban population growth rate (%)		4.18	3.61	5.17	5.40
Four-city primacy index	0.73	1.17	1.34	1.34	
Population in cities of 1 million + in 1980					
Jakarta	533,000	2,973,000	4,579,000	6,503,000	
Surabaya	342,000	1,008,000	1,556,000	2,028,000	
Bandung	167,000	973,000	1,200,000	146,000	
Medan	77,000	479,000	636,000	1,379,000	
Semarang	218,000	503,000	647,000	1,027,000	

Sources: ESCAP, 1981; BPS, 1983; BPS, 1987.

given declines in fertility, in the component of urban growth represented by net in-migration from rural areas. If these data are to be believed, for perhaps the first time in history, in-migration is contributing a higher proportion to urban growth than natural increase.[1]

Concern with overall urban growth, however, is not the only factor in this equation. The geographic and cultural diversity of the country has underscored a long-standing concern with national integration as a basis not only for development, but also for achieving political stability throughout the archipelago. Achievement of national integration, at least since the start of the New Order Government in the late 1960s, has been broadly codified in terms of a policy of 'balanced development', not only between major regions, but also, and increasingly during the 1970s, between rural and urban areas within regions and between different size classes of cities and towns. Balanced development, in turn, has been further quantified into a 'development trilogy' encompassing principles of equitable distribution of development, economic growth, and political stability. These have served as underlying principles in Indonesian development planning over the last 20 years.

During the 1970s, and borrowing heavily from European planning traditions of the 1930s and 1940s, a series of attempts were made to create various spatial planning frameworks for the country, largely defined in terms of hierarchical structures of national, regional, and local plans, and including the specification of urban systems, with individual cities and towns defined in terms of functional

[1] For the 1960s and early 1970s it is estimated that natural increase accounted for some 65 to 70% of urban population growth (ESCAP 1981: 72–4).

order within them. Unfortunately, these specifications were more often idealistic than realistic and thus provided a weak base on which to design operational programmes regarding investment in various forms of infrastructure. There also remained a high degree of confusion (a result of the limited knowledge base) over the real dynamics of urban development both within and between regions, and the linkages of these dynamics to the formulation of appropriate urban policy and to urban-development programming.

The National Urban Development Strategy: An Overview of the Basic Objectives and Approach

Basic objectives

The National Urban Development Strategy (NUDS), implemented between 1983 and 1985, was designed to address a number of these concerns. Broadly stated, the overall goal was:

To obtain a more balanced [urban] development through a more appropriate and equitable allocation of development resources to meet better spatial distribution of population in line with comprehensive objectives of the Guidelines of State Policy (GBHN) by assisting and strengthening the institutions charged with development policies (NUDS 1985b: 3).

There were a number of principles guiding formulation of the strategy which, in and of themselves, were laudable, but which in the end, helped contribute to difficulties in actually 'selling' the results to policy-makers, administrators and planners. As stated in the final report (NUDS 1985b), these included the following ideas:

1. The strategy should be designed to facilitate the achievement of established national development goals and policies, offering guidelines for their implementation.

2. The strategy should delineate the process by which change is to be achieved, not only the ends toward which it is directed—the strategy must be action-oriented.

3. The strategy should be demonstrably feasible in the light of financial and administrative constraints.

4. The strategy should recognize that the people themselves are to play the primary role in building the nation's cities. Government's role is to provide incentives that will encourage equitable and efficient development patterns and to assure that basic levels of services are provided for lower-income groups.

5. The strategy should be based on a realistic assessment of national social and economic prospects.

6. The strategy for urban areas should be based on an assessment of prospects and policies for regional development, including the development of rural areas.

7. The strategy should consider the full range of government policies that influence spatial development, including national macro-sectoral policies, national direct spatial policies, and regional and local development policies.

8. The application of the strategy's recommendations should differ for different types of policies. Those affecting national macro-sectoral and spatial policies should be intended for direct implementation. Those affecting regional and local development policies should be 'indicative'—to be used as a basis for central government guidelines to, support for, and monitoring of planning and implementing actions at lower levels of government.

9. The strategy should be designed to allow for recurrent updates and revisions in the future since conditions will inevitably vary from current expectations.

The approach

The basic methodological approach incorporated the creation of a series of urban development scenarios involving the projection of the regional (province-level) distribution of urban population based on a variety of assumptions regarding the nature and spatial pattern of economic activity. Past patterns of interregional migration were considered and the projections were linked specifically to the one quantifiable direct spatial programme; that for 'transmigration' of families from the more densely populated inner islands of Java, Madura, Bali, and Lombok to less densely populated rural areas elsewhere (see Hardjono 1978; Arndt 1983; and references cited therein).

Parallel work was carried out to define the functional role of individual cities both within their respective regions and in terms of broader national and international linkages, and including attempts to assess physical and economic conditions likely to support or constrain future growth. These were then combined to produce city-specific projections for some 500 urban areas which were, in turn, used as a basis for assessing likely policy implications, with specific attention being paid to the implied costs of inter- and intra-city physical infrastructure development and to the affordability of various sets of development targets in terms of likely levels of the national resource pool.

A 'preferred' scenario was selected, and this was then used as a basis for what might be considered as the strategy itself; the classification of cities by future functional potential and appropriate 'public-action' categories, the establishment of priorities for programme action at the province level, the estimation of specific city-level infrastructure requirements, and recommendations on institutional and financial changes required to support implementation.

Although the objectives and methodology may seem logical in this abbreviated description, in practice it was not easy to build convincing arguments linking various stages in the strategy-building process. Thus, the rather abstract and seemingly arbitrary nature of some of the outputs created their own difficulties in consensus building. This was particularly the case where these outputs posited a different way of looking at things than had been used in the past. For example, the categorization of cities proposed by NUDS led to quite different interpretations on the role and position of some medium- and smaller-sized urban areas than the more rigidly hierarchical 'City Order' system used in regional plans implemented through the Urban and Regional Planning Directorate of the Department of Public Works in the late 1970s and early 1980s. It was not easy to convince planners that these new views had more validity than the old.

More broadly, however, it can be suggested that the very comprehensiveness of the exercise required to meet the objectives outlined in the first part of this section may have been an even greater obstacle to consensus building. In this sense, irrespective of the radicalness of particular outputs, by giving the major emphasis to attempts to effectively link processes and outcomes related to urban development, it in fact made it more difficult to translate the strategy into terms understandable to administrators dealing with specific sectors or to planners who had to cope with the practical day-to-day issues involved in processes of regional or local change. Moreover, keeping the overall presentation to manageable length also meant that some of the analysis (particularly in the potentially contentious discussion of economic trends underlying patterns of spatial change) was superficial and failed to provide convincing arguments that NUDS had the most believable vision of the urban future. In some respects, this problem of superficiality applied to a number of the policy and programme recommendations as well.

This leads us to the question (one which was, in fact, raised at the end of the project) of whether it is even useful to contemplate a comprehensive strategy in an area such as this, as opposed to more restrictive (and more detailed) studies at the sectoral level. While the latter would obviously be less 'integrated,' in the sense of trying to tie together a rather complex range of processes and outcomes, they would likely be better able to express development objectives and targets in terms more readily interpretable to administrators and planners. On the other hand, there may well be longer-term impacts of the more comprehensive approach which are not yet sufficiently recognized. Even with its weaknesses, one must also consider the potential role of such an exercise in adjusting the views of planners as to the basic nature of urban development and in stimulating further work that will, over the long term, result in practical improvements in physical planning and management of urban growth and change. Nevertheless, the question of the ultimate utility of a NUDS-type exercise remains a real one. Later in the chapter we will return to some other aspects of this issue as they relate more specifically to a NUDS vision of the urban future, and, as they relate to the structure and politics of policy formulation and planning processes in Indonesia.

A New View of Urban Growth Patterns in the 1970s

It is worth noting, however, that some of the NUDS outputs did achieve a degree of visibility, if not full acceptance, among policy-makers and planners. One of these was the analysis carried out under the project of urban-growth patterns during the 1970s at the city level. Before the change in the urban definition used in the 1980 census, only designated 'administrative' urban areas could be specifically identified.[2] Even with the 1980 data, considerable work had to be done to group the units (villages) used by the Central Statistical Office as the building blocks of urban areas[3] into composite or aggregated functional urban areas, as the census itself did not include any attempt to build any data files or tabulations according to size of place. NUDS used the base information from the census to build a framework of 'Functional Urban Areas'. An attempt was also made to 'reverse project' these areas to 1971 using data on intercensal growth patterns in the lowest-level administrative units (*kecamatan*) for which relatively consistent population information was available from both the 1971 and 1980 censuses.

Based on this work, estimates of urban growth rates and the share of growth over the 1971–80 period broken down by region and city-size class are shown in Table 8.2. Estimates of the numbers of urban areas with a population of over 10,000 in 1971 and 1980, and total urban populations in 1980, classified in the same manner, are shown in Table 8.A1 at the end of this chapter.

Examination of these data, in fact, suggested a relatively balanced pattern of urban growth among different size classes of urban areas and throughout most parts of the country. There were some concerns related to relatively slow growth of small urban centres (below 50,000 inhabitants) and the weakness of urban systems (development of regional primacy) in some of the outer island regions. However, it did support the NUDS policy recommendation that urban programmes focus primarily on strengthening the existing urban areas rather than trying to push for new growth poles, even in more isolated parts of the country.

On the other hand, it can be argued that these data, and, more specifically, the rather superficial way in which they were dealt with in the NUDS final report, also obscured some legitimate questions about the suitability of this representation, even for the 1970s. Thus, even though the data indicate relatively balanced growth among different size classes of cities down to those with a population of about 50,000, this can be shown to be a result of a number of different forces, not all of which are indicative of either a general strengthening of national or regional urban systems or necessarily of sustainable growth processes at the individual city level. Broadly, these included:

1. Rapid growth of a number of smaller and medium-sized urban areas located on the fringes of major metropolitan centres. This was particularly true of urban areas surrounding the two major centres of Jakarta and Surabaya, both of which have become increasingly pre-eminent as general development nuclei and

---

[2] Purely urban administrative areas are called *kotamadya*; areas which are primarily rural administrative, but which also often contain some urban population, are called *kabupaten*.

[3] The criteria for classifying a village as urban were:

1. a population density of 5,000 persons per km[2] or above;
2. 25% or fewer agricultural households;
3. eight or more types of urban facilities.

Localities were assigned a score for each of these criteria, and the total score determined whether it should be defined as an urban village or a rural village.

Table 8.2. Urban growth rates and shares of urban growth over the 1971–80 period classified by region and city size class

City size class	Total	Sumatra	Java	Bali/ Nusa Tenggara	Kali- mantan	Sula- wesi	Maluku/ Irian
Urban growth rate (percentage)							
1 million & over	4.2	4.0	4.2				
500,000–1 million	4.3	4.6	4.0			4.7	
200,000–500,000	4.4	7.0	3.4	3.5	5.5	4.1	
100,000–200,000	4.2	3.9	3.6	9.1	8.1		6.3
50,000–100,000	4.3	4.7	4.0	5.0	7.0	3.1	6.8
20,000–50,000	4.0	5.6	3.4	4.9	6.1	4.9	4.5
Other areas	2.9	4.2	2.2	3.2	5.5	3.3	4.4
Total	4.0	4.7	3.7	4.6	5.9	4.2	5.0
Share of urban growth (percentage)							
1 million & over	34	20	47				
500,000–1 million	11	14	9			42	
200,000–500,000	13	16	8	18	53	13	
100,000–200,000	10	8	9	28	16		34
50,000–100,000	10	12	9	16	9	6	20
20,000–50,000	12	15	10	15	7	24	25
Other areas	11	16	8	24	16	16	21
Total	100	100	100	100	100	100	100

Source: Calculated from data in NUDS 1985c.

as hubs of both international and interregional trade (a sub-category of this kind of 'spillover' urban development is the urban growth on the islands of Batam and Bintan, part of the 'growth triangle' linked to Singapore). The NUDS analysis suggested that urban centres in the immediate hinterland of Jakarta (within the so-called 'Jabotabek region') were among the fastest-growing in the nation during the 1970s with several growing at annual rates in excess of 7 per cent. This process, which available evidence suggests has been continuing at perhaps an even more rapid rate in the 1980s (see Firman 1992), really reflects the start of what can probably best be termed the creation of a 'major metropolitan region' involving a chain of primary and secondary centres linked by high-density transport corridors; with significant pockets of rural area in between, but with these more rural areas themselves being gradually transformed to a more urban, or at least suburban orientation.[4]

2. Continued growth of a number of traditional coastal trade centres, both on and outside Java. Growth of these centres, particularly along the north coast of Java, was enhanced by relatively strong transport links to the major metropolitan

[4] McGee (1984) talks about the creation of zones of intense rural–urban interaction. The Jakarta–Bandung corridor and the area between the cities of Surabaya and Malang are the major Indonesian examples.

hubs and thus, by an ability to funnel goods relatively cheaply to the centre. Growth of some of these types of centres, particularly outside Java, was further enhanced by specific industrial investment (Palembang) or by service-sector development in areas such as tourism (Denpasar). This kind of urban development would seem to further the principles of both equity and efficiency. However, as Douglass (1984) and others have indicated, in many areas this growth has not been accompanied by a strengthening of urban linkages within the regions supported by these coastal cities. Inland cities and towns, notably on Java, have tended to stagnate and, in a few cases, have even become net exporters of migrants to the larger urban centres.[5]

3. Extremely rapid growth of a number of industrial enclave centres built around primary resource-based export commodities. Balikpapan (oil) and Samarinda (timber) in East Kalimantan are prime examples, although a number of smaller urban centres such as Lhoksumawae, Tarakan, and Kisaran also experienced rapid growth, particularly during the latter part of the 1970s, due to the initiation of major industrial projects.

4. Particularly in more isolated (less densely populated) regions outside Java, but also in a few areas on Java, the rapid growth of regional administrative centres, particularly province capitals, largely due to the rapid expansion of the government bureaucracy during the mid- to late-1970s. In a number of outer-island province capitals, public-service employment is still by far the largest single sector, a situation reflecting government efforts to deconcentrate the central bureaucracy as a basis for establishing regional administrative control and for implementing various centrally mandated development programmes.[6] The effects of this type of development in terms of sustaining long-term growth are, however, limited and, in any case, have been effectively curtailed in more recent years by the drastic decline in public-sector hiring resulting from the oil crises of the mid-1980s.

In summary, these patterns suggest a bipolar set of conditions guiding urban growth, with overall development supporting an increasing concentration in the largest centres on Java, and with rapid growth elsewhere being guided largely by factors (non-renewable resources, bureaucratic expansion) which are not necessarily conducive to sustained growth in the longer term. NUDS recognized a number of these problems and specifically noted some of the imbalances in urban development within specific regions. Yet, as intimated above and following some of the criticisms earlier in this chapter, the final report was arguably somewhat sanguine about the significance of some of these trends and, in particular, failed in this writer's view adequately to take account of their implications for patterns of urban growth under the new economic conditions that are now facing the country in the 1990s. We will return to this concern in the penultimate section of

---

5 This is embodied in Douglass' (1984) description of a 'crescent' pattern of development of major island port cities supporting strong trade linkages, not with each other, but primarily with the major centres of Jakarta and Surabaya.
6 Although it should be noted that growth of the central bureaucracy in Jakarta was equally if not more rapid during this period.

this chapter, but merely wish to note here that this also may have tended to limit the effect of NUDS on potential users.

The Preferred Scenario: Patterns of Urban Growth to the Year 2000

A major output of NUDS was a series of 'policy-sensitive' scenarios of urban growth in Indonesia to the year 2000 and an accompanying strategy for urban development. Among others, this strategy tried to address what Richardson (1987) referred to as 'the classical goal-conflict problem [reflecting] the trade-off between efficiency and equity'. The assumption here is that of a dichotomy between the effects of spatial patterns of urban investments designed to maximize efficiency in terms of production and between those designed to maximize equity in terms of per-capita welfare indicators. The theoretical conclusion is that these objectives are often incompatible, although as both the NUDS strategy documents and Richardson (1987: 283–5) concluded, there were indications that such compatibility was possible in the Indonesian context.

This was partly based on the view that the policies of the 1970s had, in fact, although perhaps not intentionally, led to a relative balance in patterns of urban growth both regionally and among different size classes of cities. It was also based on the view that a combination of direct spatial policies—continued moderately strong transmigration in the order of perhaps 100,000 families per year—and appropriate indirect spatial policies including an emphasis on export-oriented agro-based industries and infrastructure enhancement outside Java (both of which were thought to be consistent with economic efficiency) would lead to a reasonably balanced pattern of growth in the future. The translation of this policy scenario into urban growth rates and shares of growth over the 1980–2000 period classified by region and city-size class is shown in Table 8.3. Estimates of the numbers of urban areas for 1980 and 2000 and total urban populations in 2000, classified in the same manner, are shown in Table 8.A2 at the end of this chapter.

By and large, the results do suggest a policy framework under which a reasonably balanced growth pattern might be achieved, although the proportion of population in the medium- and large-sized city category (500,000-plus) does increase significantly over the period, from about 43 to 53 per cent of the total (Table 8.A2). This trend towards some increases in concentration of the urban population at the upper end of the scale, however, was justified by NUDS in terms of the need to take advantage of agglomeration economies in promoting efficiency. At the same time equity considerations would be met by the relatively wide spatial distribution of the medium and large urban centres and, particularly, by focusing attention on centres located outside Java or at least outside the immediate sphere of the major metropolitan centres of Jakarta and Surabaya. Questions remain, however, on the suitability of this analysis, both in terms of its methodological ability to link policies to appropriate projections of spatial distribution of urban population change and in terms of its appropriateness to actual conditions.

Table 8.3.   Urban growth rates and shares of urban growth over the 1980–2000 period classified by region and city size class

City size class	Total	Sumatra	Java	Bali/ Nusa Tenggara	Kali- mantan	Sula- wesi	Maluku/ Irian
Urban growth rate (percentage)							
1 million & over	3.3	3.5	3.3				
500,000–1 million	4.5	4.2	4.5			5.0	
200,000–500,000	4.2	4.2	3.7	4.2	5.2	4.1	
100,000–200,000	4.7	3.8	4.6	5.2	6.4		5.5
50,000–100,000	4.8	4.4	4.8	5.0	5.9	4.6	6.3
20,000–50,000	4.5	5.2	3.8	5.0	7.3	6.0	5.9
Other areas	4.0	4.1	3.3	4.0	6.4	4.5	5.2
Total	4.1	4.2	3.8	4.5	5.8	5.0	5.5
Share of urban growth (percentage)							
1 million & over	25	18	35				
500,000–1 million	12	14	11			39	
200,000–500,000	12	12	9	20	48	9	
100,000–200,000	11	8	12	21	15		28
50,000–100,000	12	13	12	17	8	7	20
20,000–50,000	14	18	11	16	10	29	30
Other areas	14	17	10	26	19	16	22
Total	100	100	100	100	100	100	100

Source: Calculated from data in NUDS 1985c.

Unfortunately, the problems of linking macro-level policy to future spatial patterns of population growth are myriad. Not only is there uncertainty about the spatial impact of indirect economic policies which are largely developed on the basis of national level priorities or objectives, but there is also the methodological difficulty of translating regionally specific patterns of economic change into patterns of population growth and redistribution. Weaknesses in data (for example, estimates of labour elasticities) commonly used in making projections are well known in the Indonesian context. Moreover, the still limited understanding of the actual decision-making process influencing migration to urban areas (and the likelihood of a variety of such processes guiding different types of migration streams) add to the problem. As noted earlier, NUDS did make an attempt to translate policy into process and process into spatial outcomes in a logical way, but it should still be stressed that technical questions about the analytical strength of this translation was probably one of the major factors influencing the credibility of the overall strategy in the eyes of potential users.

The credibility has also been affected by the results of the 1985 Intercensal Population Survey (SUPAS) which became available only a few years after the strategy was completed. Not only was the overall level of urbanization much faster than that indicated by the NUDS projections, but the difference was particularly marked on Java where, if the data are to be believed, rural growth was extremely low, at least in comparison with the previous decade (Table 8.4). The implication of these results is massive pressure on the major urban centres on Java, and particularly the main metropolitan regions, that would have severe implications for efforts to improve the coverage and quality of various social and economic services. It also raises questions about the degree to which equity or balance considerations are being met, particularly with regard to areas outside Java where urban growth rates remained, in general, more comparable to levels observed during the 1970s.

In fairness, there are also questions about the credibility of SUPAS itself; for example, how well the regional totals account for reported flows of transmigrants during the early 1980s (Gardiner and Oey 1987), and how the high urban growth rates (which apparently did not include an allowance for changes in status of individual villages from urban to rural) can be reconciled with much lower growth estimates coming from specific urban development plans being prepared at the city level under the Integrated Urban Infrastructure Development Programme (IUIDP). Nevertheless, from a purely practical standpoint, such inconsistencies make it that much more difficult for planners to determine exactly what information to use as a basis for setting priorities and estimating requirements for basic urban services.

Perhaps a more salient point is that it is not at all clear that the patterns of urban development described above, including those for the 1980s, represent in any sense

Table 8.4. Urban and rural populations (in thousands) and growth rates 1980–5 by region

	Urban		Rural		Total	
	1980	1985	1980	1985	1980	1985
Total population						
Sumatra	5,481	7,116	22,515	25,488	27,996	32,604
Java	22,926	30,317	68,291	69,536	91,217	99,852
Kalimantan	1,441	1,847	5,275	5,875	6,717	7,722
Sulawesi	1,654	1,936	8,746	9,617	10,401	11,553
Other islands	1,342	1,814	9,104	10,502	10,446	12,316
Total	32,846	43,030	113,931	121,017	146,776	164,047
Growth rates (percentage)						
Sumatra	5.22		2.48		3.05	
Java	5.59		0.36		1.81	
Kalimantan	4.96		2.15		2.79	
Sulawesi	3.14		1.90		2.10	
Other islands	6.02		2.86		3.29	
Total	5.40		1.21		2.22	

Sources: ESCAP 1981, BPS 1983, BPS 1987.

a result of integrated policy. To put it another way, to assess the utility of the policies and actions proposed by NUDS, it is necessary to look at the relation of the strategy to the way policy formulation and planning is actually carried out in Indonesia. This is not a minor issue since it does, I feel, also help explain why NUDS, even if it had succeeded as an accurate integrated statement of appropriate policies and interventions, was, at least in part, doomed to failure because of its irrelevance to the way policy-making and planning is actually carried out.

NUDS and the Indonesian Policy and Planning Process

Formal planning in Indonesia remains highly centralized and is embodied in a medium-term (five-year) and annual planning process dealing primarily with establishing sectoral patterns of public expenditure. Much of the effort here has distinct spatial components, particularly in terms of the regional distribution of direct grants (SDO, Inpres)[7] and in the regional patterns of expenditure underlying the sectoral programmes of various central government departments. Overlaying this is a mechanism for economic-policy formulation concentrated in the Ministry of Finance and among a small group of 'technocrats' which is primarily geared to providing conditions necessary to maximize and sustain overall economic growth. Outside of location-specific decisions regarding investment (for example, in state enterprises) linked to this process, there is little effort to take spatial or regional issues into account.

To the degree that these policies influence growth, they also influence the level of revenues accruing to government. Historically, almost all of these revenues have accrued to the central government which then uses the basically sectoral-planning and budgeting process alluded to above to distribute them—in a manner based, at least in some cases, on stronger equity principles—back to the various regions. Through changes in macro-economic policy from import substitution to export-driven development (particularly exports of manufactured goods), the central government has continued to remain the main source of funds for what could be termed regional development programmes, particularly those related to the provision of social and economic infrastructure and services. While this may change in the future if policies to decentralize both development planning and responsibilities for resource generation are implemented, the prognosis is for very slow change in this direction given the strong vested interests and resistance to change built into the current centralized bureaucracy.

An essential problem facing NUDS in fitting into this structure was that, to put it bluntly, it was largely irrelevant to more global economic policy-makers who had generally been concerned with spatial issues only to the degree that they were necessary to support nationally defined objectives of economic efficiency and

---

[7] SDO (*Subsidi Daerah Otonom*) are grants to support routine expenditures (salaries, etc.). Inpres are general and sectoral grants to support development activities of local governments.

growth.[8] In this respect, national economic policy supersedes spatial policy, a situation recognized by NUDS in that the process of scenario building was, in large part, merely an attempt to capture the implications of such macro-level policies in spatial terms. On the one hand, NUDS' reliance on this policy framework as essentially exogenous input, rather than being able to use spatial implications to influence macro-level policy decisions, meant that as the policy framework itself changed, the picture regarding future spatial development provided by NUDS would become increasingly out of date. On the other hand, the basic independence of macro-policy from spatial contexts meant that there was, in fact, no vested interest in recognizing NUDS relevance, and hence no demand for updating the strategy in the face of change.

On the other side of the coin, the formal planning process is more strongly equity-driven and, as noted earlier, relates to the sectoral and, where relevant, regional distribution of central government resources. The process is built around the setting up of national sectoral targets or objectives which are, in turn, broken down where appropriate into regional targets to be met through various forms of central government grants or through various central sectoral department expenditure programmes. Because programmes are initially defined on a sectoral basis, little attempt is generally made to try to integrate programmes between sectors as part of this process.

NUDS actually attempted to establish a set of more or less integrated policy actions both for different types of cities at the national level and for different provinces. This framework involved the division of the roughly 500 urban centres covered by the strategy into four main groups—national development centres, interregional development centres, regional development centres and local service centres—with the national centres playing a stronger role in medium- and large-scale industrial development (to take advantage of agglomeration economies and a more diversified labour supply) and the other centres serving to support their respective hinterlands (rural development) as well as providing linkages to the national centres through a stronger overall urban system.[9]

While the province-level specifications might have proved useful in defining regional priorities under the planning framework described above, the list of priorities produced by NUDS was, in fact, simply too general to be readily adaptable to basically sectoral needs.[10] The policy and public-action framework for different city types, with type here reflecting both size and functional characteristics, could have had relevance in a macro-policy framework, but basically could not be

---

[8] I would put, for example, efforts to increase local government financial resource generation in this category as it is seen at the centre primarily as a means of relieving pressure on scarce central government resources.

[9] See the NUDS final report (NUDS 1985b) for a more detailed discussion of policies and actions related to these types of cities.

[10] NUDS did produce detailed programmes at the province level for investment in selected forms of urban infrastructure. The model, on which this work was based was, however, questioned (particularly in terms of the quality of baseline information used) and, in any case, this was superseded by the introduction of the Integrated Urban Infrastructure Development Programme (IUIDP) which is described in Chapter 9 below.

handled in the context of vertical sectoral programming. In fact, even if it had addressed sectoral issues more effectively, the lack of intersectoral co-ordination in overall planning would still have created problems for acceptance. Thus, the fact that NUDS was executed as a project under a single ministry, that of public works, was itself enough to make the results suspect in the eyes of other sectoral departments which, in fact, should have been influenced by the results.

The end result was a limited acceptance of the basic ideas presented by NUDS as reflecting a suitable pattern for future development, and acceptance of some of the specific outputs including some of the urban-area specific demographic projections, if only because NUDS remained the only source of such figures. Indirect effects of NUDS may have been more important, in the groundwork laid for the Integrated Urban Infrastructure Development Programme (IUIDP) and in the development of policies and actions defined for implementing large-scale World Bank and other multilateral and bilateral assistance in the urban sector.

Urban Size, Distribution—Some Implications of Policy

Macro-economic policy

The problem is that macro-policy, particularly macro-economic policy, does have strong spatial implications. In fact, it is likely that the indirect effects of such policies, through their effect on the scope and distribution of various forms of economic activity, are the most significant factors in determining patterns of spatial mobility and, hence, spatial patterns of growth, including that in and around urban areas. This is even more the case where, as in Indonesia, the great majority of urban infrastructure investment is reactive to problems and demands created by past urban growth, rather than playing much of a role in stimulating new centres of development.

In general, it appears that such policies in Indonesia have tended to favour the largest urban centres. There appears to be general agreement that import substitution policies of the 1970s ultimately favoured growth in areas where markets for various locally produced products were most developed, that is, in areas where the largest concentrations of population were to be found. It is also likely that the more recent shift to an emphasis on manufactured and other non-oil exports (a shift made in the face of declining oil revenues) as the new engine of growth, and the accompanying deregulation designed to stimulate the climate for private foreign and domestic investment, will continue to draw activity disproportionately towards these same types of areas. Although accurate population figures are not yet available—the 1985 SUPAS predates the major policy changes in this direction—the dominance of Jakarta, Surabaya, and their respective hinterlands in investment proposals processed through the National Investment Co-ordinating Board (BKPM) does provide some evidence of the possible extent of this bias. More detailed information from the next census which should become available in the early 1990s will provide a much firmer basis for assessing the impact of these developments.

Reasons for this bias in business location are dealt with in the NUDS documents and in a range of other reports. A primary concern is with issues related to economic efficiency, and particularly to non-wage costs of operation. These include external and internal transport and communication costs (for example, for imported inputs or for reaching international or domestic markets), greater availability of infrastructure and financial services,[11] and the nature of costs, in particular bureaucratic costs associated with land acquisition, which (even with deregulation) make it more efficient to locate near to the administrative centre. These problems are all amenable to solution, but they are inherently long-term and require major changes in central–local administrative and financial relations as well as in patterns of development expenditure at the regional level.

More relevant to this discussion, there may also be a degree of political conflict or tradeoff between perceived needs to meet short- to medium-term growth objectives (e.g. letting the spatial chips fall where they may), and objectives of promoting greater regional balance in development which may well have positive implications for efficiency, but probably only in the longer run. This is a slightly different way of phrasing the efficiency–equity conflict discussed by Richardson (1987) but is one that is perhaps more relevant to the Indonesian policy-making and planning process which is the focus of this discussion.

Transmigration

As has already been noted, there were also forces during the 1970s drawing people away from Java; the development of industries built up around the extraction and processing of petroleum and other primary resources, the expansion of regional public bureaucracy, and transmigration.

Transmigration started slowly during the 1970s, but, as noted earlier, reached a peak during the period from 1979 to 1984 when more than 1.5 million people were moved under the programme, a level equivalent to nearly one year's natural growth of the population on Java over this roughly five-year period. Although transmigration has been a rural development programme, primarily aimed at opening up land in the outer islands for food and cash-crop cultivation, it has still had some impact on urban growth both directly through the onward movement of 'failed' transmigrants to regional urban centres (at least those who did not return to Java), and indirectly through effects on development of urban trade and services to support the rapid overall growth of population in these areas.

Although direct information does not exist, some evidence of this process can be found in the maintenance of moderate, but significant, differences between urban and rural growth rates (in favour of the former) during the late 1970s and including provinces which were significant transmigrant-receiving areas but

[11] Until recently, foreign banks were exclusively limited to Jakarta and even private domestic bank operations were severely limited outside the major cities.

which were not, at the same time, significantly affected by resource-based industrial developments that would have independently affected urban growth. A
second indicator is the role played by off-site activity in transmigrant income. A
survey conducted in 1986 by the Central Bureau of Statistics found that nearly 50
per cent of transmigrant family income was derived from off-site activity, some of
which would likely have been obtained from wage or informal-sector activity in
surrounding urban areas. Furthermore, this survey did not cover households
which had quit sites entirely, some of which would also have moved on to urban
areas in the same region rather than returning to Java.

More important to this discussion, both the booms in public-sector job creation and in fully sponsored transmigration have now effectively ended with the
severe cutbacks in government funds resulting from the oil crisis in the mid-1980s.
The transmigration programme remains in existence, but with policies geared
more towards promotion of voluntary movement which will depend far more on
levels of private investment in the receiving areas than the earlier fully sponsored
programme. Thus, if the spatial implications suggested for current macro-
economic policy are true, it seems that there could be a worsening of interregional
balance (if not interregional equity) in terms of patterns of urban growth.

Conclusions

In summary, it is suggested that while NUDS tried (even though perhaps not in
the most convincing methodological way) to propose a strategy for urban
development that, at least to some degree, combined concepts of efficiency and
equity in the spatial pattern of urban growth and development, it failed in implementation partly because it was unable to prove sufficiently responsive to the
largely political motives inherent in the real-life policy-making and planning
process. This process, it is suggested, in fact operates largely independently of the
kind of strategic spatial planning framework outlined in the NUDS report. In
short, macro-economic policies are geared more towards achieving global
efficiency through the maximizing of economic growth and are devised largely
independently of spatial considerations. Spatial policies are largely concerned
with equity, involving the sectoral distribution of central government resources in
a reasonably equitable fashion among the different regions of the country.
Technical problems in building linkages between the two are myriad and may well
prove to be beyond the scope of a single project or study.

Even so, there is interest in a number of quarters in changing this and improving the quality of spatial analysis as an integral part of the national policy and
planning process. This will not be easy; among other problems, the understanding
of the precise nature of economic linkages (wage rates, types of job opportunities)
to likely directions and volumes of migration is still imperfect, and the data base,
particularly at the regional level, necessary to support decision-making on where
to place supporting investment, particularly in infrastructure, is notoriously

weak. However, it is likely that until such changes in the basic structure come about, it will be difficult to incorporate any kind of spatially-oriented, multi-sectoral strategy (in the sense envisioned by NUDS) effectively into the planning process.

Yet it may be too early to dismiss NUDS out of hand. The information and methodological base established by the project has already had some influence, most notably within the Department of Public Works, and could serve as a basis for future improvement. One should also reflect on the rather weak publication and dissemination record of the project. It could well be that in part it failed simply because the inherent difficulties in building consensus were inadequately recognized and that it might have ultimately had a more receptive audience had more attention been given to this critical area.

Table 8.A1.   Numbers of urban areas in 1971 and 1980, and total urban area population in 1980 classified by region and city size class

City size class	Total	Sumatra	Java	Bali/ Nusa Tenggara	Kali- mantan	Sula- wesi	Maluku/ Irian
Number of urban areas, 1971							
1 million & over	3	0	3	0	0	0	0
500,000–1 million	3	2	1	0	0	0	0
200,000–500,000	6	0	4	0	1	1	0
100,000–200,000	16	4	9	1	1	1	0
50,000–100,000	22	3	15	1	2	0	1
20,000–50,000	93	14	65	3	2	7	2
10,000–20,000	157	30	94	11	5	14	3
Total	300	53	191	16	11	23	6
Number of Urban Areas 1980							
1 million & over	4	1	3	0	0	0	0
500,000–1 million	5	1	3	0	0	1	0
200,000–500,000	13	2	6	1	3	1	0
100,000–200,000	20	3	14	1	1	0	1
50,000–100,000	43	10	26	2	2	2	1
20,000–50,000	127	23	81	5	3	11	4
10,000–20,000	172	32	106	11	8	13	2
Total	384	72	239	20	17	28	8
Urban area population, 1980							
1 million & over	10,868	1,265	9,603	0	0	0	0
500,000–1 million	3,330	758	1,934	0	0	639	0
200,000–500,000	3,938	654	2,041	211	815	217	0
100,000–200,000	3,015	515	2,047	159	183	0	112
50,000–100,000	2,956	643	1,878	138	110	126	61
20,000–50,000	3,925	700	2,535	137	95	352	106
10,000–20,000	2,480	482	1,529	159	113	172	26
Other areas	2,334	466	1,360	148	125	148	85
Total	32,846	5,482	22,927	952	1,441	1,654	390
(percentage)	(100)	(17)	(70)	(3)	(4)	(5)	(1)
Cities/million + population	2.6	2.6	2.6	2.5	2.5	2.6	3.1

Source: Calculated from data in NUDS 1985c.

Table 8.A2. Numbers of urban areas in 1980 and 2000, and total urban area population in 2000 classified by region and city size class

City size class	Total	Sumatra	Java	Bali/ Nusa Tenggara	Kali- mantan	Sula- wesi	Maluku/ Irian
Number of Urban Areas 1980							
1 million & over	4	1	3	0	0	0	0
500,000–1 million	5	1	3	0	0	1	0
200,000–500,000	13	2	6	1	3	1	0
100,000–200,000	20	3	14	1	1	0	1
50,000–100,000	43	10	26	2	2	2	1
20,000–50,000	127	23	81	5	3	11	4
10,000–20,000	172	32	106	11	8	13	2
Total	384	72	239	20	17	288	
Number of Urban Areas, 2000							
1 million & over	8	2	5	0	0	1	0
500,000–1 million	15	2	9	0	4	0	0
200,000–500,000	29	5	17	3	1	1	2
100,000–200,000	52	12	27	2	2	8	1
50,000–100,000	94	19	53	5	9	5	3
20,000–50,000	205	36	124	13	14	15	3
10,000–20,000	184	48	97	11	7	16	5
Total	590	124	332	34	37	46	4
Urban Area Population, 2000							
1 million & over	21,159	2,556	18,604	0	0	0	0
500,000–1 million	8,251	1,752	4,754	0	0	1,745	0
200,000–500,000	9,085	1,500	4,273	487	2,307	489	0
100,000–200,000	7,710	1,098	5,160	454	662	0	335
50,000–100,000	7,666	1,543	4,862	374	355	315	217
20,000–50,000	9,666	1,963	5,407	369	411	1,171	345
10,000–20,000	5,382	1,108	2,964	368	431	417	93
Other areas	5,251	1,057	2,625	309	415	379	188
Total	74,140	12,577	48,649	2,361	4,581	4,516	1,178
(Percent)	(100)	(17)	(66)	(3)	(6)	(6)	(2)
Cities/million population	2.8	2.4	2.9	3.2	2.8	2.9	2.9

Source: Calculated from data in NUDS 1985c.

9 Urban Housing and Infrastructure Provision and Financing in Indonesia

MUSTARAM KOSWARA

Introduction

According to the 1990 population census, by 1990 the urban population of Indonesia had already reached over 55 million persons. Projections made by the National Urban Development Strategy (NUDS) project suggest that by the turn of the century urban population could well reach 76 million persons, representing about 36 per cent of the projected total and an average increment of over 2 million persons annually over the 1980–2000 period (NUDS 1985). Relating this to total population growth under the same set of projections implies that close to two-thirds of all the population growth over this twenty-year period will accrue to urban areas.

Projections made for Pelita V (the fifth five-year development plan covering the period from April 1989 to March 1994) are equally dramatic. As shown in Table 9.1, they indicate a rise in urban population from about 51 to 62 million persons, accounting for well over half of the total projected growth of around 17 million persons over the five-year period.

This serves to emphasize the scope of the problems facing Indonesia related to the provision of adequate housing and infrastructure to the urban population.

Table 9.1. Projections of urban population for Pelita V

Year	Total population (millions)	Urban population (millions)	Percentage urban
1988	174.9	50.4	28.8
1989	178.4	52.6	29.5
1990	181.9	54.7	30.1
1991	185.4	56.7	30.6
1992	188.7	59.1	31.3
1993	192.1	61.3	31.9
1994	195.5	63.6	32.5

Source: Unpublished projections by Directorate of City and Regional Planning, Department of Public Works. Numbers refer to end of year and do not include the population of East Timor which would add about 600,000 persons to the total and 100,000 to the urban population.

Thus, while rural development has remained an important component of national policy-making and programming, the issues involved in merely trying to cope with the basic urban transformation that is now clearly underway has meant that increasing emphasis has had to be placed on improving housing and infrastructure provision in urban areas.

This chapter attempts to highlight some of the issues and answers, as perceived by the Indonesian authorities, surrounding urban housing and infrastructure provision and financing. It starts with a few brief observations on patterns of urban development and on baseline (start of Pelita V) conditions in order to further elucidate the nature and scope of the issues being faced. Programmes and accomplishments during Pelita IV (covering the period from April 1984 to March 1989) are also touched upon to provide a background for the discussion of current initiatives which forms the main focus of this chapter. These are discussed in the third and fourth sections which deal, respectively, with housing and infrastructure policies and with the provision and financing of urban housing and services. Aspects dealt with here include efforts to improve design, implementation, and management of housing and infrastructure programmes through decentralization of planning, decision-making, and financing to local governments; and efforts to increase the role of the private sector in running and financing urban services. Finally, some summary comments are made in a concluding section which highlights the progress so far achieved and some of the problems remaining to be faced.

Development Patterns and Baseline Conditions

Historical patterns of urban growth in Indonesia have posed particular problems for housing and infrastructure development. Particularly on Java, which has long been characterized by relatively high rural-population density, urban areas have tended to develop through a process of agglomeration of existing rural settlements. These scattered settlements have become tied together through their own natural growth, and through in-migration which has often led to the spontaneous formation of new communities on areas of vacant land. The result, particularly in the larger cities, is an urban area made up of a number of largely ethnically distinct settlement areas (called *kampung*) interspersed with ribbons and pockets of planned development, including businesses, public facilities, and formal-sector housing. *Kampung* are estimated to cover more than 60 per cent of the built-up urban area in Indonesia and to account for up to 70 per cent of the urban population.

These urban *kampung*, characterized by high density and generally populated by lower-income groups, have long faced deficiencies in service provision. For example, as of 1985 roughly half of urban residents did not have direct access to clean water and almost 60 per cent lacked access to appropriate sanitary facilities (private or public toilet equipped with septic tanks). All in all, it was estimated that 73 per cent of urban residents did not enjoy a 'basic needs' standard of service provision and fully 15 per cent were classified as living below the poverty line (Directorate of Housing 1989). The statistics refer to the total urban population, but conditions in urban *kampung* would be even worse. The obvious conclusion is that, future needs aside, there is still a considerable backlog of housing and service deficiency in terms of the existing population in many, if not most, urban areas. Given this backlog, the additional housing and urban infrastructure needs arising from the projected rapid growth of urban populations are quite daunting.

Faced with these challenges, a variety of programmes and bureaucratic structures have been created to deal with provision of housing and infrastructure, all guided by the basic philosophy of improving the quantity and quality of urban service provision, particularly for the low- and middle-income groups living in urban areas. A few of these efforts are briefly described below.

Urban housing

Urban growth figures shown earlier emphasize the scope of demand for new housing in urban areas, which now exceeds 300,000 units per year. Only a small proportion of housing is provided by the formal sector (through the National Housing Development Corporation (*Perum Perumnas*) or private developers). The remainder is provided by the people themselves. This includes some informal housing development of medium to high standard, but, as might be expected, much of this housing is substandard, often of only a 'temporary' or 'semi-permanent' nature.[1] This is particularly true for families with limited financial resources who are estimated to account for up to 70 per cent of total demand (Asian Development Bank 1983).

In general, it is considered that the level of overall investment in housing (from both public and private sources) is still below levels required to meet the demands of the growing population, much less to meet the needs for substantial upgrading of existing stocks which is a recognized concern in many of the larger urban centres. Estimates indicate that only about 3 per cent of Gross Domestic Product (GDP) represents activities in residential construction. Yet, even excluding much of the upgrading required for existing stock, it has been suggested that a level of closer to 5 per cent would actually be required if all new construction were to be carried out at acceptable levels of quality (Asian Development Bank 1983).

A number of programmes have been developed in Indonesia to help meet needs for improved housing in both urban and rural areas, and aimed particularly at low-to middle-income groups in the population. These include efforts to support so-called 'formal sector' housing provision through *Perum Perumnas* and private developers, and the national programme to upgrade general living conditions in existing *kampung*, known as the Kampung Improvement Programme or KIP.

---

[1] Censuses and surveys in Indonesia classify housing as temporary, semi-permanent, or permanent based on types of construction materials used.

Housing provision by *Perumnas* and the private sector

The National Housing Development Corporation (*Perum Perumnas*) which was established in 1974 is responsible for implementing a centrally directed programme to provide housing for low- and middle-income households. As a government developer, it acts as a corporation as well as an agent for non-profit development. Thus, it builds houses not only in areas where private developers are active, but also in areas that developers do not find attractive. It also acts as the government's arm for stabilizing house and land prices in certain areas, as an agent for pioneer development of new housing options, including construction of flats, urban land consolidation, and rental housing, and as a partner of the private sector through encouragement of private efforts in particular areas in order to increase the quantity and quality of housing development.

Low-cost housing is produced to standard designs with floor areas of, for example, 15, 18, and 21 m^2 for low-income families and 45, 54, and 70 m^2 for middle-income families. Mortgage financing is organized through the State Savings Bank (*Bank Tabungan Negara* or BTN).

BTN is authorized by the government to channel funds to low- and middle-income households through a variety of housing credit schemes. BTN utilizes internally generated funds as well as money derived from Government, Bank Indonesia (the central bank), and World Bank loans. BTN is also starting to play a role in efforts to develop 'new' towns (satellite communities around major metropolitan areas) through provision of a range of credit products.

Since the mid-1970s, annual production of housing by *Perumnas* itself has averaged around 16,000 units. 70,000 units were produced during Pelita II (April 1974–March 1979), 81,000 units during Pelita III (April 1979–March 1984) and 87,000 during Pelita IV, with the latter figure including some 5,300 units of four-storey walk-up flats. Particularly in recent years, these figures have been enhanced by the provision of *Perumnas*-type housing by private developers who are required to construct low- and middle-income housing units in proportion to their total housing output. Even with these efforts, as shown in Table 9.2, formal-sector housing provision (including provision of luxury housing by private developers) still accounts for only about 20 per cent of total demand.

Table 9.2. Housing provision by *Perumnas* and the private sector during Pelita IV

Period	*Perumnas* (units)	Private sector (units)	Total (units)
1984/5	10,516	36,804	47,320
1985/6	15,072	54,421	69,593
1986/7	12,866	21,066	33,932
1987/8	21,865	56,486	78,351
1988/9	26,681	64,923	91,604
Total	87,000	233,700	320,800

Source: Government of Indonesia 1988.

As indicated in Table 9.2, during Pelita IV over 70 per cent of formal-sector housing provision came from private developers. Particularly in the major cities, medium- and large-scale developers and contractors have shown increasing capability to finance and implement relatively large-scale housing projects. Perhaps the most striking example of the role of private developers can be seen in efforts to develop the new satellite city of Serpong on the outskirts of the capital city of Jakarta. This development, being implemented by a consortium of private developers in co-operation with the government, covers some 6,000 hectares of land and upon completion, early in the next century, will provide a place of residence for some 600,000 people.

This approach to housing provision faces numerous constraints, particularly in its ability to reach lower-income groups. Perhaps the most intractable problems have to do with land acquisition and with the rising cost of urban land. In the first place, acquisition of sufficiently large blocks of suitable vacant land within or in the immediate environs of urban centres is often difficult. Even more important, urban land prices have risen rapidly, a result of increasing demand and land speculation, often precisely in those areas slated, or most suitable, for residential development. The ability of government to move quickly enough to acquire blocks of suitable land in advance of such speculation has, in practice, been limited. Among other things this has affected the ability of government to implement some of the lower-cost options to formal-housing provision (e.g. guided land development, and land consolidation[2]) which generally require fairly large contiguous blocks of land, but which also, at least in theory, would be more amenable to accommodation of existing residents and of the poor.

Another result of escalating land values (when taken in conjunction with costs of actual construction) has been effectively to price this type of housing beyond the reach of the poorest households (lowest 20 per cent in terms of income). BTN financing restrictions, at least in the past, have also tended to limit recipients of *Perumnas*-type housing loans to families with regular sources of income (e.g. employees). It is not surprising that, in many areas, public servants have been major beneficiaries of this scheme.

The Kampung Improvement Programme

The Kampung Improvement Programme (KIP) represents the cornerstone of efforts to reach the urban poor. KIP is designed to improve the living environment in existing densely settled urban *kampung* through the improvement of basic access (footpaths, and in some cases, roads), drainage and flood control, and

---

[2] Guided land development (GLD) involves public-sector acquisition, integrated planning and basic infrastructure provision on relatively large tracts of vacant or sparsely settled land. Land is segmented for different types of more intensive (private-sector) development and costs are largely recovered through rises in land values. Land consolidation is specifically aimed at minimizing problems of land acquisition. Existing residents give their land which is then developed. Sites in the developed area are then returned to the original owners with the idea that losses (in terms of area) will be more than made up for by increases in land values resulting from the development itself.

low-cost (community) water supply and sanitation services (e.g. standpipes and community bathing, washing and toilet facilities known as '*mandi, cuci, kakus*', or MCK). Community groups are formed and training is also provided on the operation and maintenance of these facilities and services. KIP was effectively born with pilot efforts carried out in the early 1970s under the *Mohammed Husni Thamrin* programme in Jakarta and Surabaya. It became a national programme during Pelita II. During Pelita IV the programme covered some 24,100 hectares of urban *kampung* and served about 6 million urban residents (Table 9.3). This represented a more than 100-per-cent increase over the roughly 11,700 hectares and 2.5 million people covered during Pelita III. Even so, the numbers reached still represent only a small fraction of the potential demand.

While KIP does not formally include the provision or upgrading of individual housing, it is still administered under the Housing Directorate within the Department of Public Works. It is also intended to have an indirect effect on housing quality to the degree that area upgrading serves to motivate residents to improve their housing and yard areas on their own. It has also been hoped that by keeping improvements relevant to *kampung* lifestyles and conditions, they would not serve to simply 'price' the poor out of the KIP areas with benefits ultimately accruing to higher-income segments of the urban population. In practice, this appears to have largely worked—the existing residents remain in the upgraded areas. Problems have generally had more to do with lack of effective community involvement in operations and maintenance and resultant deterioration of the facilities provided under the programme.

Other infrastructure

Other forms of urban infrastructure investment (water supply, drainage and flood control, community sanitation, solid waste disposal, etc.) have also largely been implemented via formal central-government programmes. Sectoral directorates within the central Department of Public Works and in its regional offices (*Kanwil*)

Table 9.3.   Kampung improvement programme (KIP) during Pelita IV

Period	KIP area (hectares)	No. of residents served
1984/5	4,040.9	1,010,225
1985/6	3,776.7	944,175
1986/7	3,778.8	944,700
1987/8	5,355.0	1,338,750
1988/9	7,150.0	1,787,500
Total	24,101.4	6,025,350

Source: Government of Indonesia 1988.

have historically been largely responsible for co-ordination of new investment, much of which continues to be drawn from large-scale foreign (multilateral and bilateral) loans. Some infrastructure improvements have been directly implemented by local governments under the various central government grant programmes (INPRES) or using locally raised revenues, but these have represented only a small proportion (generally under 15 per cent) of the total.

On the other hand, delivery of city-wide services is, in principle, the responsibility of local government, particularly of government at the regency/municipality (*kabupaten/kotamadya*) level.[3] For example, public clean-water supply is administered through locally owned regional water-supply companies (*Perusahan Daerah Air Minum* or PDAM) and there are local government offices concerned with general sanitation (e.g. street cleaning) and other services. This responsibility, including responsibility for the preparation of supporting long-term urban structure and master plans, was effectively established by a 1974 law dealing with local government organization.[4] More recent regulations (e.g. Government Regulation No. 14, 1987) have further extended the transfer of responsibilities for the implementation of specific infrastructure programmes to local government.

While steady progress has been made in the basic investment in urban services (particularly for public water supply which has been the most heavily funded area in recent years), concerns have been expressed since the early 1980s about the ultimate effectiveness of these efforts in meeting needs of target populations. Part of this had to do with questions about the ability of essentially 'top-down' vertically and sectorally oriented hierarchies to be sufficiently sensitive to local needs and conditions. Even more practical considerations had to do with the lack of management capabilities at the local level. Low cost-effectiveness due to inefficient operations and/or rapid deterioration of installed infrastructure resulting from poor maintenance have been recognized problems of efforts made so far. The declines in central-government resources in the mid-1980s (a result of the world oil-price decline) also served to reinforce concerns already present about the low level of local-government financial responsibility in the overall process and the generally poor record of cost recovery for urban services.

These concerns, stimulated by an international climate favouring deregulation and decentralization as ways to improve internal efficiency have led to a number of innovations in recent years. A number of these were actually implemented or had some effect on activities during Pelita IV, but it seems safe to say that the policy implications of these developments are largely longer term. These form the basis for the discussion in the following sections of this chapter.

---

[3] *Kabupaten* and *kotamadya* are the administrative level below the province. There are twenty-seven provinces and 300 *kabupaten* and *kotamadya* in Indonesia. The term 'local government' generally refers to this administrative level.

[4] This law, No. 5 of 1974 on Principles of Regional Government, effectively gave responsibility for housing, water supply, solid waste, drainage, human waste, building control, and local planning to province government. National and regional spatial planning, water resource management, and flood control were retained at the national level.

Housing and Infrastructure Development Policy

The period of Pelita IV saw a number of new developments affecting urban policy formulation. A National Urban Development Strategy was completed in 1985 which attempted to provide a broad picture of urban development and a strategy for sustaining economically and socially appropriate patterns of growth (including a 'balanced needs' approach to urban service provision) through to the end of the century.[5] Partly as a result of this effort, a more explicit approach to urban service delivery was developed under the Integrated Urban Infrastructure Development Programme (IUIDP) which was implemented, in its initial stages, during Pelita IV (see section on urban housing later in this chapter).

As well, at a more global level, there was concern with effectively linking the provision (public works) aspects of infrastructure to institutional capabilities within local governments (particularly in areas of planning and operations and maintenance) to manage that infrastructure over time, and development of systems for improved financing (including local government revenue generation, cost recovery and, where appropriate, privatization of service delivery). This led, in 1987, to the formation of an interdepartmental co-ordination team for urban development, known as '*Tim Kordinasi*.' This team, made up of representatives from the Departments of Public Works, Finance and Home Affairs and the National Planning Agency (*Bappenas*), is structured with a steering committee, a secretariat and four permanent working groups for policies and programmes, programme implementation, and financial and institutional resource development. It has played a major role in sector policy formulation in recent years.

Tim Kordinasi and the general approach to urban development

The principle functions of *Tim Kordinasi* as set out in Decree 16 of 1987 were:

To develop integrated policies and medium (five year) and short term (annual) programmes for the provision of infrastructure, financial resources and institutional development in a framework of cooperation between central and local government, and with community participation; and to coordinate and monitor the implementation of integrated programmes of urban development by identifying problems and seeking their solution through interagency consensus.

The decree was accompanied by a policy statement outlining policies in relation to functional arrangements for infrastructure provision, interagency coordination, IUIDP, and local government finance and institutional concerns (Government of Indonesia 1987). Key points are outlined below:

1. that development of urban infrastructure and the operation and maintenance thereof is, in principle, primarily within the authority and responsibility of local government. The role of provincial and central government lies primarily in the areas of guidance and assistance;

[5] For a more detailed discussion see Gardiner, Ch. 8, above.

2. that planning, programming and identification of investment priorities by all levels of government for urban development would continue to be improved by means of a decentralized and integrated approach based on principles established under the Integrated Urban Infrastructure Development Programme system;

3. that local government's capability to mobilize resources and optimize the use of funds for provision of infrastructure services would be expanded and strengthened;

4. that, in accordance with the principles of decentralization, central government would endeavour to improve the overall financing system for urban infrastructure delivery and management. This would include efforts to (a) strengthen central–local government borrowing schemes for local government urban infrastructure investment needs, and (b) provide incentives for local resource mobilization and borrowing;

5. that the capability of provincial and local government staff and institutions to execute urban development activities would be enhanced through organizational and procedural improvement, as well as through a co-ordinated programme of local government manpower training and development;

6. that co-ordination and consultation between the various agencies and levels of government (central, provincial and local) involved in the development of urban infrastructure and services would be strengthened in order to ensure the smooth implementation of development activities and to provide a mechanism for review and formulation of future sector policy recommendations.

These policies, at least in theory, implied a radical change from previous procedure in that they represent both a long-term commitment to decentralization and a commitment to the effective 'bottom-up' and 'top-down' integration of the major concerns in infrastructure delivery—service provision, operations and maintenance, finance and cost recovery, and human resource development. The actual implementation of this process is less certain, if only because of the major changes it implies in interdepartmental relations and patterns of operation at both the central and local levels which will not be all that easy to carry out in the field.

The integrated urban development approach in public works

Underlying the more general concerns reflected in the policy statement is a more specific set of principles related to the physical development of urban areas and to the provision of basic infrastructure and services, mainly concerning facilities and services provided under the Department of Public Works but, in some cases, those provided under other government agencies as well. These principles, which together were designed to represent an integrated approach to urban development planning and programming, evolved during the early 1980s and emphasized a number of salient objectives, many of which bear close similarity to those in the urban policy statement indicated above. These included:

1. Improved intersector co-ordination in planning and programming of different types of infrastructure in conjunction with basic development priorities and objectives. This is a particular concern at the national level where sectoral vested interests and budgeting systems continue to reinforce a sectoral approach, but it is relevant at the local level as well. Thus, integrated planning is a key element in the 'bottom-up' approach adopted by IUIDP which more broadly emphasizes the need to co-ordinate planning and programming of infrastructure delivery across all sectors consistent with objective assessments of needs and priorities within individual urban areas, rather than on a sector-by-sector basis.

2. A principle of joint funding from central, regional and local sources aimed both at generally raising the levels of regional and local financial responsibility in infrastructure development and at emphasizing the use of central funds as an incentive to support worthwhile regional and local initiatives. A long-term objective is a system whereby more generalized central government grants or revenue-sharing packages are used to support agreed-upon overall local development programmes, rather than having funding determined (as it is largely at present) on a sectoral or project-by-project basis.

3. Synchronized development of various types of infrastructure in order to promote increased efficiency in implementation. The emphasis is on increased co-ordination in infrastructure development through parallel or sequential implementation, depending on the type of infrastructure involved or on existing local conditions.

4. Improved support and guidance from the central government (e.g. the Central Office of the Directorate General for Human Settlements) through its provincial branches to Level II (*kabupaten/kotamadya*) local authorities. This guidance function, through training, technical assistance, supervision and evaluation, is seen as a key element of a closely related objective which is to nurture 'bottom-up' efforts in both planning and implementation of service delivery, in turn, essential to the overall decentralization process.

5. A focus on residential areas occupied by the urban poor with KIP as the leading sector as a basis for alleviating existing distortions in service delivery and in providing for improvement in the quality of life of the urban poor (Directorate General of Human Settlements 1984).

There is also an overall objective of mitigating growth problems in major metropolitan centres and, in particular, in the densely settled core areas of the largest cities. Thus, in addition to programmes designed to upgrade conditions in 'inner city areas' of established larger urban centres, a special spatial emphasis is being placed on satellite town development in metropolitan sub-regions where demand for individual land and related urban infrastructure/shelter already exists and where the financial and economic costs of meeting such demands in existing areas is too high; town expansion schemes where prospects of employment growth are best, particularly in medium-sized cities both on Java and in the outer islands; and integrated urban development projects in selected smaller towns with high employment growth potential due to locational advantages; as well as on the basic efforts required to deal more generally with problems of backlog and effect-ively to manage demands generated by ongoing population growth in existing built-up areas in all classes of cities and towns.

On the other hand, there are no immediate plans to move away from the basic set of more or less established programmes that have evolved over the past few decades. At least from a public works perspective, the core of the approach adopted for Pelita V still evolves around the major programmes described earlier; *kampung* improvement, urban housing, clean-water supply, drainage and sanita-tion, and, although not specifically dealt with in this discussion, urban roads. In this respect, sub-sectoral responsibilities enshrined in the current bureaucratic structure are being maintained. This provides a useful way of focusing technical skills on specific problems, but it is less clear how well a segmented, vertically ori-ented organizational structure will be able to respond to needs for more integrated 'bottom-up' planning and programming at local levels.[6]

Even so, it should be clear that the policy structure currently in place provides a relatively unequivocal framework for decentralization and increased local self-reliance; in short, a framework aimed at making urban development program-ming more responsive to patterns of social and economic change through improved co-ordination of service delivery and through strengthening organiza-tional structures at all levels, but particularly at the local levels closest to the sources of demand.

Housing and Infrastructure Provision and Financing

Urban housing

Housing provision under the programme financed by the State Savings Bank (BTN) and constructed both by *Perumnas* and the private sector remains an important component of the urban development strategy. Targets for the early 1990s (Pelita V) were actually slightly up on those for Pelita IV at some 450,000 units (Table 9.4). According to the planning document about two-thirds of this total would be smaller-sized units of under 36 m². Furthermore, about 50,000 units would be covered under a special sites and services programme (*Kapling Siap Bangun*, or KSB), leaving about 100,000 units overall for middle-income housing, virtually all of which would be constructed by the private sector. In

---

[6] The solution so far has been to establish various co-ordinating functions on top of the existing bureaucracy. Within the Directorate General of Human Settlements a separate office of programme co-ordination (*Bina Program*) was established shortly before the start of Pelita IV. Implementation of IUIDP is further built around a series of interdepartmental technical teams at various levels of government. *Tim Kordinasi* plays the primary role in co-ordination among different departments at the national level. While this has ensured improved communication, it has not always succeeded in breaking down vested interests within specific sectoral programmes.

Table 9.4. Housing provision by *Perumnas* and the private sector during Pelita V

Period	*Perumnas* (units)	Private sector (units)	Total (units)
1989/90	20,000	50,000	70,000
1990/1	22,000	58,000	80,000
1991/2	24,000	66,000	90,000
1992/3	26,000	74,000	100,000
1993/4	28,000	82,000	110,000
Total	120,000	330,000	450,000

Source: Government of Indonesia 1988.

addition there would be some 30,000 units of upper-middle-income housing which would be financed under *PT Papan Sejahtera*.[7]

Even so, it is clear that 'formal sector' housing provision will still fall far short of demand. In view of this, and considering some of the bottlenecks discussed earlier, policies are also being designed and implemented to maximize impact and benefit in this area. Among the salient points are the following:

1. Increased emphasis would be placed on low-income housing for the self-employed, both by *Perumnas* and by local government.
2. *Perumnas* would develop a modest programme of pipeline land banking whereby stocks of available land are built up to ensure that its implementation process would not be hampered by land acquisition problems. This would concentrate on sites around major cities.
3. A close linkage between housing development and industrial development would be forged. In view of the land acquisition problems in major cities, this is likely to take the shape of industrial/residential satellite towns.
4. An increased emphasis would be given to land development, not only for residential, but also for commercial and industrial purposes. Government's role would be to acquire and subdivide land and to develop basic infrastructure. Construction would largely be left to the private (formal and informal) sectors.
5. Experiments with controversial urban renewal (including construction of four-storey walk-up flats) in core areas of Jakarta would be continued only where financially and economically viable.
6. Expansion and extension of the mortgage finance system would be pursued, primarily through BTN and the creation of a credit insurance scheme. Although foreign loans would be used to establish a base, increased efforts would be made to mobilize private savings to meet the financial demands of such an expanded system.

[7] A private home-mortgage company which offers government-backed and moderately subsidized loans for middle-income housing.

7. An urban land policy would be framed to cope with problems related to government land acquisition, land banking, land development and issuing of land titles.[8]

The housing development strategy can be further summarized according to income group for both urban and rural areas. In urban areas, KIP remains the programme of choice for the very poor (bottom 15 per cent of the income distribution), but with some innovations designed to provide access to small loans for building materials for housing construction/improvement. Sites and services development under the KSB programme is also part of the strategy at this level. For the bulk of working-class and middle-class urban residents (up to the 8th or 9th income decile) *Perumnas*-type housing would be the main avenue of support; smaller sizes (under 20 m²) for the urban poor, and larger sizes for the middle class with household incomes of around US$100–400 per month. A portion of this would be implemented outside the formal sector and supported by technical guidance and individual housing loans.

The Kampung Improvement Programme

A similar, moderate expansion is envisaged for KIP during Pelita V, but again falling far short of potential demand. There is, however, an increased emphasis on quality in terms of unit (per hectare) expenditure, on flexibility in the nature of specific inputs, and on local involvement in KIP activities, implying greater attention to institution-building at the community level and, at least, recurring-cost-recovery aspects of the programme to encourage improved operation and maintenance of infrastructure supplied.

Concerns with flexibility are of particular interest. To facilitate centralized implementation, past practice has involved the creation of input 'packages' and the setting of cost standards; 'threshold' (*perintis*) standard at Rp. 2.8 million per hectare, 'minimum' standard at Rp. 6.0 million per hectare, and 'desirable' standard at Rp. 10.0 million per hectare. These standards have also been used to determine the nature of funding, with lower levels financed entirely as a grant from the central government and higher levels partly as a grant and partly as a loan (Asian Development Bank 1983). However, such rigidities have occasionally led to inefficiencies and wastage due to underfunding or inappropriate mixes of infrastructure components in specific local situations. Whether it can respond more positively to the wide variations in local conditions will thus be an acid test of the ability of the programme effectively to meet the needs of the people it has been designed to serve.

---

[8] In support of this, a new national land agency, the *Badan Pertahanan Nasional*, was created in 1989, taking over and expanding on the functions previously held in the Directorate General for Agrarian Affairs in the Department of Home Affairs.

Integrated Urban Infrastructure Development Programme (IUIDP)[9]

As noted earlier, a number of recurring concerns evolved during the 1970s and early 1980s regarding perceived problems with the implementation of infrastructure development in urban areas in Indonesia. These were largely a reflection of the limitations of central government in meeting national requirements, and which were brought to the forefront following the dramatic decline in state revenues which occurred as a result of the oil-price declines starting in 1983. These reflected, among others, the need for greater responsibility at the local government level for planning, financing and management of urban services, the need for better integration of sectoral activities, and the need for strengthening the institutional and financial capability of local government to manage their own affairs in this area.

It was essentially these concerns, supported by a favourable climate for central agency policy formulation and strong backing by international technical assistance and funding agencies (notably the United Nations Centre for Human Settlements and IBRD), that led to the launching of IUIDP as a distinct programme in 1985. In basic terms, IUIDP provides for Level II (*kabupaten/kotamadya*) and provincial authorities to establish their own priorities for urban infrastructure development within their jurisdictions, along with a mechanism for communicating these priorities to the national level and for decision-making on levels of national assistance. It also includes a strong institutional development component and places emphasis on expanded local financial participation and improved systems of cost recovery as well as on development of local capabilities for operation and maintenance of infrastructure. Thus, at least in some respects, IUIDP can be viewed as an implementation mechanism for most of the policy considerations discussed earlier.

While IUIDP, as a programme, is housed primarily within the Department of Public Works (as of 1989 it only covered Public Works sub-sectors[10]), the emphasis on integrated planning, on institutional development and on local government finance has meant that other agencies have had to be involved. This was, in fact, the impetus for the formation of *Tim Kordinasi*, which was designed in part to sanction activities that, due to jurisdictional responsibilities, could not be implemented by one department alone. Yet, this has also created the need to establish new ground rules among central government agencies, something which has not been all that easy for the Ministry of Public Works which has had effectively to admit its dependence on the commitment of other government agencies if key aspects of the programme (institutional development, finance) are to work. Even more important are difficulties of building this kind of co-ordination at more local levels, particularly the province level, where past practices have clearly emphasized vertical sectoral linkages and upward-oriented loyalties rather than

---

[9] The discussion in this section is taken primarily from Suselo and Hoban, 1988.

[10] Water supply, human-waste disposal, solid-waste disposal, KIP, urban drainage and flood control, and urban roads.

more local self-reliance and cross-sectoral responsibility.[11] Efforts have been made to deal with these problems, but it is equally clear that early optimism probably underrated these essentially bureaucratic issues as impediments to overall implementation.

Central–local financial relations

At least in the Indonesian context, central–local financial relations are at the core of the decentralization process and hence deserve some brief comment on their own. As in a number of other developing countries, the highly centralized revenue collection and disbursement system has meant that local dependence on central resources has been extremely high. As recently as 1983/4, for example, more than 85 per cent of all development expenditure was effectively derived from central government sources (including block and categorical grants). Local tax collection was extremely limited, amounting, on average, to an equivalent of just over one US dollar per capita at the province level and about 30 cents per capita among the *kabupaten* and *kotamadya*.

During the oil 'boom' there was little perceived need to emphasize local revenue generation in view of the large surpluses accruing to central government. This changed with the collapse in oil prices in the mid-1980s. Central government revenues fell sharply, development budgets were slashed, and this, along with the pressure to move toward greater decentralization of the development process, stimulated efforts to improve local capabilities to finance their own development activities.

Thus, local governments are now expected to play an increasing role in the financing of urban services. This involves the mobilization of local revenue through local taxes (e.g. property tax), cost recovery (e.g. user charges for urban services) and local government borrowing. To facilitate this process, a number of initiatives have been or are being undertaken.

1. Taxes—A large number of taxes are available to local governments, but only a few yield significant revenue. Many taxes, in fact, are negative in the sense that they produce less than the collection costs involved. Tax reform, however, has focused on only one form of tax, the property tax, which has a long tradition, but which, up to the mid-1980s was, essentially a central tax, with some 70 per cent of revenue accruing to central government.

A new Land and Property Tax Law (PBB), however, was passed in 1986 which now assigns 80 per cent of revenue to district and province levels, plus an additional 10 per cent locally to cover collection costs. The new law also consolidates several existing land taxes, simplifies procedures for determining assessments and provides penalties for failure to register or late payment. Results have been

---

[11] Province-level institutions include both *kanwil* which are offices of central government departments and *dinas* which are offices of the local government. In practice, there is considerable overlap in leadership (the head of the *kanwil* is also often the head of the *dinas*), but, as the great majority of funding flows through *kanwil* channels, this determines, in practice, where the real power lies.

encouraging, although, due to the low base, it is still not a major contributor to overall local development expenditure except in a few of the largest cities.

2. User charges—The most significant user charges accruing to local government are those for water supply, medical treatment, refuse collection, markets, parking, bus stations, taxi stands, and the supply of official documents. Attempts to rationalize some of these fees are being made in the form of a new Local Taxation and Charges Law introduced in the late 1980s. IUIDP itself emphasizes more complete costing of infrastructure expenditure, including operation and maintenance (O and M), and the need to meet at least O and M requirements from local revenues. Where appropriate, user charges are emphasized, including cross-subsidization of poorer households in order to meet equity goals of service delivery.

3. Local government borrowing—Initial steps have been taken to establish a consolidated loan fund for local governments and local government enterprises in the form of a Regional Development Fund. Outstanding local government loans would be repaid into the new fund and all new loans would be channelled through it. Basic aims of this fund are:

- to encourage local authorities to develop and increase their revenue generation capacity, and to promote cost recovery and realistic service charges. This would encourage local governments to become less dependent on central government and more involved with planning, programming, budgeting and financing of development projects;
- to rationalize and simplify the present regional government loan schemes and procedures and provide a standard channel for local and foreign aid donors to finance local government projects;
- to provide a revolving fund which would become self-generating, thus limiting contributory support by central government and provide (at a later stage) a vehicle for mobilizing and channelling private-sector funds for local government programmes.

Yet, with the possible exception of the governments in the largest cities, most of these efforts are still in their infancy and it remains clear that it will be years before the essential dependency on central government is substantially reduced. Thus efforts are also being made to rationalize the various forms of direct central government contributions to local government budgets, including those for urban infrastructure. These include:

1. Subsidi Daerah Otonomi (SDO)—a subsidy to cover routine expenditures, mostly wages and salaries of regional government staff whose appointments are centrally approved. The allocation is based on the number of officials appointed to each region.
2. Block grants—given under the INPRES programme and which can be used for a variety of development expenditures, but which are subject to broad central government guidelines. Grants to provinces are made at two levels, a

higher level for the most populated provinces (North and South Sumatra, West, Central and East Java) and a lower level elsewhere. For districts (*kabupaten*/*kotamadya*), grants are on a per-capita basis and grants to the lowest level, the village (or *desa*) are made on a pro-rata basis.

3. Categorical grants—also given under INPRES but confined to specific designated activities, including roads and bridges, primary schools, health facilities, irrigation, and reforestation. They are designed to ensure a more equitable distribution of basic services.

On top of this one needs, of course to add the substantial resources which flow through the central government departments themselves, which are used to benefit local areas, but which do not appear as part of local budgets, being entirely implemented through the regional offices (*kanwil*) structure of these line agencies.

Centrally administered grants have clearly been a significant factor in regional development over the past two decades, but they have also contributed to problems, among them distortions in the allocation of expenditures and a lack of incentive for official local resource mobilization or borrowing for development purposes. Efforts are being made to develop more effective and efficient central–local financial relations through reducing fragmentation of existing grants, streamlining grant procedures, increasing the level of local government control and raising the predictability of exactly how much local governments can expect to receive.

Conclusion

Housing and infrastructure provision are at the core of Indonesia's efforts to improve levels of human welfare. In essence, they are seen to be major tools in meeting equity-driven goals of national development, standing alongside education, health, employment and family planning in this regard. Yet, it is equally clear that these efforts are now being carried out within the context of unprecedentedly high urban growth rates as well as within the context of an ongoing process of metropolitanization in the largest cities which, itself, is helping to raise the cost of provision of many types of urban infrastructure and services.

It is, in fact, these cost considerations and the recognized limitations of government (particularly central government) to meet the costs necessary to achieve envisaged standards that are arguably driving the basic changes in the overall strategy for urban housing and infrastructure development outlined earlier in this chapter. Keys here are seen to be improved revenue generation (particularly by local governments) and improved cost recovery, where feasible, for infrastructure investment.

A key is also seen in an increased role for the private sector, in housing, through the roles played both by formal-sector developers and by individuals in improving existing houses or building new ones. Here, the basic role of government is shifting from that of a provider to that of a facilitator, through the encouragement of private initiative. Assistance in land acquisition through appropriate land regulation or more formal guided development, capitalizing and improving access to credit, and improving processing of documents leading to formal ownership, are aspects of this approach.

For other forms of infrastructure and service provision, privatization is also often relevant, particularly where there is potential for profit on the part of the operator. Solid-waste collection is an area where some pilot activities are already being carried out. But, more generally, this remains an area where little has been done and much remains to be accomplished.

There is also an increasing recognition of the importance of the management of urban development, including operations and maintenance (not just investment), and of the severe limitations of central government in dealing with these concerns. These issues are central to the philosophy embodied in the Integrated Urban Infrastructure Development Programme and in efforts effectively to decentralize responsibility for planning and management of most urban development activities to the local government level.

In some respects this remains an even more intractable issue than urban finance as it combines the need to strengthen the currently weak technical capabilities of local government agencies with that of changing fundamental aspects of a bureaucracy where status is more a function of position than of skill. It also requires the devolution of political power to make decisions (along with the financial capability to implement them) to local levels, something which it is not at all clear that a bureaucracy which is essentially vertically and sectorally oriented will be able to accomplish. While it is arguable that the overall outlook and approaches described earlier have at least established a technical framework for meeting the challenge of urban development in Indonesia, it may well be that the surmounting of essentially political and administrative issues may prove to be the biggest challenge of all.

Part III

Brazil

Map 5. Urban centres, Brazil

Map 6.   Percentage urban map by state, Brazil

Introduction

DONALD SAWYER

With an area of 8,522,965 km², Brazil is the fifth-largest country in the world. It is nearly as large as the continental United States and covers half of the territory of South America. The landscape is dominated by the Amazon basin in the north and the Brazilian highlands in the south-east and south regions. The climate is tropical and sub-tropical, humid in the Amazon, mostly covered by forest, and semi-arid in the north-east. There are vast areas of savannah in the centre-west.

With 148 million inhabitants, Brazil also contains about half of South America's population, as well as the fourth-and seventh-largest cities in the world, São Paulo and Rio de Janeiro. It boasts the world's ninth-largest economy and has a per-capita income of around US$2,000, which makes it an 'advanced developing country', although the economy has remained virtually stagnated since the early 1980s.

The average income masks extraordinary socio-economic heterogeneity and inequality. Some areas in the south-east and south regions are densely populated and have dynamic urban-industrial economies similar to those of developed countries. At the other extreme, about one-third of the population lives in misery not unlike that found in India or Africa. The poor population is concentrated in the north-east, which holds about 30 per cent of the total population and about half of its rural population, but there are also huge pockets of urban and rural poverty in the richest regions.

In spite of marked internal differences, the country is culturally united by a common language—Portuguese—and the predominant Catholic religion. The Amerindian population was decimated and most of the remainder incorporated into Brazilian society, made up of descendants of African slaves and European and Japanese settlers, with considerable intermarriage. While religion is diversifying, with the growth of Protestantism and beliefs and practices of African origin, investments since the 1960s in transport and telecommunications, especially television, have contributed to widespread diffusion of urban values regarding lifestyles and consumption patterns.

The various economic cycles which Brazil went through since colonial times did not foster lasting penetration of the interior or integrated urban networks until well into this century. Three successive frontier movements since the 1930s were responsible for the progressive incorporation of the north-west portion of the south region, the centre-west and, lastly, parts of the Amazon region. From one movement to the next, however, the cycle of absorption, stagnation and out-migration has shortened, so that migration to the frontier is no longer significant when compared with movement in the other direction. City growth and concentration are now the leading tendencies of population redistribution.

The official definition of urban places in Brazil is administrative, including all municipal and district seats, regardless of size. By these criteria, the degree of urbanization increased from 31.2 per cent in 1940 to 45.1 per cent in 1960 and 67.6 per cent in 1980. The number of cities with 20,000 or more inhabitants grew from 50 in 1940 to 390 in 1980, while the number of cities with more than half a million went from two to fourteen. During the 1970s, the ten largest urban areas were responsible for 42 per cent of Brazil's total demographic growth of 25 million people. By the year 2000, São Paulo will be one of the world's largest cities; the United Nations projects it to be the third-largest city, with a population of 23 million.

Average growth rates of GNP of 7 per cent, and significant gains in per-capita income, in spite of population growth rates of nearly 3 per cent per year, were possible in the post-war period because of import substitution and continued exporting of primary products. During the economic 'miracle', in the late 1960s and early 1970s, income became more concentrated. The high level of informal activity in the urban and rural economies continued to increase during the crises and the brief recovery of the 1980s.

In addition to providing infrastructure, the state has played an important role in economic development, directly through state-owned enterprises in sectors such as petroleum and steel, and indirectly through regulation, subsidies, and incentives.

Since declaring itself a republic in 1889, Brazil has had a federal system of government, which became more centralized during the Vargas regime in the 1930s. During a democratic interregnum, decentralization increased, but the military regime (1964–85) left the states with little power. Redemocratization in 1985 resulted in a new constitution increasing significantly the degree of decentralization.

Economic planning was emphasized in the 1950s, under President Kubitschek, and in the late 1970s, under President Geisel. Attempts at urban planning in the 1970s were later abandoned. Throughout the 'lost decade' of the 1980s the government took a short-term approach to dealing with overwhelming problems of public deficit and foreign debt. Some compensatory social policies have been adopted, without altering Brazil's deep-rooted inequality.

10 Economic and Demographic Concentration in Brazil: Recent Inversion of Historical Patterns

GEORGE MARTINE AND CLÉLIO CAMPOLINA DINIZ

Introduction

To the uninitiated, Brazil has long stood out as an immense country with a quasi-unlimited potential for growth in its many and diversified regions (see fig. 10.1). Aggressive and well-publicized efforts have been made in recent decades to occupy the interior, through the relocation of the capital city, through massive road-building programmes, through large-scale colonization projects and through regionalized fiscal-incentive policies. Undoubtedly, the agricultural frontier has expanded, while interiorization of the population and of the economy has occurred to some extent. Nevertheless, during most of this century, economic activity and population have tended to concentrate increasingly in the region dominated by the metropolitan area of São Paulo.

This pattern of concentration has evidently caused increasing concern among policy-makers. Why has it taken place? What are its consequences? More importantly, will it continue? This chapter addresses itself to the question of concentration and deconcentration, focusing on the trajectory of dominance by the São Paulo region within a historical framework. How did the economic region controlled by the city of São Paulo attain this ascendency? How has it affected demographic concentration? How has the level of domination and concentration evolved in recent years? What are the prospects for the future? The experience of São Paulo within the Brazilian context is germane to the more general issue of the interplay between shifts in economic activity, regional development and urban growth, as well as to the broader question of the limits to concentration.

The chapter begins with a capsule review of the main historical trends in economic activity which shaped the configuration of Brazil's population over space until the 1930s. This serves as background for a more detailed analysis of changes in the last half-century and, particularly, in the 1970s and 1980s. Therein, attention is focused on interregional shifts in economic activity, particularly concerning the São Paulo area, as well as on changes in population distribution and urban growth.

Fig. 10.1.   Regions, states, and capital cities of Brazil

The Long View: From Spatial Dispersion to Concentration in São Paulo

Export cycles and shifting loci

The economic and demographic history of Brazil has been marked by temporal and spatial discontinuities, prompted by shifting potentialities for insertion of Brazilian raw material and foodstuffs in the international market. Over time, the production of different goods has gone through cycles of expansion, atrophy and regression. The better-known cycles include: brazilwood in the sixteenth century; sugar in the north-east during the sixteenth and seventeenth centuries; gold in Minas Gerais (with extensions into Goiás and Mato Grosso) in the eighteenth century; rubber in the Amazon region in the late nineteenth and early twentieth centuries; and, coffee in the south-east region in the nineteenth and twentieth centuries.[1]

The dynamism of these various export cycles depended on the conditions of production, on changing circumstances in the international market, and on Brazil's comparative advantages in different sectors of international commerce. Articulation between the various regions which produced different commodities or minerals was fragile since each was directly and independently connected with the international market. On the other hand, given the nature of the relations of production which prevailed throughout much of its history—wherein slave or quasi-servile labour predominated—the internal market failed to mature. Thus, the basic stimuli for interregional communication and articulation did not develop.

Hence, during most of its history, Brazil did not form a unified economic space or even a minimally integrated unit. On the contrary, the various export-oriented experiences produced a highly decentralized demographic and economic mosaic. Consequently, it would be inappropriate to speak of an interregional division of labour, or of an urban network, until well into the mid-nineteenth century; there simply was no significant exchange, complementarity, or subordination between regions until then (cf. Castro 1975b; Singer 1977).

Coffee became Brazil's major export product from the mid-nineteenth century, thereby generating a considerable demand for manpower. But this period also coincided with a ban on the illegal slave market. The gradual relocation of coffee production from areas in which slave labour and other unsalaried forms predominated—Rio de Janeiro, Minas Gerais and the Paraiba Paulista valley—towards the elevated plateaus of São Paulo, marked an important turning-point in Brazil's economic history. This transfer, carried out in the latter half of the nineteenth century, coincided with the government-induced expansion of European immigration, the introduction of salaried labour, the commercialization of food production and the implementation of a complementary services network—such as railway transport, the introduction of coffee processing machines, urban services, etc. The net effect of these changes was to promote the state of São Paulo to the position of the most developed region in the country, thereby attracting both internal migrants and international immigrants.

The process of economic and demographic concentration in the state and city of São Paulo, begun in the nineteenth century on the basis of coffee production, persisted into the twentieth as agriculture branched out to include foodstuffs for local and urban populations, as well as raw materials for a growing industry. This dynamic and market-oriented agriculture generated surpluses which were utilized to finance productive diversification in general (banks, railways, commerce), and industry in particular. The introduction of capitalist relations of production, together with ongoing internal and external transformations, had facilitated the birth of industrial production for a growing internal market. When the First

---

[1] For a discussion of these cycles, cf. Prado, 1973; Sodré, 1976; and Furtado, 1973.

World War slowed imports to a trickle, the process of industrial concentration in São Paulo was consolidated, given the region's relative ability to respond rapidly to new stimuli. In addition to import substitution, a further demand for new industrial products was generated, thereby imposing industrial diversification. Strong migratory flows (estimated at 1.57 million people between 1900 and 1930, 82 per cent of whom were foreign immigrants) (Cano 1977: 308), favoured additional expansion.

Early trends in urban growth

Dispersion of population and the creation of new towns attended each of the different export cycles; urban growth was, however, restricted until well into the twentieth century. The prevailing Portuguese urban model, which had been transplanted to Brazil, was that of agro-commercial and maritime towns. The outward-oriented nature of Brazil's economy and its domination by the landed gentry—the anti-urban *latifundistas* (large landowners) who owned vast *sesmarias*[2]—coincided with the new nation's defensive concerns to create a number of agro-commercial coastal settlements. These towns featured few links between them, were modest in size and appearance, and generally haphazard in layout (Castro 1975a; Singer 1977; Morse 1965). It took more than two centuries of occupation before mineral strikes forced the displacement of substantial population contingents towards the interior. On the other hand, the transfer of the capital city from Salvador to Rio de Janeiro—in order to control the flow of minerals from Minas Gerais and Goiás in the mid-eighteenth century—strongly boosted city growth in Rio. Increasing administrative centralization in this city, plus its port facilities, largely explain its demographic pre-eminence over two centuries.

The different export cycles and the sporadic incursions into the interior had stamped an irregular or leapfrogging pattern on the occupation of the Brazilian interior. Interregional and interurban migrations appear to have been at a minimum during the colonial and most of the imperial periods. However, the last decades of the nineteenth century were marked by considerable population mobility; in addition to substantial international migration, largely to the state of São Paulo, considerable interregional and intraregional movement occurred— also directed to this state. Much of this ended up in urban areas. Merrick and Graham (1979) note that one of the ironies of the immigration-subsidization policies, aimed at increasing agricultural labour, is that they contributed significantly to urban swelling. They estimate that, in 1872, Rio de Janeiro was roughly eight times larger than São Paulo and that the latter was, then, only the eighth-largest city in the country. By 1900, however, São Paulo was already the second-largest city in Brazil, its size being one-third that of Rio de Janeiro (Merrick and Graham 1979: 187).

Detailed data on the size of urban localities is available only from 1940, but information on the size of municipalities—which, in the case of the more

2 A grant of land, usually large, made by the King of Portugal.

populated ones, largely reflect their urban population—is available for earlier periods. These data show that in 1872, less than 8 per cent of Brazil's population lived in *municípios* of over 20,000 inhabitants; except for São Paulo, these were all located on the coast. Only three *municípios* had more than 100,000 inhabitants (Rio de Janeiro, Salvador, and Recife). São Paulo, however, had the fastest growth, increasing from 65,000 in 1890 to 240,000 in 1900. The only other town with comparable rates of growth during this period was the rubber port of Belém (Merrick and Graham 1979: 189).

Industrialization and Urbanization after 1930

Industrial concentration in the state of São Paulo[3]

The world crisis of the 1930s served to accelerate the transformation of the Brazilian economy. It produced a major shift in the pattern of accumulation from agrarian exports to urban industry; meanwhile, the focus of production was switched from the external to the internal market. However, by the time the Depression devastated the coffee-dominated economy centred in São Paulo, the São Paulo–Rio de Janeiro axis had already accumulated enough momentum and comparative advantages, as well as sufficient human and physical capital, to allow it to consolidate its growing domination of the Brazilian economy. Moreover, the effects of the crisis were minimized in São Paulo by the government's decision to purchase coffee surpluses and thereby sustain economic levels among its producers. The abrupt severance of international ties provided the stimulus for import-substituting industrialization, which lent new significance to the internal market. The available capital and the relative advantages already accruing to the São Paulo–Rio axis, in terms of the size of local markets, access to manpower, as well as links to the hinterland and to other regional markets, increased its ability to take advantage of this new situation.

During the initial stages of Brazil's autonomous industrialization, the difficulties of communication, the heritage of various export experiences, and an incipient scattered urban growth, had led to deconcentrated industrial production. The industrial concerns which sprang up had been geared to local and regional markets, or possessed tenuous links to the international market. Within a relatively short time, however, Rio de Janeiro and São Paulo began to expand their markets. Rio's size, port facilities, and proximity to the power structure gave it an edge over most other regional centres. However, the dynamism of São Paulo's regional market, the modernization of its relations of production, its intersectoral integration, its production of a surplus, and its economies of agglomeration, which had all served to sustain its agricultural structure, now promoted its industrial production to a dominant position. Strengthened by the

[3] The discussion of concentration and deconcentration is largely based on Diniz, 1987. Cf. also Morse, 1958.

extension of rail communications and, later, of highway transport, the foundation for the integration of a national market and, consequently, for the interregional division of labour, were established in Brazil after the 1930s (cf. Cano 1977; Mello 1982; Silva 1976; and Dean 1974).

The integration of the national market generated a centre–periphery relationship between the Rio–São Paulo axis and the remainder of Brazil. As Cano (1985) and Oliveira (1977) have shown, the peripheral regions increasingly found themselves obliged to reshape their productive structures in complementarity with that of the dominant axis, with increasing emphasis on the São Paulo pole, as the interregional division of labour was intensified. From then on, industrial and demographic concentration progressed continuously in São Paulo until the 1970s, with most other states and regions showing relative losses (cf. Tables 10.1 and 10.2).

Table 10.1.   Distribution of industrial production, by selected regions and states, Brazil, 1907–80 (%)

Region or state	1907[a]	1919[a]	1939[a]	1950[b]	1960[b]	1970[b]	1980[b]
North	4.3	1.3	1.1	0.6	1.0	1.0	2.5
North-East	16.7	16.1	10.4	9.3	7.7	5.7	8.0
East (MG, RJ, ES)	42.3	34.5	28.9	28.9	23.7	22.7	18.2
São Paulo	15.9	31.5	45.4	46.6	54.5	58.1	53.4
South	19.9	16.2	13.8	14.0	12.5	12.0	15.7
Centre-West	0.9	0.4	0.4	0.6	0.7	0.5	1.2
Brazil	100.0	100.0	100.0	100.0	100.0	100.0	100.0

[a] Participation in the value of production of the manufacturing industry.
[b] Participation in the value of industrial transformation in the manufacturing industry.

Sources: 1907, 1919 and 1939—IBGE, Censos Industriais do Brasil. Apud (1977): 296.
          1950, 1960, 1970 and 1980—IBGE, Censos Industriais.

Table 10.2.   Percentage of total population, by selected regions and states, Brazil, 1907–80

Region or state	1907	1920	1940	1950	1960	1970	1980
North	4.4	4.7	3.6	3.5	3.5	3.0	4.6
North-East	38.3	36.8	35.0	34.0	31.7	30.3	29.3
East (MG, RJ, ES)	30.7	29.6	27.1	25.8	25.4	23.7	22.4
São Paulo	13.8	15.0	17.4	17.6	18.3	19.1	21.0
South	10.8	11.5	13.9	15.1	16.8	17.6	15.9
Centre-West	2.2	2.5	3.0	3.4	4.3	5.6	6.8
Brazil	100.0	100.0	100.0	99.4	100.0	99.3	100.0

Sources: IBGE, Censos Demográficos.
          IBGE, Estatísticas Históricas do Brasil.
          IBGE, Anuários Estatisticos do Brasil.

Frontier expansion and urbanization

The coffee crisis in 1930, as well as the major changes in the pattern of accumulation based on the internal market and industrialization, provoked both citywards migrations and frontier expansion. During its initial stages, the frontier movement towards adjacent regions of Parana and, later, of Mato Grosso do Sul, and parts of Minas Gerais and Goiás, constituted a geographic extension of São Paulo's agricultural production; later, it attained self-sustained dynamism, to the extent that land values increased in previously occupied regions, and that infrastructure was gradually built up. The progressive incorporation of new agricultural areas would later lead to the gradual reduction of São Paulo's predominance in agricultural production, as will be discussed below.

With respect to urbanwards migration, it has been shown that the curtailment of international immigration after 1930 was more than substituted by both intraregional and interregional movement directed towards São Paulo, particularly its urban areas (cf. Lopes 1980, esp. p. 58). Figure 10.2 shows that in 1940, Brazil had fifty urban centres of 20,000 or more inhabitants, of which sixteen were located in the state of São Paulo. The great majority of all Brazilian cities were still found on the coast or a short distance away; again, the major exception was in the state of São Paulo where several cities—including the city of São Paulo itself—were inland. The Second World War gave rise to an acceleration of internal demands for industrial products due to new import difficulties, as well as an external demand for raw materials. Existing industrial equipment was expanded and utilized to maximum capacity, resulting in increased wages and the attraction of further migration to industrial areas.

The acceleration of demographic growth, induced by a rapid decline in mortality without a commensurate reduction in fertility, helped feed both frontier movements and cityward migrations. Thus, it has been estimated that some 3 million persons moved from rural areas to the cities during the 1940s and 7 million more during the 1950s; Rio de Janeiro and São Paulo were the cities most affected by this movement. Meanwhile, the frontier state of Parana and the centre–west region were absorbing some 1.5 million more migrants in their rural areas (cf. Martine 1990a).

The 1950s were marked by a particularly intensive rhythm of urban growth. The number of cities (i.e. urban localities of 20,000 or more inhabitants) grew from eighty-two to 154 in this period; the rate of urbanization reached its highest point and the inter-class mobility of cities was also at its highest.[4] Part of this urban explosion was again attributable to demographic growth, as Brazil's fastest ever rate of increase was recorded in the 1950s. But a major part was provoked by profound social and economic transformations. After the Second World War, Brazil had set out to restructure its economy. Communications and transport were modernized and basic infrastructure was provided. Growing faith in the

---

[4] Historical patterns of urban growth in Brazil are discussed at length in Martine *et al.* (1989). The data on urbanization quoted here are based on that study.

Fig. 10.2.   Urban localities, Brazil, 1940

central planning of economic life encouraged several major undertakings during
the Kubitschek era in the late 1950s; these included State incentives to import-
substituting industrialization, the transfer of the capital city to Brasília, the introduction of a massive road-building programme, and the occupation of new
frontier regions.

The conservative modernization model implemented by the military regime
after 1964 extended and updated these major reforms, providing more effective
state support for productive activities and channelling international resources in
their direction, while simultaneously muzzling union movements and popular
unrest. In both the 1950s and 1960s, most of the planning-induced changes
favoured the São Paulo region. The accumulated locational advantages around
the city of São Paulo, based on its external economies, the size and power of its

market, as well as the talent and energy of its entrepreneurial class, in addition to its volume of resources and political clout, served to promote further concentration in the region. Improvements in the transport and communications sector also furthered the penetration of its industrial products. When the city and its surroundings were declared a metropolitan area (M.A.) in the late 1960s, the São Paulo M.A. concentrated a large parcel of the country's industrial production.

The relative decline of the Rio de Janeiro region which, in retrospect, can be perceived as early as the turn of the century, became more pronounced at this time. The economic disadvantages of the Rio region stemmed from the weakness of its intersectoral linkages with the hinterland, from the backwardness of its agricultural system (poor land, pre-capitalist relations of production and an inability to produce a surplus), from the entropy of its industrial bourgeoisie, as well as from its lack of mineral resources. All of these factors are in sharp contrast to São Paulo's overall dynamism. Thus, the transfer of the capital city to Brasília, in the early 1960s, only served to lay bare Rio's fundamental disadvantages.

Meanwhile, the concentration of population in the state of São Paulo and in its cities continued apace with the concentration of economic activity in the industrial and tertiary sector. By 1960, over 7 million people lived in forty-one cities of 20,000 or more inhabitants within the state; this amounted to 28 per cent of the country's cities and 31 per cent of their inhabitants. Although the relative share of all cities located in the state of São Paulo declined slightly in subsequent years, its proportion of the total urban population had actually increased by 1970, and the metropolitan area of São Paulo had overtaken Rio as Brazil's largest city, containing 21 per cent of the country's urban population.

Deconcentration after 1970

Economic deconcentration: indicators and causes

Agricultural production had already begun deconcentrating away from the state of São Paulo in the 1940s. The largest drop occurred in the 1950s when its participation in the national value of agricultural production fell from 34 to 24 per cent. Such shifts are in consonance with the previously discussed patterns of frontier expansion in a land-rich country which, traditionally, has always looked to the extension of cultivation to new agricultural areas as the easiest path to increased production (cf. Table 10.3). Although figures show steady increases in production within São Paulo state, and although it has always achieved some of the highest levels of productivity in the country, its share of national production was bound to decline, just by virtue of the country's large and constant increase in cultivated areas.

However, it is interesting to observe that by the late 1960s, deconcentration from São Paulo had begun to occur in other areas of activity, such as industrial transformation, which are typically capital-intensive and space-specific. Indeed,

Table 10.3. Proportion of cultivated area, value of agricultural production and geographic area, by selected regions and states, Brazil, 1940–80 (%)

Region or state	1940		1950		1960		1970		1980		
	a	b	a	b	a	b	a	b	a	b	c
North	4.9	1.1	1.3	0.6	1.5	1.2	1.7	2.7	2.7	3.2	39.2
North-East	30.6	20.6	27.6	20.1	30.4	22.1	30.4	21.4	28.9	19.8	18.2
East (MG, RJ, ES)	22.1	23.6	21.9	21.1	18.3	17.2	14.4	13.4	12.6	12.8	8.0
São Paulo	22.9	35.0	22.3	34.1	16.6	24.0	13.9	21.9	12.1	20.6	2.9
South	1.6	16.8	23.7	21.0	28.3	30.3	32.5	34.7	29.7	35.9	6.7
Centre-West	3.9	2.9	3.2	2.8	4.9	5.1	7.1	5.9	14.0	7.7	25.0
Brazil	100.0	100.0	100.0	100.0	100.0	100.0	100.0	100.0	100.0	100.0	100.0

a Proportion of cultivated area
b Proportion of value of agricultural production
c Proportion of geographic area

Source: IBGE *Censos Agropecuários.*

recently published data on regionalized national accounts for 1970 and 1980 provide a clear picture of the deconcentration process.[5] These data clearly indicate that, for the first time, the state of São Paulo's relative participation in GNP suffered a relative loss in this period (from 41.1 per cent to 38.2 per cent between 1970 and 1980). The change of direction implied by these figures is perhaps more significant than the size of the relative loss (2.9 per cent), particularly in view of the fact that it was caused by a reduction of São Paulo's prominence in both industry and agriculture, but particularly in the former (cf. Table 10.4).

The slack was taken up by most other regions. For instance, the northern region increased its share of GNP from 2.0 per cent in 1970 to 2.9 per cent in 1980; the major gain here was made in industry, which rose from one per cent to 2.9 per cent of the national total, due to the installation of an industrial complex in Manaus and of isolated projects in the state of Pará. The north-eastern region was able to maintain its relative share, basically as a result of industrial expansion in Bahia. The southern region showed an increase in industry from 12.0 per cent to 16.3 per cent during the interval, while experiencing a reduction in its relative share of agricultural production. The centre–west region increased its modest share in all sectors. The state of Rio de Janeiro continued its permanent decline, while Espirito Santo and Minas Gerais increased their relative shares at a reduced pace.

The central question to be asked at this juncture is—what prompted these trends towards deconcentration from São Paulo during the 1970s and what is their overall significance? First of all, the notion that deconcentration occurred without the concurrence, or to the detriment, of São Paulo's entrepreneurial class, should be discarded outright. Deconcentration reflected the logic and the best interests of firms from that state, inasmuch as it was prompted by the need to expand their production over a growing share of national geographic space. Indeed, this phenomenon is analogous to the world-wide movement of productive capital through multinational interests. Moreover, the impact of decentralization and deconcentration policies, or of regional development policies, should not be exaggerated; although some public policies may have helped accentuate the process of deconcentration, major changes occurred mainly in answer to the specific needs of the accumulation process at a given stage of maturity.

Secondly, the search for a single underlying cause of deconcentration is futile; it resulted from the coalescence of a number of different factors at a given historical moment. Some of the factors which, at different times and with differential impact, have helped promote deconcentration away from the São Paulo region can be singled out.[6] The mood of arrogant optimism which prevailed in the country at the beginnings of the 'economic miracle' (late 1960s) certainly favoured expansion and the 'conquest' of new markets via the integration of previously isolated regions. The very need to incorporate the natural resources frontier—which partly explains the dislocation of agricultural or mineral production—provided

[5] Data on the spatial evolution of investments as well as census data from 1970 to 1980 provided the first indicators of deconcentration but did not really permit a global view of this process.
[6] The factors affecting current decentralization are discussed in Diniz, 1987.

Table 10.4.   Structure of the GNP, according to sector, by selected regions and states: Brazil, 1960–80 (%)

Region or state	Total GNP			Industrial GNP			Agricultural GNP			Services GNP		
	1960	1970	1980	1960	1970	1980	1960	1970	1980	1960	1970	1980
North	2.2	2.0	2.9	1.9	1.0	2.9	2.0	3.9	4.5	2.5	2.2	2.6
North-East	14.8	11.6	12.2	8.0	7.0	9.5	22.1	20.9	19.5	11.7	12.5	12.8
East (MG, RJ, ES)	28.1	26.0	25.5	22.2	22.7	21.9	20.0	16.2	20.4	34.5	30.9	29.2
São Paulo	34.7	41.1	38.2	54.3	56.5	47.5	23.0	18.0	14.3	34.8	35.8	36.0
South	17.8	16.6	17.4	11.9	12.0	16.3	28.2	33.4	29.5	14.6	15.9	15.7
Centre-West	2.4	2.7	3.8	0.8	0.8	1.9	4.7	7.6	11.8	1.9	2.7	3.7
Brazil	100.0	100.0	100.0	100.0	100.0	100.0	100.0	100.0	100.0	100.0	100.0	100.0

Sources: IBGE *Estatísticas Históricas do Brasil, Vol. 3, 1987.*
IBGE *Anuário Estatístico do Brasil, Vol. 34, 1973.*

impetus for intercapitalist competition, in terms of resource appropriation and control, barriers to entry, market expansion, etc; all these factors have spatially-differentiated features and, thereby, promote integration. Interindustrial effects were amplified by technological changes and the strengthening of intersectoral relations. The launching of new packages of industrial projects—whenever existing plants reached their technical and economic scales or attained full capacity—also favoured spatial dispersement.

On another level, considerations of a geopolitical nature fostered the occupation of open spaces, as well as the construction of a new capital city in Brasília, the creation of a free commerce zone in Amazonian Manaus, and the construction of infrastructure for decentralized economic activity. Further improvement of the communications network, and particularly of transport, improved access to new regions. Demographic pressure in older areas of settlement reinforced migration streams and integration. An avalanche of fiscal incentives for regional, state and sectoral development—including massive subsidized agricultural credit—increased land values nationally and promoted all sorts of decentralized economic activity during the 1970s.

What happened to deconcentration during the 1980s? Since the last available regionalized National Accounts are dated 1980, it is difficult to provide a definitive reply to this question. It can safely be assumed, however, that the severity of the economic crisis in the 1980s is sure to have attenuated the trend towards regional redistribution of production in Brazil. This is because deconcentration here—in contrast to what generally happens in advanced industrialized countries such as the United States or England—generally results from the manipulation of new investments, and not from the relocation of existing production units. Thus, the shortage of investment resources in the 1980s hurt decentralization.

In addition to this general consideration, a few concrete elements concerning the more recent situation can be provided. In the agricultural sector, the 1980s brought several important transformations, some due to continued deconcentration and some to the economic crisis. With respect to the latter, the 1985 agricultural census shows an apparent—and, most probably, temporary—reversal in previously observed trends towards concentration of land, reduction of rural employment and heavy out-migration.[7] For the first time since the beginning of the recent modernization process, the number of agricultural establishments showed a significant increase during the 1980–5 period; meanwhile, the rate of increase in both total land area and cultivated land was significantly reduced. This was accompanied by a decline in the rate of increase of incorporation of new technology and of frontier expansion. The sum of these patterns would appear to reflect the impact of the economic crisis on the availability of subsidized credit—which had previously fed both modernization and speculation—as well as constriction of the market. Thus, the crisis appears to have re-opened, at least temporarily, interstitial spaces for small-scale producers of all types, especially the

[7] Cf. discussion in Martine, 1990b.

subsistence *minifundistas*. This is almost sure to have retarded rural–urban migration in the early 1980s.

In contrast, the latter half of the decade appears to have been marked by a return to the dominant patterns of modernization, increasing land values and heavy out-migration. Overall, however, it can be expected that the 1980s will record a lower level of rural–urban migration than the previous decade. In addition to the impact of the crisis, it should be remembered that the absolute size of the rural population is now smaller, due to heavy out-migration in the 1960s and 1970s. Moreover, rates of natural increase have declined significantly in both rural and urban areas. Although fertility decline does not produce a short-term impact on out-migration, given the age selectivity of migration patterns, some 20 years have gone by since Brazil's fertility decline first became noticeable.

Concerning the deconcentration of agricultural production, the 1980s witnessed a new shift in the locus of mechanized grain farming towards the *Cerrados* (poor-quality cattle-grazing land) of the centre-west region, as well as to adjacent areas in the north-east and Minas Gerais. Between 1980 and 1986, for example, the centre-west region increased its participation in the national production of soybeans from 12 per cent to 23 per cent, and that of corn from 9 per cent to 12 per cent, with an expected rise to 30 per cent and 15 per cent, respectively, by 1989. The current expansion of the centre-west region actually represents a more intensive and extensive exploitation of a frontier area which had been settled in a somewhat haphazard fashion some 30 years before.

Concerning industrial deconcentration São Paulo's industrial production, although declining, held its own until 1984; after 1985, São Paulo's industrial growth was considerably slower than that of other areas (cf. Table 10.5). Between

Table 10.5.   Index* of physical production in the manufacturing industry

Year	Brazil	Minas Gerais	North-East	Rio de Janeiro	São Paulo	South
1980	100	100	100	100	100	100
1981	89.62	—	—	—	—	—
1982	89.63	93.74	93.05	92.62	88.47	87.73
1983	83.91	88.81	88.79	80.96	82.77	84.52
1984	89.02	97.87	90.07	79.33	88.48	90.76
1985	96.41	105.25	100.32	82.76	96.25	96.82
1986	109.79	110.38	105.53	95.89	105.93	107.19
1987	110.58	113.52	109.69	96.05	106.20	108.33
1988	107.51	115.52	101.01	96.16	102.55	105.59
1989	110.89	116.41	105.19	100.30	104.61	109.70

* Index refers to an average of physical production weighted by its aggregate value—means that figures are unavailable.

Source: IBGE, *Indices da Produção Industrial, Séries Revistas 1975–85*. IBGE, *Indicadores*, Several numbers.

1980 and 1989, the production index for industry rose by 0.3 per cent in Rio de Janeiro, 4.6 per cent in São Paulo and 10.9 per cent in Brazil as a whole. Such figures have caused a considerable stir in the press, which tends to see in them a major crisis for São Paulo's industry.[8] Regional changes in production figures are reflected in consumption patterns; a recent study showed that the state of São Paulo suffered a decline of 5.4 per cent in its share of national income between 1975 and 1985 (cf. Amarante and Bondioli, 1987).

In addition to the various factors, listed earlier, which promote deconcentration, ongoing field research in industrial firms from São Paulo, which have recently established subsidiaries in the interior of that state or in southern Minas Gerais, revealed additional motivation for deconcentration.[9] A first such incentive is the classical one of cheaper lands outside the São Paulo M.A. A negative inducement was the perception by industrialists that labour unions in the state of São Paulo are better organized and more active, thereby demanding (and getting) better wages. A third motive adduced was the cost of the pollution controls which a relatively strong state agency in São Paulo (CETESB) has been enforcing. Lastly, the diseconomies of urbanization brought on by Greater São Paulo's excessive urban growth (cf. Tables 10.6 and 10.7) have led the present state government to promote measures aimed at industrial deconcentration within the state.

A central question which arises at this point is whether or not economic deconcentration, and particularly its industrial variety, constitutes a loss in the relative ascendency of the growth pole dominated by the metropolitan area of São Paulo, or whether it simply represents a natural extension in the radius and

Table 10.6. Rates of urban growth, Brazil and state of São Paulo

Categories	1940–70[b]		1970–80[c]	
	r (%)	Absolute increase (in '000s)	r (%)	Absolute increase (in '000s)
Brazil, cities of 20,000 + [a]	4.5	19,400	4.2	14,309
Brazil, 10 largest cities[a]	4.3	11,874	3.7	7,223
São Paulo, cities of 20,000 +	5.3	9,684	4.5	7,047
Metropolitan areas of São Paulo	5.6	6,569	4.5	4,451
Other cities of São Paulo	4.7	3,115	4.6	4,595

[a] Excludes cities in the state of São Paulo

[b] Refers to growth of 246 localities which, in 1970, had 20,000 or more inhabitants, regardless of their sizes in earlier censuses.

[c] Refers to growth of 393 localities which, in 1980, had 20,000 or more inhabitants, regardless of their sizes in earlier censuses.

Source: Computed from Martine *et al.* (1989).

[8] e.g. two leading national newsmagazines recently published detailed analyses of São Paulo's industrial crisis. Cf. *Isto É* (No. 362) and *Senhor* (Nos. 1021 and 1025).

[9] Field research carried out by Clélio Campolina Diniz in 1989. Results are, as yet, unpublished.

Table 10.7. Indices of urban concentration in the state and metropolitan area of São Paulo

	1940–70	1970–80
Percentage of country's urban growth in state of São Paulo	33.3	33.0
Percentage of country's urban growth in M.A. of São Paulo	22.6	20.8
Percentage of state's urban growth in M.A. of São Paulo	67.8	63.1

Note and sources: See Table 10.6.

perimeter of the dominant region. Before answering this question it may be necessary to differentiate between short-term financial disadvantages for the state of São Paulo and a permanent loss in the ascendency of the dominant pole. Given the structure of taxes on production and distribution of goods collected at the state level, as well as the multiplier effect that industries have on their respective local communities, there is no question but that deconcentration of industry to areas outside the state of São Paulo implies a relative loss of income for that state.

As concerns the more general question of the relative loss of ascendency, it would appear that both extension of the dominant pole's perimeter and autonomous deconcentration beyond this perimeter have occurred. Of the two, extension of the perimeter is much more frequent and important. Such concentration towards the outer rim of the dominant pole is brought about by the sum of individual entrepreneurial decisions—to take advantage of access to raw materials, manpower concentration, better living conditions, and other factors—and tends to bring a reinforcement of the dominant pole.

Most of the deconcentration towards distant regions is stimulated by government actions, solely for the purpose of creating and protecting industrial zones in these regions (such as in the case of SUFRAMA, the free commercial zone in Manaus and of the industrial pole in the north-east). This type would tend to bring about a relative loss of ascendency by the dominant pole, were it not for the fact that much of this decentralization involves the creation of subsidiary plants—to take advantage of fiscal incentives, or to facilitate access to new markets, materials or manpower pools—by industries whose headquarters are in the dominant pole. Within this framework, it is likely that both types of deconcentration have constituted a natural outgrowth of the dominant pole centred around the metropolitan area of São Paulo. Viewed in this light, deconcentration really involves expansion and strengthening of the dominant pole.

In addition to the foregoing comments, it is important to observe that deconcentration from São Paulo, particularly when resulting from entrepreneurial decision, has not led to decentralization of financial or administrative control. On the contrary, it is likely that centralization of economic decision-making has been intensified with industrial deconcentration as the control of financial capital is progressively centred in the São Paulo metropolitan area. In short, the process which is currently underway in Brazil could perhaps best be described as centralized deconcentration.

Deconcentration and urban growth

What impact have the trends towards agricultural deconcentration from São Paulo (begun in the 1940s) and industrial deconcentration (begun in the late 1960s) had on the spatial distribution of population, particularly on urban concentration?

As to the expansion of the agricultural frontier from 1940 onwards, there can be little doubt that it helped foster urban growth in previously unsettled regions. The multiplication of urban localities having 20,000 or more inhabitants, from fifty in 1940 to 393 in 1980, can, to a significant degree, be attributed to this outward expansion (cf. Fig. 10.3). Nevertheless, agricultural activity does not spawn large metropoles; moreover, it does not appear from existing data that urban concentration in São Paulo regressed because of agricultural expansion elsewhere. Indeed,

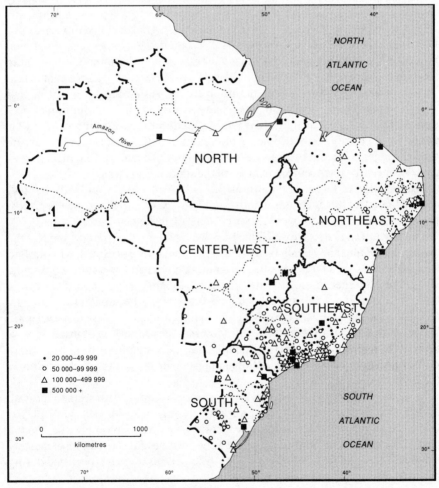

Fig. 10.3. Urban localities, Brazil, 1980

as can be seen from Table 10.6, urban growth rates in the state and M.A. of São Paulo were significantly higher than in the remainder of Brazil throughout the 1940–70 period.

The impact of industrial deconcentration has to be viewed at two levels. Given the primacy of the São Paulo M.A. in the industrialization process and its position as the nerve centre of the São Paulo dominant pole, deconcentration can be construed as movement towards the periphery of the dominant pole, or towards new poles in more distant regions. For purposes of analysing the first type of movement, the state of São Paulo can be taken as proxy for the perimeter of the dominant region. Obviously, this constitutes an oversimplification since certain areas within the state are outside the dynamic centre, while other areas outside the state are rapidly being incorporated in economic terms; nevertheless, currently-available data sources make it necessary to utilize this procedure, which is unlikely to generate serious analytical distortions.

The main question here is—how to reconcile industrial deconcentration in São Paulo with the fact that the São Paulo M.A. accounted for 17 per cent of national population growth between 1970 and 1980? Or—how did the state of São Paulo increase its share of the national population from 19 per cent to 21 per cent in that period, despite its lower rates of natural increase? A first answer might be that migration patterns tend to lag behind changes in the spatial distribution of economic activities; in that light, São Paulo's great momentum over a fifty-year period would justify continued heavy in-migration to that state and M.A. during the first stages of deconcentration. Another point to be made is that much industrial deconcentration occurred to areas in the state of São Paulo itself.

But, on another level, the data from Tables 10.6 and 10.7 would indicate that, despite huge absolute increases in the state and M.A. of São Paulo, urban growth has already slowed; moreover, it showed signs of deconcentration in the 1970s. For instance, it can be seen from Table 10.6 that, in the 1940–70 period, cities in the state of São Paulo grew much faster than in the remainder of Brazil, with the São Paulo M.A. having a large advantage over other cities in its own state. During the 1970s, the difference in growth rates between São Paulo's cities and those of the rest of the country was considerably reduced; moreover, the São Paulo M.A. grew at a slightly lower rate than the other cities in the same state. These tendencies are borne out by figures in Table 10.7 which show that the proportion of urban growth in the state of São Paulo decreased slightly and, more significantly, that the share of the São Paulo M.A. in both national and state urban growth declined during the 1970s.

In short, available data on urban growth processes would also seem to indicate a reversal in the trend towards concentration during the 1970s. The M.A. of São Paulo, despite a huge absolute increase, grew at a relatively slower pace than in the past and even lost ground to other cities within the state. It will be extremely enlightening to see, from 1990 census data, whether this trend has persisted during the more recent period. In view of the above-described process of industrial deconcentration—which tends to reduce the demand for labour in the nucleus—as well as the impact of the recent economic crisis on rural retention during the early 1980s, it can be expected that migration to São Paulo and to its M.A. will be reduced during the 1980s.

Prospects for Future Deconcentration

The above analysis indicated significant industrial and urban deconcentration from the M.A. and state of São Paulo during the 1970s. In the 1980s, this process continued at a slower pace than might have been expected, due to the economic crisis and to the overall reduction in investment. For the future, major macro-spatial alterations are not expected since most of the deconcentration which does occur tends to constitute a geographical expansion of the dominant pole, in answer to the felt needs of individual firms. Hence, the geographic expansion of the pole's radius, in response to market factors, can be expected to proceed at a fairly leisurely pace.

Those relocations which did occur far beyond the perimeter of the dominant pole took place in response to heavy government investments, and are generally proving to be ineffective. The social costs, reduced multiplier effect on the economy of outlying regions, lack of intersectoral relations, and inability to absorb technology in experiments such as the free commerce zone of Manaus—which accounts for much of the northern growth—warn against the indiscriminate repetition of such experiences. Industrial growth in the north-east was strongly influenced by a petrochemical pole established in Bahia for political reasons. Several industrial projects were set up in that region as a result of fiscal incentives. Most of these have become industrial enclaves, which benefit from incentives and raw materials, but whose capital and markets are outside the region. Consequently, further industrial growth in that region is not to be expected. Similarly, the eastern region, especially around Rio de Janeiro, can be expected to pursue its historical decline, since it offers few locational advantages.

In principle, ongoing technological transformations may affect concentration in Brazil, to the extent that they alter future locational requirements. Indeed, in the wake of the crisis of world capitalism in the 1970s, profound changes occurred in the technical base of production. Such changes may affect location patterns, particularly with the emergence of new sectors such as electronics, informatics, new materials, chemistry, precision mechanics, etc. Given their high-tech base, it is probable that their locational requirements will be different from those of traditional or heavy industry. In that sense, it is at least theoretically possible that some selective industrial activities will be deconcentrated.

But, even in the case of these new technologies, the relative development of productive forces in different regions will continue to be a central factor. From the standpoint of production, the educational, scientific and cultural base—represented by universities and research institutions—the technological ambience, the existing production base, the cultural ethos and general level of knowledge, and the availability of technically-competent personnel, are all factors which influence the relative attractiveness of different sites. From the standpoint of demand, in addition to the level and magnitude of regional income, the major determinants involve the relative stage of development of other activities or sectors (industry, agriculture, services) which can absorb the new products generated by the dynamic industries and, at the same time, stimulate their further expansion.

From this line of reasoning, it is apparent that the state of São Paulo still possesses clear relative advantages which could promote industrial expansion in this region by way of the more dynamic industries. On the other hand, the improvement of transport could reduce the friction of space, contributing to the expansion of the geographic area within the dominant pole by incorporating parts of Minas Gerais, Rio Grande do Sul, Parana, Santa Catarina, or even the centre-west. This would introduce a new spatial configuration for the dynamic centre of Brazilian industry.[10] To the extent that this enlarged pole were to become functionally integrated, it would imply a reduction of growth possibilities in other regions. Consequently, regional disparities would be increased, as would the inter-regional division of labour, thereby enhancing the subordination of other regions to the dominant pole, which has its nucleus in Metropolitan São Paulo. It will then become increasingly difficult to redress the situation of relative backwardness which prevails in the industrial sectors of the north-eastern and eastern regions, or to occupy the relatively empty northern region.

In the agricultural sector, prospects are somewhat more varied. The outlook for the Amazon region is rather bleak. The inability to resolve the enormous technological difficulties in any sort of large-scale framework, the distance factor and its corresponding transport costs, the lack of infrastructure, the absence of an organized labour market, the constant threat of debilitating tropical diseases, *inter alia*, present formidable obstacles to productive settlement, at least in the short and medium range (cf. Sawyer 1982a; Martine 1990a).

The older regions, namely the north-east and east, maintain low and stagnant levels of production and productivity. A significant proportion of their population carries on under precarious social and material living conditions. These regions are characterized by poor soils, a combination of *minifundios* (small-holdings) and *latifundios* (large landed estates), uneven terrain, low technological levels and strong cultural resistance to change. Prospects for rapid improvement in agricultural production in these areas are poor.

Major prospects for frontier development are found in the central region, which had been occupied in a non-intensive fashion during previous decades. This area includes parts of the centre-west region, as well as parts of Minas Gerais, Bahia, Piaui and Maranhão. In this vast area, the availability of relatively cheap land, the existence of adequate technology and of minimal infrastructure, as well as the

---

[10] Azzoni (1986), after analysing the spatial evolution of twelve urban services introduces the concept of 'agglomeration field' to refer to the expansion of the radius of the economies of scale of large cities.

relative proximity to markets, indicate considerable potentialities in the next stage of Brazilian development.

In sum, the main type of deconcentration which can be expected for the future will emanate outwards from metropolitan São Paulo towards the interior of that state, to southern Brazil, to Minas Gerais and the centre-west region; this will tend to intensify demographic growth and concentration in a larger region than before. Development in the centre-west will be linked to the continued dynamism of its agricultural frontier and its impact on agro-industrial development; the need for urban supporting services in this region will foster urban growth but not rapid metropolitan concentration. But industrial expansion to the southern region, to Minas Gerais and to the interior of São Paulo will occur, as Azzoni has suggested, along the lines of minimum friction, dictated by the uneven development of transport and communications (Azzoni 1986). Figure 10.4 indicates the probable axes of future decentralization, such as currently perceived by the authors of this paper.

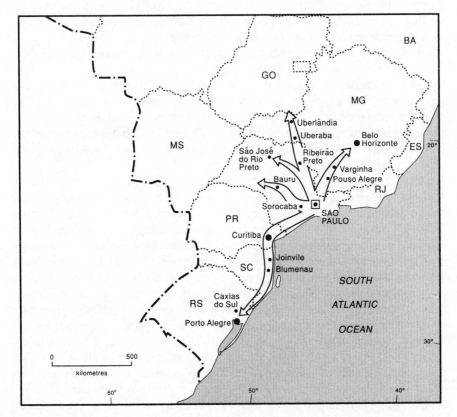

Fig. 10.4. Probable axes of future industrial deconcentration, Brazil

Concluding Remarks

Throughout most of its history, the spatial distribution of Brazil's population was moulded by a succession of settlement surges prompted by successive extractive/agricultural cycles. During much of the present century, however, economic power has become increasingly concentrated in the large hinterland dominated by the city of São Paulo, due to a combination of natural advantages and historical circumstances. In more recent years, the economic primacy of this region is apparently being challenged by the location of new industrial investments away from the São Paulo M.A. The main forces behind this deconcentration stem from agglomeration diseconomies, population density, environmental pollution, labour problems and such—whose aggregate results are prompting entrepreneurial decisions to decentralize—and, to a lesser extent, from government policies aimed at the development of outlying regions.

The significance of this trend towards deconcentration of economic activity, spatial redistribution and decentralization of political power should, however, not be overestimated. Industrial deconcentration constitutes, for the most part, an enlargement and reinforcement of the growth around São Paulo. Firms are moving out, of their own accord, in an extension of the dominant pole, but remain closely articulated with the financial and decision-making centre in its hub. In short, the main trend would appear to be towards a gradual extension of the dominant region, which only serves to increase its radius of power.

As to the impact of regional development policies, there seem to be definite limits beyond which the friction of space and accumulated historical disadvantages can be overcome by heavy government subsidies. Brazilian experience in government-sponsored industrial deconcentration is sobering. Many of the newly-relocated industries would probably fold without continued direct or indirect subsidies.

Reflection on such experiences provokes a basic question: why should industry be deconcentrated in the first place? The obvious answer is—so that population will be deconcentrated. But this only begs the question—why should population be deconcentrated? Apparently, much of regional policy has been guided by an implicit set of values which condemn spatial concentration and applaud all forms of decentralization under the assumption that territorial equity is tantamount to interpersonal equity. The premises underlying such assumptions have to be examined in more objective terms. Obviously, there are limits to concentration beyond which private and social costs increase significantly. But this limit varies enormously with historical and national contexts.

Finally, the experience of concentration and deconcentration in Brazil appears to reinforce the tenet that market economies—even of a peripheral nature—tend to establish their own limits to concentration. That is, deconcentration tends to occur whenever unspecified and intangible limits to growth are attained. Obviously, the nature and strength of the stimuli to deconcentration vary with concrete historical circumstances in a given country or region, at a given moment in time. Thus, spontaneous deconcentration is perhaps restricted to relatively dynamic capitalist societies (i.e. those which show significant growth, are currently undergoing structural and technological change, and have a large market base). Be that as it may, it is important to avoid confusing deconcentration with loss of power or dominance. In the Brazilian case at least, deconcentration implies extension of the radius of concentrated economic activity and of intensive demographic growth, as well as centralization of financial control. The result might aptly be described as centralized deconcentration.

11 Industrial Location Policies and the Urbanization Process in Brazil

PAULO ROBERTO HADDAD

Introduction

Macro-economic and sectoral economic policies are not neutral in their urban and regional effects in large countries where there are heterogeneous socio-economic and cultural contexts among the geographical areas. Policy-makers intend that these policies should be non-spatial in their conception and results; but when they are implemented across a territory with differing economic and social organization, development structures, and growth dynamics, impacts differ among the regions and urban subsystems. Therefore, in a large country, each macro-economic and sectoral policy always subsumes an implicit urban and regional policy that is sometimes even more relevant and decisive for the inter-regional distribution of growth effects than well-known explicit policies for regional and urban development.

This chapter analyses the regional and urban effects of industrial location policies in Brazil over the last three decades. It is assumed that there is a causal relation between industrialization and urbanization. Chapter 10 by Martine and Diniz has already dealt with the historical process of deconcentration of investments and production from the national dominant pole to peripheral areas in an interregional perspective, so this chapter is meant to complement such an approach by examining the relations between regional industrialization and urban subsystems. Given the territorial size of Brazil and the heterogeneity among its regions and urban centres, sometimes the analysis of the relation between industrialization and the national city-size distribution may become meaningless for specific industrial location and urban development policies.

Two main sections of this chapter are concerned with the relations between regional industrialization and urban subsystems. The first discusses the objectives, instruments and efficacy of industrial location policy in Brazil. Three subjects are emphasized: (1) the conception and the ideological traits of the development paradigm that has been adopted in the formulation and implementation of these policies in the country; (2) the roles of different federal and state agencies in formulating and implementing such policies; and (3) the fiscal incentives system for industrial promotion, the main instrument used to induce interregional movements of factors of production.

The second section presents some thoughts about three cases of industrial policy in Brazil and their impact on the urban subsystems in which they were set. Two are cases of industrial promotion in far-off regions led by the federal government to induce a process of development of peripheral areas: the formation of an export base in the Amazon region of Carajás, and the organization of industrial complexes in the depressed areas of the north-east; a third case illustrates the experience of 'decentralized deconcentration' through the expansion of industrial locations in the agglomerative field of the national dominant pole.

Industrial Location Policies in Brazil: Objectives, Instrument and Efficacy

The Brazilian economy has a long experience of more than three decades in developing and implementing industrial location policies. Their explicit objectives are mentioned in different official documents: to reduce regional development disparities, to mobilize latent resources in peripheral areas to accelerate national economic growth, to balance city-size distribution and the urban hierarchy, to generate export surplus for the payment of the foreign debt, to improve quality of life in metropolitan regions by managing congestion and environmental problems, to generate employment and income for poor people, etc. Since many of these objectives are merely rhetorical, we have to detect those that really matter by discussing the kind of development paradigm in which these industrial location policies are embedded so that the degree of conflict and ideological variance among them may be fully understood.

The instruments of public policies for industrial location depend on the alternatives of public intervention in economic and social processes, either direct or indirect, and on the nature of the institutions which control different instruments and resources to implement these policies (see Table 11.1). However, among all of these instruments, those mostly used in the Brazilian experience are: public investment in the infrastructure required to support plant location; fiscal incentives administered by national and subnational authorities; the location of industrial complexes in specific programme areas; industrial investments made directly by public enterprises; the supply of specific financial resources offered by development banks; and economic regulation. Only the efficacy of the system of fiscal incentives for industrial promotion is evaluated here.

Development paradigm

The development paradigm adopted by the political subsystem during the last two decades when industrial location policies were implemented in Brazil had some very important ideological traits. The basic analytical tools used by economists dealing with the main issues of public policies were traditional welfare theories, concerned with deriving normative criteria for the optimal interregional and interurban allocation of scarce resources from simplified hypotheses about

Table 11.1.   Brazil: mechanisms and instruments of the industrial location policies

Alternatives of public intervention	Financial, economic, technological, and institutional resources controlled by:		
	Public sector—direct administration	Public sector—indirect administration	Private capitalist sector
Direct intervention location	Infrastructure investments (to support industrial plants or industrial complexes)	Industrial investments by public enterprises (individual through regulation)	Direct control of prices and quantities
Indirect intervention	Non-relevant	Discrimination in public tariffs and prices to attract private investments to specific geographic areas	Indirect control of prices and quantities through fiscal policy, monetary and financial policies, etc.

individual consumer and entrepreneurial behaviour; since this theory has been developed assuming the absence of power in individual relations, policy recommendations derived from it are often extremely naive from a political and institutional perspective. As a consequence of isolating power relations from their analytical system, economic planners managed to split their decisions into 'economic' and 'political', with economic decisions allocating scarce resources efficiently and political decisions redistributing the results of such allocations. Equity objectives and spatial redistribution policies were therefore subordinated to the accelerated expansion of the per-capita product since, by increasing the income and the tax base of the economy, the political subsystem could manipulate greater resources allowing for solutions 'from above' to filter down to the social and economic problems of the poorest people (Haddad 1981).

In terms of interregional and interurban public policies, this paradigm takes for granted that economic growth begins—in a spontaneous or a programmed form—from a few dynamic sectors or geographical clusters and that later economic growth spreads its beneficial impacts to the other centres, sectors, or regions of the country. The growth potentialities of a peripheral area would depend on the discovery of natural resources available in this area in an adequate quantity and quality to induce the formation of an export base by transferring to it economic, technological and institutional resources from central areas. This would exploit its interregional comparative and cumulative advantages, thus deconcentrating economic activities, employment and income from the dominant poles. However, an assessment of the recent history of many countries which adopted strategies based on the theoretical conceptions of this paradigm indicates that only a few urban sectors and social groups in isolated regional centres located in the peripheral areas have been integrated into the production system of core regions.

As far as industrial location policies or the promotion of regional industrialization are concerned, empirical studies evaluating historical experiences of these (Hansen 1978; Stöhr and Taylor 1981; Kuklinski 1981) indicate, first, that the promotion of 'modern' industries in peripheral areas meant their economic activities became increasingly dependent not only on external production factors (capital and technology) but also on external demand, reinforcing the risks of high structural instability. Secondly, lack of an explicit sectoral specification in the industrial location policy made it regionally less effective, because little attention was paid to the functional relations between the 'modern' export-base activities and intraregional sectors, as well as linkages to regional resources and to regional demand. Thirdly, since growth-centre policies, including the creation of agglomeration economies, were developed within the same value and political systems prevailing nationally there was often only a shift or a reproduction of spatial disparities from one level (interregional) to another (intraregional) but little reduction of overall spatial disparities in living levels. Fourthly, investments in public infrastructure to support industrial location policies had increased accessibility between core regions and peripheral areas (by the extension of transport and communication networks), but with little emphasis on increased accessibility between and within peripheral areas. On the other hand, centrally-steered public investments did not allocate to the peripheral areas indispensable expenditures in the supply of traditional public goods (education, health, etc.) more linked to the basic needs of the regional population.

In practice, the recent Brazilian development experience has seen the official effort in public policies directed towards reinforcing the objective of economic efficiency; redistributive policies were to achieve, 'outside' the accumulation and production processes, whatever corrections were necessary to lessen the social and environmental costs incurred by the accelerated expansion of the GNP. The basic hypothesis of this strategy—which has not been proven in practice—is that any unfavourable effects upon income and property distribution can be offset, and those who lose will be more than matched by those who achieve a larger share of an increasing product. However, evidence from various social and economic indicators shows that the official policies, in timidly triggering such compensatory actions, permitted the benefits of development to be concentrated among a minority group of the Brazilian population, and that this concentration was in fact institutionalized through mechanisms such as restrictions on the freedom of trade unions to bargain for wage levels and working conditions, from 1965 to 1975. In short, industrial location policy was efficiently activated by the public administrative-bureaucratic subsystem in Brazil as far as it was 'functional' to reinforce the goal of increasing the rate of growth of GNP, notwithstanding its side effects in terms of social and environmental costs.

Concentration of decision-making powers

In large and complex countries with different levels of government, it is sometimes argued that policy instruments which affect many objectives must be centrally employed, while the instruments affecting one or a small number of objectives can be decentralized to a greater extent. The effectiveness of such decentralization will depend upon the organizational capabilities of the institutions involved. In the Brazilian case, for various reasons linked to the political logic of the 1964 military revolution, the general tendency has been towards reinforcing vertical and horizontal centralization of economic policy instruments, regardless of how ineffective or even deleterious they may be. The public bureaucracy's inexperience in specifying and executing macro-economic policies, combined with the need for getting the country's economy out of stagnation as quickly as possible, did not allow for a decentralization process which, it was believed, would result in a slow process of recycling the institutions. On the other hand, the scarcity of personnel experienced in handling such policies required that they be concentrated in a few dominant organizations within the public sector, which became the real decision-making centres. Finally, since conflicts between the objectives and goals of the different policies proposed could not be resolved at the level of open quarrel among social groups or regions, under penalty of jeopardizing the consolidation of the new political regime, it was necessary to assemble technical staff with the power to define the conditions for 'stability' of the economic system in the long run.

Two kinds of power concentration can be detected during this period which strongly affected the economic content of industrial location policies. The first is vertical concentration of decision-making power (intergovernmental relations), whereby the federal government has progressively constrained the political autonomy of states and municipalities to deal independently with economic policies by centralizing one by one the available instruments of public intervention in the processes of economic growth and distribution. The second is horizontal concentration of decision-making power (intragovernmental relations), whereby among all institutions of federal government there is a strong tendency for decisions to be taken within one or two ministries (generally, ministries of planning and/or finance), under the assumption that this is the only way to control the pressure on public resources and the fiscal and financial crises of the public sector. As a result of this intensive process of power concentration in public-policy decision-making, development programmes and projects which might meet the basic requirements of regional and local populations tend to be lost in the endless maze of a centralized bureaucracy because they are not considered to be in the critical path of 'national interest'. Public institutions which are responsible for the formulation and effectiveness of policies not directly oriented to growth and efficiency (such as social and environmental policies) have lost their political status and position in the hierarchical process of decision-making.

The efficacy of fiscal incentives in industrial location policies

In order to clarify the effect of the development paradigm on the conception and implementation of industrial location policies, a preliminary evaluation of the fiscal incentives system is now presented. Since 1963, a system of federal government income-tax incentives has been in operation to promote the industrialization of Brazilian peripheral regions: the north-east, the Amazon and the centre-west. The incentives discussed here belong to the Fundo de Investimentos do Nordeste (FINOR) and the Fundo de Investimentos da Amazônia (FINAM). FINOR and FINAM allow entrepreneurs exemption from 50 per cent of the tax due on investment projects located in the less developed macro-regions as long as they are approved by the public institutions which analyse and evaluate them. Through tax deductions for directly productive investments, public authorities have allowed for the reduction of private risks and for the decrease of the start-up costs for certain projects considered to be of high social priority and meant to promote faster expansion of the region. The fiscal incentives appear to have achieved their general targets, as the private sectors have increased their investments in the targeted geographical areas and strategic productive sectors.

Such special income-tax breaks are a means the government uses to increase investment expenditures on certain areas and activities, assigning to the private enterprises the leadership of the projects in return for the monetary benefits allowed. Even though this kind of incentive is considered by entrepreneurs as an indirect form of 'individual resources' available to finance their investment projects through the intermediary of the regional development agencies, such resources should really be treated as an implicit expenditure made by the government, that is, an expenditure tax. As they represent a reduction of the tax receipts that might have alternative allocation, this kind of implicit government expenditure should be evaluated in the same way as conventional public expenditures are treated in the fiscal budgets.

There are at least two more major reasons for us to carry out a more rigorous evaluation of the investment projects which receive fiscal incentives through reduced income tax. The first one refers to the complexity of a fiscal system which gives out subsidies through expenditure tax while its administration imposes high costs on the public sector. The second one concerns misunderstandings about the equity implications of such fiscal incentives: since the deductions for investments vary proportionally with the legal tax rate applicable to each taxpayer, the expenditure tax will have an increasingly perverse effect, the greater the degree of progressiveness in the income tax structure.

Besides, given the present stage of the Brazilian economy where the investment coefficient dropped from 26 per cent of GNP in the 1970s to about 16 per cent in the late 1980s, we must achieve greater efficiency in public resource allocation, aiming to increase the rate of net return of investment projects. However, it is not unusual to observe FINOR and FINAM industrial projects contributing to distortions, sometimes helping to reinforce the serious degree of regional income and wealth concentration and sometimes even distorting the local productive system, with perverse effects on employment levels and the regional ecosystem.

Such effects of investment projects that receive fiscal incentives arise, to a certain extent, from the crisis in the social and economic planning process in Brazil. In the 1980s, in accordance with the greater emphasis laid upon short-term issues (inflation control and equilibrium in the balance of payments), the federal government actually abandoned medium- and long-run development planning. Therefore, many government actions have gone through a disorganization phase and the political status of several institutions and public agencies within the central administrative structure has fallen. This is what has happened to fiscal system management: on one hand, projects were chosen based on an evaluation process aiming to co-ordinate them with regional and urban development objectives; on the other hand, the agents in charge of controlling such incentives lost their decisive autonomy and were exposed to increasing pressure from political and entrepreneurial lobbies in defining their priorities.

Some of the main conclusions in the evaluation of the fiscal incentives system for FINOR and FINAM industrial projects (COMIF 1986) can be summarized as follows.

1. FINOR: The industrial projects promoted by FINOR have reinforced the secondary sector of the regional economy quantitatively and qualitatively, as evidenced by changes in the industrial structure through technological

modernization, greater relative growth of dynamic sectors and increasing share of industrialized products in the regional export mix. FINOR subsidized projects have increased the industrial integration of the north-east with the rest of the country, particularly with its central dynamic pole. In terms of capitalization of new industry, or interindustry financial and marketing relations, FINOR has helped to develop in the region an industrial base which meets the interests of the hegemonic economic groups in the country. However, FINOR industrial projects have not proved relevant in solving the serious economic and social problems of the north-east region, because such incentives systems promote concentration. Moreover, inefficiencies are apparent in the administration of the incentive system; the technical procedures in evaluating and approving projects are inappropriate and the following-up of the projects inadequate and in some cases practically nonexistent; there is also no periodic evaluation of this system based upon scientifically-oriented field research using a broader approach in terms of regional development objectives.

2. FINAM: Fiscal incentives have been adopted to support two basic models of regional industrialization in the Amazon region. One model emphasizes local raw material, produces goods strictly dependent on international markets. faces unfavourable terms of trade and increasing competition from substitute products and tends to specialize in a few non-dynamic sectors: non-metallic minerals, wood processing, natural rubber, etc. The other model is based on the presence of the Free Trade Zone of Manaus, along with its modern enterprises (mainly controlled by multinational capital). It uses high technology processes, depends on inputs from extraregional markets and exports their production to the rest of the country or abroad. Although the investment and production targets have been achieved with some time delay, social and economic indicators have shown that these projects did not help to increase wage levels in the region, for the skill levels of the required workers are low and little attention has been given to improving the quality of the labour force. Apparent social benefits derived from the regional industrialization process were therefore deceptive.

Evaluation of the application of fiscal incentives in geographical areas and specific sectors of the Brazilian economy therefore show the need for broader reformulation of their institutional mechanisms to bring them into line with the objectives of national and regional planning. However, there will long be a need to maintain fiscal and financial incentives to attract entrepreneurial investment projects for the north, north-east and centre-west regions; such incentives are required to counterbalance the highly favourable locational effects of the agglomeration and urbanization economies available in many urban centres of the most developed areas of the country.

Regional Industrialization and Urban Subsystems

After 1970, two fundamental processes of economic deconcentration from the metropolitan area of São Paulo took place in Brazil: one planned and oriented by the federal government to promote industrial growth in far-off regions in the north-east and in the north; the other, towards the outer rim of the metropolitan area involving its spatial expansion and economic strengthening. The historical reasons that prompted these processes of deconcentration and their overall significance and perspectives for the Brazilian economy are analysed in Chapter 10. This section indicates how these trends towards deconcentration from São Paulo are affecting regional spatial structures, and specially the urban subsystems where regional industrialization took place. Since there are many such experiences to draw from, only three regional cases of industrial location policy are analysed: the formation of an export base; the organization of industrial complexes; and the expansion of the agglomeration field of the dominant pole.

Location Policy I: The formation of an export base

In many peripheral regions of Brazil, industrialization of available resources, normally mineral resources, is frequently necessary for development to take off, usually supported by input demands from other regions or abroad. Resource-dominated economic expansion then becomes the principal characteristic of the spatial subsystem of these regions. The geographical juxtaposition of mineral-resource endowments brings to different regions of the country first-stage resources-using manufacturers, who need to locate their plants near the accessible deposits to minimize transport costs, as this processing stage is generally the primary weight-losing point in the industrial production circuit. The role of government is basically to supply economic infrastructure to support the operation of the directly productive investments and to administer fiscal incentives to attract these projects.

However, since 1974, trends in world demand for metals and mineral alloys have been sluggish and prospects are gloomy. Changes in the product composition of income are expected to lower the relative weight of industrial products with a higher intensity of metallic inputs; on the supply side the quantity of mineral raw materials per unit of industrial production is steadily declining because of the high degree of substitutability among such materials, the possibility of their recycling and the increasing miniaturization of many final-demand industrial products.

Although, in the long run, this atrophy in demand for metals will cause resource activities to decline in relative importance, there is still an economic interest in developing mineral-metallurgical industrial activities. This is because the most conservative projections still estimate a yearly expansion of 2 per cent in the world market for the traditional and strategic primary minerals, sustained mainly by heavy industry and infrastructure growth in countries of late industrialization with less advanced technological processes.

Nevertheless, in a socio-economic context where centre–periphery relations prevail, regional economies whose export base is restricted to natural resources become extremely vulnerable and unstable since the dominating centre, by investing in transport and communications sectors in the periphery, induces a process of internal colonialism in the country's interregional system. In those geographical areas with a large resource-potential base, directly productive investment projects are financed and controlled by large extraregional corporations, aiming to generate cheaply an export surplus of raw materials and semiprocessed products, to support industrialization in other regions or to solve acute problems in the balance of payments. For such an export base to maintain a regional economic development process, however, a necessary condition is dynamism in the external demand markets, thus enabling a dispersal of growth to other productive sectors and activities inside the region.

What type of urban subsystem can we expect from a regional spatial structure in which the industrialization process has taken this form over a sufficiently long period? To answer this question we can use the methodological approach formulated by Hilhorst (1971), who bases his typology of regional spatial structures on three factors. Factor 1 is the distribution within the region of exploited natural resources other than those of importance for agriculture. Exploitation of these resources through extractive mining and initial processing will strongly influence the distribution of population. If they are spatially concentrated, the people engaged in their exploitation will tend to live in one large mining town or in a cluster of mining towns; the spatial dispersion of the mineral resources will be more advantageous to the long-term development of the region because, besides the organization of a more balanced system of cities, the transport and communication networks will influence the region's potential to start other activities along these networks. Factor 2 is the relative size of the ecologically most favourable area for exploitation within the region; settlers will tend to concentrate in this area where natural conditions are such that they result in a higher productivity per hectare than anywhere else in the region, given the same technological level. Factor 3 is the number of resource-based functions the region performs within the national system; if more than one such function is performed, there will be various development potential focuses in the region.

If these factors are assumed to have worked themselves out over a relatively long period, their effects on the type of city size distribution and the relative size of the periphery (less developed areas inside the region) can be subsumed in two extreme cases. First, if the natural resources are spatially concentrated, if the ecologically most favourable area is relatively small, and if there is only one natural resources-based activity being performed, there will be a tendency towards a primate distribution of city sizes and a relatively large territorial extent of the periphery. Second, if the natural resources are dispersed, if the ecologically most favourable area under exploitation is relatively large, and if there are various natural resources-based activities being performed, there will be a tendency towards a rank-size distribution of cities and a relatively small periphery.

An illustration of this pattern is given by the spatial structure of the Carajás region in the north of Brazil where, since 1967, surveys of the natural resources in the Carajás Mountains (in the Amazon region) have revealed the existence of huge mineral reserves of manganese, copper, nickel and gold, in addition to iron ore deposits estimated at more than 18 billion tons. Because of the external crisis in the Brazilian balance of payments, the regional economic infrastructure (a modern railroad 960 km long, improvements in port facilities, etc.) has been strongly reinforced since 1975 by federal government investments to play an important role in the export of minerals and metallurgical products. The exploitation of mineral resources in the region is most advanced and concentrated in the Carajás Mountains; the ecologically most favourable area in exploitation along the railway is quite small because of intensive deforestation in the last decade; and, so far, metallurgical production is in small and medium-sized plants for the production of pig iron, copper, ferro-manganese, nickel, ferro-nickel, etc., which have a low impact on the growth of formal urban employment markets.

The urban subsystem which is being structured under the basic influence of the Carajás export corridor has the following characteristics (SEPLAN, 1989). There is one big city (Marabá) with more than 250,000 inhabitants, located near the mining activities, which has attracted some investments in first-stage processing. There are no intermediate or medium-sized cities (subregional centres); twelve small cities with populations of under 30,000 function as central places of fourth order in the city-size distribution; and two cities with populations of between 50,000 and 70,000 tend to be zonal centres in the regional urban hierarchy.

Social and economic indicators show that impulses of economic growth are not being transmitted from higher to lower centres in the hierarchy and that there is a strong tendency for disparities in intraregional income and quality of life to increase, forming a periphery with a large territorial extent. Since the industrial policy to promote economic growth in Carajás is oriented to building an export base of mineral and metal products to help solve the country's balance-of-payments problems, public infrastructure investments are concentrated in the region only in so far as they are needed for a good export performance. More than fifty industrial projects based on the abundant primary metals have been approved by the fiscal incentives authorities. Social and environmental impacts of this industrialization process are not seriously considered; for instance, the industrial consumption of charcoal to generate energy for the metallurgical smelting plants is projected to total 10.24 million tons by the year 2000, mainly from the deforestation of over 2 million hectares in the Amazon region. The central authorities consider that the only regional problems of national interest are those related to the dynamism of the export base, so they will not pay attention to other problems of urbanization in the region such as the lack of social infrastructure in the cities to accommodate the pressure of the increasing migration flows, which they classify as a regional problem of 'regional' interest.

Location policy II: The organization of industrial complexes

In the last two decades, many developing countries have incorporated the concept of industrial complexes in their industrial location policies, with the basic objective of reducing spatial inequalities in the national development process. In Brazil, the Second National Development Plan (1975–9) proposed an industrialization strategy for the north-east which emphasized the organization and location of industrial complexes, involving sets of productive plants, technologically inter-dependent and geographically concentrated. The planning and establishment of these industrial complexes has been going on ever since in this region: the petro-chemical complex of Camaçari (Bahia); the chorochemical complex of Alagoas; the chemical-metallurgical complex of Rio Grande do Norte; and the integrated industrial complex of Sergipe.

The concept adopted in the industrial programming of the Second National Development Plan was that of an industrial complex, not of an industrial con-glomerate. The two terms are differentiated by whether the locational issue is incorporated: intensive interindustry relations with no concern as to the spatial distribution of activities are a necessary but not a sufficient condition to define an industrial complex. Therefore, an industrial complex may be characterized opera-tionally as a group of industries, or economic activities, linked by strong and significant flows of goods and services besides an important similarity as to their locational patterns (Isard 1960; Barbetto and Pistonesi 1985; Haddad 1989).

Although in a relatively developed country economic activities tend to be highly interdependent, the interdependent transactions do not follow a random pattern; interindustry relations can be restructured by different methods so that subsets of industries can be put together in different blocks; the industries belong-ing to each block maintain more intensive interindustry relations with the other industries in the same block than with those in other blocks. The basis for the organization of these blocks is certain fundamental technological elements in the production structure of modern economic systems. Recent empirical studies of the industrial structure dynamics of the Brazilian economy have tried to identify these types of conglomerates, by experimenting with different methods of ana-lysis, including graph theory, multivariate statistical analysis and mathematical programming (Haddad 1989).

However, for the analysis of regional and urban problems, it is necessary to incorporate the spatial dimension into the industrial conglomerate studies. Usually, the planning methodology adopted in Brazil to identify the industrial complexes starts from information about the engineering of products and processes, combined with locational studies to define the economic viability of deconcentrating these blocks of interlinked activities into peripheral areas. It is very difficult to explain analytically the occurrence of a significant similarity in the locational patterns of economic activities and sectors of an industrial com-plex. The basic question is whether these activities and sectors tend to locate in specific urban centres because they are linked with other activities or sectors sup-plying services (technical assistance, financial subsystems, trade networks, etc.) located in these centres, or because of primary interindustrial linkages with other plants which supply their main inputs according to technological affinities. There are many methodological difficulties in developing regression models to detect the

240 Paulo Roberto Haddad

reasons for spatial linkages between economic activities, because of the geo-graphical coexistence of the primary and secondary linkages in many urban centres. The problem is that urbanization economies are conditioning factors for the locational decisions of almost all types of large-scale industrial investments, including those which form an industrial complex.

The pre-existence and the reproduction of urbanization economies in three metropolitan areas of the north-east (Recife, Salvador, and Fortaleza) were the most important elements in explaining the strong spatial concentration of invest-ment and employment in the region since the institutionalization of the fiscal incentives system (FINOR) in the 1960s: between 1960 and 1980, these metro-politan areas cumulated 63 per cent of the investments and 56 per cent of the employment in all industrial projects approved by the fiscal incentives system. The recent geographical dispersion of industrial complexes to the capital cities in other states will avoid this excessive concentration of the 1980s; so these industrial complexes will play an important role not only in the deconcentration of indus-trial activities from the national dominant pole to far-off regions but also in a bal-anced distribution of industrial investments between metropolitan areas and medium-sized cities in the north-east, thus avoiding reinforcement of a spon-taneous process of intraregional development concentration.

Regarding the impact of industrial complexes in the urban subsystems where they are located, there are at least two types of problem: the acceleration of city population growth and the consequent informalization of the urban economy; and the deterioration of urban environment and quality of life. Impact analysis is a special form of conditional prediction which examines expected consequences of an exogenous change in a given model, under *ceteris paribus* conditions. It is difficult to isolate the effects on economic and environmental conditions of the urban centres where the complexes are located since these centres, generally, have already surpassed the threshold size required for urbanization economies to take place. Nevertheless, some important points can be made based on the experience of location policy for industrial complexes in the metropolitan areas and medium-sized cities of the north-east region in Brazil.

The fiscal incentives system for attracting private investors to that region, originating from almost 50-per-cent income-tax deduction, also promoted exemption from import duty for the importation of modern equipment, financial support to investments through negative rates of real interest, and 100 per cent income-tax exemption for the profits generated by the operation of the new plants. The result was a decreased cost of capital (compared with its opportunity cost) to entrepreneurs who based their decisions to invest on cash flow of projects calcul-ated from effective market prices. The current wage rate, on the other hand, was legally determined by a minimum subsistence level and has not reflected the relat-ive scarcity of labour in the region, where the rates of open unemployment and structural underemployment are very high. Therefore, if the authorities adminis-trating the allocation of the fiscal incentives had been able to use a system of social prices to analyse and evaluate investment projects for the region, the rise in formal employment opportunities that could be induced with a lower capital–labour relation per unit of investment might have been seen as much more significant and desirable.

Using the OECD Manual formula

$$SCL = c - 1/so\,(c - m)$$

to calculate the social cost of labour (where c = consumption level of urban worker measured at social cost; m = marginal productivity of labour in agriculture; so = present value of one unit of investment in consumption terms), we would conclude that, according to many alternative hypotheses for estimating the values of the parameters, the social cost of labour in the north-east varies from 50 to 60 per cent of the private costs. Should these values be adopted by the authorities in the project-selection process, the reduction in the relative price of labour could stimulate a higher volume of current production, an easing of the unemployment and underemployment problems and an improvement in personal income distribution. For entrepreneurs investing in the region, this reduction of labour market price might be manifest through the decrease or elimination of the firms' contribution to the costs of social insurance for the labour force or the granting of direct subsidies for the employment of labour itself. On the other hand, the capital-intensive nature of the industrial complexes has reinforced this inadequate pattern of dealing with the employment issue in the region. Besides having a less favourable labour/capital ratio for the development of the formal urban labour markets, these complexes have employed during the construction phase a large number of unskilled labourers who could not find an alternative job afterwards, increasing the rate of underemployment in the principal metropolitan areas and urban centres of the region.

After the industrialization spurt in the region, even with the presence of high rates of unemployment and underemployment in the urban labour markets, there were very strong migratory movements to the large cities from rural areas and small urban centres lacking economic and social infrastructure, where the average income is four to five times lower than the average wage level paid by the new industrial projects. Owing to insufficient dynamism in their labour markets, the metropolitan areas and medium-sized cities have developed very active informal economies, estimated to be between 30 to 50 per cent of their total economic activity (metropolitan or urban GDP). Considering as a definition of visible underemployment 'the population who work part-time but would like to work full-time, besides those who are occasionally working part-time for economic reasons', the rates of visible underemployment may be higher than 20 per cent in some of the large urban centres of the north-east. On the other hand, if under-remuneration of up to half a minimum wage is taken to define disguised underemployment (a figure which would incorporate many of those obviously underemployed), the unfortunate position of employed and self-employed workers in those urban centres is revealed, as almost 40 per cent of the labour force is in this situation, notwithstanding that a minimum wage already indicated absolute poverty at that time.

The establishment of industrial complexes in the north-east as part of the expansion of the core region or dominant pole in the country, deconcentrated a great volume of private and public investment in the production of intermediate goods in heavy industries with high capital-intensity through isolated actions controlled by extraregional capital and without articulation with a broadly-based regional development policy. Since these industrial poles are meant basically to transform large quantities of raw materials and energy, their propensity to pollute the urban environment is extremely high. In fact, since environmental regulations were quite flexible in the 1970s, when the decision to invest in these industrial complexes was made, these complexes are causing a lot of pollution problems to their city-regions. But the future prospects for public policies dealing with this issue are not so gloomy: adequate funds with support from external institutions are being offered to encourage the producers of environmental pollution to instal control equipment; regional and local public institutions propose the adoption of effluent standards tailored to each enterprise; an increasing tax is imposed on polluting industries and firms equivalent to the associated external cost. How effective this system of taxation, regulation, standards and licences will be in the future will depend on the pressure of organized groups within society and public opinion concerning the political subsystem.

Location policy III: The process of centralized deconcentration

The first two cases of industrial location policy illustrate the implications for urbanization of the process of economic deconcentration of investments and employment from the metropolitan area of São Paulo to far-off regions in the periphery of the country. This third case is somewhat related to the second type of deconcentration toward the outer rim of the dominant pole; it is called 'a process of centralized deconcentration' because the spontaneous or induced decisions of entrepreneurs to relocate activities into a new axis of regional development inside the agglomerative field of the metropolitan area of São Paulo will probably bring about a reinforcement of this national dominant pole.

There are many economic reasons to cause private entrepreneurs to leave the core region without moving on to far-off regions in the country. A simple version of the Kaldor model (Kaldor 1970; Azzoni 1986) may be used to evaluate the relative performance of different regions in a country in attracting the new industrial investment required for a process of polarization reversal. Let us assume that entrepreneurs wish to locate their plants in regions where the private profitability of investments is higher; that the lower the efficiency wage (the index of growth of nominal wages divided by the index of growth of productivity) the higher the competitive capacity of the region and the higher the growth of regional production; that the growth rate of nominal wages (among workers in the same functional activities) will turn out to be practically the same in all the regions of the country owing to the great mobility of this factor in the open regional economies of a country; and, finally, that efficiency wages tend to decrease in the regions (and in specific industries of regions) where productivity grows at a faster rate than the national average. Empirical studies show that higher growth of areas in the hinterland relatively close to the dominant pole is correlated with higher profitability of industrial investments in these areas. One of these studies compares the performance of productivity, wages and profitability in terms of national averages among industries in the metropolitan area of São Paulo and some cities in areas of industrial deconcentration in the hinterland of this state (Azzoni 1986). The results show the economic vitality of some of these areas for plant location and their better performance regarding the indicators when compared with the metropolitan area of São Paulo (see Table 11.2).

It is important to show the fundamental reasons for this regional spatial structure, looking critically into the traditional location theories which have, so far, afforded an analytical support to industrial location policies. The classical theories of location have an analytical utility mainly for the examination of sectors in which the inputs are voluminous and localized, and therefore liable to a greater spatial deconcentration. There is some consensus that such theories of industrial location must be reformulated, because of the type of productive organization

Table 11.2.   Productivity, wages and profitability in industry in the state of São Paulo, 1980

Regions and cities	Labour productivity (value added per worker)	Wages	Profitability (value added less labour costs)
I. Metropolitan area			
I.1 More industrialized cities	140	130	142
I.2 Other cities	137	121	141
II. Hinterland			
II.1 Campinas (including Jundiaí, Limeira, Piracicaba and Rio Claro)	169	131	179
II.2 Vale do Paraiba			
(a) São José dos Campos and Taubaté	147	145	147
(b) Guaratinguetá and Cruzeiro	109	105	110
II.3 Sorocaba			
(a) Sorocaba	136	116	141
(b) Itapetininga and Botucatu	148	108	157
II.4 Ribeirão Preto (including Araraquara and São Carlos)	139	102	149
II.5 Bauru	150	112	159
II.6 Marilia	126	94	134

Note: References to national averages = 100

and competitive structure implicit in them; the insufficient and inadequate treatment offered to labour; the limited view of the issue of industrial integration and disintegration; the restricted comprehension of the economies-of-agglomeration concept; and the spatial distribution of economic activities.

It is necessary to enlarge the traditional concept of economies of agglomeration in order to increase its analytical contribution to understanding the locational patterns of dynamic industrial activities. In the specialized literature, the economies of agglomeration are being given increasing importance in explaining the locational patterns of several sectors or industries which have acquired advantages in reducing their production costs because they are located in places (generally, large urban clusters) which contain several productive units, producing on a significant scale. The basic agglomerative factors affecting enterprise locational decisions have been classified into three groups: economies of scale, owing to an increase in the production scale of the firm itself; economies of localization, owing to its location next to other firms from the same sector, and economies of urbanization, regarding its location at a place where the activities of different productive sectors are concentrated, affecting population, income, employment, etc.

Some important recent research has expanded the original conception of economies of agglomeration by connecting them to the large urban centres as the summit of a polarized field, whose attractive power decreases as the distance from these centres increases. The intention is not to hold the metropolis or the urban clusters as the locational attraction centre but to consider a larger region surrounding that metropolis or that urban cluster as an agglomerative field that can produce regionalization economies. The great difference between this analysis and the traditional analysis is the distinction between urban and regional advantages and the concept that, given the level of regional attraction, the economies of urbanization are almost ubiquitous, and can be acquired by quite small towns as well as big cities. 'Regarding the costs, however, one gets great differences according to changes in the urban size. The measure to be taken is to reinforce the medium-sized cities' attractive potential inside the attraction area of the region' (Azzoni 1986).

It is to be concluded, then, that there are great opportunities for economic growth and demographic expansion of the cities (mainly those of medium size) which are on the deconcentration axis of the dominant-pole agglomerative field and that as a new expansion cycle in the Brazilian economy begins, a spatial reconcentration of development may occur, a kind of reversal of the polarization which started in the mid-1970s. This reconcentration can be greater the more the current industrial promotion policies of the state and local authorities on the borderline of the metropolitan area of São Paulo are intensified. Therefore, deconcentration to the outer rim of this area tends to be more relevant in this new cycle of economic expansion than deconcentration to far-off regions.

12 Urbanization of the Brazilian Frontier

DONALD SAWYER

The Amazon region has become the main stage for frontier expansion in Brazil in the last two decades. Although it is usually depicted as an 'agricultural frontier', in which one would expect rapid growth of rural population, the region has in fact undergone rapid urbanization, with levels similar to the rest of the country outside the urban-industrial core. It may now be more appropriate to speak of urbanization of the frontier than *of* urbanization *on* the frontier.

The present analysis deals with this apparent paradox, attempting to explain the process under way in the Amazon in the context of broader changes in Brazil as a whole and their interplay with the region's particular ecological and historical characteristics. The chapter describes levels and trends of urbanization in frontier regions, discusses causes of non-metropolitan urbanization, explains the specific characteristics of pioneer urbanization, and suggests some general conclusions. The analysis is based in large part on field observations in Acre, Rondônia, Pará, and Goiás, complemented by review of the literature (Sawyer, Montanari and Abers, 1989).

Level and Trends of Urbanization in Frontier Regions

For present purposes, 'frontier regions', which we will loosely refer to as the Amazon, are the north region or classic Amazon (states of Rondônia, Acre, Amazonas, Roraima, Pará, and Amapá) as well as the centre-west region (Mato Grosso do Sul, Mato Grosso, Goiás, Tocantins, and Brasília). These regions cover about 60 per cent of Brazil (see Figure 12.1). The north region is primarily rainforest, while the centre–west includes large areas of savannah. This definition of frontier regions corresponds roughly to 'Legal Amazônia', a planning area. We focus on the process of occupation since the 1960s, when Brazilian economic development passed from the import-substitution phase to the phase of associated and dependent development.

'Urbanization' is used not only in the strict sense of the proportion of the total population residing in urban places, but also in the broad sense of social change associated with the trend of increase in this proportion.

Earlier versions of this paper in Portuguese were presented at the Congress of Brazilian Architects in Belo Horizonte in 1985 and at the workshop 'A Formação das Cidades na Fronteira' in Rio de Janeiro in 1987 (Sawyer, 1987). The author wishes to thank Rebecca Abers for help with the translation and the members of the Amazon Studies Group (GEA) for their discussion and suggestions.

Fig. 12.1.   Brazil

Table 12.1 shows urbanization rates (urban population/total population × 100) by region for Brazil from 1940 to 1980. The south-east, which includes the large metropolitan areas of Rio de Janeiro, São Paulo and Belo Horizonte, and is Brazil's industrial core, has always been the most urban. Although in the past the populations of all regions except the south-east have been predominantly rural, in the 1970s they all became primarily urban. Unlike large developing countries in Asia and Africa, which are about two-thirds rural, Brazil, like many other Latin American countries, is approximately two-thirds urban. Internal differences are significant but not dramatic. The north region has always been more urban than the north-east, and since the 1960s the centre-west region has been more urban than the south. In terms of urbanization rates, the frontier regions are thus not

Table 12.1. Urbanization rates, by region, Brazil, 1940–80

Region	1940	1950	1960	1970	1980
North	27.8	31.5	37.8	45.1	51.7
Centre-West	21.5	24.4	35.0	48.0	67.8
North-east	23.4	26.4	34.2	41.8	50.4
South-east	39.4	47.6	57.4	72.7	82.8
South	27.7	29.5	37.6	44.3	62.4
Brazil	32.2	36.2	45.1	55.9	67.6

Source: Preliminary synopsis of the 1980 demographic census.

very different from other non-core regions. They have in all probability become much more urban during the 1980s.

Brasília, which held 15.6 per cent of the population of the centre-west in 1980, contributed to the accelerated expansion of the urban population in that region, which jumped nearly 20 percentage points in a single decade. The growth of the new national capital had little to do with the dynamics of frontier expansion as such. However, there is much more to urban growth in frontier regions than expansion of the national and state capital cities. Table 12.2 shows that the capital cities in each region were responsible for 58.5 per cent and 45.6 per cent of the urban populations, respectively. This chapter focuses especially on the remainder, more than 4 million persons, 30.1 per cent of the total population in frontier regions, especially that portion which represents pioneer urban settlement.

Table 12.2. Total, urban, capital, and other urban population, by state, north and centre-west regions, 1980

State and region	Total	Urban		
		Total	Capital[a]	Other
Rondônia	491,069	228,539	103,850	124,689
Acre	301,303	132,169	89,799	42,370
Amazonas	1,430,089	856,617	620,510	236,107
Roraima	79,159	48,734	43,786	4,948
Pará	3,403,391	1,667,356	826,776	840,580
Amapa	175,257	103,735	90,795	12,940
North	5,880,268	3,037,150	1,775,516	1,261,634
M G do Sul	1,369,567	919,123	289,853	629,270
Mato Grosso	1,138,691	654,952	198,086	456,866
Goiás[b]	3,859,602	2,401,491	704,085	1,697,406
Brasília	1,176,935	1,139,031	1,139,031	—
Centre-West	7,544,795	5,114,597	2,331,055	2,783,542
Total	13,425,063	8,151,747	4,106,571	4,045,176

[a] Sinopse Preliminar, Censo Demográfico, 1980
[b] Including state of Tocantins, created in 1989

Source: Demographic Census, 1980.

Urbanization rates in frontier areas are probably underestimated, since there is a lag between the appearance of urban nuclei and their official reclassification as district or municipal seats. This administrative criterion is used by the Brazilian census bureau to define 'urban'.

Some authors exclude from the 'urban' category those areas which do not reach a certain minimum size, such as 2,000 or 20,000 inhabitants. Using the minimum size of 20,000, the urbanization rate in 1980 falls to 39.2 per cent for the north region, 34.3 per cent for the centre-west region, and 50.6 per cent for Brazil (Faria, 1983: 125). Thus, 12.5 per cent of the population of the north region and 33.5 per cent of the population of the centre-west region lived in urban nuclei of fewer than 20,000 inhabitants.

Size criteria have different meanings in different settings. In frontier conditions, where distances are large, some nuclei that are small in demographic terms exercise important urban functions. By the criterion of 20,000 inhabitants, the cities of Guajará-Mirim, Cruzeiro do Sul, Tefé, Manacapuru, and Conceicão do Araguaia, among others, would not be considered 'urban' in 1980, in spite of being commercial and financial centres with areas of influence reaching over hundreds or thousands of square kilometres. Even nuclei with fewer than 2,000 inhabitants, such as Plácido de Castro, Barcelos, Ipixuna, and São Félix do Xingu, can be tiny metropolises within their respective enormous hinterlands.

Frontier urbanization is obviously due primarily to migration. Census data show that of the 3,623,756 inter- or intrastate migratory moves ending in frontier regions between 1970 and 1980, 64 per cent involved migration to urban areas (Sawyer and Pinheiro, 1984: 14–15). The urbanization occurs principally in the region which Martine and Carmargo (1983) called the 'consolidated frontier' (Mato Grosso do Sul, Goiás, and Brasília), but it is also predominant in most of the states they call the 'expanding frontier' (Amazonas, Acre, Amapá, and Roraima).

The spatial distribution of these changes can be better visualized if we look at population growth rates for the 1970s at the micro-regional level (Sawyer 1984). For the total population we observe three distinct belts within the frontier regions: recent, current, and former (see Figure 12.2).

1. The 'recent' frontier includes Mato Grosso do Sul, southern Mato Grosso, Goiás, and Tocantins. In the greater part of this area, growth rates, which rarely surpass 3 per cent per year, suggest a negative or near zero net migration rate for the total population. Since during the 1960s this belt had very high growth rates, there was a marked inversion of growth tendencies.
2. The 'current' frontier extends from Rondônia through northern Mato Grosso and into southern Pará. Average growth rates in the 1970s were above 6 per cent per year, in some cases above 15 per cent. Judging by rates, this belt should include Roraima as well.
3. The 'former' frontier encompasses Acre, Amazonas, northern Pará and northern Amapá. The rates for the greater part of this third belt indicate

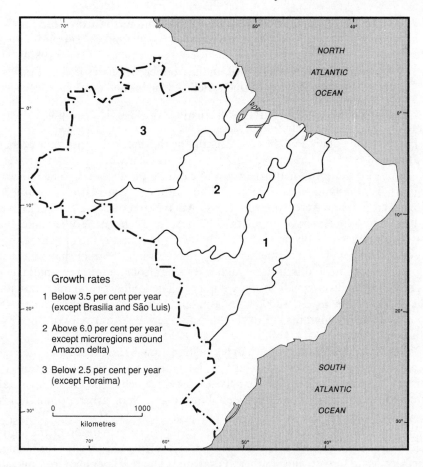

Fig. 12.2. Growth rates of rural population on the Great Frontier, Brazil, 1970–80

negative net migration for the total population. Thus, it should be considered as quite distinct from the so-called 'expanding frontier'.

In spite of net immigration at the aggregate level for the north and centre-west regions, with high growth rates in some micro-regions, in two of the three belts—practically two-thirds of the frontier regions' total area—there is negative net migration. This curious fact—emigration from 'frontier' areas—gives us pause.

Emigration from parts of the Amazon results from three migrant flows, which can be identified in the census data about prior state of residence of migrants in the last ten years:

1. Migration from the first to the second belt. The advance of the frontier can behave like a wave, leaving behind it a vacuum or 'hollow frontier' (James 1949).

2. Attraction of population from the entire frontier towards more central regions, following the national tendency of population concentration in the South-East region, especially in metropolitan areas (see Martine 1987).
3. Migration to the larger cities within the frontier regions, especially Brasília, Porto Velho, Rio Branco, Manaus, Belém, Cuiabá, and Goiânia.

Mapping rural and urban population growth rates separately facilitates understanding the spatial distribution of these flows.

For the rural population, the contrasts among the three belts are dramatic. For the first and third belts population-growth rates are clearly below natural growth, which was 2.5 per cent for Brazil as a whole during the decade. In many microregions, especially in Mato Grosso do Sul, southern Mato Grosso, southern Goiás and parts of Acre, Amazonas, and Amapá, the rates are even negative, indicating absolute losses of population. In the second belt, on the other hand, the rates are unquestionably above natural growth. This belt is the only area that absorbs rural population on the frontier, or in Brazil as a whole for that matter. It should be remembered that these high rates stem from an initially small base, representing relatively small absolute numbers. The total net rural migration for this area is of the order of 500,000 migrants, compared with approximately 16 million net urban migrants in Brazil in the same period (Wood and Wilson 1984; Martine 1987).

When we look at the map of urban population growth (Fig. 12.2), the uniformity is dramatic. The rates are very high in all frontier areas, without exception. In this respect, there is no difference between the three belts. The growth of rural population on the frontier is localized, but the growth of urban population is generalized.

We are therefore faced with a paradox. The regions of expansion of the 'agricultural' frontier in Brazil, with the exception of a belt passing through Rondônia, northern Mato Grosso and southern Pará, are losing rural population, while all are marked by accelerated urban growth. Thus it is now appropriate to speak of urbanization 'of' the frontier. The following sections of this chapter focus on the vigorous growth of small and medium cities in the interior, especially in the context of pioneer settlement.

Causes of Urbanization of the Countryside

Urbanization of the countryside in Brazil

Urbanization in frontier areas should be understood in the context of the urbanization taking place throughout Brazil. In the 1970s, the proportion of the Brazilian population living in urban areas jumped from 55.9 per cent to 67.6 per cent. This population redistribution can be divided into two principal components, the growth of metropolitan areas and the growth of medium-sized and small cities in the interior, or 'urbanization of the countryside'.

Table 12.3 shows the percentage of the urban population of each region of Brazil living in cities of over 100,000 inhabitants in 1980. The degree of primacy is not particularly high for Brazil as a whole or for the regions separately. The north and centre-west regions have higher degrees of concentration of the urban population than the north-east and south. The north stands out as the only region in which the concentration decreased over time, over the two decades 1960–80.

The only officially recognized metropolitan regions in frontier regions are Brasília and Belém. For an analysis at a regional level, we could add medium-sized cities such as Campo Grande, Cuiabá, Porto Velho, Rio Branco, Manaus, Santarém, and Goiânia, which have functions different from those of smaller cities. Even though the growth of larger cities, because of their size, represents a large proportion of urbanization at the regional level, we see in the maps of growth rates that smaller cities are also growing rapidly, not only on the frontier, but also in the rest of Brazil (the higher rates on the frontier are principally due to small initial bases).

The explanations for 'urbanization of the countryside' in Brazil, through growth of medium-sized and small cities, have to do with broader economic and demographic trends. They include partial modernization of agriculture, the need of modern agriculture for urban services, the new consumption patterns of Brazil's rural population, the need for urban consumer services, decreased access to land, and, finally, decreased access to ownership and employment in large cities.

The partial modernization of farming practices in Brazil has involved mechanization in the preparation and cultivation phases and incorporation of chemical and genetic technologies, while harvesting continues to be done manually. This unequal use of modern technology decreases the demand for labour during most of the year and increases it during the harvest season, due to higher productivity of land (Silva 1981). Technical progress also affects craftsmanship and services within farms, which used to be more autarchic, so as to decrease the occupation of the workforce in activities which are not directly agricultural and which could be performed in the off-peak seasons. Thus, incomplete technical progress

Table 12.3. Percentage of the urban population in cities with more than 100,000 inhabitants, by region, Brazil, 1950–80

Region	1950	1960	1970	1980
North	38.8	52.3	52.2	51.7
Centre-West	—	12.6	41.4	48.0
North-east	23.4	36.1	37.1	37.8
South-east	46.9	49.5	55.1	56.2
South	22.2	24.3	29.5	37.0
Brazil (total)	36.6	41.6	46.7	48.7

Source: Sinopse Preliminar, Censos Demográficos, 1950 to 1980, cited in Davidovich and Fredrich (1988: 28).

accentuates the seasonality of demand for agricultural labour. A considerable part of the labour expelled from agricultural establishments remains in small towns and cities in the interior. These rural workers who are simultaneously urban residents are called *volantes* or *bóia-frias*. The partial character of agricultural modernization is the fundamental economic explanation for this phenomenon.

On the traditional farm, services linked to production were developed largely within the establishment, but modern technology demands services of a sophistication and scale that can only be provided off the farm: machine and equipment maintenance, distribution of modern inputs, financing, technical assistance, telecommunications, etc. To this we can add services linked to consumption and to the reproduction of qualified labour (operators, technicians, administrators) who apply modern technology: schools, hospitals, supermarkets, leisure, etc. Urban services generate urban employment directly, as well as absorbing less qualified labour, such as bricklayers and washerwomen, through multiplier effects.

In the post-war period of import substitution, the consumption 'needs' of Brazil's rural population were redefined, incorporating a wide variety of industrialized products, including ready-made clothes, shoes and durable consumer goods. These consumer goods, which are perfectly transportable, are distributed in the commercial centres and markets of small cities and towns of the interior. In addition to the above-mentioned consumer goods, the rural population also seeks typically urban services such as education, health care, water, energy, and television. In the current stage of development in Brazil, access to these services, which are not transportable and are collective, requires urban residence. The proliferation of urban nuclei and roads makes possible urban residence without total disconnection from rural activities. Circular and pendular movements maintain the link with work on the land.

Concentration of land ownership and the expulsion of permanent employees and sharecroppers, for the motives discussed above, combined with the effects of labour legislation so as to restrict access to land, leaving urban residence the only alternative for a landless population.

The expansion of oligopolistic enterprise, unemployment and underemployment in metropolitan areas, because of structural characteristics of the Brazilian economy and the effects of the economic crisis of the 1980s, discourage rural–urban or urban–urban migration to large cities. On the other hand, the effects of concentration and centralization of capital and of technical progress, exacerbated by the economic crisis, also cause the expulsion of the unemployed as well as bankrupt small businessmen who seek space in smaller cities. Urban–urban migration, which already corresponded to half the total migration in Brazil in the previous decade, is not unidirectional in the sense of small to large cities, in a stepwise fashion, but also takes place in the opposite direction. Smaller cities also attract ex-proletarians in the process of becoming their own bosses and ex-proprietors who are victims of capital concentration and centralization and of technical progress which dispenses with labour.

Urbanization of the countryside in frontier regions

All the above-mentioned causes of urbanization of the countryside are present in frontier regions, although to different degrees. Some causes are accentuated because of regional peculiarities.

Although agricultural production in general is not as modern as in the Centre-South, some activities such as growing black pepper are modern except in the harvesting process. On the other hand, labour seasonality in extraction (of rubber or Brazil nuts for example) stems from a complete lack of modernization; preparation and cultivation do not take place at all, but only harvesting. In Amazonia, in addition to seasonality, we have to take into account the temporary character of deforestation: preparing the land for agriculture or cattle raising demands a great deal of labour, but during a short period of time. If they are from the region, the labourers who work in clearing are almost always urban.

Recruitment of male labour for rural activities in civil construction, deforestation or placer mining favours a sexual division between the countryside and the city. While men work in the country, women stay in the city, engaged in housework and child care or in prostitution.

New consumption patterns of the Brazilian rural population affect urbanization in Amazônia, as in the rest of Brazil, but the form of commerce deserves some comment. Previously, the consumer needs of the Amazonian rural population were typically met by the *barracão* trading posts, in the system of local monopoly-monopsony known as *aviamento*. With the expansion of the road and communication network, the tight control of the *patrão* or boss was destroyed, and commerce multiplied. The large number of small businesses existing today in Amazonian cities and towns stems in part from the need for personal acquaintance between creditors and debtors in an unbureaucratized credit market. What is more, becoming a small businessman signifies a path to social ascension, or at least additional income, for many poor people.

The restriction of access to land in frontier regions or 'closing' of the frontier stems in large part from speculation, which also restricts rural employment. Beyond the rural exodus occurring in all of Brazil, in Amazônia we see the arrival of migrant groups seeking land, which few find. Cities fill up with migrants waiting for land. The large distances make the combination of rural work and urban residence more difficult.

Two factors which have been particularly important in urbanization on the frontier are public investments, especially by the federal government, and savings brought by migrants whose expectations may exceed the economic possibilities offered by the frontier today.

Characteristics of Pioneer Urbanization

Recent pioneer urbanization can be classified according to three distinct types:

1. Company towns: some nuclei are implanted by businesses to support the development of the company's own activities or as real-estate development

projects. In the first case, we have Serra do Navio, Carajàs, Tucuruí, and Barcarena. In the second, Alta Floresta, Tucumã, and Matupá. Some cities mix support for the company and sale of land parcels and urban services.

2. Official towns: official nuclei are principally those implanted by INCRA, the federal colonization and land-reform authority, such as the *agrovilas* and *agropoli* of the Transamazon Highway (Smith 1982), the nuclei of colonization projects in Rondônia such as Ji-Paraná (Monte-Mor 1980) and Ariquemes (Wilson 1985), or Urban Nuclei for Rural Support (NUARs) such as Machadinho (Millikan 1984; Torres 1988).

3. Spontaneous towns: most nuclei are spontaneous, such as those that arose along the Belém–Brasília Highway in the 1960s: Gurupi, Paraíso do Norte, Araguaína, and Paragominas (Sawyer 1969). Others arose from agricultural occupation in areas without highways, such as Capitão Poçp (Sawyer 1979), or because of gold mining, such as Serra Pelada and Curionópolis (Pereira 1989) or Ourilândia (Monte-Mor 1984).

There are combinations among the types. Nuclei also evolve, expanding from company or official origins to include spontaneous settlement, or being regularized through official interventions as occurred in Ourilândia. There are also numerous cases of rapid expansion of new towns around older 'seed' nuclei such as Marabá, Altamira, and Ariquemes.

Even though the causes of urbanization of the countryside in all of Brazil, as detailed above, are essentially the same, with differences in emphasis, the effects are very different when we compare pioneer urbanization with urban growth in already occupied areas. Although growth in both cases can reach very high levels, with high absolute numbers in already occupied areas, the lack of a pre-existing urban base or of a network of consolidated cities creates special problems for pioneer urban nuclei. The growth near large cities or within an urban network—a simple extension of already existing urbanization—is fundamentally different from the implantation of new cities in the middle of the jungle. Peripheral urbanization is different from the urban periphery.

The principal difference is the debility of settlement in pioneer urban nuclei, as regards both population itself and public and private infrastructure. Most of the frontier urban population lives in extremely makeshift and substandard conditions. Houses are usually self-built using easily available materials: unsawn wood, refuse from sawmills, mud, and palm thatch. The floor is typically of earth. Recently, since about 1980, black plastic sheeting, often combined with palm thatch, has become the poor man's zinc. At times, wells and cesspools are dug for water and sewage. Otherwise, one appeals to neighbours, or goes to the streams and forests provided by nature. Either there are not sufficient wells and cesspools, or there is high risk of contamination, given the intense rainfall and porous soils. Dirty and stagnant water accumulates within the urban area, polluting the sources of water used for drinking, washing clothes, bathing. . . Thus, living conditions, in terms of the house itself and its surroundings, are several rungs below those of peripheral neighbourhoods of cities in southern Brazil.

The insufficiency of housing and improvements is due principally to poverty, which itself stems from the restricted access to land and employment, given the speculative character of the region's occupation and the weakness of product- ive activities. The effects of poverty are made worse by the transitory nature of frontier life. Many urban residents do not consider the city their permanent resid- ence, but as eminently temporary. They may be waiting for land from the govern- ment, working at placer mining, or have left their families while working in clearing or on some construction project. At the same time, the land-titling process is dubious or inexistent. Nothing is definitive. Thus, even when time or money are available, the deprived urban population invests little in housing or improvements.

Urban infrastructure is extremely deficient as well. This stems mostly from the rapid pace of population growth, which can reach 15 per cent per year. Nuclei of 15,000 inhabitants, such as Xinguara (Godfrey 1979) appear in a matter of months. There is little time to install roads, lighting, water or sewers in the out- lying neighbourhoods, nor to build schools, health posts, hospitals or public buildings in the city centres.

Due to the lack of a consolidated central base, the problem of accelerated growth is worse on the frontier than on the periphery of large cities, where the growth rates might be equally high and the absolute numbers even higher. In the city centres or in neighbouring cities, there are simply no collective services such as public hospitals, water and sewage systems, and schools which might at least partially attend to the recently arrived population. City governments, like the population, are very poor. They lack a basis for tax collection, which would make new public investments possible. They do not have enough officially enumerated population to receive proportional participation in federal funding. Agencies or companies responsible for water, electricity, telephone, transportation, and the like, do not exist or have very limited resources.

The deficiency of public services is exacerbated by the instability of urban growth, which has both ups and downs in frontier regions. Net overall urban growth for frontier regions includes some local decreases, if not in populational terms, at least in industry, commerce, and other services. The 'boom towns' of Amazônia are better known than the 'ghost towns', but these exist as well. Besides Beiradão, Curionópolis, Imperatriz, Ariquemes, and Barcarena, there are also towns like Peixe, Sena Madureira, Guajará-Mirim, Cristalândia, Agua Azul, and Manelao, to say nothing of other urban areas which have disappeared completely. The state of Pará, for example, has fourteen district seats, localities considered urban by the criteria of the census bureau, which have a population of zero, an insurpassable world record for the smallest 'urban' populations (1980 demo- graphic census).

The languishing or demise of urban nuclei on the frontier is rooted principally in the transitory quality of the rural economic activities. Some are transitory by nature, such as placer mining and lomber extraction through high-grading. Others, such as rubber extraction, could be permanent, but as peripheral activities with high transport costs, they are very sensitive to market oscillations. Other activities such as colonization, cattle-raising, or reforestation rarely succeed, for combined economic and ecological reasons, and because they depend to a very large extent on political support.

Even when rural activities endure, the competition between incipient nuclei causes the weakening of some and the strengthening of others, or retraction at the local and regional level. In the first moments of occupation, numerous nuclei appear, serving as construction camps, gas stations, highway junctions, river crossings, etc. Over time, some settlements lose in interurban competition to others which attract stores, banks, hospitals, schools, electric plants, airports, telephones, television, post offices, hotels, and city governments. The differentiation process is cumulative, not only in terms of the economic activities and public services, but also in terms of migration. The construction of roads, although it can stimulate growth along their borders, can provoke stagnation in adjacent areas, where relative special advantages are eliminated (cf. Sawyer 1969).

With improvements in transport and communications and the expansion of oligopolistic enterprises at the national level, it is possible as well that a complex hierarchical network of commercial entrepôts will no longer be necessary. In this new setting, orders can be placed directly to headquarters by telephone or by mail or through travelling salesmen. They can be filled by truckers making deliveries directly from the main office. This decreases the need for a complex network of intermediaries.

At the local level, numerous small general stores give way to bigger specialized businesses and to supermarkets. There is a comeback of big commercial capital in a new and modern form. Merchant capital temporarily lost its hegemony in the Amazon due to the weakening of the traditional *aviamento* system of credit and marketing of production, which linked sales and purchases in kind. The new merchant capital disentwines sales to consumers from purchases from producers and deals in cash.

The retraction of investments at a local level can be aggravated by a recent retraction at the macro-regional level, at least in the case of the northern region. With few exceptions, capitalist agriculture did not prove economically successful in Amazônia, as it requires infrastructure, especially within the ecological conditions of the humid tropics. The lack of infrastructure discourages productive investments, which thereby discourages investments in infrastructure—a vicious cycle. Without production, all that is left is speculation. This can favour population accumulation in the cities but it undermines their economic foundations. Official production incentives as well as social investments for Amazônia diminish not only because of the broader economic crisis, but also because of the weak economic role of the livestock and colonization projects and the need, within a democratic regime, to direct social expenditure to areas with a higher electoral density (Sawyer 1982, 1984).

Conclusions

In the import substitution phase of Brazilian development, Amazônia became a rural refuge for the dispossessed and disqualified from the north-east and south-south-east. Most of the migrants sought land of their own. During the 1980s, they discovered that their 'project of autonomy' via land was generally not feasible in Amazon conditions, for a combination of economic, political, and ecological reasons. They accumulated in the cities and towns because they were waiting for land or were pushed off it, or because they were unable to make a decent living with whatever land they had. In this sense, urban life was the only alternative for many migrants. Urbanization seems to have taken place without industrialization or any other kind of strong economic base.

Should 'urbanization of the frontier' be taken as a sign of failure, undesirable, pathologic? Probably not. While the 'push' factors behind rural–urban migration are undeniably important, one cannot forget the attractions of urban life. The new 'pull' factors act increasingly upon the urban population, now the vast majority in Brazil. The urban frontier attracts not only the rural folk who want or need urban services and comforts, but also urban population from the rest of Brazil. Many new migrants seek opportunities for employment or setting up their own businesses.

Demographic trends like urbanization of the frontier are the result of economic forces, but they also react back upon and alter or condition economic trends. The urban network of the frontier makes pioneer agriculture feasible for economic and social reasons, by providing productive and social infrastructure. Where the urban network is weak, the frontier is weak. Where it is vigorous, the agricultural frontier is strongest. Planners must take this intertwining and mutual reinforcement into account.

Part IV

India

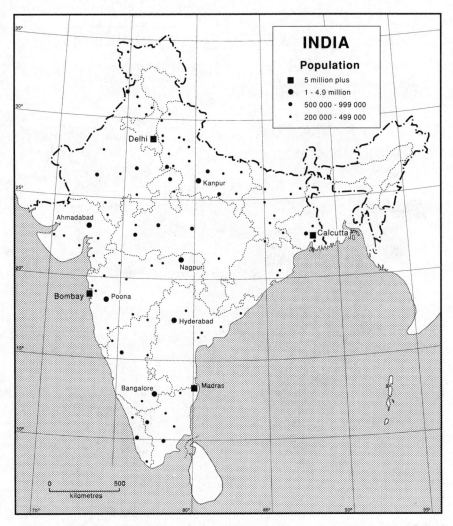

Map 7. Urban centres, India

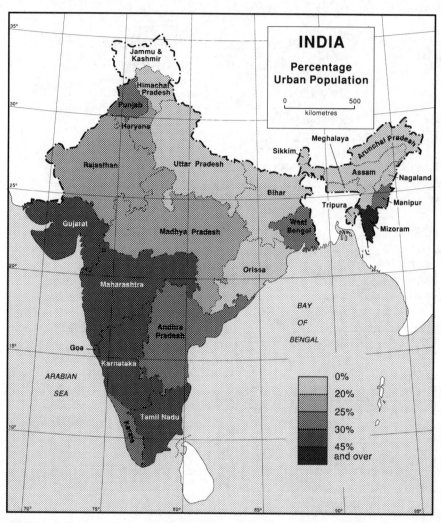

Map 8.   Percentage urban by state, India

Introduction

PRAVIN VISARIA

India, with a population of nearly 846 million according to the 1991 census, is the second most populous country in the world. Its land area of 3.23 million km² forms only 2.4 per cent of the total land on planet earth. Separated from central Asia by the Himalayas, it is dependent on the monsoon winds originating in the Indian ocean for rainfall which has a decisive impact on the productivity of its agriculture and the incomes of nearly 60 per cent of the workforce.

India has a federal political structure. It has seventeen states and one union territory with a population of more than 5 million each, and eight states and seven union territories with smaller populations. Despite a policy of narrowing inter-regional inequalities, substantial interstate and intrastate interregional inequalities persist with respect to the level of income, industrial and infrastructural development, as well as social and educational development. The perennial rivers originating in the Himalayas provide irrigation facilities to some of the most fertile soils in the northern states of Punjab, Haryana, Uttar Pradesh, Bihar, and West Bengal. The southern states have very few perennial rivers and the soil is much less fertile.

Fourteen major languages with distinct scripts and a large number of other minor linguistic groups make India unique with respect to the diversity and heterogeneity of its population. Linguistic diversity reportedly hinders the mobility of the population. Several different religious groups contribute to the high cultural diversity of the country.

The Indian states vary widely in area (from 4,000 to 443,000 km²) and population (from less than half a million to 139 million). Districts form the second level of administration within states. Their number has grown over time, along with population growth, from 412 in 1981 to 466 in 1991. The four largest districts in terms of area had over 6 per cent of the total land area of the country but less than one per cent of the population of India.

The recent archaeological discoveries indicate that the city-centred prehistoric civilization, earlier identified in the Indus Valley (now in Pakistan), had spread widely in western India. Throughout subsequent history, the Indian native princes or local rulers (and most of the Muslim rulers during the twelfth to eighteenth centuries) were patrons of arts and crafts and helped to support a system of towns that serviced the farmers in the countryside. During British rule, there was some de-urbanization when colonial rulers tried to protect the producers of industrial goods, particularly textiles, in England against the more efficient Indian workers.

After 1947, when India gained independence from British rule which had lasted nearly 200 years, the liberal Western-educated leadership tried to usher in a welfare state with a socialist orientation. India began to formulate five-year plans for social and economic development through a central Planning Commission set up in 1951. With the plans for certain years undergoing major revisions because of varied exigencies, it is now implementing the eighth five-year plan.

Partly because of the scarcity of foreign exchange to pay for imports and partly to ensure maximum social gain from the relatively limited investable surplus, India instituted a fairly rigid industrial licensing system. Attempts were made to regulate industrial location and to slow down the pace of population growth in large cities but the decisions were often influenced by political factors. While Indian planning was never as centralized as that in the former USSR, the past few years have witnessed a dismantling of many of the industrial licensing procedures and controls.

Nearly five decades after the British left India its urban centres continue to reflect the colonial influence. The three largest cities of India (excluding the national capital Delhi) happen to be port cities, which were centres of international trade. Cities that have grown relatively rapidly since the end of British rule include port sites as well as major industrial complexes set up by the central and state governments.

India's national income (at 1980–1 prices) increased at an average annual rate of 3.8 per cent between 1950–1 and 1991–2. With population growing at 2.2 per cent, per-capita income rose at an average annual rate of 1.6 per cent (or a modest 93 per cent over the 40-year period). Yet India achieved a substantial expansion of the infrastructure and a diversification of its industrial base and foreign trade over this period. The share of agriculture in the GDP declined from 55 to 31 per cent; and those of the industrial and services sectors rose from 16 to 29 and from 29 to 40 per cent, respectively.

Conversion of India's national income into dollar terms according to the prevailing rates of currency exchange does not indicate the living conditions of the people. The level of living is better reflected in figures that take account of the purchasing power of currencies in terms of non-trade goods and services as well. Estimates by the World Bank suggest that taking into account the differences in purchasing power, the Indian per-capita income in 1990 was close to US$1150, rather than around US$290 during 1991–2 (using the average exchange rate of Rs. 24.47 per US dollar).

India also shows considerable diversity with respect to the level of demographic parameters. An official family planning programme, implemented effectively since about 1966–7, has contributed to a fall in the level of fertility (TFR) from 6.0 to 3.8 in 1990 in rural areas and from 6.0 to 2.8 in urban areas (with a population of 217 million). However, the decline in the infant mortality rate from 225 to 250 around 1950 to 80 by 1991 and also in child and adult mortality rates raised the life expectancy at birth from about 32 years during the 1940s to 60 by 1991. The decline in birth rates has lagged behind the fall in death rates but the latter has largely offset the former. As a result, the rate of natural increase has remained more or less stable at around 2.1–2.2 per cent. India's main achievement has been to avoid the rise in the rate of natural increase to the 3 per cent or more that has been seen in several other countries of the world.

Within India, Kerala and Goa states (with 1991 populations of 29 million and 1 million) have already achieved a below-replacement level of fertility. The other southern state of Tamil Nadu, with a population of 56 million, has also witnessed a marked decline in its fertility. The four large north Indian states of Bihar, Madhya Pradesh, Rajasthan, and Uttar Pradesh, with low levels of literacy and socio-economic development, have higher fertility than the national average. However, even in these states, urban fertility levels during 1988–90 fell 25 to 33 per cent below the rural levels. These emerging differentials are indicative of the ongoing process of demographic transition.

13 Urbanization in India: An Overview

PRAVIN VISARIA

India, the second most populous country of the world, had a population close to 820 million on 1 October 1989 when the seminar organized by the IUSSP was held in Ahmedabad. By 1992, the population had grown to about 870 million. The proportion of urban population in India increased from about 11 per cent in 1901 to 18 per cent in 1951 (a few years after independence) and to a modest 26 per cent at the time of the 1991 census. The total urban population in India (including an estimated figure for the state of Jamu and Kashmir where the 1991 census was not conducted) was about 217 million. Had it formed a separate country, urban India alone would have been the fourth most populous country of the world (after China, India, and USA).

Criteria to Define an Urban Area

India defines towns and urban areas primarily in terms of the form of local self-government. All places with a municipality, corporation, cantonment board, or notified area committee are considered towns. Other places to be considered urban ordinarily satisfy the three criteria of (a) a minimum population of 5,000; (b) at least 75 per cent of the male working population being engaged in non-agricultural activities; and (c) a density of population of at least 400 persons per km^2. In addition, some places not satisfying these three criteria are also classified as urban, if they have distinct urban characteristics. The marginal cases include major project colonies, areas of intensive industrial development, railway colonies, important tourist centres, etc.

The 1991 census identified a total of 2,996 statutory towns and 1,693 non-statutory or census towns (an increase of 238 or 9 per cent and 422 or 33 per cent, respectively, relative to the 1981 census). The statutory towns generally tend to be larger and they accounted for an estimated 85 per cent of the urban population enumerated by the 1991 census. (In many states of the country, the statutory towns are under the jurisdiction of and receive grants from the urban development department, whereas the non-statutory towns have to deal with and receive assistance from the department of local self-government and/or Panchayats.)

Thanks are due to Anil Gumber, Paul Jacob, and Leela Visaria for their assistance in preparing and revising the paper and to A. S. Oberai of the International Labour Office, Geneva, for his comments on the draft of this chapter.

The Indian census also uses a concept of urban agglomeration (UA), and the census figures often relate to UAs and towns together. The UA forms 'a continuous urban spread' and normally consists of a town and its adjoining urban out-growths, if any. The 4,689 towns in 1991 formed 3,768 urban agglomerations and towns. Of them, 3,387 towns were not included in any urban agglomerations whereas 381 agglomerations included 1,302 towns.

Level of Urbanization

Towns with a population of 20,000 or more are generally supposed to have distinct urban characteristics. Table 13.1 therefore shows the percentage of urban population resident in towns with 20,000 or more persons. The proportion was nearly 53 per cent in 1901, 70 per cent around 1951 but over 89 per cent in 1991. There has been a steady decline in the share of urban population resident in localities which may not have distinct urban characteristics.

Table 13.1.   Key statistics on Urbanization in India, 1901–91

Census year	No. of towns	Urban popu- lation (mill.)	Urban- ization level (%)	Percentage urban population in towns 20,000 or more persons	Intercensal annual growth rate (%)		
					Urban popu- lation	Rural popu- lation	Difference between urban and rural growth rates
1901	1,916	25.9	10.8	52.9	—	—	—
1911	1,908	25.9	10.3	55.4	0.0	0.6	−0.6
1921	2,048	28.1	11.2	56.1	0.8	−0.1	0.9
1931	2,220	33.5	12.0	59.7	1.7	1.0	0.7
1941	2,422	44.2	13.8	66.0	2.8	1.1	1.7
1951	3,060	62.4	17.3	70.4	3.5	0.8	2.6
1961	2,700	78.9	18.0	79.6	2.3	1.9	0.4
1971	3,126	109.1	19.9	84.1	3.2	2.0	1.2
1981	4,029	159.5	23.3	86.4	3.8	1.8	2.0
1991	4,689	217.6	25.7	89.4	3.1	1.8	1.3

Notes: Number of towns shown above is taken from Planning Commission, *Eighth Five Year Plan*, Vol. 2, p. 345. In Jammu and Kashmir no census could be conducted in 1951. The towns which had continued between 1941 and 1961 are considered in the 1951 figures. Their population in 1951 is assumed to be the arithmetic mean of the 1941 and the 1961 figures. The 1981 Census was not conducted in Assam; the 1981 population figures for India include interpolated figures for Assam. The 1991 Census was not conducted in Jammu and Kashmir; the 1991 population figures for India include projected figures for Jammu and Kashmir.

Sources: Census of India 1991, Series 1, Paper 2 of 1991, Provisional Population Totals: Rural Urban Distribution. Also, Census of India, 1971, Series 1-India, Part II-A(i) General Population Tables; Census of India, 1981, Series-1, India, Part B(i), Primary Census Abstract: General Population; Census of India, 1981, Series-1, Paper-1 of 1982, Final Population Totals.

The average annual rate of population growth for the country as a whole remained stable at 2.0–2.2 per cent during 1951–91. The growth rate of urban population increased from 2.3 during 1951–61 to 3.2 and 3.8 during 1961–71 and 1971–81 respectively, but declined to 3.1 per cent during 1981–91. As a result, the differential between the rates of growth of rural and urban populations had widened during 1951–81 but narrowed during 1981–91.

Interstate Differences in Urbanization

There are significant interstate differences in the proportions of urban population. Table 13.2 presents these data, and also the projections for 1991, prepared prior to the last census, for the sixteen major states (which had a population of 5

Table 13.2.   Level of urbanization in different states of India, 1961–81 and projected values for 1991–2001

India/State Union Territory	Percentage of urban population/total population					
	1961	1971	1981	1991 P	R	2001
*India**	18.2	20.2	23.7	27.5	25.7	33.1
States						
Andhra Pradesh	17.4	19.3	23.3	27.9	26.8	32.9
Bihar	8.4	10.0	12.5	15.6	13.2	19.9
Gujarat	25.8	28.1	31.1	34.4	34.4	38.3
Haryana	17.2	17.7	21.9	27.8	24.8	37.4
Himachal Pradesh	6.3	7.0	7.6	8.3	8.7	8.9
Jammu and Kashmir	16.7	18.6	21.0	23.8	23.8	27.1
Karnataka	22.3	24.3	28.9	34.6	30.9	42.3
Kerala	15.1	16.2	18.7	21.9	26.4	26.2
Madhya Pradesh	14.3	16.3	20.3	25.4	23.2	32.6
Maharashtra	28.2	31.2	35.0	39.3	38.7	44.1
Orissa	6.3	8.4	11.8	16.5	13.4	23.2
Punjab	23.1	23.7	27.7	32.8	29.7	40.5
Rajasthan	16.3	17.6	21.0	25.4	22.7	31.7
Tamil Nadu	26.7	30.3	32.9	35.8	34.2	38.7
Uttar Pradesh	12.8	14.0	17.9	23.5	19.9	32.1
West Bengal	24.4	24.7	26.5	28.6	27.4	31.6
Union Territories						
Delhi	88.7	89.7	92.7	95.2	89.9	97.3

* Excluding Assam; P: Projected; R: Reported by the 1991 Census

Source: Census of India, 1991 (b and c).

million or more in 1991). Among these major states, Maharashtra, with Bombay as its capital, has the highest level of urbanization (39 per cent). Three other more urbanized states are Gujarat, Tamil Nadu, and Karnataka, which include the large metropolitan cities of Ahmedabad, Madras, and Bangalore. West Bengal, which includes Calcutta, ranks sixth among the large states in terms of the level of urbanization. At the other end, the five 'union territories' (for which the central government shoulders the administrative and financial responsibilities) including Delhi, Chandigarh, Daman, and Diu, and the states of Mizoram and Goa have a higher level of urbanization than even the most urbanized Maharashtra state.

The less urbanized states of Himachal Pradesh, Assam, Orissa, Bihar, and Uttar Pradesh have an urbanization level of 9–20 per cent. The relatively low urbanization in Kerala is an artifact of definitions in so far as the rural–urban distinction is difficult to make in a state with a high density of population everywhere. Almost 90 per cent of the population of Kerala in 1981 lived in villages with a population of 10,000 or more. In 1981, the country had a total of 1,834 such villages accounting for 15 per cent of the rural population; 49 per cent of these large villages were in Kerala and another 36 per cent were in Bihar, Tamil Nadu, Andhra Pradesh, and Maharashtra.

Table 13.2 also shows the projections of urbanization prepared prior to the 1991 census, which envisaged that by 2001, the share of urban population in the country would approach about one-third, very nearly the level observed in the two most urbanized states of India in 1981 (Maharashtra and Tamil Nadu). The 1991 census proportion of urban population has corresponded to the projected value in Jammu and Kashmir, as a result of an assumption by the Office of the Registrar General, and for Gujarat the two values are very close. (Gujarat reported a sharp decline in the average annual rate of population growth from 2.5 per cent during 1971–81 to 1.9 per cent during 1981–91. The decline is seen in both rural and urban areas and the rural–urban growth differential during 1981–91 was almost the same as during 1971–81). Among other states, only Kerala has reported a higher percentage of urban population than was projected. All other states have reported a lower actual percentage of urban population than was projected. The special case of Kerala is a result of reclassification of localities or the addition of 92 towns to the list.

The projections for 2001 have been modified in the light of the results of the 1991 census. According to the Planning Commission, by 2001, about 30.5 per cent of Indians would be resident in urban areas (India, Planning Commission 1992). (The state-level projections are yet to be revised.) However, with the total population expected to exceed 1 billion by 2001, the absolute addition to the urban population during the 1990s will approximate to no less than 90 million. Besides, it is quite likely that an extensive reclassification of localities or large villages as towns will become necessary during the 1990s and it would be a mistake to presume that urbanization will continue to be slow during the 1990s and beyond.

Concentration of Urban Population in 'Cities'

A striking feature of urbanization in India has been the increasing concentration of urban population in relatively large cities. The 300 UAs, or cities with a population of 100,000 or more (called Class 1 cities), in the 1991 census, accounted for almost 65 per cent of the urban population. This process of concentration of urban population has been continuing steadily since at least 1901 when only 26 per cent of the urban population was resident in cities with more than 100,000 persons.

Within the category of Class 1 cities, the number of metropolitan cities with a population of one million or more has steadily increased from only one in 1901 to five in 1951, twelve in 1981 and twenty-three in 1991. The number of these million-plus cities is projected to rise to 40 by 2001, when they would account for 36 per cent of the urban population.

These metropolitan cities include six agglomerations/cities (Bombay, Calcutta, Delhi, Madras, Hyderabad, and Bangalore) with a population of 4 million or more. The first three of them had a population of 8 million or more, and met the United Nations criterion to be termed 'mega-cities' (United Nations 1991). The Indian census of 1991, however, used a lower cut-off line of 5 million, which classifies four cities as mega-cities (Census of India 1991). Among these mega-cities, Greater Bombay with a population of 12.6 million appears as the most populous because of the addition of five urban areas in 1991. Calcutta urban agglomeration with 129 constituent units in 1991 had a population of 10.9 million. Delhi, the seat of the national capital, had a population of 8.4 million. The three Indian mega-cities rank sixth, tenth and twenty-second among the world's largest metropolises (United Nations, 1990).

Are Large Indian Cities Growing Faster than Small Towns?

Over the past forty years, Indian urban policy has been guided by a mistaken impression that the population of larger cities has been growing faster than that of smaller towns. The impression has been a result of the census authorities' practice, until recently, of presenting rates of growth of urban population by size class of towns without any adjustment for changes in the number of towns in different size class categories. Table 13.3 shows for 1971–81 and 1981–91 the unadjusted indicators of urban growth as well as those with the requisite adjustment in which the number of towns is held unchanged.

There is little evidence of a decay of small and medium towns or of a very rapid growth of cities with a population of 100,000 or more. Further, during 1971–81, when cities with 100,000 or more persons are considered in five disaggregated classes, there was little difference between the rates of growth of cities of 500,000–999,999 persons and those with 4 million or more; they had grown at the rate of about 3 per cent per year. Cities with a population of 250,000–499,999 persons and 1–4 millions had an average annual growth rate of 4.0 per cent per year

Table 13.3. Growth of urban population by size (population) class of towns, India, 1971–91

Size class category according to population	Population (millions) and number of UA/towns at each census			Inter-censal growth (%)			
	1971	1981	1991	1971–81		1981–91	
				(a)	(b)	(a)	(b)
Class I	61.2	94.5	138.8	54.4	41.4	46.9	34.5
(100,000 +)	(148)	(216)	(296)				
Class II	11.7	18.2	23.3	55.7	36.2	28.1	31.6
(50,000–99,999)	(173)	(270)	(341)				
Class III	17.1	22.4	28.1	30.8	39.5	25.3	29.6
(20,000–49,999)	(558)	(738)	(927)				
Class IV	11.7	14.9	16.5	27.5	35.0	10.7	28.4
(10,000–19,999)	(827)	(1053)	(1135)				
Class V	4.8	5.6	5.5	17.8	37.0	–1.3	30.0
(5,000–9,999)	(623)	(739)	(725)				
Class VI	0.5	0.8	0.6	65.7	47.7	–21.7	43.9
(< 5000)	(147)	(229)	(185)				
Total	107.0	156.4	212.8	46.2	39.7	36.1	32.8
	(2476)	(3245)	(3609)				

Notes: The figures exclude Assam state where the 1981 Census could not be held and the state of Jammu and Kashmir where 1991 Census had not been held. Figures in parentheses show the number of UA/towns. (a) Figures refer to the growth of urban population according to the size class given in each census. (b) Figures refer to the growth of urban population according to initial population of each town. It eliminates the shift of a town to a higher or lower size class category.

Source: Census of India, 1991, Paper 2 of 1991.

and cities with a population of 100,000–250,000 grew at the second highest rate of 3.8 per cent (India, Planning Commission 1983: 16).

Overall, there is no 'exodus' from rural to urban areas and the big cities are not really growing much faster than smaller towns. Of course, the rates presented in Table 13.3 are averages and can be misleading. When 2,295 towns were distributed by their rate of population growth during 1971–81, the frequency distributions showed a tendency for a large proportion of small towns to be slow-growing. There is a tendency for larger towns and cities to grow somewhat faster. (Yet, the rate of population growth during 1971–81 was between 1.0 and 2.0 per cent for only seventeen towns and less than 1.0 per cent for only six towns.)

Components of Urban Growth

Urbanization can result from (a) rural–urban differentials in the rate of natural increase, (b) net migration from rural to urban areas and (c) reclassification of villages as towns as a result of changes in the nature of economic activities, avail-ability of infrastructure, or acquisition of urban characteristics and/or the spill-over of urban population growth beyond designated boundaries (which usually leads to an extension of the boundaries of towns and cities).

To examine the contribution of natural increase, Table 13.4 summarizes the average birth and death rates in rural and urban India during 1971–80 and 1981–90 according to the Sample Registration System (SRS). (Separate estimates of rural and urban vital rates are not available for earlier years because the civil registration of vital events has remained deficient.) Both birth and death rates tend to be lower in urban areas than in villages.

During 1970–1985, the expectation of life at birth (for both sexes together) in urban India is estimated to be almost nine years higher than in rural India (Office of the Registrar General 1989). During 1986–90, the rural–urban gap in the expectation of life at birth narrowed to seven years but it is still quite large (Office of the Registrar General, 1994). The infant mortality rates have declined both in rural and urban areas but during 1990–2, the rate in urban India (42) was three-fifths that in rural India (86) (*Sample Registration Bulletin*, 28/2: 51, 57). But the differences in vital rates largely offset each other and the urban rate of natural increase was only a little lower than the rural. Interestingly, the rate of natural increase (RNI) in rural India seems to have risen a little during 1981–90 (relative to 1971–80), while that in urban India has remained stable. The underlying factor is the larger decline in the rural death rate than in the rural birth rate, while in urban areas the decline in the birth rate has offset the fall in the death rate during the 1980s. (The impression of a rise in rural RNI may be a spurious product of deficiencies in SRS data for the 1970s; but it is difficult to examine the issue in the present chapter.) In the absence of any rural–urban migration or reclassification, the rise in the rate of natural increase in rural India during the 1980s would have added nearly 8.4 million persons to the rural population; it has contributed to the slower urbanization during the 1980s than during the 1970s.

Table 13.4.   India: birth and death rates and rates of natural increase by rural–urban residence, 1971–80 and 1981–90

Years	Birth rate	Death rate	Rate of natural increase
1971–80			
Rural	35.8	15.8	20.0
Urban	28.5	9.2	19.3
1981–90			
Rural	33.9	12.6	21.3
Urban	27.0	7.7	19.3

Note: We have taken account also of the provisional SRS estimates for 1990.

Sources: Census of India, paper 2 of 1991, *Provisional Population Totals; Rural–Urban Distribution*, New Delhi, 1991, p. 52; various issues of the annual publication of the Office of the Registrar General entitled Sample Registration System.

The process of reclassification of localities from rural to urban also slowed down after 1981. The 1981 census had added 1,043 new towns and, with a declassification of eighty-seven former towns, the net addition to the number of towns was 956. The new towns of 1981 had a population of 7.4 million. The 1991 census added 856 new towns and declassified ninety-three towns, with a net addition of 763 towns having a population of 5.3 million. The reclassification of localities had accounted for almost 15 per cent of the urban growth during 1971–81 but its share declined to 9.5 per cent during 1981–91.

On the basis of the data about the rate of natural increase in urban areas and the net effect of reclassification, we can make some preliminary estimates of the different components of urban growth during 1981–91. To estimate net rural–urban migration, it is assumed that the flow of migration was more or less even throughout the decade and that the rate of natural increase among migrants was the same as among non-migrants. The effect of possible refinement of these assumptions on the results would probably be small. The results, summarized in Table 13.5, are compared with corresponding estimates for 1961–71 and 1971–81. (The latter estimates are taken from Visaria and Kothari 1987.)

It is evident from Table 13.5 that net rural–urban migration accelerated during the 1980s. It contributed nearly 17 million persons to the urban population during the 1980s whereas the figure for the 1970s was 10 million. The average annual rate of net out-migration from rural India is estimated to have been almost 3.0 per

Table 13.5. India: components of urban growth, 1961–71, 1971–81 and 1981–91 (millions)

Component	1961–71		1971–81[a]		1981–91[b]	
	Number	%	Number	%	Number	%
1. Absolute increase	30.2	100.0	49.9	100.0	57.7	100.0
2. Net reclassification of localities from rural to urban	4.5	14.9	6.7	13.4	5.3	9.2
3. Net rural-urban migration	6.3	20.9	9.8	19.6	16.6	28.8
4. Natural increase (i) of initial urban population	18.8	62.3	24.5	46.1	34.0	58.9
(ii) of intercensal migrants (net figure)	0.7	2.3	1.1	2.2	1.8	3.1
5. Residual (including errors and changes in boundaries)	–0.1	–0.3	7.8	15.6	—	—

[a] Excluding Assam
[b] Including Assam as well as Jammu and Kashmir.

1000 during 1981–91 and 2.1 per 1000 during 1971–81. The contribution of migration to urban growth has increased from 20 per cent during the 1970s to 29 per cent during the 1980s. The contribution of natural increase to urban growth during 1981–91 also seems to have risen, but perhaps not too much can be read into this finding because the estimates for 1971–81 had attributed nearly 16 per cent of urban growth to residual factors.

Our discussion of urbanization has presumed that the 1991 census count has not been more deficient than the 1981 count. Admittedly, the growing difficulties of ensuring a complete count of population during a census tend to be particularly acute in urban areas and especially in metropolitan cities. The concentration of urban population in big cities can, therefore, lead to an increase in the net undercount of urban population. According to the post-enumeration check (PEC) conducted after the 1991 Census, the net omission rate in urban India in the 1991 Census was 1.9 per cent, higher than in rural India (1.6 per cent), but lower than the corresponding rate in the 1981 Census (2.8 per cent). The net undercount in the three large urban agglomerations of Bombay, Delhi, and Madras together was 4.0 per cent (Census of India 1991e). So the level of urbanization is indeed slightly understated because of the somewhat higher undercount of urban population, but the understatement might have declined compared to 1981. The pace of urbanization during the 1980s is not, therefore, understated because of this factor.

Why Was Urbanization During the 1980s Slower than Projected?

There is considerable interest in India in identifying the reasons for the slower-than-projected urbanization during the 1980s. Two contributory factors noted above have been a slower reclassification of localities and a slightly higher rate of natural increase in rural areas during the 1980s than during the 1970s. The pace of rural–urban migration seems to have risen a little. However, there is also evidence that some of the rural workers seek and find opportunities to work in urban areas. They retain their rural habitations and commute to urban centres to work. According to one estimate, about 4.3 per cent of the urban workforce during 1987–8 was actually resident in the adjoining rural areas (NSSO 1990: 18). (The counter-flow of urban residents working in rural areas was much smaller.) Assuming a worker population of 34 per cent observed during both 1983 and 1987–8, if the commuter rural workers working in urban areas had in fact migrated to the towns, they would have added about 10 million persons to the estimated urban population of 217 million persons. (The level of urbanization would have been higher by 1.2 percentage points.) Such commutation is a low-cost alternative to migration. It is partly a response also to the acute scarcity of urban housing and is facilitated by relatively inexpensive or subsidized transport facilities. It is also possible that the policies to encourage the location of new industrial units outside the cities with a population of more than 1 million and other incentives to develop the backward areas have contributed to a slowing down of the growth of urban employment opportunities. (Chapter 14 below by Rakesh Mohan reviews the policies relating to industrial location.) These policies have aimed at relieving the pressures on urban housing and infrastructure, which have deteriorated over the years and need improvement. We shall first examine the level and pattern of employment in urban India.

Level of Employment in Urban India

The level of employment in urban and rural areas of India is indicated by worker–population ratios summarized in Table 13.6. These ratios are based on the decennial censuses and the usual status concept used in four quinquennial national surveys of employment and unemployment conducted by the National Sample Survey (NSS) Organization. Briefly, the NSS estimates seem comparable with those of the 1961 census while the decline in female worker–population ratios suggested by the 1971 and the 1981 censuses is not confirmed by the national surveys conducted by better-trained investigators. (All the NSS estimates are based on the usual status approach, essentially similar to that of the 1961 census. The 1971 and the 1981 censuses attempted to distinguish workers for whom work was the main activity from other workers but the instructions evidently proved too difficult to follow and/or implement for the essentially honorary enumerators numbering more than 1 million.) Given the problems with the 1971 and the 1981 censuses, highlighted by Table 13.6, it would be best to concentrate attention on the results of the 1961 Census and the four NSS surveys. The stability of the urban worker–population ratios was a concomitant also of the absence of any significant rise in the level of unemployment measured in terms of alternative concepts of usual status, current weekly status, or the activities of the previous (reference) week, and the current daily status or the activities of each day of the reference week (Visaria and Minhas 1991). There was, however, a decrease between 1972–3 and 1987–8 in the share of regular employees and an increase in the share of the self-employed and casual labourers among male workers (NSS 1990:92). These trends are suggestive of the growth of the informal sector with its tendency to conceal under-employment.

To look at changes in the nature of economic activities being pursued by workers, Table 13.7 presents the broad sectoral classification of workers by sex and rural–urban residence. Interestingly, the changes in the sectoral distribution of urban workers appear to be small. It is the distribution of rural workers that appears to have begun to change.[1] Further, the changes in the distribution of

---

[1] These data shed interesting light on the dynamics of change in the sectoral pattern of work. A fall in the percentage of workers engaged in the primary sector has begun particularly after 1972–3. The process has been faster among male workers than among female workers. Quite likely, there is some substitution of female workers for male workers in the primary sector. Also, activities relating to animal husbandry which tend to absorb female workers have expanded relatively fast because of what is called the white revolution. Of course, even in the case of male workers, with their numerical strength growing at the average annual rate of 1.8% the absolute number of even the male workers engaged in

Table 13.6.   India: crude worker population ratios by sex and rural–urban residence, 1951–91

Area/Sex	1951 Census	1961 Census	1971 Census	1972–3 27th round	1977–8 32nd round	1981 Census	1983 38th round	1987–8 43rd round	1991 Census
India									
Both sexes	39.1	43.0	34.0	40.7	41.6	36.8	41.8	40.9	37.6
Males	53.9	57.1	52.7	52.7	53.4	52.6	53.5	53.0	51.5
Females	23.4	28.0	13.9	27.8	28.9	19.8	29.3	28.0	22.7
Rural Areas									
Both sexes		45.0	36.1	42.8	43.8	38.9	44.2	43.3	40.1
Males	n.a.	58.2	53.6	53.6	54.4	53.8	54.3	53.9	52.4
Females		31.4	15.5	31.4	32.6	23.2	33.7	32.3	27.1
Urban Areas									
Both sexes		33.5	29.6	32.6	33.9	30.0	34.0	34.0	30.4
Males	n.a.	52.4	48.9	49.4	50.0	49.1	50.9	50.6	49.0
Females		11.1	7.1	13.2	15.3	8.3	14.9	15.2	9.7

Note: The ratios based on the NSS have been obtained by weighting the worker–population ratios for broad age-groups by interpolated population figures from the smoothed age distributions of the population enumerated in 1971 and 1981 and the projected population for 1986. The estimates for 1987–8 take account of the projected population as on 1 January 1988 but not of the age-specific worker-population ratios.

Sources:
1. Census of India, 1961, Vol. 1, *India*, Part II-A(i), *General Population Tables: and Part II-B(i), General Economic Tables*
2. Census of India, 1971, Series-1, *India*, Part II-8(i) and 8(ii), *General Economic Tables*, pp. 20–74 and pp. 291–304.
3. National Sample Survey Organization, Sarvekshana, Vol. 1, No. 2, October 1977; Vol. 5, Nos. 1 & 2, July–October 1981; Vol. 11, No. 4, April 1988.
4. Census of India, 1971, Series-1, *India*, Part II-C(ii), *Social and Cultural Tables*, pp. 106–129.
5. *Census of India, 1981, Series-1, India*, Part II-B(i), *Primary Census Abstract: General Population*, (New Delhi, 1983), pp. xliv–lvi.
6. Census of India, 1991, Series 1, Paper 3 of 1991, Provisional Population Total: *Workers and Their Distribution*.
7. K. C. Seal, 'Women in the Labour Force in India: A Macro Level Statistical Profile' in: International Labour Organization, ARTEP, *Women in the Indian Labour Force*. Bangkok, 1981, p. 43.
8. National Sample Survey Organization, Special Report No. 1, Key Results of Employment and Unemployment Survey: All India (Part-I), NSS 43rd Round (July 1987–June 1988), New Delhi, January 1990.

workers in the country as a whole are sharper than those in the distribution of either rural or urban workers because the relative share of urban workers in the total has been on the increase. The corresponding process in the sectoral distribution of female workers appears slower than among males because the female worker–population ratios in urban areas tend to be much lower (less than half those in the rural areas), and the urban female workers with a predominance of

the primary sector continues to grow because the rate of decline in the share of the primary sector has been rather slow. (The absolute number of rural male workers engaged in agriculture rose from 89.3 million in 1961 to 120.1 million by 1987–8.)

Table 13.7. Broad sectoral distribution of the workforce in India by sex and rural/urban residence, 1961–83 (%)

Sector	1961	1972–3	1977–8	1983	1987–8
Rural Areas					
Male Workers					
Primary Sector	83.7	83.3	80.6	77.8	74.6
Secondary Sector	7.8	7.8	8.8	10.0	12.1
Tertiary Sector	8.5	8.8	10.6	12.2	13.3
Female Workers					
Primary Sector	89.7	89.8	88.1	87.8	84.8
Secondary Sector	7.2	5.9	6.8	7.4	10.0
Tertiary Sector	3.1	4.3	5.1	4.8	5.2
Urban areas					
Male Workers					
Primary Sector	10.2	10.8	10.6	10.4	9.2
Secondary Sector	33.9	33.0	33.8	34.4	34.2
Tertiary Sector	55.9	56.3	55.6	55.3	56.6
Female Workers					
Primary Sector	28.6	33.0	31.9	31.2	29.5
Secondary Sector	33.0	29.3	32.4	30.9	31.8
Tertiary Sector	38.4	37.6	35.6	37.9	38.7
All Areas					
Male Workers					
Primary Sector	71.0	68.9	64.0	61.4	57.9
Secondary Sector	12.4	12.8	14.2	15.8	17.7
Tertiary Sector	16.6	18.3	21.8	22.8	24.4
Female workers					
Primary Sector	85.8	84.5	81.7	80.9	77.2
Secondary Sector	8.9	8.1	9.7	10.2	13.0
Tertiary Sector	5.3	7.4	8.6	8.9	9.2

Note: Unrecorded cases have been distributed pro-rata

Sources:
1. Census of India, 1961, Vol. 1, *India*, Part II-8(i), *General Economic Tables*.
2. National Sample Survey Organization, Special Report No. 1, *Key Results of Employment and Unemployment Survey: India* (Part-1), NSS 43rd Round (July 1987–June 1988), New Delhi, January 1990, pp. 100–1.

non-agricultural employment form a rather small proportion of all female workers.

The changes in the structure of the rural workforce are a result partly of the growing density of workers on land and the steady decline in the average size of holding. Even the rural population responds to these changes partly by shifting to non-farm activities. As the share of time devoted to these activities and that of income derived from them change, the erstwhile agricultural workers (who probably considered the label of a cultivator a source of prestige), begin to report themselves as engaged in non-farm activities. The differences in the elasticity of demand for different goods and services and the process of specialization also underlie the shift in the pattern of economic activities. A logical consequence of this process is a change in the composition of the national product by source.

Urban–Rural Differentials in Productivity per Worker

The contribution of different sectors of economic activity to the gross domestic product (GDP) of India changed significantly over four decades. Table 13.8 shows the distribution of GDP by sector of economic activity between 1950–1 and 1990–1. It shows marked shifts in the sectoral distribution of GDP, sharper than those in the workforce. The share of the primary sector in the GDP has fallen from 55 to 32 per cent whereas the shares of the secondary and the tertiary sectors have risen from 16 to 26 and 29 to 32 per cent, respectively. These shifts reflect marked differentials in the capital intensity of different activities, (taking due account of both physical and human capital). The relative concentration of capital-intensive

Table 13.8.   India: shares in Gross Domestic Product by economic activity, 1950/1–1990/1 (at 1980–1 prices) (%)

Sector of economic activity	1950–1	1960–1	1970–1	1980–1	1990–1
Primary Sector					
1. Agriculture, forestry, and fishing	55.4	50.9	44.5	38.1	31.6
Secondary Sector	15.8	19.4	22.4	24.2	26.4
2. Mining and quarrying	1.1	1.3	1.3	1.5	1.7
3. Manufacturing	11.4	13.9	16.1	17.7	20.6
4. Construction	3.3	4.2	4.0	5.0	4.1
Tertiary Sector	28.8	29.7	33.1	37.7	42.0
5. Utilities	0.3	0.6	1.2	1.7	2.3
6. Trade, hotels, etc.	8.5	9.7	10.8	12.0	12.7
7. Transport, storage and communications	2.5	2.9	3.5	4.7	5.4
8. Financing, insurance real estate, and business	9.0	8.2	8.0	8.8	10.3
9. Community, social, and personal services	8.5	8.3	9.6	10.5	11.3
All	100.0	100.0	100.0	100.0	100.0
Per capita GDP (Rs.)	1194	1449	1671	1808	2490

Source: India, Central Statistical Organization, *National Accounts Statistics* for various years.

manufacturing and services in urban areas leads to differentials in the per-capita domestic product. According to the eighth five-year plan prepared by the Indian Planning Commission, the contribution of urban sector to the National GDP increased from an estimated 29 per cent in 1950–1 to 47 per cent in 1980–1 (India, Planning Commission 1992: 344). The basis of these estimates is not, however, known. According to the national accounts prepared by the Central Statistical Organization, the ratio of per-capita incomes in rural and urban areas was 1: 2.4 in 1970–1 and 1: 2.32 in 1980–1. Some analysts believe that the urban–rural disparity is likely to have increased rather than declined after 1971. Rakesh Mohan has suggested that the disparity between rural and urban per-capita income has increased from about 1.8 in 1950–1 to 'about three now' (Mohan 1992b).

Table 13.9 shows for different sectors of economic activity (a) the share of urban workers in the total reported to be working in a sector—according to the 1981 census and according to the average of the NSS surveys during 1977–8 and 1983; (b) the urban share in the total net domestic product (NDP) estimated to be originating in different sectors of economic activity during 1980–1; and (c) the NDP per urban worker as a percentage of NDP per rural worker. Two alternative sets of estimates are presented for the share of workers in urban areas because the estimates of female workers by the NSS and the censuses differ significantly. The differences between the two sources of estimates in the share of urban workers among all workers (of both sexes together) are generally small, except in the case of (a) mining and quarrying and (b) utilities.

Estimates of the NDP for some sectors have been obtained partly on the basis of the number of workers estimated by the 1981 census. The urban contribution to the total NDP exceeds the urban share of the national workforce because of the higher productivity of urban workers. The NDP per urban worker exceeded that per rural worker by 222 per cent in all economic activities taken together. Among sectors, the differences are of the order of 24–25 per cent in mining and quarrying and utilities and 117 per cent in manufacturing and repair.

The higher implicit productivity of urban workers suggested by the national income estimates is often viewed in India as a result of the exploitation of rural workers by town-dwellers. The latter are criticized for imposing adverse terms of trade on the producers of agricultural commodities. The underlying concerns date back to India's struggle for independence from British rule, when the urban areas were seen as the agents of foreign rulers who 'siphoned off' the raw materials produced in rural areas and exported them. Partly as a result, India's efforts at economic and social development through five-year plans have laid considerable stress on raising the productivity of agriculture and on rural development. However, many analysts continue to discern an urban bias in India's development plans and argue that the level of investment in agriculture has been lower than desirable (Lipton 1980; Genesh Kumar 1992).

While the debates on these issues continue, the level of urbanization and particularly the growing concentration of population in larger cities are considered serious problems leading to a decline in the quality of life. The cost of

Table 13.9. Contribution of urban workforce to the total Net Domestic Product (NDP) of India and NDP per urban worker as percentage of NDP per rural worker by industry, 1980–1

Industry division	Urban share of the workforce (%)		Urban contribution to NDP (%)	NDP per urban worker as percentage of NDP per rural worker
	1981 Census	NSS 1981[a]		
0. Agriculture, hunting, forestry, and fishing[b]	3.5	4.1	5.0	148
1. Mining and quarrying	40.0	33.3	45.2	124
2 and 3 Manufacturing and repair	49.8	49.2	69.2	216
4. Electricity, gas and water	54.5	62.5	59.9	125
5. Construction	44.7	39.3	54.4	148
6. Wholesale and retail trade and restaurants and hotels	59.3	55.7	69.6	158
7. Transport, storage and communication	66.7	66.2	77.0	168
8. Financing, real estate and business, services[c]	78.6	⎱ 55.4[d]	84.6	150
9. Community, social, and personal services	53.6	⎰	60.9	135
Total	17.6	18.7	40.7	322

[a] The NSS-based estimates of the number of workers have been obtained by using an average of the worker-population ratio and the industrial distribution of workers reported by the 32nd (1977–8) and 38th (1983) Rounds.

[b] Minor Groups of 'soil conservation' (035), 'agricultural services not elsewhere classified such as land clearing, land draining etc.' (039) and 'planting, replanting and conservation of forests' (050) are included in Division 5 (except for col. 4).

[c] Excluding the contribution from 'Ownership of Dwelling'. Since the percentage of rented dwelling units is much lower in rural areas than in urban areas, the urban share of NDP originating in industry division 8 declines sharply from 84.6 to 62.5 per cent when the NDP attributed to the ownership of dwellings is taken into account. This is so despite the high value of owned dwellings in urban areas.

[d] The corresponding figure based on the 1981 Census is 55.2.

Sources: Central Statistical Organisation, *Monthly Abstract of Statistics*, Vol. 42, No. 7, July 1984, Tables 1/2; and National Sample Survey Organisation, *Sarvekshana*, Vol. V, Nos. 1 and 2, Vol. XI, No. 4 and Special Number, September 1990.

providing the various basic amenities to the growing number of urban residents is said to be higher in real terms. The obvious argument that the high density of population in urban areas (relative to rural areas) leads to a fall in the per-capita cost of provision of various services because of agglomeration economies is generally overlooked and the diseconomies are emphasized instead. Indian cities suffer from acute problems of deteriorating infrastructure in the form of poor housing, inadequate availability of drinking water, paucity of drainage and sewerage facilities, virtual breakdown of local public transport, and pollution. The growth of urban population, erroneously regarded as a result primarily of migration from rural areas (rather than of natural increase), is blamed for growing unemployment and underemployment leading to crime and anti-social behaviour (National Institute of Urban Affairs 1988).

The critics overlook that the rates of unemployment in fact tend to be lower among migrants than among non-migrants (Papola, Chapter 15, below). Furthermore, the growth of the informal sector in urban areas is a valuable complement to other economic activities. Likewise, better co-ordinated planning and management can bring about a significant improvement in living conditions in urban India. Even the problems of housing and the non-availability of basic amenities in urban India need to be viewed from the perspective of conditions prevailing in rural India from where many of the migrants come.

Housing Shortage

Since shelter is a basic need, India aims at the goal of 'shelter for all'. Estimates of housing shortage in India differ according to the source. The decennial censuses have estimated the homeless population as rising from 1.3 million in 1961 to 2.3 million in 1981. They formed less than 1 per cent of the total population of the country in both 1961 and 1981. About 26.5 per cent of the homeless in 1981 were resident in urban areas. The censuses have reported only a small number of the homeless partly because they collect information on the material of the walls and the roof of the dwelling units of households and do not apply any normative judgement. On the other hand, the National Buildings Organization (NBO) has estimated a housing shortage in 1991 of the order of 9.6 million dwelling units in urban India and 21.2 million in rural India. These estimates of shortages aim at ensuring certain minimum standards of amenities and divide dwelling units made of non-permanent materials into two categories: serviceable and unserviceable. Of course, the NBO does not have the resources to make any significant dent in the problem it has identified. The low incomes and extensive poverty lead to a wide variability in the standards of quality and durability as well as spaciousness of housing acceptable to millions of people, particularly urban residents who have migrated from and retain close links with rural areas of the country. The rising cost of construction materials and urban land makes it unlikely that most or all of them would aspire to the level of standards that have been envisaged by the National Buildings Organization. In any case, the severe scarcity of financial resources available to the government is unlikely to permit any major initiative in the public sector to reduce the housing shortage. A realistic assessment of the need and scope for public intervention requires a careful review of the realities of the situation on the ground.

Estimates of Slum Population

According to a task force on housing and urban development constituted by the Planning Commission, between one-fifth and one-fourth of the urban population of the country in 1981 was living in slums. The estimates ranged between one-third and 40 per cent for the twelve metropolitan cities; between 18 and 25 per cent in cities with a population of 100,000 or more (excluding the metropolitan cities); and between 15 and 20 per cent in the smaller towns with fewer than 100,000 inhabitants (India, Planning Commission 1983, iv: 20). The document relating to the National Housing Policy placed the estimate of the slum population in 1981 at 18.8 per cent (India, Ministry of Urban Development 1988). According to some other estimates, in the three largest metropolitan cities of Bombay, Calcutta, and Delhi, 57, 40, and 50 per cent of the population in 1988, 1980, and 1981, respectively, was reported to be living in slums (Oberai 1992). However, according to a large national survey conducted during 1988–9, only about 15 per cent of the urban households were living in slums and the figures for three metropolises ranged between 19 and 31 per cent (see Table 13.10). The survey has also indicated that except in Madras, a majority of the households resident in slums had permanent pucca or semi-permanent (semi-pucca) dwelling units and had some drainage facilities.

Table 13.10. Percentages of households living in slums and the distribution of their residential dwelling units by type of structure in urban and rural India and in four mega-cities (NSS 44th round, 1988–9)

| Area | Percent-age of HHS living in slums | Distribution of households in slums by: | | | | | |
| | | Structure Type | | | Drainage facilities | | |
		Pucca or perman-ent	Semi-pucca or semi-perman-ent	Katcha or non-perman-ent	No drain-age	Open Drain-age (katcha and pucca)	Others (covered or under ground)
Urban India	14.6	43.4	30.6	26.0	44.8	43.6	11.6
Bombay	30.6	61.4	30.2	8.4	11.1	76.4	12.5
Calcutta	28.9	85.2	12.6	2.2	17.2	45.2	37.6
Delhi	19.4	61.6	29.4	9.0	23.0	58.9	18.1
Madras	15.3	24.2	9.2	66.6	79.7	9.4	10.9
Rural India	6.2	15.5	37.5	47.0	78.8	19.7	1.5

Notes: A pucca structure has its outer walls and roof made of materials such as cement, concrete, oven-burnt bricks,stone or stone blocks, galvanised iron, zinc or other material sheets, timber, corrugated iron, asbestos, cement sheet, etc. A katcha structure has its walls and roof made of materials other than those noted above. A semi-katcha structure is one which cannot be classified as pucca or katcha structure.

Source: *Sarvekshana*, Vol. XV, No. 3.

Housing Conditions According to NSS Survey

Table 13.11 summarizes the results of two housing surveys conducted by the National Sample Survey (NSS) in 1973–4 and 1988–9. The dwelling units were classified into three categories of pucca or permanent, semi-pucca or semi-permanent, and katcha or non-permanent according to the durability of the materials used for the construction of walls and roof. The results indicate that both in 1973–4 and 1988–9, the proportion of dwelling units constructed out of non-permanent materials was much lower in urban India than in rural India. Further, the percentages of such dwelling units declined over the 15-year period between the two surveys, and faster in urban areas than in rural areas.

The 1988–9 survey also attempted to evaluate the condition of dwelling units. While these evaluations may be criticized as involving some subjective element depending on the background and experiences of the individual investigators, the survey identified that about 23 per cent of the semi-permanent and 56 per cent of the non-permanent dwelling units in urban India were in a 'bad' condition and needed major repairs. The percentage of such bad dwelling units was 13.5 in urban India and 22.1 in rural India although it was lower within each category (permanent, semi-permanent and non-permanent) in rural India than in urban India.

Table 13.12 summarizes the 1988–9 survey data relating to some critical characteristics of residential households such as:

- exposure to the risk of flooding or water-logging;
- lack of direct access to a road;
- non-availability of latrine facility;

Table 13.11. Percentage distribution of households by type of structure of their residential dwelling units, urban and rural India, NSS data

Area	1973–4 (28th Round)			1988–9 (44th round)		
	Pucca or permanent	Semi-Pucca or semi-permanent	Katcha or non-permanent	Pucca or permanent	Semi-pucca or semi-permanent	Katcha or non-permanent
Urban India	64.5	19.6	15.8	71.1	18.0	10.9
				(4.6)	(23.0)	(55.7)
Bombay	—	—	—	84.6	12.0	3.4
Calcutta	—	—	—	90.3	8.6	1.1
Delhi	—	—	—	89.1	8.7	2.2
Madras	—	—	—	70.1	10.0	19.9
Rural India	18.4	32.4	49.1	27.1	33.5	39.4
				(4.1)	(13.4)	(41.9)

Note: Results for four cities were not compiled for the 28th Round of the NSS. Figures in parentheses show the percentage of dwellings in bad condition (i.e. needing major repairs).

Table 13.12. Some characteristics of 'residential housing' in the four mega-cities of Bombay, Calcutta, Delhi, and Madras and in urban and rural India (NSS 44th round, 1988–9) (%)

Characteristics of dwellings	Bombay	Calcutta	Delhi	Madras	Urban India	Rural India
Exposed to the risk of flood water, logging, etc.	15.5	24.9	15.1	26.9	13.1	18.6
With no direct opening to road	27.6	12.3	6.8	16.1	17.7	37.5
With no drainage arrangement	5.1	11.5	9.4	26.8	28.7	66.8
Source of drinking-water other than tap, tube-well or hand-pump	1.6	0.0	2.5	15.1	10.7	45.5
Without latrine facility	5.2	2.8	18.7	17.6	31.1	89.0
Not using electricity for lighting	8.4	21.1	13.6	18.8	25.6	73.0
Not owned by household	56.7	67.4	47.3	61.3	45.5	9.0

- use of a source other than a tap, tube-well or hand-pump for drinking water;
- use of a source of energy other than electricity (mainly kerosene lamps) for lighting.

The data for urban India and for four mega-cities are compared with rural India. Evidently, the conditions in urban India are indeed much better than in rural India and those in the four mega-cities tend to be generally better than in urban India as a whole. However, the data also indicate that the exposure to risk of flooding or waterlogging in Calcutta and Madras was higher than even in rural India. Because of the generally heavy rainfall during the monsoon in both these cities, these problems need urgent attention.

Of course, the 1988–9 survey results do not suggest that the problems of slums or of providing adequate amenities in urban India are not serious. The non-availability of latrine facilities is a much more serious problem in crowded high-density urban areas than in rural areas where open spaces or fields are accessible. Likewise, safe potable water becomes more difficult to get in towns and cities because inadequate drainage and sewerage leads to contamination of water and creates serious health hazards. Several metropolitan centres such as Bombay, Delhi, Calcutta and Ahmedabad experience recurrent outbursts of jaundice and hepatitis B because of contaminated water. The high density of motorized vehicles on urban roads, with no check on the pollutants emitted in the exhaust, aggravates air pollution. According to the Department of Environment and Forests, Government of India, about 70 per cent of the industries in India fail to meet the pollution-control standards. The problem is more acute with small- and medium-scale industries which have not yet modernized plants and machinery to check pollution because of want of technology and funds. If immediate action is not initiated, Indian towns and cities will suffer a substantial worsening of the already degraded environment and an increase in the associated morbidity and ill health.

Assuming the results of the 1988–9 survey to be valid for 1991, the absolute number of households resident in slums in urban India in 1991 exceeded 6.3 million. According to the NSS data collected during 1976–7, the average size of households in slums tends to be a little lower (4.7) than in other urban areas; according to this figure, the number of slum dwellers was about 30 million or 13 per cent of the total urban population in 1991. According to these estimates the total magnitude of the problems seems to be a little smaller than was suggested earlier, but the scale and seriousness of the problems have indeed grown over the years.

Difficulties of Providing Basic Services in Urban Areas

The widespread concern about the difficult challenges of maintaining and improving the basic amenities provided to the people in the face of prospective urban growth is well founded. Further, given the competing claims for scarce public resources for investment, the slums cannot be 'cleared' by providing to their occupants alternative accommodation in 'built houses'. The alternative approach of providing sites for construction along with basic services such as approach roads, water, electricity, drainage, and sanitation has also not proved effective because the serviced sites tend to be on the periphery of towns and the poor consider them to be expensive. To overcome these problems, some low-interest credit will have to be provided as a complementary input because housing constitutes long-term investment. However, the requirements for serviced sites far exceed the rate at which they are being developed and it is extremely difficult to prevent the growth of squatter settlements on public lands. The latter will continue to absorb recent rural migrants while the sites and services programme can cater to persons who have already attained some economic stability after working in the urban areas for a few years. At the same time, a pragmatic approach can encourage individual and group (or community) initiatives with strategic support from the public-sector institutions such as the National Housing Bank in the form of credit to expedite an improvement in the living conditions of even the slum population. The possibilities have been demonstrated by the Bustee Improvement Programme in Calcutta, which has paved the lanes and provided common services such as water supply and sanitation. Elsewhere, in Hyderabad, an urban community-development programme has provided low-interest loans to the slum dwellers and has assisted them in the procurement of materials (Mohan 1992a).

A critical constraint in the provision of urban housing is land. Well-motivated intentions to limit the speculative gains from the inevitable rise of land values in or in the vicinity of growing urban centres have led to the enactment of laws such as Urban Land (Ceiling and Regulation) Act of 1976, Transfer of Property Act and the Rent and Accommodation Control Act. These laws have created serious impediments to the operation of the market for urban land as well as for rented housing in urban areas. The central government has declared its intention of amending these laws and also the regulatory framework relating to the payment of compensation for land acquired by it. However, action has been extremely tardy and the problems continue to be aggravated.

A Perspective for Urban Planning in the 1990s

The 1990s have brought about a marked change in the Indian perceptions about the scope, nature, and effectiveness of planning activities. It is now recognized that in a continental economy only indicative planning is really possible. Furthermore, the need to encourage private initiatives through market-based signals is considered imperative.

A cornerstone of the new environment is an emphasis on a realistic assessment of the situation, without any reliance on altruistic motivations of the people or a utopian vision of an idyllic society. In this perspective it is essential to recognize that a basic goal of the public policies relating to the infrastructure must be to reduce and eventually to eliminate the rural–urban differentials in the availability of various basic amenities. An important element of progress in this direction has been the electrification of 84 per cent of India's villages, which now have access to a connection for the supply of electricity. (Centre for Monitoring Indian Economy 1993). The percentage of rural households using electricity for lighting their residence has risen from 15 in 1983 to 27 in 1988–9 and further to 31 in 1991.

The prospects in regard to population growth in India imply that even if the country succeeds in lowering the total fertility to 2.1 by about 2016–21, the population will continue to grow for the next 60–70 years. A simultaneous substantial increase in urbanization is inevitable. The associated increase in the density of population will reduce the per-capita cost of providing various services to the people. Therefore, the growth of urban centres must be welcomed and the emphasis of policy and public investment must shift towards minimizing the unfavourable aspects of urban growth and removing the critical bottlenecks.

The planning activities also need to consider the requirements of various urban centres in the larger framework of their hinterland. Such a regional approach to the identification of various linkages in the provision of goods and services needed by the people can be adopted at the sub-state level. A recognition of the essentially fluid nature of the administrative boundaries of districts and states would help to enhance the efficacy of such region-based urban planning.

Need for Better Urban Management and Cost Recovery

Many problems of urban development in India can be tackled at least partially by convincing the beneficiaries or users of services about the simple fact of life that there can be no 'free lunch' for any society. The delivery of services of high quality cannot be ensured without recovering at least the variable costs (including maintenance) and in the long run without paying also for the fixed or developmental costs which would contribute towards an expansion of the infrastructure. The subsidies cannot continue indefinitely for more than a very small segment of the population who are destitutes and must receive public transfers.

The urban local bodies also need to strengthen their capacity for enforcing the basic regulations in regard to land encroachment; traffic laws; pollution of water, air and land; as well as waste disposal. Problems of water supply can be relieved partly by requiring industries to recycle the water used by them. Water used for disposal of human waste can also be reused for irrigation after requisite treatment. Bio-gas plants at various levels can also be used to convert human and animal wastes into sources of energy as well as fertilizers. In brief, a judicious mix of better management and use of available technology can significantly improve the living conditions in urban India. Such an improvement will help the evolution and adoption of policies for facing the inevitable substantial growth of the urban population in India during the 1990s and beyond.

Conclusion

To conclude, a large majority of Indian scholars and policy-makers rightly lament the worsening of the living conditions in Indian cities and towns. Yet, the population in cities continues to grow faster than in rural areas and net in-migration from rural areas continues.

There is no doubt that many Indian towns or cities include incredibly filthy sections with extremely poor sanitation. The residents in these areas seem to have developed an inexplicable degree of tolerance or adaptability to unhygienic living conditions. It is possible that they fail to recognize the implications of their environment for the health and longevity of their family and themselves and put the short-term gain of higher money incomes before their long-term interests. But the usual assumption of economic rationality on their part would suggest that the alternatives open to them are less attractive.

While the case for public or state intervention to eliminate urban squalor is extremely strong, an appalling inaction has persisted for several decades. The recent initiatives (supported by a constitutional amendment) for decentralized planning bodies will not alter the situation unless adequate funds are mobilized. The relatively limited plague epidemic that began in Surat (reputed to be one of the filthiest Indian cities) in 1994 had created a serious scare in India about the consequences of unregulated urban growth. However, the Indian capacity to meet the crisis and perhaps sheer luck or chance factors that led to a quick subsidence of the epidemic have made most policy-makers overlook the seriousness of the problems faced by Indian cities. These problems cannot be ignored for long in view of the imminent large additions to the urban population. The Planning

Commission has recently identified urban waste disposal as a serious problem needing urgent attention during the 9th Plan (1997–2002). A special study commissioned by it is still under review. However, the problem of sanitation is likely to need and receive more focused attention in both rural and urban areas. In a long-run perspective, a simultaneous effort at a balanced rural and urban development, which narrows (and eventually eliminates) the differentials in the basic amenities available to the people of different areas, is imperative.

14 Industrial Location Policies and Their Implications for India

RAKESH MOHAN

The Rationale and International Experience of Industrial Location Policy: A Review

Since independence India has followed a path of rapid industrialization in a very conscious, planned manner. At the time of independence, industrial production in the organized sector of the economy was very concentrated in a few industries and in just a few regions, and was mostly centred around large cities. At the same time, there was a relatively even spread of household industry across the country. The main centres of industrial production were Calcutta, Bombay, Madras, Ahmedabad, and Kanpur, with some concentration of the steel- and coal-related industries in eastern Bihar and West Bengal. Most of the industries located in and around the port cities were export-related processing of basic items such as tea and jute. Given this background of the industrialization pattern in the country there has been a long-standing concern with the location of industry in India. It is probable that this concern is more serious than in many other countries since the pre-independence concentrations of industry were also linked with colonial domination and exploitation. Before independence it is difficult to find any indication of any location policy being followed by British India. As time has progressed the government has adopted an increasingly interventionist stance in the location of industries.

Although the location policies that have been followed in India may be somewhat more stringent than in many other countries, one of the interesting facets of industrial policy of most countries, whether developed or developing, whether socialist or capitalist, has been a manifest desire of the state to intervene in the location decisions of industrial entrepreneurs. Equally interesting is the finding of most studies that explicit spatial policy concerning industrial location has been relatively ineffective in governing the eventual concentration pattern of industry. One of the intrinsic patterns of economic development and industrialization has been the concentration of development in certain regions and not in others. In order to make the design of industrial location policy more intelligent it is

I am grateful to V. P. Bhatia and V. K. Garg, Chief Research Officers in the Office of the Economic Adviser, who provided invaluable help in the preparation of this paper. (The views expressed in this paper are those of the author and may not be attributed to the Government of India)

therefore necessary to understand some of the reasons behind concentration of industry. This can be done from a careful examination of the principles governing the decisions behind the choice of location for different economic activities, and by empirical work which attempts to find out through survey methodology why firms locate where they do. I review some of the basic issues in this introductory section.

To begin with, it is useful to understand that almost all industries exhibit some level of scale economies. This implies the existence of plants of a certain optimal size. Of course different industries have different levels of optimal size. This itself means that each plant implies some level of concentration of resources, be they capital resources or labour. Thus a plant which requires a thousand industrial workers implies concentration of that level. Furthermore it also requires other complementary manufacturing facilities for the working of efficient backward and forward linkages. Those industries which supply inputs to the core plant find it profitable to locate near the plant so as to reduce transport costs. Similarly the consumers of the products of the plants also benefit by being located near the plant. There are other facilities such as banking, insurance, and transport services which exhibit greater levels of efficiency over some minimum threshold size. It is economical for these services to be located in a centre only if there is a reasonable number of customers for their services. Similarly a new entrepreneur wishing to locate a new plant finds it much easier to locate in a centre which already provides him with the relevant forward and backward linkages in terms of the ease of obtaining his inputs as well as increasing the probability of selling his output. The existence of the complementary services also reduces his costs of operation. The provision of infrastructure services such as power, water supply, and roads also benefits from the existence of some level of concentration of the users of these services. The effective price of these services is therefore reduced if there is some level of concentration. Lastly it is also important to appreciate that one of the most important considerations in the location of manufacturing industry is the availability of an adequate quantity and quality of labour. Again, the establishment of the new plant is made much easier if it is located in an area where there is already some concentration of industrial labour so that the new plant can start work with relative ease. Given these issues of principle it is not surprising that there is a natural tendency all over the world for there to be a snowball effect in the location of industry. The issue for policy is essentially to find means by which such concentration is, on the one hand, encouraged, while at the same time the spread of industrialization across the country is also promoted such that the benefits of industrialization become widespread. In summary, some industries induce concentration of economic activity because they exhibit high economies of scale in operation, while others benefit from concentration because of the operation of agglomeration economies.

Turning to a review of industrial location policies, it is useful to record that almost all OECD countries followed some kind of location policy through the 1950s, 1960s, and 1970s (OECD 1974, 1976a, b). This is of interest since all the

European countries are relatively small compared with India. Even in such small countries it was found necessary by the state to intervene in influencing location decisions which went behind the establishment of new plants and the relocation of existing plants.

The OECD review had concluded that the history of regional policies was one of mixed success: '[We] cannot point to any country that has been able, despite determined and considerable effort over long periods, to achieve the objectives it has set for itself.' However, it was also concluded that regional policies are a very necessary and important element of national policies. In a sense, the main conclusion to be drawn from this review and other available reviews of industrial location policies is that expectations about the effectiveness of such policies should be made more realistic. In particular, it was found that 'regional policies based on incentives alone cannot achieve the desired results'. Industrial location policies typically followed can be classified in a few types. The main objective of policy is to induce a firm to locate in a desired location X rather than Y which would otherwise be preferred by the firm. A policy action attempting this would be successful if the costs to the firm of locating at X are reduced to below those of locating at Y; or that the benefits accruing at X would exceed those at Y such that the cost disadvantage of X would be compensated for. In order to accomplish this, the government can offer subsidies which reduce the costs of the three factors of production: capital, labour, and land. The other inducement can be to make infrastructure investments, so that the costs of operation are reduced. Tax benefits can be provided, so that the benefits of location are increased. In principle, most types of inducement that governments typically offer can be categorized within these three classifications. Another kind of policy, of a negative kind, depends on mandates and prohibitions which administratively limit the places where industry can be located.

An exhaustive study attempting to evaluate the effectiveness of location policies was carried out by a group of researchers led by Kyu Sik Lee at the World Bank. This study made a detailed examination of industrial location policies and their effectiveness in South Korea, particularly those aimed at inducing firms to locate away from the Seoul region. The general conclusions of these studies are quite instructive (Murray 1988; Lee 1985; Lee, Choe and Pahk 1987):

1. Subsidize that input which is used extensively by the firm and is a poor substitute for other inputs.
2. If infrastructure investment has to be made, subsidize that public input for which the firm is otherwise more willing to pay high prices, and which is a good substitute for other inputs.

In the case of Korea it was found that capital subsidies were successful in the form of loan guarantees to small and medium-sized enterprises since these enterprises cannot otherwise get bank credit and have to operate on the expensive curb market. In this case the policy was effective since it amounted to a very high level of subsidy for these firms. It was also found otherwise that wage-bill subsidies were much more efficient than land-price subsidies. Finally, in terms of public infrastructure investment it was found that the government is best-off limiting its infrastructure investment to the provision of goods and services that can be widely shared by several firms in an area. One conclusion drawn by Lee is that industrial location policy which restricts location of new industries in cities can end up inhibiting industrial growth itself since the incubator functions of cities as spawning grounds for new industry would then be denied to new entrepreneurs. Decentralization of manufacturing employment away from such city centres to outlying areas and to outlying regions is, however, a general pattern observed in most cities and countries and it takes place naturally as cities become larger and firms need to expand or change operations.

The general conclusion from this very sketchy survey of industrial location policy is that an intelligent design of industrial location policies would attempt to reflect an understanding of the reasoning behind the industrial location decisions of firms. Policies would then be tailored to reinforce firms' natural economic decisions through means which do not grossly violate economic rationality and efficiency. Moreover, the operation of successful industrial location policy is also crucially dependent on co-ordination with other regional policies. In practical terms this means that location decisions can, at best, be affected at the margin and that a large reorientation of industry can take place only over a long period. Hence expectations about the efficacy of policies should be tempered with this kind of understanding.

Industrial Location Policies in India

A very competent review of industrial location policies in India has been provided by Sekhar (1983). Vast differences existed between different regions in terms of the infrastructure and industrial endowment that was in place at the time of independence. Once the Union of India was formed it was therefore to be expected that political and equity considerations would induce the Government of India to attempt to influence industrial location in a planned manner. Apart from the uneven distribution of industry between states, the concentration of industry in certain metropolitan regions was most glaring. It has been felt that the agglomeration economies and economies of scale that originally led to the existence of these concentrations have now been exhausted. Continued expansion of these concentrations would then imply an inefficient allocation of resources. There has also been a high degree of concern for the unemployment and underemployment that characterizes large parts of India. It has been felt that industry must be dispersed in the interests of employment generation in all the different states and regions of India and that this would also promote a more equitable distribution of income.

Sekhar reviewed at some length policies such as industrial licensing, the location of public sector plants, the distribution and pricing policies for intermediate industrial inputs, and other government locational incentives. These policies were aimed at influencing inter-state distribution of industry. One important policy has been the policy of the control of distribution and pricing of key industrial products through the operation of the freight equalization scheme. Prices of key products such as cement, steel and coal have been made equal throughout the country (cement however was partially decontrolled in 1982 and fully decontrolled in February 1989). Some of the natural competitive advantage that the eastern region possessed through the location of the major iron ore and coal deposits has been lost through the operation of these schemes. Conversely, other regions such as the northern, southern, and western regions have been the main beneficiaries of this price equalization scheme. However, a proper evaluation of the functioning of the scheme requires a more detailed effort than is being attempted here.

Among the policies influencing intraregional distribution of industries Sekhar has included policies encouraging small-scale enterprises; the industrial estates programme; the rural industries project; metropolitan planning in the major states; and incentives to promote industrial development in backward areas: these include central government subsidies, concessional finance from all-India financial institutions and additional state government incentives).

According to the information provided by the various studies reviewed by Sekhar, the industrial estates programme was judged as not having been successful. As late as the mid-1970s as many as 30 per cent of completed sheds in industrial estates were not operating. The industrial estates in rural areas fared even worse, with almost half the completed sheds not functioning. The estates in semi-urban areas were only slightly better, with 40 per cent of the sheds not functioning. The urban industrial estates were working more satisfactorily, with only about a quarter of the sheds not operating. Sekhar argued that the most important factor in the indifferent performance of the industrial estates was the wrong choice of location. Proximity to markets, availability of raw materials, labour, transport facilities etc. were often inadequate for the successful functioning of these estates. Another case of economic irrationality cited by Sekhar was the idea of locating industrial estates outside the municipal limits in order to encourage dispersal. Whereas these efforts may have been advisable in the case of large cities, some states decided to locate these estates two to four miles away from the centre even in the case of small towns. Hence the estates encountered typical problems in terms of the lack of infrastructure facilities such as water, electricity, and transport. These problems were recognized within the government when the industrial estates programmes were reviewed. Overall, the industrial estates programmes were assessed to have been relatively unsuccessful, with their share in total output being only 1.7 per cent and in employment 3 per cent by the mid-1970s. In particular, the performance of rural and semi-urban industrial estates was rather poor.

The desire to promote the dispersal of industry gathered momentum during the 1970s and continued with greater force during the 1980s. In 1971, the Planning Commission identified a large number of districts as 'backward' in the country. Districts classified as backward in 1971 accounted for about 60 per cent of the total population of the country and about 70 per cent of the area. The central government announced a capital-investment subsidy scheme in 1971 under which new industrial investment in backward districts was entitled to a subsidy of 10 per cent of their total or additional fixed capital investments. This was, however, subject to certain investment limits beyond which the subsidy would only be given at the discretion of the government. The rate of subsidy was raised to 15 per cent in 1973.

Along with the introduction of the capital investment subsidy in 1971, a transport subsidy was also announced to aid industrial development in hilly, backward areas. This applied to specific hilly districts in the country. The transport subsidy accounted for 50 per cent of the transport costs of raw materials and finished goods for units located in these areas.

Income-tax concessions for new industrial units in backward districts were announced in 1974. The tax concession was available to all projects commencing operation after 1970 for a period of ten years. Eligible units were to be allowed a deduction of 20 per cent of profits in the computation of taxable income.

The other most important scheme for encouraging investment in backward areas was introduced by the all-India financial institutions: the Industrial Development Bank of India (IDBI), the Industrial Finance Corporation of India (IFCI), the Industrial Credit and Investment Corporation of India (ICICI), the Industrial Reconstruction Corporation of India (IRCI), and the National Small Industries Corporation. Each of these institutions provided interest-rate concessions of about 1 or 2 per cent under the normal interest rate charged, also allowing long grace and amortisation periods. The response to these schemes has been quite encouraging and the share of backward areas in the financial assistance sanctioned and disbursed by the all-India financial institutions has consistently been in the region of 40 to 50 per cent since the mid-1970s.

The disbursal of the capital investment subsidy and the concessional finance scheme suggests that they have been quite successful in inducing industry to locate in backward areas. However the National Committee on the Development of Backward Areas (India 1981) found that of the 247 districts that qualified for concessions, only fifteen districts accounted for about 56 per cent of the central investment subsidy disbursed until 1978–9. Similarly twenty-two districts received almost half of the total disbursal of concessional finance given by the financial institutions. Many of these backward districts were located in the backyards of some of the large states. Given the convenience of locating in the vicinity of large cities it should not be regarded as surprising that entrepreneurs would locate in areas closest to large cities but where they could take advantage of all the incentives provided.

Since the late 1970s the licensing mechanism has also been used to restrict the location of new industrial units within certain limits of large metropolitan cities. The Statement on Industrial Policy announced in 1977 prohibited the location of new industrial units above a certain size in all cities with a population of more than 500,000. Furthermore the financial institutions have also been instructed to deny finance to new industries which do not require an industrial licence and which would like to locate in these areas.

The use of backward-area incentives in concentrations in the vicinity of some large cities has led to the further refinement of industrial location policy. Two kinds of new guidelines have been designed. Backward areas have been redesignated in three categories depending on their level of backwardness.

In 1988 when some deregulation of industry was carried out, the locational constraints were extended further. According to an announcement made on 30 June 1988, all industrial investment was delicensed apart from a negative list of 26 industries and subject to a number of provisos. The delicensing facility was available for investments up to Rs. 500 million if located in backward areas but up to only Rs. 150 million if located in non-backward areas. Furthermore, the delicensing was only applicable if the investment were to take place at a distance of 50 km from metropolitan areas with a population of over 2.5 million, 30 km from metropolitan areas with a population of between 1.5 and 2.5 million, 15 km from cities with a population of between 0.75 and 1.5 million, and if it was outside all standard urban areas or municipal limits of all other cities and towns. It should be obvious from this that the government has been very serious in promoting the location of industries away from existing concentrations.

The central investment subsidy scheme has been amended a couple of times and has now been finally discontinued. In 1983, the investment subsidy was placed on a sliding scale with a higher subsidy being given to the more backward areas. Backward areas were divided into three categories, A, B, and C; the subsidies made available were 25, 15, and 10 per cent, each subject to their respective maximum limits. Other incentives for location in backward areas included various exemptions given to 'large industrial houses', allowing them to set up industries in which they would not otherwise be permitted to invest according to the licensing regulations. These exemptions were also related to the imposition of export obligations on these firms. The firms referred to here are those which were classified as large according to the Monopolies and Restrictive Trade Practices Act (MRTP) and other firms with dominant foreign ownership (FERA), which were generally restricted to investing in certain preferred industries only. In 1986, these MRTP/FERA companies were allowed to invest in a number of new industries without export obligation if they agreed to locate in designated backward areas. Similarly, all industries in which MRTP/FERA companies could invest after obtaining a licence were delicensed in 1986 if the investments were to be made in backward areas. Obviously, the guidelines for industrial location have added further complexities to the relatively complex industrial regulatory system of India.

The New Industrial Policy announced in 1991 has made far-reaching changes in Industrial Location Policy along with the other major changes that are taking place in all aspects of economic policy in the country. Along with the large-scale delicensing of industry, all location restrictions described above have been lifted, except for the location of industries within 25 kilometres of twenty-three cities with a population greater than 1 million according to the 1991 census. A licence is required for any industry to locate in any of these metropolitan areas even if the industry is otherwise delicensed. However this condition is not applicable for areas designated as industrial areas before the announcement of the new policy in July 1991. Secondly, a 'flexible location policy' is to be implemented for cities requiring industrial regeneration. Thus very few location restrictions now exist under the new policy regime. Environmental, pollution and other local land-use-related restrictions will naturally continue to be enforced. Along with this change in policy, almost all other incentives for location in backward areas have also been withdrawn. There are no longer any interest rate or income-tax incentives available for location in backward areas. The new philosophy is that the development of backward areas should mainly be assisted through the development of appropriate infrastructure. The key issue now is whether the government will be able to provide such infrastructure investment in selected backward areas.

Overall, the Indian industrial location policy has emphasized incentives as inducements to firms to change their locational preferences. Among the incentives offered, those to which greatest importance has been attached have been capital-cheapening ones. Subsidies for employment have been conspicuous by their absence. Even indirect labour subsidies such as programmes for labour training, retraining, or redeployment have not been utilized in India. Subsidies for land have also been made available mainly through the development of industrial estates: but this particular intervention has not been found to be too successful. Income-tax concessions have also been provided, in an attempt to increase the benefits available to firms locating in backward areas. Besides these incentives, the licensing system has been used to induce investment in backward areas. Finally, there has also been some attempt to use the public-sector investments in a more equitable manner.

There has been a remarkable lack of co-ordination of Indian industrial location policy with other aspects of regional policies. This is all the more noteworthy since, among market economies, India otherwise has had one of the more intensively planned systems. There are no regional development plans attempting to co-ordinate all the elements necessary for a successful regional or industrial location policy. The co-ordination of education or health programmes with any industrial programme has not even been attempted. Even direct inputs such as labour have not been organized in backward areas in order to induce industry to locate in these areas. Similarly, there has also not been any attempt to co-ordinate housing or urban development programmes with industrial location policies except in a negative sense in that industry is prohibited from locating in metropolitan areas. The most conspicuous lack of co-ordination is visible in the green-fields investment of large public-sector enterprises. In the case of all the public-sector steel plants, for example, the planned investment allocations are limited to the specific industrial investments and the creation of company townships. There has been little attempt to co-ordinate the other urban infrastructure and social infrastructure investments required in the environs of these large industrial townships.

However, some light is now beginning to be visible. With the cessation of the central government's capital subsidy scheme, the approach now is to programme co-ordinated investments in 100 selected growth centres during 1992–7 in the interest of industrial dispersal. The existence of agglomeration economies has therefore been explicitly recognized. Moreover, public investment in these selected growth centres is also to be used to improve social infrastructure. Since the scheme has yet to begin, it is not possible to make any conjecture on its likely efficacy. However, the growth centre concept is akin to the Spanish attempt at developing industrial poles: these growth centres are not embedded in a more comprehensive regional planning approach.

It is difficult at this point to make a proper evaluation of the success of all these efforts. It is only recently that data relating to licensing procedures have become available in computer-readable form. Moreover, it is difficult to find information relating to the actual investment after the original licence for investment was granted. With the delicensing of industry in recent years, the monitoring of industrial investment has become even more difficult. The most easily available and reliable series of data on current industrial investments in the country relates to the sanctions and disbursements made by the all-India financial institutions. These institutions are the main source of term loans since the banking system is nationalized. However, their data are available only at the all-India level or at the state level. It is difficult to find more disaggregated data where the investment and production in backward areas can be monitored without conducting a research project of some magnitude.

The following discussion reviews the results of all these industrial location policies by examining the distribution of industries across the fifteen major states of India with a population of 10 million or more. The effort is to compute indices of concentration and evaluate their trend over time since the early 1970s when locational policies first came into operation.

The Dispersal of Manufacturing in India: The Record

It is only possible to evaluate dispersal across states rather than at a more disaggregated level across backward regions within states. In other work (Mohan 1983), I have demonstrated that the variance in levels of urbanization between states has reduced over the years. The rate of growth of urbanization in the older industrialized states of West Bengal, Tamil Nadu, and Maharashtra has slowed down while it has accelerated in the hitherto less urbanized states. As for the spread of manufacturing in the different states of the country, the data from different sources give somewhat different results. Overall, there is evidence of some deconcentration from the older industrialized states, but the picture gets somewhat blurred with the onset of the 1980s. On the spread of employment, the main sources of data used are the population censuses; on value added, the main sources are the state accounts published by the Central Statistics Office (CSO). In both cases, data on the organized sector are available from the Annual Survey of Industries (ASI) as well. Finally, investment data are available from the financial institutions which, perhaps, points to the shape of things to come.

I first examine the spread of manufacturing employment from the census data. Since the various definitional changes between the 1961 and the 1971 censuses affected the data on female employment, only the data on male main workers are used. Looking at the spread of household industry first (Table 14.1), it is clear that it is only in West Bengal that there was growth of any consequence. It is striking that the overall growth rate of about 1.2 per cent is of about the same magnitude as the growth rate of male agricultural employment during the 1971–81 period (see Visaria, Chapter 13, Table 13.6 above). Even in the green-revolution areas of Uttar Pradesh, Punjab, and Haryana, employment growth in household industry in rural areas was negative, but it was highly positive in urban areas. Thus, the main conclusion is that household industry has steadily declined all over India, and particularly in the rural areas, with the notable exception of West Bengal. Looking at the growth in non-household manufacturing employment in different states (Table 14.2) is of greater interest since the growth rates are much higher. It is remarkable that the highest rates of growth in non-household manufacturing employment are in Haryana, Orissa, and Rajasthan (these are also the states which exhibit the highest rates of urban population growth). Similarly, there is direct correspondence at the other end: the states of Maharashtra, Tamil Nadu, West Bengal, and Kerala show the slowest growth in non-household manufacturing

Table 14.1. Employment in household industry by state, males only, 1961–81 ('000)

States	1961		1971		1981		Rates of Growth		
	No.	%	No.	%	No.	%	1961–71	1971–81	1961–81
Andhra Pradesh	1,149	15.60	653	13.00	697	12.34	−5.50	0.66	−2.47
Bihar	603	8.19	373	7.43	410	7.26	−4.69	0.96	−1.91
Gujarat	343	4.66	209	4.16	222	3.93	−4.83	0.60	−2.15
Haryana	146	1.98	82	1.64	96	1.70	−5.61	1.57	−2.07
Karnataka	451	6.13	308	6.13	335	5.93	−3.76	0.86	−1.48
Kerala	189	2.56	148	2.94	124	2.20	−2.42	−1.70	−2.06
Madhya Pradesh	529	7.18	420	8.36	484	8.57	−2.28	1.43	−0.44
Maharashtra	560	7.60	424	8.45	445	7.89	−2.73	0.48	−1.14
Orissa	286	3.88	189	3.76	206	3.64	−4.06	0.86	−1.63
Punjab	247	3.35	119	2.37	119	2.10	−7.04	−0.02	−3.59
Rajasthan	398	5.40	246	4.89	297	5.26	−4.69	1.91	−1.45
Tamil Nadu	681	9.25	486	9.69	561	9.94	−3.31	1.44	−0.96
Uttar Pradesh	1,319	17.91	893	17.78	1,054	18.66	−3.83	1.67	−1.12
West Bengal	300	4.07	290	5.78	430	7.61	−0.33	4.00	1.81
Total[a]	7,337	100.00	5,021	100.00	5,648	100.00	−3.72	1.18	−1.30

[a] The column percentages for the fourteen states may not add up to 100 because of the exclusion of the data for some small states and the union territories with a total population of about 2 to 3 per cent.

Source: Census of India.

Table 14.2. Employment in non-household industry by state, males only, 1961–81 ('000)

States	1961		1971		1981		Rates of growth		
	No.	%	No.	%	No.	%	1961–71	1971–81	1961–81
Andhra Pradesh	388	5.40	637	6.46	1,031	6.51	5.08	4.94	5.01
Bihar	385	5.36	434	4.41	772	4.88	1.20	5.93	3.53
Gujarat	500	6.96	737	7.48	1,358	8.58	3.95	6.31	5.12
Haryana	102	1.42	171	1.74	356	2.25	5.30	7.60	6.45
Karnataka	359	5.00	527	5.34	910	5.75	3.89	5.62	4.75
Kerala	393	5.47	533	5.41	622	3.93	3.10	1.55	2.32
Madhya Pradesh	303	4.21	433	4.39	789	4.99	3.64	6.20	4.91
Maharashtra	1,192	16.59	1,705	17.30	2,549	16.10	3.64	4.10	3.87
Orissa	73	1.02	142	1.45	280	1.77	6.91	7.01	6.96
Punjab	225	3.13	311	3.16	506	3.20	3.29	4.99	4.14
Rajasthan	151	2.10	245	2.48	551	3.48	4.93	8.45	6.68
Tamil Nadu	751	10.45	1,166	11.84	1,720	10.86	4.50	3.96	4.23
Uttar Pradesh	771	10.73	961	9.76	1,662	10.49	2.23	5.63	3.91
West Bengal	1,244	17.31	1,361	13.82	1,900	12.00	0.91	3.39	2.14
Total[a]	7,173	95.16	9,852	95.04	15,834	94.77	3.21	4.86	4.04

[a] See note to Table 14.1.

Source: Census of India.

(and in urban population growth). Indeed, all the states increase their shares at the expense of these older industrialized states. Among the relatively industrialized states only Gujarat exhibits fast growth in manufacturing employment. The fall in share is the highest for West Bengal, which also has a very low rate of urban growth, a clear indication of the decay of Calcutta. Note that this is in contrast to its record in household industry.

The record of growth of factory employment (Table 14.3) presents a similar picture, showing the greater spread of manufacturing employment away from the older industrialized states. The decline of West Bengal emerges in even sharper focus in these data. The share of West Bengal, Maharashtra, and Tamil Nadu falls from just over 50 per cent in 1961, to 47 per cent in 1971, to just over 40 per cent in 1981. The gains of the other states are relatively well distributed: most of the dispersal appears to have taken place during the 1970s.

It is now of interest to look at the distribution of 'unorganized' employment (Table 14.4); which may be defined as the residual resulting from the subtraction of census sector employment as obtained from the ASI from non-household manufacturing employment. Employment in household industry is also excluded from 'unorganized' employment here. Although the highest growth rates are still in Punjab (including Haryana), Rajasthan, and Orissa, the fall in the share of the old industrialized states is less obvious. The share of Maharashtra, Tamil Nadu, and West Bengal falls only negligibly, from about 40 per cent in 1961, to 39 per cent in 1971, and 38 per cent in 1981. There is a clear fall only in the share of West Bengal. Thus, the dispersal of industrial employment is mostly in the factory

Table 14.3.   Factory employment in the census sector, 1961–81 ('000)

States	1961		1971		1981		Rates of growth		
	No.	%	No.	%	No.	%	1961–71	1971–81	1961–81
							% per year		
Andhra Pradesh	142	4.66	255	5.99	448	7.19	6.03	5.80	5.91
Bihar	176	5.77	232	5.45	347	5.57	2.80	4.11	3.45
Gujarat	308	10.10	363	8.53	548	8.80	1.66	4.20	2.92
Karnataka	116	3.80	195	4.58	321	5.15	5.33	5.11	5.22
Kerala	140	4.59	161	3.78	222	3.56	1.41	3.26	2.33
Madhya Pradesh	102	3.34	173	4.06	267	4.29	5.43	4.44	4.93
Maharashtra	650	21.31	830	19.50	1,072	17.21	2.47	2.59	2.53
Orissa	25	0.82	78	1.83	117	1.88	12.05	4.14	8.02
Punjab[a]	76	2.49	173	4.06	307	4.93	8.57	5.90	7.23
Haryana	—[b]	—[b]	89	2.09	139	2.23	—[a]	4.56	—[a]
Rajasthan	44	1.44	87	2.04	150	2.41	7.05	5.60	6.32
Tamil Nadu	227	7.44	441	10.36	599	9.61	6.87	3.11	4.97
Uttar Pradesh	252	8.26	317	7.45	678	10.88	2.32	7.90	5.07
West Bengal	679	22.26	749	17.59	854	13.71	0.99	1.32	1.15
Total[c]	3,050	100.00	4,257	100.00	6,230	100.00	3.39	3.88	3.64
Coefficient of variation		0.97		0.80		0.67			

[a] Including Haryana. Numbers shown separately against Haryana are considered as part of Punjab while estimating the annual average growth rates of employment for the latter
[b] Included in Punjab
[c] See note to Table 14.1.
Source: Annual Survey of Industries 1961, 1970, 1980–1; Census of India.

sector: the distribution of unorganized manufacturing employment has remained relatively stable.

This can be seen in sharper focus in Table 14.5 which gives the share of major states in labour employed in manufacturing in the organized factory sector. It may be observed that the share of Maharashtra, Tamil Nadu, and West Bengal fell consistently during the 1970s, with that of West Bengal being the most pronounced. Among the industrially advanced states, only Gujarat consistently kept up its share during the 1970s. In the 1980s, the picture is less clear, but West Bengal continued its loss of share, along with Maharashtra, the latter's record of decline being less pronounced. The record with respect to the gainers is clearer in the 1970s than in the 1980s. Andhra Pradesh, the green revolutionaries Punjab and Haryana, along with Uttar Pradesh and Rajasthan, showed consistent gains in the share of organized-sector manufacturing employment during the 1970s. During the 1980s, the list of gainers is smaller, with Punjab and Haryana continuing their industrializing path, along with newer entrants, the backward states of Orissa and Madhya Pradesh. The share of the top four, Maharashtra, West Bengal, Tamil Nadu, and Gujarat fell from about 58 per cent in 1970–1, to 50.5 per cent in 1980–1, and to just 49 per cent in 1986–7. The pace of dispersal clearly slowed down in the 1980s.

Table 14.4. Workers in the unorganized sectors (as computed from census and ASI data), 1961–81 ('000)

States	1961		1971		1981		Rates of growth		
	No.	%	No.	%	No.	%	1961–71	1971–81	1961–81
							% per year		
Andhra Pradesh	334	6.78	500	7.74	767	6.85	4.13	4.37	4.25
Bihar	250	5.08	223	3.45	479	4.28	−1.15	7.96	3.31
Gujarat	228	4.63	413	6.40	873	7.79	6.12	7.76	6.94
Karnataka	306	6.21	405	6.27	778	6.94	2.84	6.75	4.78
Kerala	389	7.91	551	8.53	606	5.41	3.53	0.96	2.24
Madhya Pradesh	235	4.77	292	4.52	601	5.37	2.21	7.49	4.81
Maharashtra	654	13.29	1,002	15.51	1,705	15.22	4.35	5.46	4.90
Orissa	61	1.24	79	1.23	196	1.75	2.63	9.49	6.00
Punjab[a]	278	5.65	323	4.99	583	5.20	1.51	6.08	3.77
Haryana	—[b]	—[b]	89	1.37	230	2.05	—[a]	9.97	—[a]
Rajasthan	128	2.60	171	2.64	440	3.92	2.91	9.93	6.36
Tamil Nadu	621	12.62	861	13.34	1,399	12.49	3.32	4.97	4.14
Uttar Pradesh	549	11.15	673	10.42	1,044	9.32	2.06	4.49	3.27
West Bengal	640	13.00	657	10.17	1,172	10.47	0.26	5.97	3.07
India[c]	4,924	100.00	6,460	100.00	11,202	100.00	2.75	5.66	4.20

[a] Including Haryana. Numbers shown separately against Haryana are considered as part of Punjab while estimating the annual average growth rates of employment for the latter.
[b] Included in Punjab.
[c] See note to Table 14.1
Note: Unorganized manufacturing = employment in non-household industry − employment in factory sector (census sector)
Source: Annual Survey of Industries 1961, 1970, 1980–81; Census of India.

This examination of Table 14.5 is confirmed by the three systematic indexes of concentration computed. The coefficient of variation (standard deviation/mean), the Theil index and the Hirschman–Herfindahl index. The Theil index measures the extent of departure of the distribution of any item from the population distribution between states: if the two distributions were identical, the Theil index would be 0. The Hirschman–Herfindahl index also indicates the level of concentration. In the present context, it is the sum of the squared values of the share of each state in total value added in the specified sector. A rise in the value of the index indicates a rise in the level of concentration. All three indexes demonstrate a clear decline in concentration during the 1970s, whereas during the 1980s, the indexes show that the fall in concentration was marginal.

The regional spread of value added in manufacturing

How does the spread of manufacturing employment compare with that of value added in manufacturing? Table 14.6 shows that most states gain at the expense of West Bengal which suffers a drastic fall in share of value added in manufacturing from 18 per cent in 1961, to 13 per cent in 1971, and to just under 10 per cent in

Table 14.5.   Labour employed in manufacturing, Annual Survey of Industries, 1970–86 (% shares of states)

State	1970–1	1971–2	1973–4	1974–5	1975–6	1976–7	1977–8	1978–9	1979–80	1980–1	1981–2	1983–4	1984–5	1985–6	1986–7
Andhra Pradesh	6.56	6.46	6.93	7.51	7.54	8.73	8.58	9.18	9.46	9.09	9.72	9.87	9.63	9.13	9.17
Assam	1.81	1.82	1.53	1.83	1.94	1.88	1.92	1.81	1.71	1.65	1.60	1.46	1.56	1.49	1.63
Bihar	5.32	5.28	4.86	5.15	5.68	5.41	5.43	5.56	4.76	5.06	4.87	4.93	4.72	4.60	4.77
Gujarat	9.55	9.21	9.47	9.62	9.51	9.24	9.27	9.45	9.63	9.41	8.97	9.85	10.27	9.10	9.24
Haryana	0.21	2.07	2.49	2.05	1.88	1.93	1.98	1.97	2.20	2.47	2.67	2.83	2.97	2.97	3.28
Karnataka	4.99	5.21	5.37	5.00	5.32	5.38	5.25	5.13	5.03	5.30	4.81	5.10	5.16	5.23	5.22
Kerala	4.03	4.26	4.25	4.15	3.95	3.98	4.11	3.78	3.84	3.71	3.89	3.38	3.28	3.24	3.24
Madhya Pradesh	4.09	4.05	4.29	4.35	4.40	4.21	4.32	4.28	4.25	4.32	4.49	4.63	4.87	5.16	4.80
Maharashtra	20.19	19.60	19.82	19.89	18.85	18.80	18.09	18.26	18.07	17.87	17.47	16.61	16.78	16.59	16.65
Orissa	1.80	1.80	1.81	1.67	1.75	1.71	1.77	1.62	1.59	1.77	1.83	1.80	1.82	1.85	2.11
Punjab	2.80	2.68	2.85	2.80	2.90	3.08	3.06	3.33	3.48	3.24	3.55	3.45	3.88	4.14	4.34
Rajasthan	2.25	2.09	2.17	2.09	2.33	2.38	2.38	2.35	2.62	2.55	2.65	3.04	2.98	2.92	3.01
Tamil Nadu	11.46	10.96	10.29	10.29	10.37	10.38	10.24	10.30	10.65	10.67	11.09	10.55	10.73	11.68	11.88
Uttar Pradesh	7.88	7.79	7.86	8.65	8.79	9.20	9.97	9.69	9.59	10.26	10.21	10.44	9.52	9.89	9.48
West Bengal	17.06	16.72	16.00	14.96	14.79	13.70	13.61	13.30	13.08	12.62	12.18	12.07	11.85	12.01	11.19
India	100.00	100.00	100.00	100.00	100.00	100.00	100.00	100.00	100.00	100.00	100.00	100.00	100.00	100.00	100.00
Indices of Concentration															
CV	0.84	0.79	0.78	0.77	0.73	0.72	0.70	0.71	0.70	0.69	0.68	0.66	0.65	0.65	0.63
HH Index	11.32	10.83	10.68	10.59	10.26	10.12	9.95	10.00	9.95	9.84	9.71	9.54	9.48	9.46	9.32
Theil Index	8.40	7.49	7.47	6.79	6.07	5.78	5.32	5.56	5.85	5.38	5.30	5.08	5.54	5.34	5.40

Note: 'India' includes only the states listed above (states with over 10 m. population)

Source: Central Statistical Organisation.

Table 14.6.   Manufacturing value added by states, 1961–81 (Rs Lakhs in 1970–1 prices)

States	1961		1971		1981		Rates of growth		
	No.	%	No.	%	No.	%	1961–71	1971–81	1961–81
							% per year		
Andhra Pradesh	13,328	5.01	22,135	5.21	36,559	5.31	5.20	5.15	5.17
Bihar	12,178	4.58	22,177	5.22	34,414	5.00	6.18	4.49	5.33
Gujarat	26,425	9.93	34,939	8.23	58,072	8.43	2.83	5.21	4.02
Haryana	3,820	1.44	8,587	2.02	18,425	2.68	8.44	7.93	8.19
Karnataka	15,591	5.86	28,588	6.73	53,395	7.75	6.25	6.45	6.35
Kerala	7,861	2.95	15,632	3.68	25,227	3.66	7.12	4.90	6.00
Madhya Pradesh	8,840	3.32	17,880	4.21	26,990	3.92	7.30	4.20	5.74
Maharashtra	60,456	22.71	102,777	24.21	175,504	25.48	5.45	5.50	5.47
Orissa	2,829	1.06	8,331	1.96	13,103	1.90	11.41	4.63	7.97
Punjab	6,411	2.41	11,494	2.71	26,176	3.80	6.01	8.58	7.29
Rajasthan	11,005	4.13	12,666	2.98	16,007	2.32	1.42	2.37	1.89
Tamil Nadu	26,267	9.87	45,871	10.80	75,834	11.01	5.73	5.16	5.44
Uttar Pradesh	23,143	8.70	37,925	8.93	62,058	9.01	5.06	5.05	5.06
West Bengal	48,007	18.04	55,587	13.09	66,899	9.71	1.48	1.87	1.67
India[a]	266,160	100.00	424,589	100.00	688,663	100.00	4.78	4.96	4.87

[a] Only including states above

Source: Central Statistical Organisation National Accounts Statistics.

1981. Both Maharashtra and Gujarat actually increase their share during these two decades, in contrast to their record in manufacturing employment. The implication is that labour productivity in these states grew much faster than in other states. The highest growth is recorded by the green revolutionaries, Haryana and Punjab. The one major anomaly relative to the record of employment growth is Rajasthan: growth in value added during the 1970s is only 2.4 per cent a year, less than half of the national average of 5 per cent a year, despite the extremely high rates of growth in manufacturing employment. Except for the fall of West Bengal, and the rise of Haryana and Punjab, there is little redistribution of manufacturing in terms of value added. One must conclude that much of the dispersal of manufacturing employment must be of low productivity.

This is investigated in Table 14.7 which shows the annual value added per employee. The evidence is of a mild trend towards increasing inequality between states, but not of a marked one. The value added per employee in Maharashtra, for example, shows a clear trend towards increase as a multiple of average productivity across all states. The industries sprouting in Punjab and Haryana are presumably of a labour-using nature: their labour productivity is consistently below the national average. Other states showing consistent low productivity are Andhra Pradesh, Orissa, and Uttar Pradesh. This offers some corroboration of the idea that some of the industrial dispersal may be of low-productivity industries: it may be recalled that these low-productivity states were among the chief gainers in manufacturing employment.

Table 14.7.   Ratio of value added per worker in states to the all-India figure, Annual Survey of Industries, 1970–86 (rupees per employee per year)

State	1970–1	1971–2	1973–4	1974–5	1975–6	1976–7	1977–8	1978–9	1979–80	1980–1	1981–2	1983–4	1984–5	1985–6	1986–7
Andhra Pradesh	0.63	0.63	0.75	0.59	0.68	0.60	0.59	0.55	0.55	0.56	0.51	0.64	0.69	0.78	0.61
Assam	0.80	0.74	0.86	1.01	0.98	1.12	1.23	0.94	0.83	0.61	0.62	0.65	0.82	1.15	1.25
Bihar	1.09	1.11	1.04	1.24	1.41	1.03	0.92	1.01	1.09	0.86	1.34	1.42	1.74	1.23	1.17
Gujarat	1.00	0.93	1.03	1.07	0.96	1.05	1.14	1.02	1.02	1.05	0.99	0.96	1.17	1.16	1.04
Haryana	1.04	1.30	0.89	1.09	1.29	1.34	1.39	1.39	1.37	1.21	1.19	1.14	1.29	0.98	0.92
Karnataka	1.21	1.19	0.97	0.93	0.98	0.94	0.96	1.28	1.07	0.99	0.99	0.99	1.13	1.00	1.00
Kerala	0.74	0.75	0.69	0.69	0.66	0.65	0.73	0.77	0.86	0.91	0.80	0.89	0.82	1.05	0.93
Madhya Pradesh	0.91	0.83	1.16	1.11	1.01	1.17	1.03	0.91	1.01	1.21	1.25	1.28	1.08	1.02	1.26
Maharashtra	1.39	1.44	1.39	1.35	1.34	1.34	1.42	1.42	1.42	1.45	1.37	1.35	1.35	1.42	1.61
Orissa	1.10	0.86	1.12	1.06	0.93	1.31	1.17	1.23	1.38	0.97	0.89	0.80	0.86	0.62	0.71
Punjab	0.84	0.83	0.78	0.82	0.94	0.92	0.94	0.91	0.97	1.03	0.86	0.83	0.72	0.74	0.77
Rajasthan	0.98	1.03	0.87	0.95	1.08	1.01	1.01	1.10	1.19	1.13	0.99	0.81	1.09	0.93	0.94
Tamil Nadu	0.90	0.88	0.93	0.95	0.84	0.94	0.99	1.00	0.96	1.00	0.91	1.00	0.87	1.00	0.90
Uttar Pradesh	0.88	0.81	0.84	0.77	0.76	0.82	0.66	0.66	0.67	0.63	1.03	0.89	0.66	0.69	0.65
West Bengal	0.84	0.88	0.85	0.89	0.93	0.91	0.88	0.87	0.87	0.94	0.84	0.84	0.71	0.76	0.77
India	6,069	6,360	8,039	10,119	10,076	11,033	11,479	13,202	14,173	15,202	18,521	20,402	25,244	26,268	31,224
CV	0.19	0.23	0.18	0.20	0.22	0.22	0.23	0.24	0.24	0.24	0.24	0.24	0.29	0.22	0.27

Note: 'India' includes only the states listed above (states with over 10m. population). The figures given are as a proportion of the India average.

Source: Central Statistical Organisation.

The spread of manufacturing activity in terms of value added is worth investigating in a little more detail during the 1970s and 1980s, the decades of accelerated urbanization and dispersal of manufacturing employment. This is because the results are not all consistent and point to areas for further research.

The main source of data used is the CSO compilation of state accounts. The data reveal that all the states increased their level of industrialization during the 1970s and 1980s, with the exception of West Bengal and, possibly, Rajasthan. A slow structural transformation is evident in all the major states, although there were some ups and downs for some states during the period.

Value added in manufacturing may be divided into registered manufacturing and unregistered (or unorganized) manufacturing. Tables 14.8 and 14.9 show the share in manufacturing of different states in the registered and unregistered sectors respectively. In registered manufacturing, there are clearly some gainers and losers in the shares of different states. The biggest consistent loser is West Bengal whose share fell by almost half from about 15 per cent in 1970–1 to less than 8 per cent in 1986–7. The consistent gainers include Andhra Pradesh, Haryana, Karnataka, Punjab, and Uttar Pradesh in the 1980s. There has clearly been some dispersal. But, according to the computed indices of concentration, little overall change is observed in the distribution over the whole period.

In the case of unregistered manufacturing (Table 14.9), the main feature to note is the generally low level of inequality between states and the lack of any clear trend throughout the period. There are no very clear gainers or losers throughout the period, except for the striking increase in share of Uttar Pradesh in the 1980s. A Theil index of less than four is quite low, demonstrating that the distribution of unregistered manufacturing is not too different from that of population.

The data from the state accounts can be compared with those from the Annual Survey of Industries (Table 14.10) which should roughly correspond with the manufacturing value added in the registered sector. The state accounts reveal a consistently higher level of inequality between states, with Maharashtra showing a consistently higher share than recorded by the ASI data. A decentralizing trend is recorded from 1970–1 to 1976–7 but the picture since then is inconclusive. Again, Andhra, Haryana, Punjab, and Rajasthan are consistent gainers in the 1970s whereas no clear pattern emerges in the 1980s.

The main results that emerge from this analysis are that whereas the results for factory employment were quite conclusive in demonstrating a trend towards a better distribution across states during the 1970s, the evidence for value added is more mixed. There is some evidence of dispersal but it is not very strong. In the 1980s, however, whatever trend there was towards dispersal was arrested. The only trend that continued unabated is the loss in share of West Bengal. Further, corroborative evidence is also offered by the distribution of power consumption per capita by industry across states; the coefficient of variation fell between 1960–1 and 1970–1 but has since been fluctuating. Similarly, no significant trend is visible in overall power consumption per capita during the 1980s.

Table 14.8. Value added in manufacturing, state accounts registered manufacturing, 1970–87 (% shares of states) (constant prices)

State	1970–1	1971–2	1972–3	1973–4	1974–5	1975–6	1976–7	1977–8	1978–9	1979–80	1980–1	1981–2	1982–3	1983–4	1984–5	1985–6	1986–7
Andhra Pradesh	3.75	3.84	3.76	3.75	4.31	4.35	4.11	3.99	4.05	4.28	4.06	4.51	4.11	4.05	5.31	5.88	5.20
Assam	1.53	1.57	1.57	1.57	1.62	1.49	1.36	1.31	1.27	1.22	1.12	1.24	1.19	1.24	1.32	1.25	1.14
Bihar	5.85	6.06	5.91	5.85	5.87	5.66	5.43	5.31	4.99	4.86	5.46	5.41	5.27	5.64	5.78	5.31	5.24
Gujarat	9.57	8.68	10.10	10.74	10.90	9.69	9.54	10.31	9.82	9.78	10.01	9.90	11.48	11.83	8.15	8.03	8.03
Haryana	2.11	2.48	2.43	2.45	2.74	2.57	2.45	2.52	2.55	2.80	2.94	2.94	2.82	3.02	3.17	3.13	3.20
Karnataka	5.37	5.51	5.32	5.08	5.19	5.67	6.27	6.01	6.79	6.76	6.49	6.51	6.35	6.47	6.60	7.47	7.26
Kerala	2.54	3.13	2.89	2.69	2.56	2.45	2.44	2.48	2.25	2.47	2.84	3.18	3.26	3.38	2.12	2.07	2.20
Madhya Pradesh	3.37	3.36	4.07	5.19	5.00	4.10	4.35	3.91	3.60	3.70	3.52	3.82	3.86	4.03	4.62	4.00	3.82
Maharashtra	28.88	29.05	28.35	27.23	29.56	29.44	28.67	29.45	30.67	30.55	30.61	31.24	31.26	30.35	28.85	29.65	30.54
Orissa	2.06	1.48	1.25	1.75	2.04	1.39	2.04	1.88	2.06	1.94	2.12	1.90	2.00	2.02	0.90	0.83	0.82
Punjab	2.05	2.05	2.29	2.28	2.24	2.54	2.36	2.49	2.54	2.70	2.78	2.87	2.88	3.08	2.82	2.61	2.51
Rajasthan	1.83	1.89	1.87	1.84	1.86	1.81	1.73	1.71	1.66	1.65	1.49	1.49	1.46	1.51	2.60	2.41	2.56
Tamil Nadu	9.56	9.84	9.77	9.64	7.38	9.96	10.61	10.63	10.86	11.23	10.24	9.77	9.40	8.67	11.15	11.27	11.15
Uttar Pradesh	6.76	6.15	5.94	5.90	5.37	6.34	5.98	5.85	6.19	5.68	5.62	4.91	4.92	5.05	8.00	7.89	8.38
West Bengal	14.76	14.90	14.48	14.04	13.38	12.54	12.66	12.16	10.70	10.39	10.71	10.29	9.73	9.67	8.60	8.20	7.95
India	100.00	100.00	100.00	100.00	100.00	100.00	100.00	100.00	100.00	100.00	100.00	100.00	100.00	100.00	100.00	100.00	100.00
Indices of Concentration																	
C V	1.04	1.05	1.03	0.98	1.04	1.04	1.01	1.04	1.07	1.07	1.06	1.08	1.08	1.05	0.99	1.02	1.05
HH Index	13.94	13.98	13.67	13.10	13.89	13.84	13.53	13.91	14.35	14.25	14.21	14.41	14.50	13.99	13.19	13.64	14.07
Theil Index	11.90	12.07	12.09	11.33	12.16	11.82	11.58	12.44	12.88	13.09	13.10	13.44	13.98	13.39	10.39	11.22	11.69

Note: 'India' includes only the states listed above (states with over 10m. population).

Source: Central Statistical Organisation.

Table 14.9. Value added in manufacturing, state accounts unregistered manufacturing, 1970–87 (% shares of states) (constant 1970–1 prices)

State	1970–1	1971–2	1972–3	1973–4	1974–5	1975–6	1976–7	1977–8	1978–9	1979–80	1980–1	1981–2	1982–3	1983–4	1984–5	1985–6	1986–7
Andhra Pradesh	7.59	7.68	7.71	7.91	8.28	8.07	6.92	6.74	7.55	7.22	7.44	7.46	7.70	7.39	7.94	8.01	8.04
Assam	1.81	1.87	1.82	1.91	2.03	2.09	1.88	1.92	1.93	1.76	2.06	2.15	2.34	2.45	2.72	3.00	2.95
Bihar	3.86	3.67	3.26	3.82	3.74	3.94	3.79	3.67	4.05	3.75	3.91	3.82	3.86	3.86	3.23	3.44	3.45
Gujarat	5.47	5.44	5.64	5.84	6.13	5.78	5.61	5.43	5.27	5.22	5.09	5.09	5.19	5.09	4.62	4.39	4.57
Haryana	1.77	1.95	1.99	1.96	2.14	2.13	2.03	2.18	2.21	2.00	2.07	2.00	2.20	2.20	2.27	2.27	2.28
Karnataka	8.85	9.26	9.08	9.76	9.83	9.29	9.47	11.01	10.45	10.43	9.82	9.07	9.46	9.10	9.03	8.25	8.05
Kerala	5.55	5.40	5.88	5.83	5.61	5.76	5.34	4.54	4.44	4.42	5.07	4.69	4.92	4.99	3.59	3.72	3.22
Madhya Pradesh	5.52	6.09	5.47	5.96	3.99	4.40	5.79	5.31	5.32	4.39	4.51	4.45	4.44	4.57	6.21	6.21	6.46
Maharashtra	14.76	15.10	15.10	14.93	14.49	14.84	15.60	15.13	15.58	14.47	14.73	13.70	13.53	13.38	13.19	13.94	14.04
Orissa	1.70	1.72	1.74	1.77	1.71	1.65	1.64	1.58	1.54	1.54	1.41	1.44	1.41	1.33	1.30	1.26	1.23
Punjab	3.76	3.89	4.42	4.57	4.78	5.15	5.36	5.58	5.40	5.05	5.57	6.00	6.17	5.81	4.77	4.81	4.73
Rajasthan	4.91	4.92	4.73	4.74	4.89	4.77	4.62	4.41	4.29	3.84	3.80	3.76	3.84	3.74	2.98	2.94	3.22
Tamil Nadu	12.53	11.98	11.55	10.16	10.62	10.84	10.65	9.40	9.50	15.78	12.02	14.04	10.88	11.46	11.29	10.73	10.19
Uttar Pradesh	12.41	11.74	12.48	11.62	12.54	12.26	12.09	14.09	14.34	13.01	15.06	15.10	16.79	17.33	19.81	20.31	20.68
West Bengal	9.52	9.28	9.14	9.22	9.23	9.01	9.22	9.01	8.12	7.12	7.44	7.22	7.29	7.31	7.06	6.71	6.90
India	100.00	100.00	100.00	100.00	100.00	100.00	100.00	100.00	100.00	100.00	100.00	100.00	100.00	100.00	100.00	100.00	100.00
Indices of Concentration																	
CV	0.60	0.59	0.59	0.56	0.58	0.57	0.58	0.61	0.62	0.67	0.64	0.65	0.64	0.65	0.73	0.74	0.75
HH Index	9.09	8.99	9.02	8.76	8.88	8.83	8.94	9.17	9.22	9.69	9.39	9.46	9.36	9.48	10.17	10.30	10.38
Theil Index	3.87	3.97	4.27	3.98	4.29	4.21	4.30	4.41	4.08	5.74	4.58	4.92	4.26	4.18	4.00	3.90	3.73

Note: 'India' includes only the states listed above (states with over 10m. population)

Source: Central Statistical Organisation.

Table 14.10. Value added in manufacturing, Annual Survey of Industries, 1970–86 (% shares of states)

State	1970–1	1971–2	1973–4	1974–5	1975–6	1976–7	1977–8	1978–9	1979–80	1980–1	1981–2	1982–3	1983–4	1984–5	1985–6
Andhra Pradesh	4.07	4.06	5.18	4.42	5.12	5.21	5.04	5.08	5.20	5.06	4.92	6.31	6.69	7.10	5.61
Assam	1.43	1.34	1.31	1.84	1.89	2.10	2.36	1.71	1.47	1.01	0.99	0.95	1.28	1.70	2.04
Bihar	5.67	5.85	5.04	6.41	7.98	5.55	5.01	5.60	5.17	4.34	6.52	6.98	8.22	5.67	5.57
Gujarat	9.37	8.54	9.75	10.27	9.17	9.67	10.55	9.63	9.78	9.87	8.90	9.47	12.01	10.58	9.57
Haryana	2.27	2.69	2.21	2.23	2.42	2.59	2.76	2.74	3.01	3.00	3.17	3.23	3.83	2.92	3.04
Karnataka	5.90	6.18	5.21	4.64	5.20	5.04	5.01	6.56	5.38	5.23	4.77	5.06	5.82	5.20	5.21
Kerala	2.94	3.20	2.93	2.85	2.60	2.61	3.00	2.89	3.31	3.39	3.10	3.01	2.67	3.39	3.00
Madhya Pradesh	3.64	3.38	4.96	4.84	4.45	4.91	4.47	3.89	4.29	5.22	5.59	5.94	5.28	5.27	6.06
Maharashtra	27.47	28.14	27.46	26.84	25.23	25.12	25.75	25.99	25.70	25.88	23.94	22.37	22.61	23.61	26.76
Orissa	1.94	1.55	2.02	1.77	1.62	2.24	2.07	2.00	2.19	1.72	1.63	1.44	1.56	1.16	1.50
Punjab	2.31	2.21	2.24	2.29	2.71	2.83	2.88	3.03	3.38	3.35	3.04	2.85	2.80	3.06	3.33
Rajasthan	2.15	2.15	1.88	1.97	2.51	2.41	2.42	2.59	3.10	2.89	2.62	2.45	3.26	2.73	2.82
Tamil Nadu	10.08	9.62	9.57	9.73	8.74	9.72	10.17	10.34	10.21	10.65	10.11	10.51	9.34	11.68	10.67
Uttar Pradesh	6.78	6.33	6.58	6.66	6.66	7.58	6.57	6.42	6.47	6.49	10.50	9.29	6.26	6.84	6.16
West Bengal	13.99	14.76	13.66	13.25	13.68	12.42	11.95	11.52	11.34	11.92	10.20	10.15	8.37	9.09	8.66
India	100.00	100.00	100.00	100.00	100.00	100.00	100.00	100.00	100.00	100.00	100.00	100.00	100.00	100.00	100.00
Indices of Concentration															
C V	0.98	1.01	0.98	0.96	0.89	0.87	0.89	0.90	0.88	0.90	0.83	0.78	0.78	0.82	0.90
HH Index	13.12	13.46	13.02	12.75	11.98	11.75	12.00	12.03	11.80	12.08	11.29	10.76	10.70	11.14	12.05
Theil Index	10.76	11.39	10.56	9.99	8.53	8.31	9.48	9.45	9.21	9.97	6.94	6.61	7.94	8.39	9.37

Note: 'India' includes only the states listed above (states with over 10m. population). For 1964–5 the data for labour are from the 1961 census; for 1970–1 from the 1971 census; for 1980–1 from the 1981 census, and for 1986–7 from the 1981 census.
Source: Central Statistical Organisation.

A final footnote to this examination of the spread of manufacturing across states is provided by the record of inequality of agricultural productivity across states. In comparison with some mild evidence pointing to decreasing inequality between states in terms of manufacturing activity, the interstate disparities in agriculture have shown a rise. Some of the apparent stagnation of agricultural productivity in all the industrially advanced states of Maharashtra, West Bengal, Tamil Nadu, and Gujarat may be weather-induced impact of droughts. If their agricultural productivity had not stagnated, their manufacturing growth might perhaps have been higher. West Bengal showed some signs of an agricultural revival in the 1980s, but the overall picture is of large and consistent increases in agricultural productivity in Haryana, Punjab, and Uttar Pradesh alone. These states are the ones showing consistent gains in manufacturing as well. The dispersal of manufacturing observed may be partly related to the pattern of agricultural productivity changes across states.

The regional spread of manufacturing investment

The most powerful lever affecting the spread of manufacturing in the country is probably the geographical pattern of financial assistance offered by the all-India financial institutions offering term loans for industrial investment. The distribution of sanctions and disbursements is given in Tables 14.11 and 14.12.

The share of the top four states, Maharashtra, West Bengal, Tamil Nadu, and Gujarat, in sanctions showed a clear falling trend in the 1970s, but this trend was arrested during the 1980s. Interestingly, the disbursement pattern exhibits this falling trend up to 1984–5: presumably a reflection of the sanctions pattern until the early 1980s. The share in disbursements of these top four states began to rise again during the second half of the 1980s, reflecting the sanctions pattern since the early 1980s. Another feature of interest is that although Punjab's share in sanctions and disbursements showed a clear upward trend during the 1970s, it stagnated during the 1980s, probably because of the terrorist activities in the state. The share of Haryana shows no trend throughout the 1970s and 1980s, despite the clearly increasing shares in value added manufacturing and employment. This evidence corroborates the idea that the pattern of industrialization in Punjab and Haryana is more labour-using with low degrees of capital intensity.

Table 14.13 confirms the dispersal pattern stated above. The financial institutions diversified their sanctions and disbursements quite fast during the 1970s but that trend did not continue during the 1980s. The indication provided by the sanctions pattern was that the inequality in the distribution of manufacturing investment between states was not likely to decrease in a striking manner in the next few years.

In summary, the initial efforts in dispersing industry away from the older industrialized states were quite successful during the 1970s, but this effort seems to have lost some steam during the 1980s. This is not easy to understand since dispersal measures certainly continued to become more stringent during this period. One

Table 14.11. Sanctions of all India financial institutions (% shares of states) 1970–88

State	1970–1	1971–2	1972–3	1973–4	1974–5	1975–6	1976–7	1977–8	1978–9	1979–80	1980–1	1981–2	1982–3	1983–4	1984–5	1985–6	1986–7	1987–8	Cumulative 1969–88
Andhra Pradesh	2.83	3.19	3.41	3.62	3.82	5.12	10.00	5.14	6.82	4.56	8.71	10.14	7.15	11.56	10.82	5.69	12.07	11.21	9.21
Assam	0.03	6.02	0.52	3.50	0.89	1.30	1.06	0.37	0.45	0.37	0.34	0.45	1.15	0.85	0.84	0.71	0.77	0.59	0.75
Bihar	11.92	5.44	5.06	4.61	2.24	3.28	4.15	4.17	3.79	2.24	3.63	3.50	2.35	3.50	2.03	1.95	2.45	3.56	2.96
Gujarat	14.38	20.60	7.98	13.15	10.89	10.91	11.01	24.04	15.33	16.10	10.48	12.10	15.86	15.87	8.04	12.36	13.67	12.86	13.08
Haryana	3.45	2.77	2.80	2.91	2.54	2.04	3.01	3.25	1.95	2.50	2.65	2.51	3.59	3.55	3.15	2.24	2.49	3.00	2.80
Karnataka	1.97	9.83	9.29	8.62	11.49	9.01	6.58	8.36	6.18	8.86	9.21	6.64	7.25	7.40	7.64	7.57	5.55	5.95	7.03
Kerala	1.82	1.77	4.93	1.43	3.96	5.02	2.71	3.54	2.55	5.41	2.51	1.74	2.64	2.18	3.07	1.90	2.27	2.01	2.49
Madhya Pradesh	5.70	2.34	1.68	1.96	3.88	2.04	3.42	2.52	2.72	4.05	3.10	2.95	6.13	4.87	6.38	5.53	6.72	6.71	5.32
Maharashtra	29.49	18.88	29.74	21.73	25.17	17.72	17.68	13.87	21.89	22.29	20.36	18.41	17.38	16.02	15.33	19.09	17.10	18.67	18.24
Orissa	3.06	0.69	2.76	0.64	1.54	3.21	2.12	1.53	2.40	2.34	2.75	4.79	3.72	3.63	5.53	2.06	2.31	2.09	2.93
Punjab	0.27	1.40	1.43	2.68	2.52	2.78	2.91	1.90	3.73	3.44	6.74	2.98	3.24	3.51	2.68	2.95	4.36	3.14	3.41
Rajasthan	1.53	2.27	1.65	1.70	5.31	2.54	4.29	4.50	4.11	4.39	7.73	5.60	5.75	5.11	3.41	4.50	4.41	4.00	4.53
Tamil Nadu	7.21	15.34	8.66	11.90	12.22	14.82	9.70	8.37	10.35	8.13	9.27	13.67	10.34	9.60	8.95	12.44	6.88	11.04	10.11
Uttar Pradesh	8.71	4.18	11.08	6.59	7.16	11.84	12.46	10.03	6.32	8.23	7.68	7.55	7.53	7.40	16.42	12.64	13.96	11.46	11.06
West Bengal	7.63	5.28	9.00	14.96	6.36	8.37	8.89	8.40	11.40	7.10	4.84	6.96	5.91	4.93	5.71	8.37	5.00	3.72	6.07
Others	3.79	2.70	5.84	2.78	6.83	8.07	6.98	5.05	4.23	0.65	1.28	0.82	0.78	4.34	5.15	6.38	6.44	5.53	4.59
Share of Top 4	58.71	60.09	55.38	61.74	54.64	51.82	47.29	54.68	58.97	53.61	44.94	51.14	49.50	46.42	38.02	52.26	42.64	46.28	47.50
Total	100.00	100.00	100.00	100.00	100.00	100.00	100.00	100.00	100.00	100.00	100.00	100.00	100.00	100.00	100.00	100.00	100.00	100.00	100.00

Note: 'Others' is not included in 'Total'. 'Top 4' includes Gujarat, Maharashtra, Tamil Nadu, and West Bengal.

Source: Industrial Development Bank of India.

Table 14.12. Disbursements of all-India financial institutions (% shares of states) 1970–88

State	1970–1	1971–2	1972–3	1973–4	1974–5	1975–6	1976–7	1977–8	1978–9	1979–80	1980–1	1981–2	1982–3	1983–4	1984–5	1985–6	1986–7	1987–8	Cumulative 1969–88
Andhra Pradesh	4.57	4.39	4.02	3.97	3.43	3.40	6.07	8.05	8.48	7.74	6.63	6.92	9.84	8.71	9.48	8.50	7.88	8.60	8.11
Assam	0.59	0.17	1.93	3.51	3.17	2.31	1.92	0.78	0.53	0.59	0.34	0.38	0.54	0.44	0.86	1.09	0.97	0.64	0.81
Bihar	4.64	3.61	10.30	7.68	2.98	4.06	4.64	3.98	2.31	2.11	2.27	2.63	2.91	3.08	2.02	1.53	2.31	3.05	2.66
Gujarat	13.38	10.95	12.67	13.40	13.28	11.21	11.50	15.39	21.50	13.44	11.99	13.38	13.12	10.78	9.98	13.40	15.11	13.28	13.16
Haryana	3.51	5.06	4.00	1.93	2.06	2.30	3.35	3.06	3.36	2.83	2.22	2.77	2.75	2.97	4.31	2.37	2.83	2.02	2.76
Karnataka	5.38	4.46	5.37	9.59	10.68	13.04	8.40	6.53	7.99	9.82	8.74	7.78	7.65	8.82	10.01	9.28	6.51	5.00	7.73
Kerala	1.39	2.08	1.87	2.93	2.77	4.34	6.88	3.41	3.35	2.81	3.31	3.49	2.91	2.55	2.97	2.19	2.31	2.06	2.67
Madhya Pradesh	5.13	6.17	3.71	1.62	1.39	2.43	2.43	2.54	2.75	4.02	3.30	3.54	4.28	5.60	6.01	7.18	5.32	6.08	5.16
Maharashtra	34.19	31.91	27.37	21.36	22.64	23.46	18.00	20.66	15.84	20.04	22.20	20.27	19.63	17.53	17.69	18.23	17.59	19.85	19.16
Orissa	2.01	2.59	1.67	1.61	1.98	1.51	1.39	1.60	1.52	2.24	2.73	3.08	3.81	3.32	2.88	3.57	3.22	2.27	2.84
Punjab	0.52	1.23	1.51	2.29	2.00	2.00	2.73	2.99	2.59	3.96	3.97	4.50	4.17	4.14	3.19	2.43	3.17	4.18	3.47
Rajasthan	2.11	2.18	2.06	2.26	1.80	4.38	3.71	3.83	3.66	5.72	5.73	5.02	6.01	6.13	4.35	4.09	4.90	3.91	4.63
Tamil Nadu	11.30	10.92	9.47	14.16	13.93	11.73	12.98	9.54	8.43	7.88	10.64	9.56	10.49	13.14	11.88	10.71	9.68	10.19	10.59
Uttar Pradesh	5.31	7.45	7.61	7.39	8.20	4.73	7.12	10.06	9.74	8.32	8.10	8.28	6.90	7.51	8.94	10.54	12.38	14.43	10.28
West Bengal	5.97	6.84	6.42	6.29	9.69	9.10	8.88	7.55	7.96	8.48	7.84	8.39	4.99	5.27	5.45	4.91	5.83	4.42	5.98
Others	6.94	4.86	3.59	3.68	5.87	7.73	6.36	7.31	6.22	5.04	4.77	6.10	7.06	6.22	5.66	6.76	5.94	5.43	5.95
Share of Top 4	64.85	60.61	55.93	55.21	59.53	55.51	51.35	53.15	53.73	49.83	52.66	51.60	48.23	46.73	45.00	47.25	48.21	47.75	48.88
Total	100.00	100.00	100.00	100.00	100.00	100.00	100.00	100.00	100.00	100.00	100.00	100.00	100.00	100.00	100.00	100.00	100.00	100.00	100.00

Notes: see Table 14.11.

Source: Industrial Development Bank of India.

Table 14.13.   Sanctions and disbursements of All India financial institutions, indices of dispersal, 1970–88

	Sanction		Disbursements	
	HH Index	Theil Index	HH Index	Theil Index
1970–1	14.76	14.37	16.61	17.25
1971–2	12.58	17.63	14.93	14.49
1972–3	13.98	11.99	12.96	11.04
1973–4	12.00	13.10	11.38	10.77
1974–5	12.20	12.21	12.14	12.86
1975–6	10.41	7.94	11.78	12.48
1976–7	9.84	5.43	9.74	8.44
1977–8	11.81	13.13	10.91	9.17
1978–9	11.45	11.11	11.36	12.41
1979–80	11.33	11.66	10.32	9.43
1980–1	10.02	9.68	10.85	9.91
1981–2	10.18	8.84	10.23	9.16
1982–3	9.78	8.99	10.06	9.24
1983–4	9.74	8.87	9.56	8.02
1984–5	9.72	4.82	9.59	7.87
1985–6	10.68	8.04	10.21	8.35
1986–7	10.30	7.18	10.15	7.59
1987–8	10.43	7.75	10.94	7.68
1969–88	9.92		10.10	

explanation could be that these dominant states simply tightened up their machinery for attracting investment to their own backward areas, and, therefore, began to regain some lost ground. However, the evidence at hand is not adequate to provide such an explanation.

Policy Implications

The review of Indian industrial location policy has shown that, although great attention has been paid to influencing industrial location in the country, particularly since the early 1970s, it is possible that the instrument of policy used may have been somewhat inadequate in greatly altering the distribution of industries across the country. The quantitative evidence on the actual record of industrial dispersal in India is somewhat incomplete. Most policies designed to influence industrial location have been directed towards inducing industries to locate away from large cities and towards areas defined as backward areas rather than at achieving a specific interregional distribution. The data examined however, were available only at the state level. Policies influencing the location of industries across states have probably been much weaker than those mentioned above. Hence the empirical work presented in this chapter is clearly inadequate to evaluate the thrust of India's industrial location policies. None the less, the evidence suggests that India has probably done as well as, if not better than, most other countries in dispersal of industry across the different states in the country. The fact that the older industrialized states have lost some ground in their hitherto dominant shares in industry is itself a creditable achievement for Indian industrial location policy. Over a period of about forty years the number of concentrations of industries certainly increased from about half a dozen to forty or fifty. The level of industrialization increased consistently in almost all states. This was achieved even though the pace of industrial growth as a whole was not very high. This was important particularly during the 1970s when industrial growth had slowed down perceptibly compared with the 1950s and the early 1960s. It was also during this period that industrial location policies were first brought into force with some level of seriousness. In a sense, there simply has not been enough industry to spread around.

Even more noteworthy is the increase in the level of inequality between different states or regions in India in terms of agricultural production and productivity. The dispersal of industry would probably have been much more impressive if the dispersal of agricultural growth had been much more even. The level of inequality between states in industrial productivity is very low relative to the agricultural productivity inequalities. Successful dispersal of industrial growth also requires the availability of adequate quality of industrial labour which is capable of being employed in modern industry. Similarly, the availability of infrastructure is also very important if entrepreneurs are to be induced to locate in backward areas. A more focused approach to spreading agricultural productivity across the different regions in India might have been more fruitful and might have promoted the dispersal of industry.

One of the more interesting features of Indian industrial location policy has been the willingness of the government to review past policies and to change them in view of new evidence and difficulties encountered in the administration of these policies. Hence industrial location policy in India has exhibited an evolutionary process probably resulting in net improvements over time. The idea of promoting 100 growth centres in the country by providing adequate resources for infrastructure investment in these centres along with attention to the social dimensions of location policy such as health and education is clearly a step in the right direction. However, it may prove too ambitious, and if politically feasible, concentration on a small number of substantial growth centres may be advisable. This scheme is also more likely to achieve some level of success if it is embedded in a more comprehensive regional approach to urban and industrial development planning. At the level of the state governments in India it would be desirable to organize specific regional-level co-ordinated planning to promote industrial and urban development in the selected regions as industrial concentrations.

One key disquieting feature of Indian industrial location policy is its excessive attention to locating industries away from cities. There is little doubt that industry has to be weaned away from the largest four or five metropolitan cities in the country. However, it is probably unwise to discourage industries from locating in the next rung of thirty to fifty cities. India is fortunate to have a good distribution of large cities. It would be more practical and efficient to encourage industries to locate in cities of some substantial size. It is only cities of such size that can function effectively as incubators for new industrial investment, specially of small and medium-sized industries, and generators of new industrial entrepreneurship. A misguided industrial location policy could well end up retarding industrial growth if the incubators are not allowed to function.

Of course, environmental and safety considerations must receive the greatest importance in industrial location policies. Some of the concerns about excessive concentration of industries in large cities are related to their pollution potential. If well-designed and strictly enforced pollution laws and practices could be implemented at the city or town level, it would be unnecessary to control industrial location at the national level.

Locating industries away from existing town and city limits prematurely can cause a host of unnecessary difficulties. If industries do locate outside town and city limits, the infrastructure service lines are stretched prematurely and excessive expenditures are incurred. Labour also encounters considerable transport difficulty along with housing problems. The experience of the industrial estates programme provides enough evidence that the objective of locating industries away from urban areas seldom succeeds.

An important issue is the decline of some of the older industrial centres such as Ahmedabad, Kanpur, and Calcutta. Under the new industrial policy, the state government can declare these and other declining cities as cities requiring industrial regeneration. New industries can then be encouraged to locate within these cities. However, to regenerate industrial activity in these older industrial centres will require a co-ordinated review of other laws which inhibit the re-use of industrial land for new industry, such as the Urban Land Ceiling Act. In addition, the legal requirements for closure and industrial restructuring will also need to be addressed. The record of industrial regeneration in other countries suggests that such revival takes a long time and requires considerable effort. This is similar to the reversal of British policy after the Second World War when an attempt was made to revive the older industrial concentrations in the North and North-West of England through area plans and inducements to industry to locate in these areas. It is not far-fetched to advocate that some of these older depressed industrial concentrations should be now designated backward areas!

Finally, given the very difficult employment situation in India, industrial location related incentives need to encourage labour use. It may be advisable to devise new programmes and schemes to subsidize employment effectively through training of labour, provision of housing, and even provision of wage subsidies promoting inefficient use of labour. This assumes even more importance once it is recalled that the major objective of industrial dispersal is to spread the benefits of industrialization over a large section of the population through enhanced earnings and spread of industrial employment.

15 Extent and Implications of Rural–Urban Migration in India

T. S. PAPOLA

India has a relatively low degree of urbanization. About one-fourth of its population is located in urban areas. The extent of urbanization has been increasing over several decades; and a part of the increase is contributed by migration from rural areas. Increasing urbanization, particularly rural–urban migration, is often viewed as a 'problem'. This chapter represents a preliminary attempt to examine the nature and extent of this problem on the basis of available evidence from the population censuses and other sources of data and studies undertaken by other scholars on related aspects.

The Issues

Migration from rural to urban areas is a phenomenon that is found to accompany economic development universally. Rural areas have agriculture as their principal activity which normally has a lower productivity per worker than the non-agricultural activities which are mainly located in urban areas. Further, being based on a relatively fixed factor of production, namely land, agriculture tends to grow at a slower rate than other activities. Thus rural–urban migration, to a large extent, is a reflection of a structural shift in economic activities from agriculture to non-agriculture, which has historically characterized the process of economic development. Besides, by definition, urban areas provide better access to non-economic facilities and amenities of life, which also attract rural population.

Despite being a logical concomitant of economic development, rural–urban migration is quite often viewed as a 'problem'. For one thing, a high rate of such migration is seen to reflect not only a high degree of rural–urban differences in incomes and economic opportunities, but also absolute poverty and destitution in rural areas, which are obviously negative characteristics of the structure and development of an economy. Then there are the social costs of migration, in terms of dislocation of family and community life in the rural areas, and congestion and stress on services in urban areas. Furthermore, in some instances, there is the possibility of a negative effect on productive activities in rural areas in that migration is mostly selective, depriving rural areas of the relatively more productive, skilled and enterprising workers.

It is for these reasons that rural–urban migration is often considered an undesirable phenomenon. In general, rural–urban migration could be so viewed if (i) such migration is very high, causing disruption in productive activities in the rural areas; (ii) inflow into urban areas is far in excess of the demand for labour beyond the capacity of the native urban population to supply; and (iii) the destination pattern of migration, in terms of size-class of towns and cities to which rural people migrate, is concentrated mainly in favour of large cities. A rational view on rural–urban migration could, therefore, be formed on the basis of an examination of these aspects.

Migration from Rural Areas: Extent and Trends

In absolute terms, rural–urban migrants in India constitute a large number. In 1961, rural-born urban residents numbered about 20 million; their number rose to 24 million in 1971 and 34 million in 1981. These numbers, however, refer to life-time migrants who migrated from rural areas to urban areas over the last several decades. Rather than the 'stock' of the migrant population which these members represent, it is the 'inflow' which indicates the dynamics of migration. If we take the urban residents of rural origin, by period of their residence in urban areas, we get an idea of the extent of such 'inflow'. According to the decennial censuses, 11.62 million rural persons migrated from rural to urban areas during 1950–61, 10.98 million during 1961–71 and 15.78 million during 1971–81, yielding average annual figures of 1.06, 1.10, and 1.58 million for the three periods respectively. As a proportion of the rural population, the annual rural–urban migration averaged to 0.32, 0.27, and 0.32 per cent during the three decades respectively. Thus, about three persons per thousand of the rural population are found to have migrated annually to the urban areas during 1950–81. This rate does not seem to have changed significantly over the period, though it declined during 1961–71 as compared to the earlier decade, but rose to the level of 1951–61 during 1971–81. In fact, *net* rural–urban migration is found to have slowed down over these decades, as there has been a significant increase in urban–rural migration (Visaria and Kothari 1985: 55–6; Kundu 1986).

Thus, the rate of migration from rural to urban areas has not accelerated and, if anything, has shown a declining tendency. Several demographic and economic reasons have been advanced to explain the deceleration of rural–urban migration. A persistent high rate of natural increase in the urban population, slow growth of employment opportunities in urban areas, growth of suburban populations, railway and road transport, etc. (Visaria and Kothari 1985: 61–3) are some of the factors which could account for deceleration in the rate of migration. Moreover, of course, general development leading to improvements not only in economic conditions but also in educational and health services in rural areas is expected to have contributed to the non-acceleration of rural–urban migration over the decades (Mehrotra 1974).

That the force of 'push' from rural areas has started to weaken to some extent is also reflected in the pattern of migrants' motivations. Over the years, there seems to have occurred a change in the pattern of reasons for rural–urban migration. From the data available from the tabulation of the 5 per cent sample of the 1981 census, it is observed that persons migrating to seek employment constituted 27 per cent of all those who migrated from rural to urban areas before 1971; their proportion declined to 26 per cent among those who migrated during 1971–6 and 25 per cent among the migrants of the 1976–81 period. The percentage of those migrating for education increased from 2 per cent among migrants of the first period, to 5 and 11 per cent among those migrating in the subsequent two periods respectively (Census of India 1981). The proportion of those migrating to accompany or rejoin family members is significantly higher among recent than among earlier migrants but those migrating for marriage constitute only 17 per cent of the migrants in the period 1976–81 as compared with 36 per cent of those who migrated before 1971. The proportion of those migrating for 'other' reasons significantly increased over the period.

The composition and characteristics of migrants are thus changing over the years. A decline in the proportion of those migrating for employment, though small but consistent, could be considered significant. So is the increasing proportion of those migrating for education. Among the pre-1971 migrants, marriage constituted the most important reason (36 per cent), followed by employment (27 per cent) and movement of family (22 per cent). Among post-1976 migrants movement of family accounts for the largest number (32 per cent), followed by employment (25 per cent); marriage is the third but much less important reason (17 per cent). If movement of family and marriage are taken together as basically non-economic, socio-demographic reasons, we find that they accounted for 56 per cent of the rural–urban migration before 1971, whereas in the post-1976 period they account for 49 per cent. However, education and other reasons have very significantly increased. It therefore seems that over the years the incidence of 'distress' migration has declined, while that for improvement in educational and living standards has increased.

One implication of these trends is that the effect on rural–urban migration of general development and improvement in economic conditions in the rural areas would be more of a qualitative than of a quantitative character: to some extent, it would check acceleration in the rate of rural–urban migration, but more significantly, it would change the pattern of motivations for migration and of the characteristics of the migrants. The educated and economically better-off would form an increasingly larger proportion of new migrants. These trends are significant in so far as they tend to suggest that rural–urban income differentials are not necessarily the only important cause of rural–urban migration.

The extent of rural–urban migration in India is too small to have any significant impact on the productive potential of the rural population. No doubt, the out-migrant males are in the most productive age-group and educated, but they form a small proportion of the rural labour force. Some recent studies in selected rural

areas suggest that out-migration had no adverse impact on agricultural productivity and, in fact, the worker–land ratio still continues to be higher than what can
be regarded as optimal in the given technological and organizational condition.

Migration and the Urban Areas

Migrants from the rural areas, however, constitute a larger proportion of the
urban population than of the rural population, because the former is much
smaller than the latter. In 1961 about one-fourth of the urban population con-
sisted of migrants from rural areas. Their proportion declined to about 20 per cent
and remained almost at that level in 1981. Yet the magnitude of the annual inflow
of rural migrants into the urban areas hardly warrants as serious a concern as is
often voiced in general discussions on the subject. And what is significant to note
is that over the decades the rate of inflow has declined. During the 1950s, the number of rural people who migrated into the urban areas in a year constituted about
1.50 per cent of the urban population. During the 1960s, their percentage declined
to 1.17 and remained almost at that level during the 1970s. As a proportion of the
urban labour force the percentage would be almost three times as high. Using NSS
data from its 28th Round, it is estimated that rural migrants 'in search of work in
urban areas' constituted about 1.28 per cent of the urban labour force at the all-
India level—1.37 per cent in urban Maharashtra, 1.69 per cent in urban Tamil
Nadu, and 1.30 per cent in urban West Bengal, during 1973 (Sundaram).

Thus the evidence does not suggest that rural–urban migration is the *main*
cause of 'overcrowding' in the urban areas. In fact, rural–urban migration has
contributed only about one-fifth of the urban growth during 1961–81; it contributed 20.9 per cent of the total increase in urban population during 1961–71
and 19.6 per cent during 1971–81 (Visaria and Kothari 1985: 65). There are, however, a few qualitative dimensions which are often highlighted to emphasize that
even quantitatively small rural–urban migration leads to deterioration in the lives
both of migrants and the urban residents. It is contended that migration tends to
swell the ranks of the unemployed in the urban areas or then force the migrants to
take up work in 'unproductive' and low-income activities in the 'informal sector'.
It leads to squatter settlements and slums and puts severe strain on the urban utility systems. Problems of urban congestion, social disorders and crime are often
attributed to the phenomenon of migration from rural areas.

What is usually ignored in these assertions is that most of these problems which
affect urban areas are only marginally accentuated by rural–urban migration and
are mostly caused by the lack of planning in urban areas to take care of the natural growth of urban population. In fact, unemployment rates in the urban areas
might be higher in the absence of in-migration from rural areas, as the incidence
of unemployment is likely to be lower among migrants than among non-migrants.
There is also no evidence to suggest or reason to believe that productivity of
migrant labour is lower than that of the natives. No doubt, a good proportion of

rural migrants work in the 'informal sector', but so do a large proportion of non-migrants. And the 'informal sector', far from being 'unproductive', provides very essential goods and services to sustain the urban economy and life. An equally large proportion of both migrants and non-migrants finds a permanent source of livelihood in this sector, which goes to show its utility on the one hand, and non-selectivity of migrants and non-migrants to either one of the two—formal and informal—sectors, on the other (Papola 1981, 1984).

Even a relatively smaller magnitude of rural–urban migration could, however, significantly accentuate the problems of unemployment, congestion, and pressure on services in urban areas, if it is concentrated mainly in a few urban areas, particularly the large metropolitan cities which are already overstretched in terms of their capacity to productively absorb and suitably accommodate further additions to their population. In fact, the major part of the concern about rural–urban migration and urban growth in India seems to stem from the apprehension that most migrants tend to go to the large cities. This apprehension is founded on the apparently high rate of growth of population observed in the *group* of large cities as compared with those of medium-sized and small ones. But a closer look at the data, after making adjustments for the mobility of towns and cities from one size class to another, reveals that towns and cities of all sizes grew at similar rates over a thirty-year period (Mohan and Pant 1982). In fact, it was the towns in the smaller-population size-group of 10,000 to 20,000 which showed the highest growth rate during 1971–81 (Mohan and Pant 1982). This trend is corroborated in a study of Uttar Pradesh where the towns in the population range of 20,000 to 50,000 are found to have the fastest growth, at least during 1971–81, and the growth of the cities with a population of over 500,000 has slowed down as compared with the earlier decades (Sinha 1987).

Another study based on a sample of fifty-five towns from different regions of the country also found a similar pattern of growth of towns and cities by size-class. Towns in the population group of 2 million and above and 300,000 to 2 million grew at the rate of around 4 per cent per annum while those in the size classes of 20,000–50,000 grew at 4.4 per cent per annum during 1971–81 (Sinha and Mehta 1987).

Since the natural growth of population is not likely to be significantly different among urban areas of different sizes, differentials in growth of different groups of cities and towns could be attributed to variations in the rates of migration to them. Two developments in recent decades tend to suggest that migration into the larger urban areas has somewhat slowed down while it has accelerated to the towns of medium and smaller sizes: (1) many of the large cities have experienced a stagnation or even a decline in employment opportunities in their traditionally major industrial activities and entry of large factories has been prohibited as a matter of policy; (2) some of the traditional rural activities, such as agro-processing, have tended to shift to urban areas as a result of extension of markets and emergence of economies of scale in production, but have mostly gone to the smaller and medium-sized towns in the rural hinterland (Papola 1987: 102). There is some evidence also to show that the rate of growth of employment (male workers) rose much faster during 1971–81 as compared with 1961–71 in towns with populations of under 100,000; and the highest growth of employment over 1971–81, at 49 per cent, was observed in the towns with populations of 20,000–50,000 (Sinha and Mehta 1987).

Conclusion

These trends, which are based on the limited evidence available so far, suggest the emergence of a more balanced pattern of urbanization in future. At the same time, it has to be recognized that even a smaller growth of larger cities entails a large volume of population, as compared with similar or somewhat faster growth of smaller towns, and leads to severe problems of management of urban systems. Therefore, an active policy for strengthening the trends towards more balanced urbanization becomes necessary. And an important aspect of such a policy would consist of ways of redirecting rural–urban migration away from large cities to the relatively smaller towns.

Rural–urban migration in itself does not need to be viewed as a 'problem' in the Indian context. Rural areas are characterized by a significant degree of surplus labour, and out-migration from rural areas, a small proportion of rural population and labour force as it is, is not likely to have any adverse effect on the productive capacity of the rural economy. The overall extent of urbanization is still very low; less than a quarter of the population lives in the urban areas: and with economic development an increase in its extent could inevitably be expected. Agricultural growth and rural development, which are important goals in themselves, would not necessarily check the pace of rural–urban migration, though the pattern of motivations and characteristics of migrants may change with rising income levels in rural areas. Diversification of the rural economy into non-agricultural activities, of which some positive evidence is seen in recent years, would be an essential ingredient of development of rural areas: but that would also lead to some shift of activities and workers to nearby urban areas. It is this trend that needs to be strengthened by supporting development of infrastructure and services in the towns of the rural hinterland so as to redirect the destination pattern of rural–urban migration to them and away from the larger cities where a faster growth of population is likely to lead to accentuation of socio-economic problems.

16 Conclusion: The Prospects

GAVIN JONES AND PRAVIN VISARIA

One of the three countries covered in this book—Brazil—has reached a high level of urbanization, with about 75 per cent of its population resident in urban areas. The percentage is not likely to increase beyond 85 per cent. Moreover, natural increase of Brazil's population has been declining rapidly in recent years. This, allied with the limited scope for further rural–urban migration as a result of the contraction of the rural population, implies that growth rates of urban populations will not be very high in future.

By contrast, the other three countries are at levels of urbanization in the vicinity of 30 per cent. They are all experiencing declining fertility and declining population growth rates. Even so, very substantial population growth is expected before population finally stabilizes. In India, for example, the population is expected to grow to 1.4 billion by 2025. Should the level of urbanization reach 50 per cent by then, which is entirely possible, this implies a rise of 484 million in the urban population, or more than a trebling of its present level. Indonesia could face much the same kind of increase, China rather less because of the smaller population growth expected before population stabilizes.

How this urban population increase takes place—its speed, the location of the growth, and how the needs of this increased population are provided for—will have enormous implications for human welfare. A range of issues emerge. One is certainly that mega-cities will grow larger, that large numbers of smaller cities and towns will grow bigger and new towns will emerge. Unlike many countries dominated by a primate city, these four countries have developed hierarchies of urban places, and the massive urban growth expected can therefore be spread over many places. Even so, the growth prospects of the mega-cities are daunting. Supposing that, in each country, the four largest metropolitan regions simply maintain their present share of the total urban population, this could mean a trebling in the populations of the largest Indian and Indonesian cities by 2025, raising their populations to 25 million or more. Provision of transportation and other infrastructure will provide major planning headaches, complicated by the likelihood that the metropolitan areas concerned will cover a number of administrative jurisdictions. Polynucleation is certain to emerge in such giant metropolises; what is not yet clear is whether it should be allowed simply to take its course, or should be fostered by policy to a greater or lesser extent.

The urban planning issues posed by these large countries are important, not only because they will directly influence the lives of vast numbers of people, but also because other developing countries will have much to learn from the experience of the giants. Even if certain of the issues they face are specific to these countries for reason of scale, many are not. The large urban and regional planning bureaucracies which large countries can sustain should enable them to examine some issues at greater depth than can smaller countries, which should therefore be able to profit from their analyses and planning initiatives.

The urban planning literature is somewhat myopic on the need to control overall population growth. As noted in several chapters in the book, natural increase is an important force driving urban growth. The demographic transition is in full swing in all these countries, though it has proceeded less far in India than in others. Already, the declines in fertility have damped down the likely ultimate size of their urban populations. An important factor for urban planning is rural–urban fertility differentials and trends. In all the countries covered in this book, urban fertility is well below rural, thus damping down the natural increase of the urban population. For example, the total fertility rate in Indonesia in 1986–9 was 2.7 in urban areas compared with 3.6 in rural areas. In China, urban fertility has long been below rural (Lavely and Freedman 1990). However, better-focused programmes to accelerate the fall in urban fertility might help. Certainly, family-planning services in the slums of the large cities tend to be very inadequate. High rural fertility is also likely to translate into urban growth in time, through rural–urban migration and reclassification of densely-populated, formerly rural areas. Rural fertility levels are therefore an appropriate focus of concern for urban planners.

As for migration, given the substantial rural–urban inequalities in the availability of basic amenities, the real question is why the rate of rural–urban migration is not higher than that actually observed. Part of the answer may be that commutation is often a low-cost and socially advantageous alternative to rural–urban migration. Its effect is similar to that of the Chinese government's advice to agricultural workers to leave the land but not the village. Such a policy continues to be a socially desirable option not only for China but for India and Indonesia as well. Gradually, of course, the goal of social policy must be to eliminate the rural–urban differentials in living conditions or at least availability of basic amenities. Technological advances in the form of micro-wave or satellite-based communication have opened up unprecedented possibilities for a relatively dispersed population-settlement pattern although there will remain some threshold levels of concentration up to which the provision of amenities and services will prove relatively expensive.

This brings us to the need for social science research on urbanization to stress the components of the process. In the introductory chapter, we stressed the complexities in really factoring out the influence of natural increase as opposed to rural–urban migration. But it is reclassification which has the greatest potential to change measured urban growth rates and to confuse analysts and planners. Nowhere is this more evident than in China, where academics and planners in the 1980s were at odds over the realities of the extraordinary jump in measured urbanization levels from 23.5 per cent in 1983 to 49.3 per cent in 1988. The Chinese government has now revised its official urban proportion down to 26 per cent. Confusion abounded in China in the late 1980s over the 'real' level and trend of urbanization. Some argued that much of the rise in the 'official' urbanization level was real, because rapid industrialization was taking place at the time. Excessive 'definitional' growth of urbanization through re-classification, such as took place in China, can cause policy to be biased by giving the misleading impression that both the pace of urban growth and the percentage of population living in urban areas are higher than they actually are.

It must be kept in mind that, as stressed in many places in this book, urban–rural distinctions are becoming very blurred in many parts of the four largest developing countries. This does not obviate the need for continued attention to issues of urbanization, but it does highlight the need for adaptation of policy and research interest to the real issues, which in some cases will have more to do with regional policy than with urban policy *per se*. Urban policy, too, may need to be focused more on the zone of influence of urban areas, including peri-urban, 'fringe', and truly rural zones, but in all of which the influence of the city is felt to greater or lesser degree.

Policy Directions

As we look ahead, technology for innovative policy initiatives to ameliorate urban living conditions seems to be available in the area of pollution control as well as supply of safe potable water. Inexpensive building materials and cost-effective energy-saving designs for better housing are also available, though the required level of investment may pose a formidable challenge.

In the relatively long-term perspective, not only better management but also technological developments can help to mitigate several of the problems of megacities. Development of automobiles that can run on liquefied petroleum gas (LPG) or rechargeable batteries, and/or solar power can mitigate many problems of air pollution. In the less developed countries, solid-waste disposal can be improved through extensive use of bio-gas plants, which would also reduce the need to use fuel based on organic matter such as wood or grass. Similarly, recycling of water after requisite treatment by industrial units can relieve at least a part of the acute scarcity of water. Recycled water can be used, too, for flushing toilets and for watering lawns, gardens, and parks. Such recycling has not so far made any headway because of inadequate understanding of the real costs of transporting fresh water over long distances or the long-term implications of drawing out underground water at a rate exceeding the recharge rate.

Better management and decisive action by local governments, with appropriate dialogue with consumers about the real costs of providing various services, can facilitate better cost recovery. Coupled with a process of polynucleation in the larger metropolises, better-informed and well-co-ordinated urban policies can safeguard (and improve) the living conditions in towns and cities where a continuation of the process of population growth appears inevitable.

The problem of feeding the growing urban population through adequate marketable surplus no longer appears serious. Quite apart from the possibilities of international trade between Argentina and Brazil (for wheat and meat) for example and/or between India and neighbouring Thailand (for rice), improvements in the food-production frontier have generally helped to ensure virtual self-sufficiency of the four large countries with respect to the production of food. To meet the needs of the poor vulnerable section of the population, India operates a large chain of nearly 400,000 'fair-price shops', (at the end of March 1991) many of them in urban areas. These shops supply certain basic needs relating to such staples as wheat and/or rice, sugar, edible oil, and kerosene. In China, one driving force behind the effort to reclassify several localities as urban was to lower the liability of the state for subsidised supply of food rations.

Prospects for Population Deconcentration

Martine and Diniz rightly question the tendency to equate spatial deconcentration of population with territorial equity and interpersonal equity. While one can presume limits to concentration beyond which private as well as social costs rise substantially, these limits are likely to vary significantly with historical and natural perspectives. Martine and Diniz see the deconcentration of São Paulo as an extension of its radius of influence or centralised deconcentration because of the continuing close links with (if not dependence on) units located far away, with the financial and decision-making centre in the dominant metropolitan area or region.

An important point, which needs to be considered and discussed, is the remarkable tolerance by humankind of a very high level of spatial concentration of population. Continuing population growth in mega-cities is a telling demonstration of this. The advantages of such concentration seem to outweigh the costs noticed or felt by the concerned population. However, the Brazilian experience suggests the possibilities of a slowing-down of the rate of growth beyond a certain, albeit unspecifiable, point. A similar indication is given by the changes in the UN list of mega-cities on the basis of the assessments in 1990 and 1992. Bangalore (the sixth-largest urban agglomeration of India according to the 1991 census), was expected in 1990 to become a mega-city with a population of 8.2 million by the year 2000. The reassessment of 1992 suggests, however, that even in 2010, Bangalore might have a population of only 7.3 million. Hyderabad (which now ranks fifth among India's urban agglomerations), on the other hand, is expected to be a mega-city by 2020 (with a population of 9.4 million). Such variations in the list of mega-cities are a normal and, indeed, necessary consequence of the objectives of projections. A projection essentially helps to assess the implication of alternative rates of population growth, including changes in some of the underlying parameters. As such, policy-makers can well make thwarting of the projections based on an extrapolation of past trends a goal of programmatic action.

Final Word

The studies in this book, then, have dealt with a range of complex issues facing urban and regional planning in the largest developing countries. Because circumstances differ so much between the four countries, few generalizations apply to them all. Even less so is it possible to generalize from these studies to the rest of the developing world. Nevertheless, we believe that an emphasis on the urban issues of the largest developing countries has been justified, not only because they themselves contain a very significant share of the world's population, and therefore provide a very important study in themselves, but also because the book has gone some way towards identifying aspects of urban planning issues that are related to scale and geographic extent and others that are not. We trust the book can therefore be read, not only with interest, but also with some profit, by those concerned with urban planning issues in other developing countries.

Bibliography

Amarante, Luis Antonio M., and Bondioli, Paulo (1987), 'A apropriação regional da renda nacional no Brasil—1975–1985' in *São Paulo em Perspectiva*, Revista da Fundação SEADE, 1(3), Oct./Dec.: 84–5.

AMPO (1980), 'Special Issue on Japanese Transnational Enterprises in Indonesia', 12(4).

Aragon Vaca, L. E. (1981), 'Despovoamento Rural da Amazônia Brasileira', paper presented at Seminário Regional Expansão da Fronteira Agrícola e Meio Ambiente na América Latina, Brasília.

—— and Mougeot, L. J. A. (eds.) (1986), *Migrações Internas na Amazónia: Contribuições Teóricas e Metodológicas*, Belém: Universidade Federal do Pará, Núcleo de Altos Estudos Amazônicos.

Arndt, H. W. (1983), 'Transmigration: Achievements, Problems, Prospects', *Bulletin of Indonesian Economic Studies*, 19(3): 50–73.

Asian Development Bank (1983), *Indonesia: Urban Sector Profile*, Manila: Social Infrastructure Division.

Aubertin, C. (1986), 'Industrialiser les frontières', *Cahiers des Sciences Humaines*, 22(3/4): 419–28.

AWSJW (Asian Wall Street Journal Weekly) (1994), 'Indonesia Attract, Foreign Investment with Hard Sell', 26 Sept.: 14–15.

Azzoni, Carlos R. (1986), *Indústria e Reversão da Polarização no Brasil*, São Paulo: IPE/USP.

Bai Jianhua (1986), 'The Situation of China's Population', *Population Research 1986*, 2: 11–14.

Bank of Indonesia (1982), 'Penanaman Modal Asing Dari Tahun 1967' S/D 30 Sept., Jakarta.

Barbetto, Alberto, and Pistonesi, Héctor (1985), 'Complexos Industriais, Industrialização e Desenvolvimento Regional', *Revista Econômica do Nordeste*, 15(3): 445–510.

Barlow, Melinda (1988), *Urban Housing Reforms in China: A First Overview*, World Bank Working Paper, Washington, DC: World Bank.

—— and Renaud, Bertrand (1989), 'Housing Reforms and Commercialization of Urban Housing in China', *Review of Urban and Regional Development Studies*, 1: 81–4.

Bauer, John (1990), 'Demographic Change in Asian Labor Markets in the 1990s', *Population and Development Review*, 16(4): 615–45.

Becker, B. K. (1978), 'Uma Hipótese sobre a Origem do Fenômeno Urbano Numa Fronteira de Recursos no Brasil', *Revista Brasileira de Geografia*, 40(1): 111–22.

—— (1985), 'Fronteira e Urbanização Repensadas', *Revista Brasileira de Geografia*, 47(3/4): 357–71.

Bengbu City Housing Reform Office (1988), 'Several Methods on Reforming the Housing System in Bengbu City', *Jingji Guanli (Economic Management)*, 3: 38–40.

Bitoun, J. (1980), 'Ville et développement régional dans une région pionnière au Brésil; Imperatriz, Maranhão', Thesis 3 cycle, Human Geography, Université de Paris I.

Booth, Anne (1992), 'Income Distribution and Poverty', in Anne Booth (ed.), *The Oil Boom and After: Indonesian Economic Policy and Performance in the Soeharto Era*, Singapore: Oxford University Press: 323–62.

BPS (Biro Pusat Statistik) (1979), *Definisi Desa Urban Dalam Sensus 1980 (Urban Definition in the 1980 Census)*, Jakarta.

—— (1983), *Population of Indonesia, Results of the 1980 Population Census*. Series S, No. 2, Jakarta.

—— (1986), 'Survey of Industry', Jakarta.

—— (1987), *Population of Indonesia, Results of the 1985 Intercensal Population Survey*. Series Supas, No. 5, Jakarta.

—— (1988), *Proyeksi Penduduk Indonesia per Provinsi 1985–1995*, Series Supas, No. 34, Jakarta.

Browett, John G. (1986), 'Industrialization in the Global Periphery: The Significance of the Newly Industrialising Countries of East and Southeast Asia', *Environment and Planning D: Society and Space*, 4(4): 401–18.

Brown, Lester R., and Jacobson, Jodi L. (1987), *The Future of Urbanization: Facing the Ecological and Economic Constraints*, Worldwatch Paper No. 77.

Butler, J. R. (1986), 'Land, Gold, and Farmers: Agricultural Colonization and Frontier Expansion in the Brazilian Amazon', Ph.D. thesis, University of Florida, Gainesville.

Cano, Wilson (1977), *Raízes da Concentração Industrial em São Paulo*, São Paulo: Difel.

—— (1985), *Desequilíbrios Regionais e Concentração Industrial no Brasil—1930/70*, Rio de Janeiro: Difel.

—— (1989), 'Urbanização: Sua Crise e Revisão de seu Planejamento', *Revista de Economia Política*, 9(1): 62–82.

Carleial, Liana M., and Nabuco, Maria R. (eds.) (1989), *Transformações na Divisão Inter-Regional do Trabalho no Brasil*, São Paulo: ANPEC/CAEN/CEDEPLAR.

Carlson, Eric (1986), *Housing Finance Development in China: An Overview of Issues and Prospects*, Illinois: International Union of Building Societies and Savings Associations.

Castro, Antônio Barros de (1975a), 'A Industrialização Descentralizada no Brasil', in *7 Ensaios sobre a Economia Brasileira*, Rio de Janeiro: Forense.

—— (1975b), 'A Herança Regional no Desenvolvimento Brasileiro', in *7 Ensaios Sobre a Economia Brasileira*, Rio de Janeiro: Forense.

Census of India (1981), *Special Report and Tables Based on 5% Sample Data, Table D-3*, New Delhi.

—— (1991a), Paper 1, *Report on Past Enumeration Check*, New Delhi: Office of the Registrar General.

—— (1991b), Paper 2 of 1991, *Provisional Population Totals: Rural–Urban Distribution*, New Delhi: Office of the Registrar General.

—— (1991c), Paper 2 of 1992, *Final Population Totals*, New Delhi: Office of the Registrar General.

—— (1991d), Paper 2 of 1993, *Housing and Amenities: A Brief Analysis of the Housing Tables of the 1991 Census*, New Delhi: Office of the Registrar General.

—— (1991e), Paper 2 of 1994: 10–11.

Central Bureau of Statistics, Industrial Survey (data tapes) 1978 and 1981.

Central Bureau of Statistics, SUSENAS (data tapes), SUPAS, 1987; SENSUS, 1971 and 1980.

Centre for Monitoring Indian Economy (1993), *Basic Statistics Relating to the Indian Economy: States*, Table 4.14.

Chakraborty, Satyesh C. (1991), 'Extended Metropolitan Areas: A Key to Understanding Urban Processes in India', in Norton Ginsburg, Bruce Koppel, and T. G. McGee (eds.), *The Extended Metropolis: Settlement Transition in Asia*, Honolulu: University of Hawaii Press.

Chambers, Robert (1983), *Rural Development: Putting the Last First*, London: Longman.

Chang Qingwu (1986), 'A Preliminary Probe into China's Floating Population' (in Chinese), *Renkou yujingji (Population and Economy)* 3 (May): 3–7.

Chang, Sen-dou, and Kim, Won Bae (1989), 'A Preliminary Analysis of Urban Systems in China', paper presented at the International Conference on China's Urbanization, East-West Center, Honolulu.

Chen Xuexi (1988), 'To Consolidate the Sources of Capital for Housing Reform', *Zhongguo Jinrong (China's Finance)*, 12: 24.

China State Statistics Bureau (1983), *Statistical Yearbook of China*, Beijing: Statistics Press.

—— (1984), *Statistical Yearbook of China*, Beijing: Statistics Press.

—— (1986), *Statistical Yearbook of China*, Beijing: Statistics Press.

—— (1987), *Statistical Yearbook of China*, Beijing: Statistics Press.

—— (1988), *China Statistical Yearbook, 1988*, Hong Kong: International Centre for the Advancement of Science and Technology.

—— (1989), *Statistical Yearbook of China*, Beijing: Statistics Press.

—— (1993), *Synopses of Chinese Statistics*, Beijing: Statistics Press.

China's Urban Housing Problem Study Society (1987), *Chengzhen Zhufang Zhidu Gaige Diaocha Yanjiu Ziliao Huibian (A Collection of Data on the Reform of Urban Housing System)*.

Clark, W. A. V. (1986), *Human Migration*, Beverly Hills: Sage.

Collier, William, Soentoro, Wiradi, Gunawan, Pasandaran, Effindi, Santoso, Kabul, and Stepanek, Joseph (1982), 'Acceleration of Rural Development of Java', *Bulletin of Indonesian Economic Studies*, 28(3): 84–101.

—— Wiradi, Gunawan, Makali, and Santoso, Kabul (1988), 'Employment Trends in Lowland Javanese Villages', Jakarta: USAID.

—— Santoso, Kabul, Soentoro, Wibowo, Rudi (1993), *A New Approach to Rural Development in Java: 25 Years of Village Studies*, Jakarta: PT Intersys Kelola Maju.

Comissão de Incentivos Fiscais (COMIF) (1986), *Avaliação dos Incentivos Fiscais*, Brasília: IPLAN.

Conselho Nacional de Desenvolvimento Urbano (CNDU) (1985), *Evolução da Rede Urbana no Brasil: Período 1970–1980*, Brasília.

Crone, Donald (1989), 'Around the Southeast Asia Region', *Southeast Asia Business*, 19, Winter/Spring: 5–15.

Davidovich, F. R., and Fredrich, O. M. B. L. (1988), 'Urbanização no Brasil', in S. T. Silva, *Brazil: Uma Visão Geográfica nos Anos 80*, Rio de Janeiro: IBGE, pp. 13–85.

Dharmapatni, Ida Ayu Indira, and Firman, Tommy (1996), 'Mega-Urban Regions in Indonesia: The Case of Jabotabek and Bandung Metropolitan Regions', in T. G. McGee and Ira Robinson (eds.), *Mega-Urban Regions in ASEAN*, Vancouver: University of British Columbia Press, forthcoming.

De Jong, W., *et al.* (1983), 'The Role of Banjarnegara as a Small Regional Centre in Central Java', *Indonesian Journal of Geography*, 13(45): 37–52.

Dean, Warren (1974), *A Industrialização de São Paulo*, São Paulo: Difel.

Dias, C. V. (1972), 'Vida Urbana na Amazônia', *Revista Econômica BASA*, 2(1): 13–20.

Dick, Howard, and Forbes, Dean (1992), 'Transport and Communications: A Quiet Revolution' in Anne Booth (ed.), *The Oil Boom and After: Indonesian Economic Policy and Performance in the Sœharto Era*, Singapore: Oxford University Press, 258–82.

Dickie, Robert, and Layman, Thomas (1988), *Foreign Investment and Government Policy in the Third World: Forging Common Interests in Indonesia and Beyond*, New York: St Martin's Press.

Diniz, Clélio Campolina (1987), 'Capitalismo, Recursos Naturais e Espaço', Ph.D thesis, University of Campinas.

—— and Lemos, Mauricio B. (1986), 'Mudanças no Padrão Regional Brasileiro: Determinantes e Implicações', *Análise Conjuntural*, 8(2), Curitiba.

Directorate General of Human Settlements, Dept. of Public Works (1984), *Report of Workshop on the Integrated Urban Development Planning Approach in Urban Services*, Puncak.

Directorate of Housing, Ministry of Public Works (1989), *Summary Report on the National Kampung Improvement Strategy Seminar*, Jakarta.

Douglass, Mike (1984), 'National Urban Development Strategy Scenarios', Jakarta: National Urban Development Strategy Project.

—— (1985), 'The Regional Impact of Transmigration', Washington, DC: World Bank.

—— (1986), 'Structural Change on the Pacific Rim: Perspective on Japan', Discussion Paper No. 1, Dept. of Geography, Vancouver: Simon Frazer University.

—— (1987), 'The Impact of Structural Change and Population Growth on Land Use Patterns in Indonesia', Washington, DC: World Bank.

—— (1988), 'Transnational Capital and Urbanization on the Pacific Rim: An Introduction', *International Journal of Urban and Regional Research*, 12(3): 343–55.

—— (1989a), 'The "New" Tokyo Story: Restructuring Space and the Struggle for Place in a World City', Discussion Paper No. 14, Dept. of Urban and Regional Planning, Honolulu: University of Hawaii.

—— (1989b), 'The Environmental Sustainability of Development: Coordination, Incentives and Political Will in Land Use Planning for the Jakarta Metropolis', *Third World Planning Review*, 11(2): 211–38.

—— (1991), 'Transnational Capital and the Social Construction of Comparative Advantage in Southeast Asia', *Southeast Asian Journal of Social Science* 19(1 and 2): 14–43.

—— (1996), 'Global Interdependence and Urbanization: Planning for the Bangkok Mega-Urban Region', in T. G. McGee and Ira Robinson (eds.), *Mega-Urban Regions in ASEAN*, Vancouver: University of British Columbia Press, forthcoming.

Du Wulu (1986), 'An Exploration of the Floating Population in Beijing's City Proper' (in Chinese), *Renkou yujingji (Population and Economy)*, 1 (Jan.): 12–14.

Ebanks, G. Edward, and Cheng Chaoze (1990), 'China: A Unique Urbanization Model', *Asia-Pacific Population Journal*, 5(3): 29–50.

ESCAP (Economic and Social Commission for Asia and the Pacific) (1981), *Migration, Urbanization and Development in Indonesia*, Paper No. 3 in Comparative Study on Migration, Urbanization and Development in the ESCAP Region, New York.

——/UNCTC (1988), *An Evaluation of Export Processing Zones in Selected Asian Countries*, Bangkok: United Nations.

Fan Lida (1988), 'The City's Functions, Development Impetus and Realistic Options in Urbanization', *China City Planning Review*, 4(3): 24–32.

Faria, V. E. (1983), 'Desenvolvimento, Urbanização e Mudanças na Estrutura do Emprego: A Experiência Brasileira dos Ultimos Trinta Anos', in B. Sorj and M. H. T. de Almeida (eds.), *Sociedade e Política no Brasil pós-64*, São Paulo: Brasiliense, pp. 118–63.

FEER (Far Eastern Economic Review) (1991), 'Investment: Twixt Cup and Lip', 10 Jan.: 52.

Ferreira, I. C. B. (1986), 'Ceres et Rio Verde: deux moments de l'expansion de la Frontière Agricole dans l'état de Goiás', *Cahiers des Sciences Humaines*, 22(3/4): 281–95.

Ferreira, J. F. S. (ed.) (1977), *Rede Urbana Amazônica: Subsídios para uma Política de Desenvolvimento Regional e Urbano*, Belém: Universidade Federal do Pará, Núcleo de Altos Estudos Amazônicos.

Fincher, John (1981), *Chinese Democracy*, London: Croom Helm.

Firman, Tommy (1992), 'The Spatial Pattern of Urban Population Growth in Java, 1980–1990', *Bulletin of Indonesian Economic Studies*, 28(2): 95–109.

Fisher, C. A. (1967), 'Economic Myth and Geographical Reality in Indonesia', *Modern Asian Studies*, 1(2): 155–89.

Fuchs, Roland J., Jones, Gavin W., and Pernia, Ernesto M. (eds.) (1987), *Urbanization and Urban Policies in Pacific Asia*, Boulder, Colo.: Westview Press.

Fuller, Theodore D. (1981), 'Migrant-Native Socioeconomic Differentials in Thailand', *Demography*, 18(1): 55–66.

Furtado, Celso (1973), *Formação Econômica do Brasil*, 13th edn., São Paulo: Nacional.

Gao Bingkun (1988), 'The Deregulation and Regulation of Real Estate Market', *Jingji Guanli (Economic Management)*, 3: 31–5.

Gao Liugen (1988), 'Comprehensive Management of Modern Cities', *Caijing Yanjiu (Finance and Economics Research)*, 2: 19–20.

Gao Shangchuan (1987), 'Ten Years of China's Economic Reforms', Report on the State Commission of Economic System Reform, January, Beijing.

Gardiner, Peter (1985), 'Provincial Population Projections; Requirements, Methodology, Results', Jakarta: National Urban Development Strategy Project.

—— and Oey, Mayling (1987), 'SUPAS 1985: Some Preliminary Observations', unpublished paper, Jakarta.

Geertz, Clifford (1963), *Agricultural Involution: The Process of Ecological Change in Indonesia*, Berkeley and Los Angeles: University of California Press.

Genesh Kumar, A. (1992), 'Falling Agricultural Investment and Its Consequences', *Economic and Political Weekly*, 27(42), 17 Oct.: 2307–12.

Godfrey, B. J. (1979), 'Road to the Xingu: Frontier Settlement in Southern Pará, Brazil', Master's thesis, University of California, Berkeley.

Goldstein, S., and Goldstein, A. (1985), *Population Mobility in the People's Republic of China*, Paper of the East-West Population Institute, No. 95, Honolulu: East–West Center.

Government of Indonesia (1987), *Statement of Policies for Urban Development in Indonesia*, Jakarta.

—— (1988), *Fifth Five Year Development Plan*, Jakarta.

Gu Wen (1989), 'Several Suggestions on Furthering the Privatization of Housing', *Chengxiang Jianshe (Urban Rural Construction)*, 1: 16–17.

Gu Yunchang (1988), 'China's On-going Housing Reform', *Building in China*, 1(3): 36–41.

Guan Jian (1988), 'An Analysis of Our Country's Rural Urbanization', *Nongye Jingji Wenti (Problems of Agricultural Economics)*, 5: 47–51.

Guimarães, Eduardo A. (1980), *Acumulação e Crescimento da Firma*, Rio: Zahar Editions.

Guimarães, M. R. S. (1987), 'Sistema Urbano', in IBGE, *Geografia do Brasil*, iv, *Região Centro-Oeste*, Rio de Janeiro: IBGE, pp. 329–58.

Gwatkin, Davidson R. (1979), 'Political Will and Family Planning: The Implications of India's Emergency Experience', *Population and Development Review*, 5(1): 29–59.

Haddad, Paulo R. (1981), *Participação, Justiça Social e Planejamento*, Rio: Zahar Editions.

—— (1985), *Dimensões do Planejamento Estadual no Brasil*, Rio de Janeiro: PNPE/IPEA.

—— (ed.) (1989), *Economia Regional: Teorias e Métodos Operacionais*, Fortaleza: Banco do Nordeste do Brasil.

Hamer, Andrew M., Steer, Andrew D., and Williams, David G. (1986), *Indonesia: The Challenge of Urbanization*, World Bank Staff Working Paper No. 787, Washington, DC: World Bank.

Hansen, Miles M. (ed.) (1978), *Human Settlement Systems*, Cambridge, Mass.: Ballinger Publishing Co.

Hardjono, Joan (1986), 'Transmigration Looking to the Future', *Bulletin of Indonesian Economic Studies*, 22(2): 28–53.

Hauser, Phillip M., Suits, Daniel B., and Ogawa, N. (eds.) (1985), *Urbanization and Migration in ASEAN Development*, Tokyo: National Institute for Research Advancement.

Hay, Donald A. (1979), 'The Location of Industry in a Developing Country—The Case of Brazil', *Oxford Economic Papers*, 31(1): 93–120.

Hilhorst, Jozef G. M. (1971), *Regional Planning: A Systems Approach*, Rotterdam: Rotterdam University Press.

Hill, Hal (1988), *Foreign Investment and Industrialization in Indonesia*, Singapore: Oxford University Press.

—— (ed.) (1989), *Unity in Diversity: Regional Economic Development in Indonesia Since 1970*, Singapore: Oxford University Press.

—— (1992), 'Manufacturing Industry', in Anne Booth (ed.), *The Oil Boom and After: Indonesian Economic Policy and Performance in the Soeharto Era*, Singapore: Oxford University Press.

Ho Yiwen (1988), 'An Analysis of the Rising Cost of Commercialized Housing', *Jingji Daobao* (*Economics Reporter*), 21 Mar.: 10.

Hu Huan Yong (1984), 'China's Population Growth and Population Economic Development in Eight Regions of Last Fifty Years', in *Population and Development*, 1987, Beijing: People's University Press.

Hua Sheng, Zhang Xue Jun, and Lao Xiao Peng (1988), 'Ten Years of China's Reforms', *Economic Research*, 9: 13–37.

Hugo, Graeme (1978), *Population Mobility in West Java, Indonesia*, Yogyakarta: Gadjah Mada University Press.

—— (1985), 'Structural Change and Labour Mobility in Rural Java', in G. Standing (ed.), *Circulation and the Labour Process*, London: Croom Helm, 46–88.

—— Hull, Terence H., Hull, Valerie J., and Jones, Gavin W. (1987), *The Demographic Dimension in Indonesian Development*, Kuala Lumpur: Oxford University Press.

Hull, Terence H., and Yang, Quanhe (1991), 'Fertility and Family Planning', in Wang Jiye and Terence H. Hull (eds.), *Population and Development Planning in China*, Sydney: Allen & Unwin.

India, Government of (1981), *Report of the National Committee on the Development of Backward Areas*, New Delhi: Government of India Press.

India, Ministry of Urban Development (1988), *National Housing Policy*, New Delhi.

India, National Sample Survey Organisation (1990), 'Results of the Fourth Quinquennial on Employment and Unemployment (All India)', NSS 43rd Round (July 1987–June 1988), *Sarvekshana*, Special Number.

India, Planning Commission (1983), 'Task Forces on Housing and Urban Development', *Planning of Urban Development*, i, New Delhi.

—— (1992), *Eighth Five Year Plan, 1992–93*, i and ii, New Delhi.

Instituto Brasileiro de Geografia e Estatística (IBGE)/MHU (1987), *Regiões de Influência das Cidades*, Rio de Janeiro.

Isard, Walter (1960), *Methods of Regional Analysis*, Cambridge, Mass.: MIT Press.

Jakobson, L., and Prakash, V. (1971), 'Urbanization and Urban Development: Proposals for an Integrated Policy Base', in L. Jakobson and V. Prakash (eds.), *Urbanization and National Development*, Beverly Hills: Sage Publications.

Jardim, A. P. (1987), 'Aspectos do Processo de Urbanização Recente na Ragião Centro-Oeste', in L. Lavinas (ed.), *Textos Apresentados no Workshop a Formação das Cidades na Fronteira*, Rio de Janeiro: PUBLIPUR/UFRJ, ii, pp. 101–28.

—— and Teixeira, J. B. (1985), *Aspectos do Processo de Urbanização nas Regiões Norte e Centro-Oeste na Década de 70*, Rio de Janeiro: IBGE.

Jones, Gavin W. (1983), 'Structural Change and Prospects for Urbanization in Asian Countries', *Papers of the East-West Population Institute*, No. 88, Honolulu: East-West Center.

—— (1984), 'Structural Change and Prospects for Urbanization: South-East and East Asia with Special Reference to Indonesia', Paper presented at the Conference on Urban Growth and Economic Development in the Pacific Region, Academia Sinica, Taipei, January 9–14.

—— (1984), 'Links between urbanization and sectoral shifts in employment in Java', *Bulletin of Indonesian Economic Studies*, 20(3): 120–57.

—— (1988), 'Urbanization Trends in Southeast Asia: Some Issues for Policy', *Journal of Southeast Asian Studies*, 19(1): 137–54.

—— (1990), 'Structural Economic Change and its Relationship to Urbanization and Population Distribution Policies', *Regional Development Dialogue*, 11(1): 1–18.

—— (1991), 'Urbanization Issues in the Asian-Pacific region', *Asian-Pacific Economic Literature*, 5(2): 5–33.

—— and Manning, Chris (1992), 'Labour Force and Education During the 1980s', in Anne Booth (ed.), *The Oil Boom and After: Indonesian Economic Policy and Performance in the Soeharto Era*, Singapore: Oxford University Press.

Kaldor, Nicholas (1970), 'The Case for Regional Policies', *Scottish Journal of Political Economy, 17: 337–48*.

Kano, Hiroyoshi (1981), 'Employment Structure and Labour Migration in Rural Central Java: A Preliminary Observation', *Developing Economies*, 19(4): 348–66.

Katzman, Martin T. (1977), *Cities and Frontiers in Brazil: Regional Dimensions of Economic Development*, Cambridge: Harvard University Press.

Kelley, Allen C., and Williamson, Jeffrey G. (1984), 'Population Growth, Industrial Revolutions, and the Urban Transition', *Population and Development Review*, 10(3): 419–41.

Kelly, Roy (1985), 'Foreign and Domestic Investment in Indonesia', Ph.D. diss., Harvard University, Cambridge, Mass.

Keyfitz, N. (1980), 'Do Cities Grow by Natural Increase or by Migration?', *Geographical Analysis*, 12(2): 142–56.

Keyfitz, N., and Philipov, Dimiter (1981), 'Migration and Natural Increase in the Growth of Cities', *Geographical Analysis*, 13(4): 287–99.

Kim, Won Bae (1989), 'Large Cities and Urban Economy in China', Paper presented at the International Conference on China's Urbanization, East-West Center, Honolulu.

Kinoshita, Toshihiko (1986), 'Japanese Investment in Indonesia: Problems and Prospects', *Bulletin of Indonesian Economic Studies*, 22(1): 34–55.

Kitazawa, Yoko (1977), 'Asahan Project: Whose National Project?', *AMPO*, Spring: 145–59.

Kleinpenning, J. M. G., and Volbeda, S. (1984), 'Recent Changes in Population Size and Distribution in the Amazon Region of Brazil', in John Hemming (ed.), *Changes in the Amazon Basin*, ii: *The Frontier after a Decade of Colonization*, Manchester: Manchester University Press.

Kojima, Reeitsu (1987), *Urbanization and Urban Problems in China*, Tokyo: Institute of Developing Economies.

Kuklinski, Antoni (ed.) (1981), *Polarized Development and Regional Policies*, The Hague: Mouton.

Kundu, Amitab (1986), 'Migration, Urbanization and Inter-regional Inequality: The Emerging Social Political Challenge', *Economic and Political Weekly*, 15 Nov.

Lau Yeefui (1977), *Glossary of Chinese Political Phases*, Hong Kong: United Research Institute.

Lee, Kyu Sik, 1985, 'Decentralization Trends of Employment Location and Spatial Policies in LDC Cities', *Urban Studies*, 22(2): 151–62.

—— Choe, S. C., and Pahk, K. H. (1987), 'Determinants of Locational Choice of Manufacturing Firms in the Seoul Region: Analysis of Survey Results', *Journal of Environmental Studies*, 21: 1–25.

Lee, Yok-shiu F. (1988), 'The Urban Housing Problem in China', *China Quarterly*, 115: 387–407.

—— (1989), 'Small Towns in China's Urbanization Level', *China Quarterly*, 120: 771–86.

Levy, Victor, and Newman, L. (1989), 'Wage Rigidity: Micro and Macro Evidence on Labor Market Adjustment in the Modern Sector', *World Bank Economic Review*, 3(1).

Lewis, W. A. (1955), *The Theory of Economic Growth*, London: Allen & Unwin.

Li Cheng Rui (1987), 'Some Remarks on the Classification of Urban Population and Rural Population', Preface to *Demographic Atlas*, Beijing: Chinese Statistics Publishing House.

Li Jing Neng (1987), 'The Review, Observation and Perspective of China's Urbanization since 1949', in *Proceedings of International Conference on Urbanization and Urban Population Problems (ICUUP), 25–30 October, Tianjin*, 1–19.

—— (1988a), 'Urbanization through the Development of Small Towns in Recent China', PSTC Working Paper Series 89–108, Population Studies and Training Center, Providence, R. I.: Brown University.

—— (1988b), in China State Statistical Bureau, *China Statistical Yearbook, 1988*, Hong Kong: International Centre for the Advancement of Science and Technology.

Li Weijie (1991), 'Housing Consumption is the Direction for Household Consumption', *Chengxiang Jianshe (Urban Rural Construction)*, 3: 16.

Li Ximing (1982), Statement of the Minister of Urban and Rural Construction and Environmental Protection, reported in *China Daily*, 13 July.

Liang Xiaoqing (1989), 'A New Solution to Resolve the Problem of "Extra Difficult Households" ', *Chengxiang Jianshe (Urban Rural Construction)*, 1: 18–19.

Lin Mingxin (1984), 'Several Necessary Conditions for the Commercialization of Housing', *Caijing Yanjiu* (*Study of Finance and Economics*), 4: 23–4.

Lin You Su (1986), 'A Study of Migration to and from Beijing', MA thesis, Australian National University, Canberra.

Lin Zhiqun (1984), 'Looking at Our Country's Housing Construction Standards from the Perspective of National Income', *Zhongguo Chengshi Zhuzhai Wenti* (*China's Urban Housing Problem*), China's Architectural Society, 15–16.

—— (1988), 'The Reform and the Development of Our Country's Real Estate Industry', *Chengshi Guihua* (*City Planning*), 6: 3–7.

Linge, G. J. R., and Forbes, D. K. (1990), *China's Spatial Economy: Recent Developments and Reforms*, Hong Kong: Oxford University Press.

Linn, Johannes F. (1987), 'Success and Failure in Urban Management: Some Lessons from the East Asian Experience', in Roland J. Fuchs, Gavin W. Jones, and Ernesto Pernia (eds.), *Urbanization and Urban Policies in Pacific Asia*, Boulder, Colo.: Westview Press.

Lipton, Michael (1973), 'Urban Bias and Rural Planning in India', in Henry Bernstein (ed.), *Underdevelopment and Development*, Harmondsworth: Penguin, 235–53.

—— (1977), *Why Poor People Stay Poor: Urban Bias in World Development*, Cambridge, Mass.: Harvard University Press.

—— (1980), *Why Poor People Stay Poor: Urban Bias in World Development*, New Delhi: Heritage Publishers.

Liu Shuhui and Wang Jian (1987), 'A Discussion on Housing System Reform', *Xueshu Yanjiu* (*Academic Research*), 6: 41–4.

—— and Xie Yiwen (1987), 'A New Form of Credit for Commercialized Housing', *Jingji Guanli* (*Economic Management*), 7: 27–8.

Liu Zheng *et al.* (1989), 'Small Towns Development and Urbanization in China', Report on a Research Project Submitted to the Canadian International Development Research Centre, People's University, Beijing, mimeo.

Lopes, Juarez Brandão (1980), *Desenvolvimento e Mudança Social*, 5th edn., São Paulo: Companhia Editora Nacional.

Lowry, Ira S. (1989), 'World Urbanization in Perspective', Paper presented at Conference on Human Demography and Natural Resources, Hoover and Morrison Institutes, Stanford University, February.

Lu Dehua (1986), 'The Development and Migration of West Part of China', *Renkou Yanjiu* (*Population Research*), 2 (Mar.): 51–6.

Lu Wei (1988), 'The Basic Characteristics of Urban Housing Market', *Jingji Guanli* (*Economic Management*), 3: 26–30.

Luo Changren (1987), 'Basic Ways for Urban Construction in Shenzhen', *China City Planning Review*, 3(1/2): 26–47.

Luo Maochu (1988), 'A Review and Evaluation of China's Policy for Development of Small Towns', *China City Planning Review*, 4(4): 22–37.

Ma Minjia (1988), 'Quickly Establish the Housing Finance System', *Zhongguo Jinrong* (*China's Finance*), 3: 51–2.

Ma Piao (1988), 'Develop Real Estate, Promote Housing Reform', *Gaige* (*Reform*), 2: 97–100.

Ma Xia (1986), 'The Analysis of Urban Development in China', unpublished paper, Population Research Institute, Chinese Academy of Social Sciences, Beijing.

—— and Wang Weizhi (1988), 'A Study of Urban Population Migration and Urbanization in China' (in Chinese), *Renkou yanjiu* (*Population Research*), 2, 29 Mar.: 1–7.

Machado, L. O. (1982), 'Urbanization and Migration in Legal Amazonia: Suggestion for a Geopolitical Approach', *Brazilian Geographic Studies*, 1: 179–83.

Malecki, Edward J. (1985), 'Industrial Location and Corporate Organization in High Technology Industries' *Economic Geography*, 61 (4): 345–69.

Manna, S. Y., Pereira, P. A., and Monte-Mor, R. L. M. (1980), 'Sistema de Cidades na Região Norte', Paper presented at NAEA/CEDEPLAR Seminar on Recent Urbanization in Amazonia, Belém.

Manning, Chris (1993), 'Structural Change and Industrial Relations during the Soeharto Period: An Approaching Crisis?' *Bulletin of Indonesian Economic Studies* 29(2): 59–95.

Martine, G. (1987), 'Exodo Rural, Concentração Urbane e Fronteira Agricola', in G. Martine and R. C. Garcia (eds.), *Os Impactos Socials de Modernização Agricola*, São Paulo: Caetés, pp. 59–79.

—— (1990a), 'Brazil', in Charles B. Nam, William J. Serow, and David F. Sly (eds.), *International Handbook on Internal Migration*, New York, Greenwood Press, 31–46.

—— (1990b) 'The Fate of Small Farmers in Rondonia', in David Goodman and Anthony Hall (eds.), *The Future of Amazonia: Destruction or Sustainable Development?*, London: Macmillan, 3–43.

—— (1990c), 'Fases e faces da modernização agrícola brasileira', *Planejamento e Políticas Públicas*, Brasília: IPEA, 3.

—— Camarano, Ana Amélia, Neupert, Ricardo, and Beltrão, Kaizô (1990), 'Urbanização no Brasil: Retrospectiva, Componentes e Perspectivas', in *Para a Década de 90: Prioridades e Perspectivas de Políticas Públicas*, Brasília: IPEA/IPLAN, iii. 101–28.

—— and Camargo, L. (1983), *Crescimento e Distribuição da População Brasileira: Tendências Recentes*, Brasília: Centro Nacional de Recursos Humanos/IPEA.

McGee, T. G. (1984), 'Rural-Urban Relations: Some Considerations for the National Development Strategy Project of Indonesia', Jakarta: National Urban Development Strategy Project.

—— (1991), 'The Emergence of *Desakota* Regions in Asia: Expanding a Hypothesis', in Norton Ginsburg, Bruce Koppell, and T. G. McGee (eds.), *The Extended Metropolis: Settlement Transition in Asia*, Honolulu: University of Hawaii Press.

McNicoll, Geoffrey, and Singarimbun, Masri (1983), *Fertility Decline in Indonesia: Analysis and Interpretation*, Washington, DC: National Academy Press.

Mehrotra, G. K. (1974), 'Birth Place Migration in India', in *Census of India 1974*, New Delhi.

Mello, João Manuel Cardoso (1982), *O Capitalismo Tardio*, São Paulo: Brasiliense.

Merrick, Thomas W., and Graham, Douglas H. (1979), *Population and Economic Development in Brazil: 1800 to the Present*, Baltimore: Johns Hopkins University Press.

Millikan, B. H. (1984), *Diagnóstico de Dez Núcleos Urbanos de Apoio Rural: Avaliação PDRI-RO/POLONORDESTE*, São Paulo: Fundação Instituto de Pesquisas Econômicas, Universidade de São Paulo.

Milone, P. D. (1966), *Urban Areas in Indonesia: Administrative and Census Concepts*. Research Series No. 10, Institute of International Studies, Berkeley: University of California.

Ministry of Information, *Lampiran Pidato Presiden*, various issues.

Ministry of Public Security (1987), *The Statistical Data of Chinese Population: 1986*, Beijing: China Map Press.

MOA (Ministry of Agriculture) (1983), 'Statistical Information on Indonesian Agriculture 1968–1980', Jakarta: German Agency for Technical Cooperation Funding.

Mohan, Rakesh (1983), 'The Regional Pattern of Urbanisation and Economic Development in India', Paper presented to the Conference on Recent Population Trends in South Asia, New Delhi, February.

—— (1992a), 'Population and Urbanisation: Strategies to Cope with City Growth', in Vasant Gowariker (ed.), *Science, Population and Development: An Exploration of Interconnectivities and Action Possibilities in India*, Pune: Umresh Communications, pp. 244–72.

—— (1992b). 'Housing and Urban Development: Policy Issues for 1990s', *Economic and Political Weekly*, 27(36–7): 1913–1920.

—— and Pant, Chandra Sekhar (1982), 'Morphology of Urbanization in India', *Economic and Political Weekly*, 17(38–9).

Moir, Hazel (1976), 'Relationships between Urbanization levels and the Industrial Structure of the Labour Force', *Economic Development and Cultural Change*, 25(1): 123–36.

Monte-Mor, R. L. M. (1980), 'Espaço e Planejamento Urbano: Considerações sobre o Caso de Rondônia', Master's thesis, Universidade Federal do Rio de Janeiro.

—— (1984), 'São Félix do Xingu: O Avanço da Fronteira Amazônica e um Novo Espaço em Formação', in CEDEPLAR, *São Félix do Xingu: Estudos Econômicos e Demográficos*, Belo Horizonte, 1–35.

Montgomery, Mark R. (1988), 'How Large is Too Large? Implications of the City Size Literature for Population Policy and Research', *Economic Development and Cultural Change*, 36(4): 691–720.

Morse, Richard (1958), *From Community to Metropolis, A Biography of São Paulo, Brazil*, Gainesville: University of Florida.

—— (1965), 'Recent Research on Latin American Urbanization: a Selective Survey with Commentary', *Latin American Research Review*, 1: 35–74.

Mougeot, L. J. A. (1983), 'Retenção Migratória das Cidades Pequenas nas Frentes Amazônicas de Expansão: Um Modelo Interpretativo', in L. J. A. Mougeot and L. E. Aragon Vaca (eds.), *O Despovoamento do Território Amazônico: Contribuições para Sua Interpretação*, Belém: Falangola, pp. 123–46.

—— and Aragon Vaca, L. E. (eds.) (1983), *O Despovoamento do Território Amazônico: Contribuições para Sua Interpretação*, Belém: Falangola.

Murray, Michael P. (1988), *Subsidizing Industrial Locations: A Conceptual Framework with Application to Korea*, Baltimore: Johns Hopkins University Press.

National Institute of Urban Affairs (1988), *State of India's Urbanisation*, New Delhi.

National Urban Development Strategy (1985), *NUDS Final Report*, Report T2.3/3, Jakarta: Directorate of City and Regional Planning, Dept. of Public Works.

Nie Yan (1987), 'Reform the Current Housing System, Gradually Realize the Commercialization of Housing', *Zhongguo Jingji Tizhi Gaige (China's Economic System Reform)*, 4: 22–3.

NSSO (National Sample Survey Organization) (1988), 'A Note on Source of Drinking Water and Energy Used for Cooking and Lighting', *Sarvekshana* 12/3 New Delhi.

—— (1990), 'Results of the Fourth Quinquennial on Employment and Unemployment (All India), NSS 43rd Round (July 1987–June 1988)', *Sarvekshana*, Special Number, New Delhi.

—— (1992), 'Report on Housing Conditions, NSS 44th Round (July 1988–June 1989)', *Sarvekshana*, 15/3, New Delhi.

NUDS (National Urban Development Strategy Project) (1985a), *The Pace of Urban Growth and Urbanization in Indonesia*, Report T1.6/C1, Jakarta.

NUDS (1985b), *NUDS Final Report*, Report T2.3/3, Jakarta.

—— (1985c), *Urban Population Projections: Methodology and Results*, Report T1.6/C4, Jakarta.

Oberai, A. S. (1992), 'Population Growth, Employment and Poverty in Third World Mega-Cities: Analytical and Policy Issues', Paper presented at European Conference on Migrants, Development and Metropolis, Berlin, 26–9 Mar.

OECD (1974), *Reappraisal of Regional Policies in OECD Countries*, Paris.

—— (1976a,b), *Regional Problems and Policies in OECD Countries*, i and ii, 2 Paris.

Office of the Registrar General of India (1989), The SRS-Based Life Tables, New Delhi.

—— (1994), Occasional Paper No.1 of 1994. *SRS Based Abridged Life Tables, 1986–90*, Vital Statistics Division, New Delhi.

Oliveira, Francisco (1977), *Elegia para um Re(li)gião*, São Paulo: Paz e Terra.

Oliveira, L. A. P. (1982), 'Notas e Particularidades sobre a Dinâmica Demográfica Recente na Fronteira Amazônica', in *Encontro Nacional de Estudos Populacionais, 3, Vitória, 1982, Anais*, São Paulo: Associação Brasileira de Estudos Populacionais, pp. 477–8.

—— and Simoes, C. C. S. (1981), 'Aspectos Recentes da Dinâmica Demográfica na Amazônia Urbana', in *Seminario NAEDA/CEDEPLAR sobre Urbanização Recente na Amazonia*, iii, Belo Horizonte.

Oong, Khong Cho (1986), *The Politics of Oil: Foreign Company-Host Government Relations*, Cambridge: Cambridge University Press.

Paauw, Douglas (1984), 'Employment Generation in Repelita IV: Agriculture Based Exports and Import Substitutes', Jakarta: Department of Manpower.

Pan Qiyuan (1989), 'Do not Let Buyers Take up Worries', *Chengxiang Jianshe (Urban Rural Construction)*, 1: 25.

Panglaykim, J. (1983), *Japanese Direct Investment in ASEAN: The Indonesian Experience*, Singapore: Maruzen Asia.

Pannell, C. W., and Veeck, Gregory (1991), 'China's Urbanization in an Asian Context: Forces for Metropolitanization', in Norton Ginsburg, Bruce Koppel, and T. G. McGee (eds.), *The Extended Metropolis: Settlement Transition in Asia*, Honolulu: University of Hawaii Press.

Papola, T. S. (1981), *Urban Informal Sector in a Developing Economy*, New Delhi, Vikas.

—— (1984), 'Rural-Urban Migration, and Urban Migration, and Urban Informal Sector', Paper presented at the Indo-Soviet Seminar on Problems of Migration in the Process of Urbanization, Osmania University, Hyderabad, 16–23 Sept.

—— (1987), 'Rural Industrialization and Agriculture Growth: A Case Study on India', in Rizwanual Islam (ed.), *Rural Industrialization and Employment in Asia*, New Delhi: ILO-ARTEP.

Parsonage, James (1992), 'Southeast Asia "Growth Triangle": A Subregional Response to Global Transformations', *International Journal of Urban and Regional Research*, 16(2): 307–170.

Peet, Richard (ed.) (1983), 'Restructuring in the Age of Global Capital', *Economic Geography*, 59(2), Special Issue.

Pereira, Alberto Carlos Lourenço (1990), 'Garimpo e fronteira amazônica: as transformações dos anos 80', Master's thesis, Center for Regional Development and Planning (CEDEPLAR), Federal University of Minas Gerais, Belo Horizonte, Minas Gerais.

Pinheiro, S. M. G., Silva, N. M., and Silva, H. C. C. (1986), 'Mudança no Quadro Domiciliar da População Brasileira: Estimativas Para a Década de 70', in *Encontro*

Nacional de Estudos Populacionais, 5. *Agyas de São Pedro, 1986*, São Paulo: Associação Brasileira de Estudos Populacionais, i. 521–39.

Population Research Centre (1985), *Almanac of China's Population*, Beijing: Chinese Social Sciences Publishing House.

Poston, Dudley L., Tian Yong, and Jia Zhongke (1989), 'The Urban Hierarchy of China', 1989 Working Paper Series 1.13, Population and Development Program, Ithaca, NY: Cornell University.

Prado, Caio Jr. (1973), *Formação do Brasil Contemporâneo*, 13th edn., São Paulo: Brasiliense.

Premi, M. K., and Tom, J. A. L. (1985), *City Characteristics, Migration, and Urban Development Policies in India*, Paper of the East-West Population Institute, No.92, Honolulu: East–West Center.

Qi Kang and Xia Zonggan (1986), 'Urbanization and Urban System in China, 1949–2000', *China City Planning Review*, 2(1): 1–20.

Qi Mingshun (1989), 'The Inequality in Housing', *Chengxiang Jianshe (Urban Rural Construction)*, 1: 23–4.

Quanguo Chengzhen Jumin Jiating Shouzhi Diaocha Ziliao 1987 (1987 Survey Data on the Income and Expenditure of Families in the Country's Cities and Towns) (1988), Beijing: China's Statistical Publishing Society.

Redwood, J. (1968), 'Internal Migration, Urbanization and Frontier Region Development in Brazil since 1940', Master's thesis, University of California, Berkeley.

Ren Suhua (1988), 'A Brief Analysis of Migration of China's City Population' (in Chinese), *Renkou yanjiu (Population Research)*, 3 (May): 19–23.

Richardson, Harry W. (1980), 'Polarization Reversal in Developing Countries', *Papers of the Regional Science Association*, 45: 67–85.

—— (1981), 'National Urban Development Strategies in Developing Countries', *Urban Studies*, 18(3): 267–83.

—— (1987), 'The Goals of National Urban Policy: The Case of Indonesia', in Roland J. Fuchs, Gavin W. Jones, and Ernesto M. Pernia (eds.), *Urbanization and Urbanization Policies in Pacific Asia*, Boulder, Colo.: Westview Press.

Rimmer, Peter (1994), 'Regional Economic Integration in Pacific Asia', *Environment and Planning A*, 26: 1731–59.

Robison, Richard (1985), 'Imperialism, Dependency and Peripheral Industrialization: the Case of Japan in Indonesia', in R. Higgott and R. Robison (eds.), *Southeast Asia: Essays in the Political Economy of Structural Change*, London: Routledge, pp. 195–225.

—— (1986), *Indonesia: The Rise of Capital*, Sydney: Allen & Unwin.

Santiago, Carlos E., and Thorbecke, E. (1988), 'A Multisectoral Framework for the Analysis of Labor Mobility and Development in LDCs: An Application to Postwar Puerto Rico', *Economic Development and Cultural Change*.

Santos, M. (1978), *Espaço e Urbanização no Território de Rondônia: Realidades Atuais, Perspectivas e Possibilidades de Intervenção*, São Paulo.

—— (1982), 'Organização do Espaço e Organização Social: O Caso de Rondônia', *B. Carioca Geogr. Amazônia: Problemas e Impasses*, 32: 51–77.

Sawyer, D. R. (1969), 'Penetration Roads and Population Growth: Patterns of Migration and Settlement along the Belém-Brasília Highway', honors thesis, Harvard University, Cambridge, Mass.

—— (1979), 'Peasants and Capitalism on an Amazon Frontier', Ph.D. thesis, Harvard University, Cambridge, Mass.

Sawyer, D. R., (1982a), 'A Fronteira Inacabada: Industrialização da Agricultura Brasileira e Debilitação da Fronteira Amazônica', in *Anais do III Encontro Nacional de Estudos Populacionais*, Vitória: ABEP.
—— (1982b), 'Industrialization of Brazilian Agriculture and Debilitation of the Amazon Frontier', in R. Misra *et al.* (eds.), *Regional Development in Brazil: The Frontier and its People*, Nagoya: UNCRD.
—— (1984), 'Frontier Expansion and Retraction in Brazil', in Marianne Schmink and Charles H. Wood (eds.), *Frontier Expansion in Amazônia*, Gainesville: University of Florida Press, 180–203.
—— (1987), 'Urbanização da Fronteira Agricola no Brasil', in L. Lavinas (ed.), *Textos Apresentados no Work-shop a Formação das Cidades na Fronteira*, Rio de Janeiro: PUBLIPUR/UFRJ, 41–57.
—— Montanari, R. V., and Abers, R. N. (1989), *Urbanização na Amazônia: Bibliografia Comentada*, Belo Horizonte.
—— and Pinheiro, S. M. G. (1984), 'A Dinâmica Demográfica das Regiões de Fronteira', *Encontro Nacional de Estudos Populacionais*, 4: 2017–47.
Sayer, Andrew (1986), 'Industrial Location on a World Scale: The Case of the Semiconductor Industry', in Allen J. Scott and Michael Storper (eds.), *Production, Work, Territory*, Boston: Allen & Unwin, 107–23.
Schoenberger, Erica (1986), 'Competition, Competitive Strategy and Industrial Change: The Case of Electronic Components', *Economic Geography*, 62(4): 321–33.
Scott, Allen J. (1983), 'Industrial Organization and the Logic of Intra-Metropolitan Location, I: Theoretical Considerations', *Economic Geography*, 59(3): 233–50.
Secretaria de Planejamento (SEPLAN) (1989), *Plano-Diretor da Área de Influência do Corredor da Estrada de Ferro Carajás*, Brasília: PGC/CVRD.
Sekhar, A. Uday (1983), *Industrial Location Policy: The Indian Experience*, World Bank Working Paper No. 620, Washington, DC: World Bank.
Setheraman, S. V. (1974), *Urbanization and Employment in Jakarta*, WEP2-19/WP6, Geneva: ILO.
Shukan Toyo Keizai (1988), 'Gyoshubetsu Kaigai Shinshitsu Kigyo 1988' (Industrial Classification of Foreign Invested Firms, 1988), Tokyo.
Silva, E. M. D. (1980), *Evolução da Rede Urbana na Região Norte no Periodo de 1950/1970*.
Silva, José Graziano da (1981), *Progresso técnico e relações de trabalho na agricultura*, São Pualo: Editora Hucitec.
Silva, Sérgio (1976), *Expansão Cafeeira e Origens da Industria no Brasil*, São Paulo: Alfa-Omega.
Simoes, C. C. S., and Oliveira, L. A. P. (1981), 'Aspectos Recentes da Dinâmica Demográfica na Amazônia Urbana', *B. Demográfico IBGE*, 12(4): 51–86.
Singer, Paul (1977), *Desenvolvimento Econômico e Evolução Urbana*, 2nd edn., São Paulo: Companhia Editora Nacional.
Singh, S. N., Premi, M. K., Bhatia P. S., and Bose, Ashish (eds.) (1989) *Population Transition in India*, Delhi: B. P. Publishing Corporation.
Sinha, R. C. (1987), 'Urban Growth and Urbanization: A Study with Special Reference to U.P.', Paper presented at International Conference on Human Settlements in Developing Countries, Bombay, January.
—— and Mehta, G. S. (1987), 'Urbanization and Urban Employment Growth', Study prepared for National Commission on Urbanization, Giri Institute of Development Studies, Lucknow.

Skeldon, Ronald (1986), 'Hong Kong and Its Hinterland: A Case of International Rural-to-Urban Migration?', *Asian Geographer*, 5(1): 1–24.

Smith, Nigel J. H. (1982), *Rainforest Corridors: The Transamazon Colonization Scheme*, Berkeley and Los Angeles: University of California Press.

Sodré, Nelson Werneck (1976), *Formação Histórica do Brasil*, 9th edn., Rio de Janeiro: Civilização Brasileira.

Soegijoko, B. T. S. (1992), 'Jabotabek as Part of the Indonesian and Asia-Pacific Urban Systems', presented at the Workshop on the Asian-Pacific Urban System towards, the 21st Century, Chinese University of Hong Kong, Hong Kong.

Soesastro, M. Hadi, and Drysdale, Peter (1990), 'Survey of Recent Development', *Bulletin of Indonesian Economic Studies*, 29(3): 3–36.

Standing, Guy (1978), *Labour Force Participation and Development*, Geneva: International Labour Office.

Stöhr, Walter B., and Taylor, R. Fraser (eds.) (1981), *Development from Above or Below? The Dialectics of Regional Planning in Developing Countries*, New York: John Wiley.

Stopford, John M., and Dunning, John H. (1983), *Multinationals: Company Performance and Global Trends*, London: Macmillan.

Stromberg, Jerome H. P., Peyman, Habib, and Dowd, John E. (1974), 'Migration and Health: Adaptation Experiences of Iranian Migrants to the City of Teheran', *Social Science and Medicine*, 8(5): 309–23.

Suhartoyo (1983), 'New Directions of Industrial Investment Policy: Opportunities for Japan', *Indonesian Quarterly*, 11(1): 68–75.

Sun Xun (1987), 'The Problems in Housing System Reform', *Shehui* (*Society*), 1: 34–5.

Superintendencia do Desenvolvimento do Nordeste (PIMES/SUDENE) (1984), *Desigualdades Regionais no Desenvolvimento Brasileiro*, 4 vols, Recife.

Suselo, Hendropranoto, and Hoban, Des (1988), *Decentralizing the Municipal Services: The Indonesian Experience*, Washington, DC.

Tao Youzhi, Zhou Yifeng, Gu Cunwei, and Zhen Li (1988), 'A Comparative Study of the Southern Jiangsu and Wenzhou Models', *China City Planning Review*, 4(4): 38–55.

Tian Fung, and Lin Fuata (1986), *Migration in China* (in Chinese), Beijing: Knowledge Press.

Tian, Xue Yan (1987), 'Economic Reforms and the Vigour of Urbanization in Recent China', in *Proceedings of International Conference on Urbanization and Urban Population Problems, Tianjin, 25–30 October*, 47–64.

Tien, H. Yuan, *et al.* (1992), 'China's Demographic Dilemmas', *Population Bulletin*, 47(1), Washington, DC: Population Reference Bureau.

Tong Zengyen (1988), 'Housing System Reform and Finance System Reform', *Zhongguo Jinrong* (*China's Finance*), 4: 11–13.

Torres, H. G. (1988), 'A Urbanização e o Migrante de Origem Urbana na Amazônia', in *Encontro Nacional De Estudos Populacionais*, 6, *Olinda, 1988*, São Paulo: Associação Brasileira de Estudos Populacionais, i. 521–30.

Tsurumi, Yoshi (1980), 'Japanese Investment in Indonesia: Ownership, Technology Transfer, and Political Conflict', in Gustav Papanek (ed.), *The Indonesian Economy*, New York: Praeger, 295–323.

Uhalley, Stephen, Jr. (1990), 'China's Urban Housing Reform', in D. J. Gayle and J. N. Goodrich (eds.), *Privatization and Deregulation in Global Perspective*, New York: Quorum Division of Greenwood Press.

UN (United Nations) (1988), *Population Growth and Policies in Mega-Cities: Jakarta*, Population Policy Paper 18, Dept. of International Economic and Social Affairs, New York.

UN (1993), *World Urbanization Prospects 1991*, New York.

—— (1980), *Patterns of Urban and Rural Population Growth*, Population Studies 68, Dept. of International Economic and Social Affairs, New York.

Universidade de Brasília (1971), *Rodovias como Fator de Desenvolvimonto do Processo do Urbanização da Região Centro-Oeste do Brazil*, Brasília.

Vance, Rupert B., and Smith Sutker, Sara (1957), 'Metropolitan Dominance and Integration', in Paul K. Hatt *et al.* (eds.), *Cities and Society: The Revised Reader in Urban Sociology*, New York: Free Press of Glencoe, Ill.

Van der Eng, Pierre (1993), 'Survey of Recent Development', *Bulletin of Indonesian Economic Studies*, 29(3): 3–36.

Van Gelder, Paul, and Bijlmer, Joep (eds.) (1989), *About Fringes, Margins and Lucky Dips: The Informal Sector in Third-World Countries: Recent Developments in Research and Policy*, Amsterdam: Free University Press.

Vining, Daniel R., Jr. (1985), 'The Growth of Core Regions in the Third World', *Scientific American*, 252(4): 42–9.

Visaria, Pravin, and Kothari, Devendra (1985), 'Data Base for Study of Migration and Urbanization in India: A Critical Analysis', Working Paper No. 2, Ahmedabad: Gujarat Institute of Area Planning.

—— (1987), 'Data Base for the Study of Migration and Urbanization in India: A Critical Analysis', in S. Manzoor Alam and Fatima Alikhan (eds.), *Perspectives on Urbanization and Migration: India and USSR*, New Delhi: Allied Publishers Private Ltd.

—— and Minhas, B. S. (1991), 'Evolving an Employment Policy for the 1990s: What Do the Data Tell Us?', *Economic and Political Weekly*, 26(15), 13 Apr.

Vogel, Ezra F. (1989), *One Step Ahead in China: Guangdong Under Reform*, Cambridge, Mass.: Harvard University Press.

Volbeda, S. (1982), 'Urbanisation in the "Frontiers" of the Brazilian Amazon and the Expulsion of Pioneers from the Agricultural Sector from 1960 to the Present', *Boletin de Estudios Latinamericanos y del Caribe*, 33: 35–57.

—— (1984), *Pionierssteden in het Oerwoud: Stedelijke Ontwikkelingen aan een Agrarisch Kolonisatiefront in het Braziliaanse Amazonegebied*, Nijmegen: Katholieke Universiteit Nijmegen.

Wang Dongjin (1988), 'The Basic Policy for Urban Housing Reform Should Place a Higher Priority on Renting', *Jingji Guanli (Economic Management)*, 3: 34–5.

Wang Xiang Ming (1987a), 'The Path of China's Urbanization', in *Proceedings of International Conference on Urbanization and Urban Population Problems (ICUUP), 25–30 October, Tianjin*, 547–60.

—— (1987b), 'The Impact of China's Rural Industrialization on Urbanization and Its Theoretical Significance', *China Population Science*, 1.

Wang Zuxin (1988), 'Speed up Housing Reform', *Chengxiang Jianshe (Urban Rural Construction)*, 12: 20–21.

Weiner, Myron (1978), *Sons of the Soil: Migration and Ethnic Conflict in India*, Princeton: Princeton University Press.

—— (1983), 'The Political Demography of Assam's Anti-Immigrant Movement', *Population and Development Review*, 9(2): 279–92.

Wilson, J. F. (1985), 'Agriquemes: Settlement and Class in a Brazilian Frontier Town', Ph.D. thesis, University of Florida, Gainesville.

Wiradi, Gunawan, and Manning, Chris (1984), 'Landownership, Tenancy, and Sources of

Household Income: Community Patterns from a Partial Recensus of Eight Villages in Rural Java', Bogor: Yayasan Penelitian Survey Agro Ekonomi.

Wood, Charles H., and Wilson, J. F. (1984), 'The Magnitude of Migration to the Brazilian Frontier', in Marianne Schmink and Charles H. Wood (eds.), *Frontier Expansion in Amazônia*, Gainesville: University of Florida Press, 142–52.

—— and de Carvalho, José Alberto M. (1988), *The Social Demography of Inequality in Brazil*, Cambridge: Cambridge University Press.

World Bank (1983), *Indonesia: Selected Aspects of Spatial Development*, Report No. 4776-IND, Annex I, Note A, Washington, DC.

—— (1986), *Indonesia: Strategy for Economic Recovery*, Washington, DC: IBRD.

—— (1988), 'Indonesia Country Report', Washington, DC: IBRD.

—— (1993a), 'Indonesia—Environment and Development: Challenges for the Future', Washington, DC.

—— (1993b), 'Indonesia: Urban Public Infrastructure Services', Washington, DC.

Wu Cunzhong and Wu Cunxiao (1980), 'Some Preliminary Thoughts on How to Alleviate the Urban Housing Problem', *Jilin Daxue Xuebao (Journal of Jilin University)*, 6: 49–53.

Wu Wanqi (1988), 'The Urban Housing Problem in China and the Solution', *Chengshi Guihua (City Planning)*, 1: 13–17.

Wu Zhaoxing and Wen Wanping (1989), 'A Discussion on the Problem of Buying Housing by Cadres and Intellectuals', *Chengxiang Jianshe (Urban Rural Construction)*, 2: 19–20.

Xiao Liang (1988), 'Reform of Rental System and the Commercialization of Housing', *Jingji Tizhi Gaige (Economic System Reform)*, 3: 18–21.

Yang Xiushi and Goldstein, Sidney, (1989), 'Population Redistribution in Zhejiang Province, China: The Impact of Development and Government Policies', Providence, R.I: Population Studies and Training Center, Brown University.

Yantai City Economic Research Center (1988), 'The Choice on Ideas of Reforming the Housing System', *Jingji Guanli (Economic Management)*, 3: 36–9.

Yap, Lorene (1975), *Internal Migration in Less Developed Countries: A Survey of the Literature*, World Bank Staff Working Paper No. 215, Washington, DC: World Bank.

Ye Shunzan (1986), 'Regional Perspectives of the Relationship of Development of Two Metropolises: Beijing and Tianjin', *China City Planning Review*, 2(1): 21–32.

Yeung, Yue-man (1988), 'Great Cities of Eastern Asia', in Mattei Dogan and John D. Kasarda (eds.), *The Metropolis Era*, i, Beverly Hills: Sage, 155–83.

—— and Hu Xu-wei (eds.), (1992), *China's Coastal Cities: Catalysts for Modernization*, Hong Kong: Oxford University Press.

Yin Wen Yao (1987) 'On Scale Composition of Urban Population and Socio-economic Development', *Population Research*, 4: 9–13.

Yoshihara, Kunio (1978), *Japanese Investment in Southeast Asia*, Honolulu: University of Hawaii Press.

Yu Zhengxing (1988), 'To Search a Strategy for Commercializing Housing with Chinese Characteristics', in *Chengshi Gaige yu Fazhan (City Reform and Development)*, Beijing: China's Finance Economics Publishing Society, 81–94.

Zachariah, K. C. (1968), *Migration in Greater Bombay*, Bombay: Demography Training and Research Centre.

Zhang Jian Shan (1987), 'Analyses on the Population Industrial Structures of China's Three Economic Zones', *Population Information*, 2: 24–31.

Zhang Jinzhong *et al.* (1988), 'To Lower the Sale Price of Housing to Achieve the Goal', *Zhongguo Jinrong (China's Finance)*, 9: 26–8.

Zhang Libo (1985), 'An Analysis of the Necessity, the Feasibility, and the Socio-economic Benefits of Commercialized Housing', *Jingji Wenti* (*Economic Problems*), 7: 18–22.

Zhang Qiufang (1986), 'Housing Commercialization is a Major Policy in our Country's Economic System Reform', *Beijing Daxue Xuebao* (*Beijing University Journal*), 6: 23–9.

Zhang Xiouzhi and Zhang Zhixin (1988), 'Housing Reform's "Shock Wave" in Yantai', *Building in China*, 1(3): 42–4, 50.

Zhao Baozhen (1987), 'A Prediction and Analysis of Our Country's Urban Housing Construction Investment', *Jingji Guanli* (*Economic Management*), 2: 16–18.

Zhao Jincheng (1985), 'An Inquiry into the Commercialization Scheme of Urban Housing', *Jingji Wenti Tansuo* (*Inquiry into Economic Problems*), 9: 11–14.

Zheng Fuheng and Zuo Ling (1988), 'The Ideal and the Reality of Housing System Reform', *Gaige* (*Reform*), 3: 143–6.

Zhong Feng Gan and Zhu Yun Cheng (1987), 'Areal Variations of China's Urbanization', in *Proceedings of International Conference on Urbanization and Urban Population Problems (ICUUP), 25–30 October, Tianjin*, 526–46.

Zhongguo Tongji Nianjian 1981, China's Statistical Yearbook 1981 (1981), Beijing: China's Statistical Publishing Society.

—— *1988, China's Statistical Yearbook 1988* (1988), Beijing: China's Statistical Publishing Society.

Zhou Ding (1987), 'Review of the Urban Planning and Development of Shenzhen', *China City Planning Review*, 3(1/2) (Special Issue): 10–22.

Zhou, Yixing (1991), 'The Metropolitan Interlocking Region in China: A Preliminary Hypothesis', in Norton Ginsburg, Bruce Koppel, and T. G. McGee (eds.), *The Extended Metropolis: Settlement Transition in Asia*, Honolulu: University of Hawaii Press.

Zhou Zheng (1985), 'The Method of Subsidized Sale of Housing Needs to Be Corrected Soon', *Jingji Wenti Tansuo* (*Inquiry into Economic Problems*), 9: 76–7.

Zhou Zhengqing (1987), 'Finance Department: Need to Participate in Housing System Reform', *Zhongguo Jinrong* (*China's Finance*), 9: 17–19.

Zhu Yin (1989), 'The Ability to Purchase Housing and the Psychology of Beijing Residents', *Chengxiang Jianshe* (*Urban Rural Construction*), 2: 17–18.

Zong Lin (1988), 'On the Scale, Structure and Development Strategy', *China City Planning Review*, 4(4): 13–21.

Index

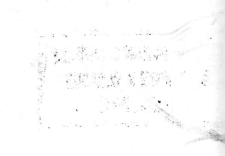